'Karen Donders has established herself as the leading academic analyst of the challenges facing public service media in contemporary Europe. Here she combines careful normative theory with in-depth case studies, providing an account that everyone concerned with this topic will have to read.'

David Hesmondhalgh, *Professor of Media, Music and Culture, University of Leeds*

'This book asks some tough and much-needed questions about the difference between the public service media we would like and the public service media we actually have. Donders argues that if PSM is to serve democracy, we will need to consider profound changes to the governance, funding and the very stranding of public media in our respective countries. A rich, comprehensive and critical account of our changing media landscape.'

Des Freedman, *Professor of Media and Communications, Goldsmiths University of London*

'The debate on Public Service Media (PSM) is conducted on many different levels: political, journalistic and academic. Karen Donders' book seems to combine all of the above. Experts' statements and the author's knowledge enabled the creation of a book that presents an in-depth reflection not only on what PSMs are like in Europe, but what they could and should be like in order for their presence to regain a strong democratic legitimacy.

The existence of the PSM is not only a non-commercial alternative to private media, but also a common denominator for the social debate in which PSMs are responsible for "giving the tone" to other broadcasters. In the choir of increasingly polarized media in Europe, the PSM's voice is not only still important, but can be an antidote to the "information smog" and disinformation. The work of Karen Donders fits into the debate about the obligations of media, which is important for the quality of democracy.'

Alicja Jaskiernia, *Professor at the Faculty of Journalism, Information and Book Studies, University of Warsaw*

'A thought-provoking book on public service media by one of the absolute experts in the field. Karen Donders brings her extensive knowledge of theories, legal realities and practices as well as her research rigor to a topic she is utterly familiar and totally passionate about. Inviting us to start from the practice and law to come to a future proof theoretical understanding of Public Service Media, Karen Donders has produced a book that is at once an instant classic and that will be of interest to academics, policymakers and professionals well beyond Western Europe.'

Hilde Van den Bulck, *Professor and Department Head, Department of Communication, Drexel University College of Arts and Sciences*

Public Service Media in Europe

Contributing to a rethink of Public Service Media, this book combines theoretical insights and legal frameworks with practice, examining theory and policy development in a bottom-up manner.

It explores the practices of Public Service Media across Europe, assessing the rules that govern Public Service Media at both the EU and the National Member State level, identifying common trends, initiated by both the European Commission and individual countries, illustrating the context-dependent development of Public Service Media and challenging the theories of Public Service Broadcasting which have developed an ideal-type public broadcaster based on the well-funded BBC in an atypical media market. Seeking to further explore the actual practices of Public Service Media and make recommendations for the development of more sustainable policies, this book offers case studies of rules and practices from across a variety of EU Member States to consider the extent to which public broadcasters are making the transition to public media organisations, and how public broadcasters and governments are shaping Public Service Media together.

This book is a must-read for all scholars who take an interest in Public Service Media, media policy and media systems literature at large. It will also be of interest to practitioners working in government, Public Service Media and commercial media.

Karen Donders is Associate Professor of Media Policy, Media Markets and Political Economy of Journalism at the Communication Sciences Department of the Vrije Universiteit Brussel. She is a member of research group imec-SMIT at the same university. Her expertise areas are Public Service Media, competition law and media, European media policy and platformisation.

Routledge Research in Media Law

Public Service Media in Europe

Law, Theory and Practice

Karen Donders

Routledge
Taylor & Francis Group

LONDON AND NEW YORK

First published 2021
by Routledge
2 Park Square, Milton Park, Abingdon, Oxon OX14 4RN

and by Routledge
605 Third Avenue, New York, NY 10158

Routledge is an imprint of the Taylor & Francis Group, an informa business

© 2021 Karen Donders

British Library Cataloguing-in-Publication Data
A catalogue record for this book is available from the British Library

Library of Congress Cataloging-in-Publication Data
A catalog record has been requested for this book

ISBN: 978-1-138-47705-6 (hbk)
ISBN: 978-1-032-01124-0 (pbk)
ISBN: 978-1-351-10556-9 (ebk)

Typeset in Bembo
by Newgen Publishing UK

To Jan, for his support and love,

To Lynn and Mats, who show me every day that Public Service Media is not the most important thing and at the same time so necessary,

To Caroline, who saw me and continues to mentor me.

Contents

Illustrations

Figures

Tables

Preface

Article 5 of the German Constitution endorses freedom of expression, press freedom and the freedom of broadcasting and film. It is the basis of a dual media system that sets out from the premise that private media cannot or should not exist without a Public Service Media system of which the editorial as well as financial independence is safeguarded by government. As such, the German system is the antithesis of the 'free market place of ideas' paradigm, which has been so dominant in the US and also has its supporters across the EU, notably in Western Europe. Most European countries still hold on to a dual media system, consisting of organisations driven by the public interest and companies acting on the basis of profit-seeking motives. This combination has served citizens well in many countries, definitely in countries where public broadcasters can act in an independent manner and where private media have sufficient means to act professionally and employ highly trained media makers and journalists.

Most Public Service Media systems have been inspired by the BBC model and the Reithian adage 'to inform, educate and entertain'. In countries such as Poland, Spain and Hungary, when describing the failure, the erosion or even collapse of Public Service Media organisations, reference is often made to the UK system. Admittedly, the British Public Service Media system is somewhat atypical, being embedded in a political system that is closer to the US than it is to most mainland European countries, is part of a media market that is very much export-oriented, and works within a highly commercialised environment. That makes one wonder whether the law and practices of Public Service Media in small countries such as Belgium, Norway and Portugal, and also Central and Eastern European countries such as Poland and Slovenia should indeed be meaningfully inspired by the British experience or rather the somewhat idyllic appreciation we have of the BBC. One can also critically reflect on whether the massive amount of and highly interesting scholarship on Public Service Media in the UK is adequate to sustain theories on public intervention in the media if not profoundly complemented with scientific work on other parts of Europe.

When I finished my Ph.D., which focused on European State aid rules and Public Service Media, in 2010, I already felt that there was more to say about Public Service Media. Quite some scientific journal articles later, that feeling had not yet left me. That is why I decided a couple of years ago to start working on a new monograph. Essentially, my main aim with this monograph was/still is to make three points. First, there is more to Public Service Media than what happens in the UK. That does not make what happens in the UK less relevant. It rather means we need to devote more attention to what is happening elsewhere as well and connect these experiences to each other. We have habitually put cases next to each other, more often than not setting out from a supposedly superior Western model of Public Service Media compared to the fiasco of and disappointment we feel about the development of Public Service Media in Southern and Central and Eastern Europe. Second, there is a need to see the gaps between Public Service Media theory, the law and practice. The ideal of Public Service Media is of course utopian. It is in fact a mission impossible to fully achieve in practice. However, that does not mean we should not reflect on the theoretical values underlying Public Service Media, which many authors in fact have done and are doing. It also means we need to connect the values and principles more with the regulatory frameworks and actual practices of Public Service Media across Europe. Moreover, there is a definite need to understand better what explains these gaps. We all know the situation of Public Service Media in Poland is deplorable to the extent one can hardly talk of a Public Service Media system at this point. But why is that the case? Can we move beyond fairly one-dimensional explanations that attribute the re-emergence of a state broadcasting system to the Party of Law and Justice only? Third, and perhaps one of the main objectives of my book, was to explore how public broadcasters themselves shape their own project. Often depicted as 'victims' of evil and malevolent governments, I am convinced that public broadcasters knowingly and unconsciously co-shape their own project as well as institution. Public broadcaster and government cannot always be neatly separated, not per se exclusively because of the latter's intention to control public broadcasters, but because of an intricate process of institutionalisation and socialisation that in some circumstances makes public broadcasters part of Structures rather than enablers of Agency.

I have to admit that the chapters in front of you do not entirely live up to the ambitions I set for myself. I fell in the trap I confront many of my master thesis students with: over-reaching. It is unmanageable to write a book that covers all of the theoretical, legal and practical aspects of Public Service Media. One can try to contribute with meaningful insights on all of these levels, though, and I hope this book does exactly that.

Many people contributed to this book, not in the least my husband, my children, my family and friends. They supported me along the way and accepted more book-time and less them-time. I would like to thank my colleagues at the Vrije Universiteit Brussel. A special thank you (although I hardly dare, risking to forget someone) to Tim and Anne-Sofie, who are Public Service Media scholars-in-crime and provided such useful comments on the manuscript; to Wim, who always tells me to calm down; to my Ph.D. students, who keep me on my toes and who inspire me to continue research myself; to Ike, Wendy and Simon, who also always tell me to calm down; to the many people at

SMIT and the department of communication sciences who have suggested interesting literature to me over the past few years; and to Pieter for giving me the time to do research and not only research management. I want to express my gratitude to all people I interviewed for this book, many of them I already know for quite some time. They are genuine supporters of research, even when inquiries are not always positive to them or the companies, institutions and agencies they work for. I realise that sharing insights with a researcher that is too or not sufficiently critical (depending on one's perception) of Public Service Media is not evident at all. While some scholars feel that there is insufficient interest in scholarly work on media, I can only say that most, if not all people I talked to did so with the intent to help advance scientific research on Public Service Media. I encountered a lot of passion for Public Service Media, frustration with letdowns and also fury regarding public broadcasters' position in markets. It is that raw emotion that drives not only industry and policy, but also science, and it is thus something we share. There are also some colleagues from other countries, all of which I call my friends, I would like to mention here. Phil Ramsey for his help on my work on Ireland; Michal Glowacki for his amazing hospitality during my stays in Warsaw and his enthusiasm to bridge the gap between Public Service Media research on the West and East of Europe; Hilde Van den Bulck for telling me 100 times every month to stop working so much (but not really leading by example); and Ben Van Rompuy for his genuine indignation about the European Commission's flaws in applying State aid law to Public Service Media and for giving me positive books on commercial media giants such as Disney. Nearing the end of this lengthy thank you list, I would like to acknowledge how much my students have contributed to this book, perhaps not directly, but by asking questions, providing new and fresh perspectives during class and giving me the energy to continue even amidst a Covid-19 pandemic that resulted in lockdowns, working at home with two toddlers that have no interest in Public Service Media at all, quarantine, and so on. The pandemic, by the way, has forcefully shown the importance of independent public broadcasters that can provide factual information and go beyond polarisation on, for example, the need to wear masks or not (obviously, yes). Siobhan and her team at Routledge also deserve my gratitude for their patience and encouragement. I would like to thank Flemish public broadcaster VRT. As you will read further in this book, I have had the opportunity to provide the public broadcaster with advice on notably the negotiation of its management contracts 2016-2020 and 2021-2025. That has given me invaluable insights in Public Service Media *from within* and also in the interaction and dialogue (and sometimes also manifest lack thereof) between public broadcasters and policy-makers. It is not easy to open the doors to a scientist that is convinced she knows better because of the sheer number of articles and books she has read on Public Service Media. Nonetheless, they – and in first instance Lut Vercruysse, former Director of Strategy of VRT – did it and it made me a better researcher and teacher. Having said that, my connection to VRT also required a constant re-balancing of the own position and mainly taking some mental distance from the research subject, something I struggled with when writing my chapter on Public Service Media in Flanders. Finally, Caroline Pauwels, rector of the Vrije Universiteit Brussel and the supervisor of my Ph.D. thesis, deserves all of my appreciation and admiration. She inspired me years and years ago when I was still an undergraduate student to research and critically think about Public Service Media in our society. She has been my mentor ever since and is one of the biggest, yet also a highly critical, advocates for Public Service Media organisations and the emancipatory role that they play/ought to play in democracy.

This book marks a pause in my academic career. Mid-2020 the Flemish Government appointed a new CEO for public broadcaster VRT. Frederik Delaplace asked and convinced me to join the public broadcaster's Board of Directors as Director of Public Value. That, I have to admit, was by no means an easy decision. Education and research are two things I am passionate about and I have been rather fanatical in both. Nonetheless, the last few years I have gradually felt more and more disappointed with some of the practices in academia. Likewise, in Public Service Media, there is a gap between what we stand for and what we do. I will not go further into that, but overall, I think it has become extremely difficult for young professors like myself to find their place, to advance and to really be judged on merit. Do not get me wrong: universities are a haven for free thinking. They are a place where people can rise above themselves and where social mobility takes shape, although we have to do better in the latter area. It is a place I hope to return to, that I feel privileged to have worked in for 15 years. I am now changing sides, but not really. Public Service Media pursue the public interest as do universities. Both do wonderful things and fail miserably in some domains. Both are based on highly aspirational objectives, work within regulatory frameworks and with funding arrangements that can make the achievement of their task more or less difficult, and are people-driven and thus imperfect. Both can push boundaries, add to the emancipation and imagination of citizens and strengthen creativity, innovation and markets.

1 Introduction

A mismatch between Public Service Media theory, law and practice

Should Public Service Broadcasting/Media be part of our societies?

For many decades, proponents of Public Service Broadcasting have argued it is not there to address market failure, but to further a societal project that prioritises citizen needs over consumer preferences (Garnham, 2000). It is there to contribute to the 'good society' (Galbraith, 1996). While this view has indeed suffered from the neoliberal upsurge in the 1980s, it remains at the core of most scholarly work on Public Service Broadcasting and its more modern version, Public Service Media. And, admittedly, most Western and Northern European governments cling to the idea of an informing, educating and entertaining public broadcaster (Donders, 2012). Public Service Broadcasting as well as the institutions traditionally entrusted with its delivery have proven to be resilient. Public broadcasters are an essential, if not in many countries the main, part of 'cultural policy toolkits' (Gibbons and Humphreys, 2012: 1-17). Nevertheless, quite some research on this issue has forecasted the 'decline and fall of Public Service Broadcasting' (see Tracey, 1998; see also Jakubowicz, 2007a; Bardoel and Lowe, 2007). While such a scenario has not become a reality so far, pessimist views on the future of Public Service Broadcasting often reign in scholarly debates (for an evaluation see Collins et al., 2001). They take away attention from a necessary and to some extent basic re-evaluation of Public Service Broadcasting in the 21st century. Equally tricky has been the huge attention for public broadcasters' presence online and the shift from Public Service Broadcasting to, what is commonly referred to as, Public Service Media. Alternative concepts to describe the transition for public broadcasters offering radio, television and – on top – online services are public service content and public service communication. Contributions on specific Internet services (Steemers, 2003), public value tests (Donders and Moe, 2011), radio and television versus online offers (Ramsey, 2018), public service algorithms (Bonini, 2019), and so on, have their merit. The digital 'turn' presents significant challenges for public broadcasters. However, theoretical, political, and strategic reflections on the future of Public Service Broadcasting deal also with other profound choices made in, for and by society.

As proclaimed by Bauer (2012), communication policy research should not stick to a reactive, descriptive approach, but engage more in normative, prescriptive endeavours (see also Puppis and Just, 2012). Focus should thus be on fundamental questions. Specifically, we should ask ourselves what type of society we want and whether Public Service Broadcasting is part of that society. In his provocative, much celebrated, but also fiercely criticised and disputed essay, 'Ill Fares the Land', Tony Judt (2010) essentially asks very similar questions. Obviously the subject of Judt's work is not the media. Rather, Judt is concerned with trends in capitalist societies at large and the mounting inequality therein. His work, moreover, makes apparent he sets out from a conflict theoretical vision on society, assuming that the exploitation of one class really and effectively serves the interests of the ruling class. I would argue such a view runs the risk of being overly reductionist, as are several political economy studies, whether concerned with the research of the media, be it from critical leftist or rather neoliberal and right-wing perspective (Curran, 2014: 28). Nevertheless, Judt points at very pertinent trends such as the increasing reliance on the, supposedly, optimal functioning of markets, our unceasing over-focus on efficiency and an upsetting ignorance of inequality at the macro, meso, micro and personal levels of society. Whereas these are 'big' questions about life and the way we collectively organise it, the answer to the questions Tony Judt asks are directly related to the manifold questions that are raised in academic, policy and practitioner debates on Public Service Broadcasting.

> Something is profoundly wrong with the way we live today. For thirty years we have made a virtue out of the pursuit of material self-interest: indeed, this very pursuit now constitutes whatever remains of our sense of collective purpose. We know what things cost but have no idea what they are worth. We no longer ask of a judicial ruling or a legislative act: Is it good? Is it fair? Is it just? Is it right? Will it help bring about a better society or a better world? Those used to be the political questions, even if they invited no easy answers. We must learn once again to pose them. The materialistic and selfish quality of contemporary life is not inherent in the human condition. Much of what appears 'natural' today dates from the 1980s: the obsession with wealth creation, the cult of privatisation and the private sector, the growing disparities of rich and poor. And above all, the rhetoric that accompanies these: uncritical admiration for unfettered markets, disdain for the public sector, the delusion of endless growth.
>
> (Judt, 2010: 1–2)

'Disdain for the public sector' (cf. quote above) is apparent in discussions on Public Service Broadcasting and, more recently, similar concepts to talk about it such as Public Service Media. There is still audience support though, albeit that varies significantly across countries and regions. While over 70 per cent of citizens voted for the Swiss public broadcaster in the *No Bilag* referendum in 2018, inhabitants of Valencia in Spain hardly protested against the government's decision to abolish the regional public broadcaster where 1,800 people worked and replace it with a much smaller organisation of about 350 employees later on. While massive outcry followed the abolition of Greek public broadcaster ERT in 2013 (Donders, 2013), much less noise is being made in Poland where the PiS government effectively and legally turned the public into a state broadcaster. This mixed stance of audiences has to do with the extent to which the public broadcaster actually represents their interest, but also the hope that the public interest is or could be at the heart of what the public broadcaster will do in the future. In other words: does the practice of Public Service Broadcasting match with the theory? And is the law the glue to ensure that match or the opposite?

For each argument against the evolution from Public Service Broadcasting to a policy project that is more future-proof, there is an argument in favour. Several disruptions, notably those linked to digitisation and internationalisation of media, have put pressure on the existing theory supporting Public Service Broadcasting. Even those scholars setting out from a social responsibility view on - as it is now most often referred to - Public Service Media, call for a fundamental rethinking of the policy idea, project and responsible institutions that are so 'near and dear' to many European citizens' hearts.

Aim of the book

This book aims to contribute to the rethinking of Public Service Media, confronting theoretical with insights on Public Service Media laws and practices. Its main aim is to contribute to theory development in a bottom-up manner, looking at the laws governing and the actual practices of Public Service Media across Europe. Largely, I set out from the observation that most work on Public Service Broadcasting and, in extension, Public Service Media has developed theories that depict an ideal-type of public broadcaster instead of explanatory theories. These theories offer guidance as to what we want Public Service Media to be. However, they do not tell a lot about why the law and practice deviate from that. Moreover, the main inspiration for this ideal-type public broadcaster remains the BBC (Enli, 2008). It is legitimate to argue that the BBC and the media market of the United Kingdom is admittedly one of the most atypical in Europe. The resources of the BBC are outnumbered only by the German public broadcasters; the UK media market is the biggest in Europe and much more export-oriented than all others; the political traditions are more similar to the US than to mainland Europe, and so on (Hallin and Mancini, 2004). Because of these reasons, I consider most theories on Public Service Broadcasting and also Public Service Media valuable, but essentially in need of an update. A specific point of attention is the suitability of theory development for Public Service Media regimes in South, Central and Eastern Europe.

In case we want to further explanatory theories on Public Service Broadcasting and Public Service Media, it is necessary to ask whether the

Public Service Media concept is a useful elaboration of the Public Service Broadcasting notion at all. We need to relate it more explicitly to notions of citizenship and democracy, especially to capture worrying trends in several European countries that see an erosion of the rule of law and thus the basics of democracy. Moreover, we should start looking at actual practices, and this across a variety of European Member States. Such an endeavour is far from easy as Public Service Media is, in practice, a highly contextual phenomenon – its status impacted by a complex interaction between economic, social, political, cultural and historical factors. This book can, of course, only partially meet the challenge sketched above. It will provide a theoretical value-based framework for Public Service Media, it will study changing Public Service Media laws across Europe as well as engage in in-depth case study research. On that basis, I will define explanatory factors for diverging Public Service Media regimes in Europe. But more work will still be needed afterwards.

Where do grand theories and day-to-day practice meet?

The first question I seek to answer in this book is whether a shared set of theoretical values is still necessary and feasible for Public Service Media. With 'theoretical' I do not refer to a systematic, 'true', 'grand theory' or explanation of human conduct and the functioning of society. Indeed, as pointed out by Sibeon (1996, 13ff), social sciences have somewhat shifted away from grand theories such as Parsonian structural-functionalism and Marxism, largely because 'they produce large, sweeping generalisations that bear little relation to concrete empirical happenings in particular times and particular places' (1996, 13–14). Rather, I see this first research question as the quest for an explanatory (as is) and normative (should be) appreciation of human conduct (related to the functioning of public broadcasters and policy-making) and the functioning of society (related to the values underpinning Public Service Media). Important therein is the necessity and possibility of identifying sufficient communality at the level of values should one seek to evolve from the *as is* to the *should be* situation. The first part of the book (see later) will devote attention mainly to the *should be* situation, whereas the second and third parts of the book zoom in on the *as is* situation as a basis for further theory development.

Setting out from some major disruptions, being the, in several ways, problematic framework Public Service Media 'has to work with', the aim is to identify the main values underlying Public Service Media and the goals institutions and people in charge of public broadcasters have to strive after. Related, I subsequently ask how and whether such a vision can be transposed into reality. In other words, and referring again to Galbraith's 'good society', I seek to identify 'what might be perfect and what is achievable' (Galbraith, 1996: 2). I will focus on both legal/policy answers and concrete public broadcasters' strategies in the digital age. The challenge, as I will point out, is to find a 'match' between theory, the law and practice. Seeking such an alignment is a shared responsibility of scholars, politicians, public broadcasters and even citizens. Indeed, as I will illustrate in this book, while public broadcasters might still be the most effective and efficient solution for delivering Public Service Media or, better, for serving the public interest in media, that might not be the case in each and every European country. The notions Public Service Broadcasting and Public Service Media concern the contribution made by a public broadcaster, but potentially also by other actors, to the public interest. Are public broadcasters, in charge of Public Service Media, contributing to informed citizenship, challenging post-truth politics and disinformation? Is a radio show, television programme or an app strengthening social cohesion in society or adding to further polarisation? Are on-demand services reinforcing the filter bubble or stimulating diversity at the point of consumption too? In case it is difficult, perhaps even impossible, to get rid of the heritage of state broadcasters, should we, under such circumstances, not abandon the practice of keeping in place a public broadcaster and think on another means of implementing Public Service Media? These are the questions to be addressed when talking about the value or lack thereof of an institutionalised form of Public Service Media through the existence of a public broadcaster. Additional and complementary kinds of public service delivery in the form of, for example, a Public Service Publisher system for public service journalism (Humphreys, 2012), can and should be considered also - notably in larger countries. An alignment between theory, the law and practice is, in addition, only possible if one, while on the one hand fiercely defending the ideal of achieving the public interest in media, realises on the other hand the need to be critical when public broadcasters do not live up to their ideals and fail to comply with relevant legislative provisions. With the welfare state being under pressure the latter is a *sine qua non* for the survival of public broadcasters as an exponent of Public Service Media in the long term. Resilience of the welfare state model implies not so much its success to inhibit change, but lies rather in its ability to adapt (Taylor-Gooby, 2001: 3).

Methods

This work is based on an extensive (yet, not exhaustive) study of literature on the role of media (companies) in society, Public Service Media, digitisation and internationalisation, and so on. The book is situated within the so-called 'political economy of media' strand of communications research (for an overview of the political economy of the media, see Hardy, 2014). Whereas attention is devoted to cultural and organisational praxis, the attention is first and foremost directed at the control of media, the structure and interactions in media markets and the impact of digitisation and commercialisation on the former two (2014: 39). While not being fatalist or utterly pessimist, the economic and, in particular, political choices made as a (so one says) consequence of digitisation and commercialisation are concerning, as will be pointed out later in this book, and go, regardless of any 'leftist' or 'right-wing' ideology, against the 'good society', social justice and the critical importance of emancipation. More so then influenced by Marxism and the Frankfürter Schule, this research aligns with democratic theory, which insists that 'democracy is based on an informed, participating citizenry' and, accordingly, 'such political culture can only be generated by a more, diverse, democratised media system' (2014: 48). The challenge then obviously is how to align a capitalist organisation of media markets with this ideal of informed citizenship (see also Pickard, 2019).

The empirical work in Part II of the book, which concerns the legal frameworks for Public Service Broadcasting in place in Europe, is to a large extent based on an analysis of a variety of documents such as the resolutions of the Council of Europe, management contracts between governments and public broadcasters, European Commission decisions on the funding of public broadcasting, media laws, publications of media regulators, speeches of key players, strategy documents of public broadcasters, annual reports of public broadcasters, and so on.[1] Complementary use of expert interviews is being made.

I attempt to provide an overview of the main aspects of Public Service Broadcasting law, policy and strategy in Europe. Attention is devoted to both European and national rules, policies and related public broadcaster strategies. Several countries, albeit with different intensity, are included in the analysis: Belgium, Poland, Ireland, the United Kingdom, Spain, the Netherlands, Finland, Switzerland, Germany, and so on, will appear in some chapters. The selection of Public Service Media systems touched upon is lightly inspired by Hallin and Mancini's taxonomy (Hallin and Mancini, 2004) and Terzis' (2007) elaboration of it. Poland is part of the Central and Eastern European group of countries that share a communist past and seem to struggle with basic aspects of democracy (e.g., freedom of the press). These countries are also categorised as 'competitive authoritarianist', given that, although democratic institutions exist in these countries, they are still often manipulated by the ruling elites (Levitsky and Way, 2010; Vladisavljević, 2016). Ireland and the United Kingdom are situated in the liberal model, at the crossroads with the democratic corporatist model. Both have a strong public broadcasting system, but are very open to market forces. Ireland is a small language neighbour of the United Kingdom, which comes with specific competitive issues such as high rivalry with UK broadcast channels. The United Kingdom is the biggest audiovisual market in Europe, exporting to other countries worldwide (Donders and Van den Bulck, 2016). Belgium (the Flemish community), Germany, Switzerland and the Netherlands are part of the democratic corporatist group, showing strong levels of government intervention and a historical inclination to protect domestic content industries. They are open to market forces as a consequence of European liberalisation processes. Both the Flemish and Dutch public broadcasters are active in radio, television and online advertising. The German public broadcasting system is admittedly more complex with competencies shared by the Länder governments, no commercial funding, a complex public value test regime in place and the organisation of ARD and its member organisations (Donders, 2012). Spain is part of the polarised pluralist model, showing high levels of government intervention, a rather weak commercial media market and a heavily politicised public broadcaster (Fernandes Alonso and Fernandes Viso, 2012). Finally, Finland can be seen as part of the demo-cratic corporatist tradition, although other scholars would argue it fits within the separate model of 'the media welfare state' (Syvertsen et al., 2014). Given the diversity of political traditions selected, we expect to see diversity of legal approaches also. Levy (1997: 24) showed there was little policy convergence between German and British broadcasting policies in the 1990s. He said that this was due 'to the strong national institutional structures and intense politi-cisation that characterise the broadcasting sector'. The question essentially is whether that observation holds today. Focus of the analysis is on the definition of public broadcasters' mission, the inclusion of new media services in the public service remit and public value tests of new media services, public broadcasters' governance structure and how it safeguards impartiality and pluralism, and the level of funding and the technique used to compensate for public service costs (license fee, subsidies, mixed). The aim of the analysis is not to provide an over-view of dozens of legislative frameworks concerning Public Service Media. Rather, I use case studies to study certain trends as well as different approaches across Europe.

Part III, looking at the practice of Public Service Media in Europe, is largely based on document analysis (with documents relating to public broadcasters' own internal strategies, multi-platform working plans, annual reports, etc.) and expert interviews with past and present key management staff of public broadcasters, private media companies, policy-makers in charge of Public Service Media policies, consultants working or having worked for Public Service Media organisations and important scholars in the field. The interviews were carried out in 2017, 2018 and mainly in 2019 (more information in the respective chapters). There is one chapter dealing specific-ally with the difficulty for public broadcasters to adopt a Public Service Media rather than Public Service Broadcasting approach to what they are doing. Next to that, I adopted a case study design allowing for thick description on the other, diverse questions asked throughout this book. A case study approach is par-ticularly relevant when investigating the implementation of complex concepts into practice (Vennesson, 2008). The case studies are descriptive and theory generating at the same time. For the two cases under investigation, I looked at public broadcasters relating to (1) their audiences, (2) other public institutions, (3) competitors, (4) politicians and other policy-makers and (5) themselves and their mission. Of course, the actual chapters on Flanders (Belgium) and Poland are structured in a different way as the key questions on the Public Service Media regimes in these countries are highly context-specific.

All types of interaction that guided the data collection for the 'practice' section of this book (often addressed separately in scholarly works; see Murdock, 2005; Lowe and Bardoel, 2007; Lowe, 2010; Hanretty, 2011; Donders, 2012) are prone to particular fields of tensions (seen from the perspective of public broadcasting institutions) that need to be dealt with (Table 1.1); or at least public broadcasters should be aware of these fields of tension in case they want to adapt to the changed circumstances. The abovementioned fields of tension

Table 1.1 Public broadcasters' relations related to fields of tensions

Public broadcasters relating to:	… are confronted with the following fields of tension:
Their audiences	taking popularity for relevance
Other public institutions	relying on the exclusive claim on 'Public Service Media' or delivering Public Service Media in an inclusive manner
Competitors	putting competition first or seeking partnerships to deliver (social and/or economic) value
Politicians and other policy-makers	inclination to legitimise towards politics instead of evaluating policies
Themselves and their mission	self-protective justification of or genuine reflection on their existence

do not exist in a vacuum. They should continually be evaluated against, among others, the changing context of renewed polarisation in politics, the impact of social media on public debate and new types of political agency.

The cases selected are the main, national public broadcasters from Belgium (Flemish community) and Poland. These two countries are also included in the legal analysis that is the subject of Part II of this book. We selected them because they each stand for a different media model. Given the embedded nature of Public Service Media, they cannot be seen as representative for other countries. They will provide some insights on trends, events, political choices, public broadcasters' decisions, and so on, that are relevant beyond their national boundaries though. I conducted site visits to Poland in Spring, Summer and Autumn 2019. The methods of document analysis and expert interviews will be explained more in detail in each of the empirical chapters. The selection of two cases in this part of the book allows for thick description. At the same time, it also makes that the identification of explanatory factors for the behaviour of public broadcasters might be a bit binary and of course explanatory theory needs more country studies to become more granular. The inclusion of more cases in Part II of the book, that is, the analysis of changing Public Service Media laws, to some extent alleviates that concern.

I interviewed 50 people for this book. As already hinted at, the main effort was spent on interviews with Flemish, Polish and Irish experts. Their insights are anonymised throughout the different chapters. I also talked about the main ideas and findings of the book with experts from the United Kingdom, the Netherlands, and Switzerland. People I talked to are, in alphabetical following order, Ben Appel (Director of Legal and Public Affairs, DPG Media), Ross Biggam (Vice President Public and European Affairs, Discovery Communications), Karen Braeckmans (former Director of HR, VRT), Sally Broughton-Micova (Lecturer in media policy, East Anglia University), Bart Caron (former member of Flemish Parliament, Green Party, and member of the Board of Governors of VRT), Peter Claes (at the time Director Media and Production, VRT), Celene Craig (Deputy Chief Executive Officer,

Broadcasting Authority Ireland), Beata Chmiel (head, Obywatele Kultury), Yaël de Haan (professor journalism, HU University of Applied Sciences Utrecht), Sandra Depreter (former CEO,VRT), Bert De Graeve (former CEO, VRT), Allan Esilemont (Director General, TG4), Tom Evens (Professor of Media Economics, Ghent University), Michal Glowacki (Professor of Media Policy, Warsaw University), Ladina Heimgartner (former Deputy Director General of SRG SSR and former Director of RTR), James Hickey (former Chief Executive, Screen Ireland), Luc Jansegers (chef de cabinet for former Minister of Media Sven Gatz, Liberal Party), Alicja Jaskiernia (Professor of Media Policy, Warsaw University), Stanislaw Jedrzejewski (Professor of Media Studies, Kozminski University and former Executive at Polish Radio), Tadeusz Kowalski (Professor of Media Economics, Warsaw University) – wrote the new financing law for Public Service Media in 2008), Andrzej Krajewski (former journalist, TVP and media activist), Paul Lembrechts (at the time CEO,VRT), Bruno Machiels (CEO, Efeso Consulting), Angela Mills Wade (Director General, European Publishers Council), Dorota Nygren (former journalist, Polish Radio), Willie O'Reilly (former RTE Group Commercial Director), Grégoire Polad (Director General, ACT), Manuel Puppis (Professor of Media Studies, Freibourg University), Phil Ramsey (Lecturer in Media Policy, Ulster University), Slawomir Rogowski (Professor at University of Warsaw, former member of the National Broadcasting Council), Paul Romer (former CEO, Dutch public broadcasting organisation NTR), Katia Segers (member of Flemish Parliament, Socialist Party), Sean Sherlock (Irish Labour Party, spokesperson on justice, children and youth affairs), Dagmara Sidyk (Ph.D. student in media regulation, Warsaw University), Gavan Titley (Lecturer in Media Studies, Manooth University), Pauric Travers (Chair, Broadcasting Authority Ireland), Luc Van den Brande (former Minister President of the Flemish Government, Chairman of VRT's Board of Governors), Hilde Van den Bulck (Professor studying Public Service Media, Drexel University), Eric Van Rompuy (former Flemish Minister of Media, Christian Democrat Party), Christian Van Thillo (Chairman of the executive committee, DPG Media), Lut Vercruysse (former Director of Strategy, VRT), Inge Vrancken (at the time Editor-in-Chief, VRT News), Liesbet Vrieleman (Director Information and Sports, VRT), Gert Ysebaert (CEO, Mediahuis), a manager with a regional section of the BBC (who chose to remain anonymous), and a journalist with Polish Radio (who chose to remain anonymous). All interviews were transcribed in full.

It will be noticeable that the interviews with experts from Flanders and Ireland are more diverse in terms of whom I talked to. For Poland, I was largely able to talk to academics, civil society, media activists and some former or current employees of the public broadcaster. One of them, a journalist at Polish Radio, asked to remain anonymous and is not mentioned with first name and surname in this introduction. I contacted Public Service Media management and government officials in Poland, but several scheduled interviews were in fact cancelled upon my arrival in Warsaw. In a personal communication with the head of international affairs at TVP on 11 April 2019 I was told that there was no interest within government and the public broadcaster TVP to talk with scientists from the West who had no genuine curiosity in understanding the Polish system and the guaranteed independence of TVP and other public broadcasting organisations at the national and regional level. I add this as some sort of disclaimer because I can imagine that the selection of interviewees might seem a bit biased, but it is in fact rather exemplary of some of the analyses on Poland and Public Service Media that readers will find later on in this book. For Poland, I relied on the extensive help of Michal Glowacki (lecturer at Warsaw University, Poland) to contact people and get acquainted with the Polish 'situation' beyond what I had already read in numerous books and journal articles. My plunge into Irish Public Service Media was aided enormously by Phil Ramsey (lecturer at Ulster University, Ireland). I am indebted to Michal Glowacki, Phil Ramsey and all of the interviewees, each of which shared valuable insights and several of them challenging my ideas.

The sound methodological approach underlying this book also serves as a guarantee against a self-protection reflex that is manifest, understandable and retraceable both in Public Service Broadcasting research and in public broadcasters themselves (and, in fact, in all other big societal institutions, see Bonnell, 1989: 651). For a good comprehension, I do not seek to protect an institution that has been around since the 1920s. Rather, I want to explain in a scientifically solid manner why Public Service Media is a societal project worth fighting for and how public broadcasters can contribute to its crystallisation in reality in some contexts, while this will most likely be a mission impossible in other settings. The observation that public broadcasters have been bureaucratic, often politicised institutions, that have indeed sometimes been over-focused on market shares, that have definitely engaged in commercial practices that do not sit easily with their public service remit (Elstein et al., 2004) and that resist structural organisational changes with an eye on the self-protection of their institution, rather than their public service remit is valid. It does not make the fight for the preservation of the public interest in media, for some sort of system that contributes to strengthening citizenship and democracy less necessary or less valuable. On the contrary, we need to invest more time in finding a realistic compromise between theory, rules and practice. We need to think beyond existing concepts and beyond the longstanding arrangements to transpose these in practice. That requires an open attitude and the intellectual honesty to recognise that in some European countries the DNA of state broadcaster instead of public broadcaster is hard to change. Moreover, it implies adding to theory development on the basis of the actual practice of Public Service Media in Europe.

Structure

The book is divided in three parts on theories, rules and practices respectively. Part I starts with an analysis of disruptions that are in fact the framework within which the choice for or against (what kind of) Public Service Media is made.

In Chapter 2, I consider two main disruptions extensively elaborated upon in communication sciences literature: first, the digitisation of media; second, the internationalisation of media. Both limit the toolkit of national governments to intervene in media be it for economic, political, social or cultural reasons. The gaps in Public Service Media theories as well as in more narrow conceptions of Public Service Broadcasting ('light scenarios') are identified and critically evaluated in Chapter 3. Essentially, most scholars seem to agree that 'one day Public Service Broadcasting was in, but today it is out'.[2] However, the plethora of other concepts, ranging from Public Service Media, public service communication and public service content on the social responsibility side to Public Service Publisher, public service light, and so on, on the market failure side has minimum-minimorum given rise to a lack of perspective on and directions for Public Service Broadcasting. The latter cannot be a public service 'anything' (Donders, Pauwels and Loisen, 2012) if it seeks to establish its relevance in the 21st century. There is a difference between Public Service Media being a holistic, democratic and broadly supported project on the one hand and it being an umbrella concept that is moulded to every day realities on the other hand. In fact, I consider the 'umbrella-isation' of Public Service Media one of the main threats for its sustainability in the long run. For example, when German public broadcasters justified the online sales of cookery equipment, linking this service to an existing television show, they in fact (ab)used the existing legal framework (at that time requiring a link between new activities and existing radio or television programmes) to their own financial benefit, while at the same time excavating their public service remit more effectively than a private competitor could have done. What is more important, they did not serve the public interest in media while, from a legal point of view, providing public media services. Similarly, when government authorities expect public broadcasters to cooperate with a plethora of public institutions on the basis of ill-defined objectives and mainly as a means to deal with budgetary restraints (Raats, 2013), they are inhibiting the emergence of a clear, collaborative role for Public Service Media in the digital age.

Based on the findings in Chapters 2 and 3, I will subsequently fill some of the gaps in Public Service Media theory, relating it not to genres or platforms, but to specific values and objectives. Some of these will be identical to values and objectives identified in their most basic form already in the 1930s by John Reith and subsequently elaborated upon in, among others, Hoffmann-Riem (1991), Raboy (1995), Price and Raboy (2003), Jakubowicz (2007b), and so on. Other values will, however, be more responsive to the needs of society in light of the digitisation and internationalisation of media. I do not per se position my work as a new theory on Public Service Media but rather as a theoretical basis with which the law and practice can be compared. What emerges from that confrontation is addressed in the conclusion of this book and already exploratively addressed in Chapters 4 and 5.

Chapter 6, kicking of Part II of the book, takes a bird's-eye perspective on legal frameworks governing Public Service Media. It ties these to ideological divisions in national Public Service Media law, discerning the variety of systems in Europe. Setting out from Hallin and Mancini's (2004) original media system typology, the chapter is structured around four main observations. Some of these are dividing the EU in the Northern and Western European Member States on the one hand and the Southern and Central European Member States on the other hand. The first observed trend is the evolution from democratic corporatist models towards liberal media systems, in which the functioning of the market is set as a standard and government intervention increasingly becomes the exception to that rule. Second, one can notice a persistence of government capture of media and also public broadcasters in notably Southern, Central and Eastern European countries. Often these countries share an authoritarian (be it fascist or communist) past. They are sometimes categorised as 'competitive authoritianist' given that, although democratic institutions and, from a legal point of view, independent media exist in these countries, they remain manipulated by the ruling elites (Levitsky and Way, 2010; Vladisavljević, 2016). Third, and related to both the first and the second observation, it is apparent that there is a thin blue line between Public Service Media laws and politics across media models. That is challenging as one might tentatively argue that achieving the public interest in media is not always a primary objective of politicians. That in itself could lead to a somewhat provocative and bold statement, being that the project of Public Service Media is intrinsically flawed as one of its key values, being independence of political capture, cannot be realised because of its very own institutional arrangement. Related to that, I, fourth, fleetingly discuss the potential of non-profit, alternative media as a complement or substitute to mainstream media, including public broadcasters.

This bird's eye perspective on legal traditions will provide a more solid basis for a more in-depth analysis of legal frameworks in place that affect public broadcasters across Europe. Chapter 7 commences with explaining how Public Service Media policies have been shaped by European institutions. First, the Council of Europe's approach is addressed. The Council, founded on 5 May 1949 (so, genuinely, a post-WWII institution), is a member-driven organisation. Forty-seven European countries make up its membership. Based in Strasbourg, it is concerned with the development of European-wide principles based mainly on the European Convention on Human Rights and has been particularly active in putting forward some shared principles on Public Service Media. In this chapter, I address the most important resolutions the Council has drafted on Public Service Media. Attention is devoted to their main underlying values, articulated principles and weaknesses (the latter mainly in terms of enforcement). Second, and more elaborately, the European Commission's actions with regard to Public Service Media are analysed. This part of the chapter sets out from the huge scholarly attention for the intervention of the Commission's Directorate General for Competition and its impact on public broadcasters (see, among others, Holtz-Bacha, 2005; Moe, 2008; Bardoel and Vochteloo, 2012; Donders, 2012; Van den Bulck and Moe, 2012;). It discusses the impact of the European Commission's State aid policies and its legal basis to act upon in this area, roughly until 2010. I discuss in Chapter 8 what impact (positive and negative) DG Competition has been making over the last ten years through State aid cases concerning the funding of public broadcasters. Notably, the European Commission dismisses the context of internationalisation and digitisation (trends discussed in relation to Public Service Media in Chapter 2) when Member States argue for Public Service Media. It nonetheless often uses these same trends to frame internal market policies on media.

Setting out from this broader reflection on the interplay between the law, political ideology and media systems, Chapter 9 deals with national and subnational governments' development, implementation and evaluation of Public Service Media policies for the digital age. It thus focuses on the legal frameworks in place at the national and subnational level. It does not necessarily confront these with relevant European guidelines (although this aspect is touched upon), but rather identifies what can be considered (new) highly relevant tools in the Public Service Media toolkit today and in the future. Issues touched upon are the definition of public broadcasters' mission, the inclusion of new media services in the public service remit and public value tests. Chapter 10 zooms in on funding arrangements for public broadcasters in Europe, specifically the shift from license fee to subsidy systems in a multitude of European countries, the pressure on revenues and some public broadcasters' quests to find other, notably commercial, revenues and the tensions that arise from this. A final chapter in this part on Public Service Media law, Chapter 11, looks at the governance of public broadcasters. It provides a sketch of governance in relation to independence and pluralism. I do not only study legal changes in the chapters on new media services, funding and governance, but also how these match with the theoretical basis for Public Service Media identified earlier and also if there is a level of consistency that can be observed across Europe. Something that is also exploratively dealt with is the extent to which politics is a determining factor in all of the legal changes and constancies studied. Des Freedman (2008: 1) argues that media policy is essentially political in/by nature, saying 'Media policy, the systematic attempt to foster certain types of media structure and behaviour and to suppress alternative modes of structure and behaviour, is a deeply political phenomenon.' Agreeing with his proposition, the purpose of these three chapters on rules for 'the digital', funding and governance is thus not only to describe and evaluate national policy practices with regard to Public Service Media, but also to uncover the interplay between media law and politics – an aim that unavoidably connects to questions of public broadcasters' independence (see Hanretty, 2011).

Part III turns to public broadcasters' own practices, elaborating on several strategies to deal with the evolution to Public Service Media. In Chapter 12, I confront public broadcasters' own digital strategies with the rather elaborate legal frameworks in place in this area. This will show that not only politicians struggle to deal with public broadcasters going digital, but also public broadcasters themselves face difficulties in so doing. Focus of the analysis is on public broadcasters in Flanders, the Netherlands, Ireland and the United Kingdom. Subsequently, there are two more chapters: one presenting the results from a comprehensive case study on the practice and also future of Public Service Media in Flanders; the other zooming in on Poland. The notions of political, social, cultural and civic citizenship form the backbone of both chapters, which present a granular analysis of the past, present and future of Public Service Media in both cases.

The conclusions will tie together the book's theoretical and empirical findings with the aim to explain what Public Service Media can and should stand for before, in and after 2020. In so doing, this book goes beyond the analysis of theory, law and practice. It's objective is to formulate sensible answers for policy as well (on the difference between policy analysis of and for, see, among others, Dunn, 2015; Sibeon, 1996: 17ff). The book's main argument is that public broadcasters delivering the public interest in media will be more necessary in the 21st century than public broadcasters have ever been in the past. They need to adapt to changing circumstances, however, and profoundly – at the level of policies, organisation and practices – so. Moreover, their underlying objective should be to serve the public interest in media, to contribute to citizenship, rather than to consider the delivery of public services as a goal in itself, instead of a means. At the same time, policy-makers need to adjust and, sometimes, even transform the way in which they develop policies for the media sector: long-term vision, formalised and visible stakeholder (including audience) involvement and a balanced appreciation of the interplay between public intervention and market forces are among the important ingredients of a more future-proof media policy framework. Importantly, public broadcasters and politicians have shared responsibilities in transposing the value-based project of Public Service Media in practice. In case public broadcasters structurally fail to live up to their obligations – and I mean this in the most fundamental way: that is, when public broadcasters fail to be public broadcasters – it is necessary to reconsider the choice for this institutional arrangement in a specific setting. In case politicians do not take care of their end of the bargain, it should become possible for European Courts to step up and hold national governments liable.

This book points at a number of trends, and policy and Public Service Media practices that are troublesome; that might render objectives related to universality, independence, quality, creativity, innovation, diversity, national identity, conversation … mere window dressing and that will, ultimately, if not remedied, undermine the trustworthiness and legitimacy of public broadcasters in contemporary society. Having said that, I am hopeful about the future of public broadcasters and even more so about the future of the public interest in media. The title already gives away to some extent that theory, rules and practice are (essentially and necessarily) three different things though. With this book I aspire to bridge the gap between them – albeit it only partially and most likely imperfectly – developing theories that can be inspiring and instructive for practice, and learning from practice what theory can never teach us.

Notes

1 A complete list of documents can be found in the reference list. More information on the methodological approach follows in the beginning of the chapters in Parts II and III.

2 Analogy with 'In fashion, one day you're in, the next day you're out' – a phrase used by presenter and former top model Heidi Klum in each episode of the television reality show 'Project Runway', which has run for over ten years now on commercial broadcasting stations around the globe.

References

Bardoel, J. and Lowe, G.F. (2007). From public service broadcasting to public service media: The core challenge. In G.F. Lowe and J. Bardoel (eds), *From Public Service Broadcasting to Public Service Media* (pp. 9–28). Göteborg: Nordicom.

Bardoel, J. and Vochteloo, M. (2012). Conditional access for public service broadcasting to new media platforms: EU State aid policy vis-à-vis public service broadcasting – the Dutch case. In N. Just and M. Puppis (eds), *Trends in Communication Policy Research: New Theories, Methods & Subjects* (pp. 301–315). Bristol: Intellect.

Bauer, J. (2012). Comments on subjects for communication policy research. Intervention in the 4th ECREA European Communication Conference, 24-27 October, Istanbul.

Bonini, T. (2019). Public Service Media (PSM) in the Age of Platform Society: From PSM to 'Convivial' Public Service Platforms. Paper presented at the IAMCR Conference 'Communication, Technology and Human Dignity: Disputed Rights, Contested Truths', 7-11 July, Madrid.

Bonnell, R. (1989). *La vingt-cinquième image. Une économie de l'audiovisuel.* Paris: Gallimard/ Femis.

Collins, R., Finn, A., McFayden, S. and Hoskins, C. (2001). Public service broadcasting beyond 2000: Is there a future for public service broadcasting? *Canadian Journal of Communication* 26(1).

Curran, J. (2014). Foreword. In J. Hardy (ed.), *Critical Political Economy of the Media: An Introduction* (pp. 17–36). London: Routledge.

Donders, K. (2012). *Public Service Media and Policy in Europe.* Basingstoke: Palgrave Macmillan.

Donders, K. (2013). Een regelrechte tragedie. In *De Standaard*, 13 June. [*A downright tragedy*].

Donders, K. and Moe, H. (eds) (2011). *Exporting the Public Value Test.* Göteborg: Nordicom.

Donders, K. and Van den Bulck, H. (2016). Decline and fall of public service media values in the international content acquisition market: An analysis of small public broadcasters acquiring BBC Worldwide content. *European Journal of Communication, 31*(3), 299–316.

Donders, K., Pauwels, C. and Loisen, J. (2012). Introduction: All or nothing? From public service broadcasting to public service media, to public service 'anything'? *International Journal of Media and Cultural Politics, 8*(1), 3–12.

Dunn, W. (2015). *Public Policy Analysis: An Integrated Approach.* London: Routledge.

Elstein, D., Cox, D., Donoghue, B., Graham, D. and Metzger, G. (2004). *Beyond the Charter: The BBC after 2006.* London: The Broadcasting Policy Group.

Enli, G.S. (2008). Redefining public service broadcasting: Multi-platform participation. *Convergence: The International Journal of Research into New media Technologies, 14*(1), 105–120.

Fernández Alonso, I. and Fernández Viso, A. (2012). Internal pluralism in the governance of public service broadcasters in Spain and the role of social groups and professionals: The case of RTVE. *Communication & Society, 25*(2), 203–230.

Freedman, D. (2008). *The Politics of Media Policy*. Cambridge: Polity Press.

Galbraith, J.K. (1996). *The Good Society: The Humane Agenda*. New York: Mariner Books.

Garnham, N. (2000). *Emancipation, the Media, and Modernity: Arguments About the Media and Social Theory*. Oxford: Oxford University Press.

Gibbons, T. and Humphreys, P. (2012). *Audiovisual Regulation Under Pressure: Comparative Cases from North America and Europe*. New York: Routledge.

Hallin, D.C. and Mancini, P. (2004). *Comparing Media Systems: Three Models of Media and Politics*. Cambridge: Cambridge University Press.

Hanretty, C. (2011). *Public Broadcasting and Political Interference*. New York: Routledge.

Hardy, J. (2014). *Critical Political Economy of the Media: An Introduction*. London: Routledge.

Hoffmann-Riem, W. (1991). Rundfunk als public service – ein überaltertes Konzept. In R. Weiss (ed.), *Aufgaben und Perspektiven des öffentlich-rechtlichen Fersnsehens* (pp. 21–47). Hamburg: Nomos. [*Broadcasting as a public service – An outdated concept. Tasks of and perspectives on public television*].

Holtz-Bacha, C. (2005). The EU, the Member States and the future of public broadcasting. *Doxa, 3*, 231–237.

Humphreys, P. (2012). A political scientist's contribution to the comparative study of media systems in Europe: A response to Hallin and Mancini. In N. Just and M. Puppis (eds), *Trends in Communications Policy Research* (pp. 157–176). Bristol: Intellect.

Jakubowicz, K. (2007a). Public service broadcasting: a new beginning, or the beginning of the end. Retrieved from www.knowledgepolitics.org.uk (accessed 20 October 2020).

Jakubowicz, K. (2007b). Public service broadcasting in the 21st century: What chance for a new beginning? In G.F. Lowe and J. Bardoel (eds), *From Public Service Broadcasting to Public Service Media* (pp. 29–50). Göteborg: Nordicom.

Judt, T. (2010). *Ill Fares the Land*. New York: Penguin Publishing.

Just, N. and Puppis, M. (2012). Introduction. In N. Just and M. Puppis (eds), *Trends in Communication Policy Research*. Bristol: Intellect.

Levitsky, S. and Way, L. (2010). *Competitive Authoritarianism: Hybrid Regimes after the Cold War*. Cambridge: Cambridge University Press.

Levy, D. (1997). Regulating digital broadcasting in Europe: The limits of policy convergence. *West European Politics, 20*(4), 24–42.

Lowe, G.F. (ed.) (2010). *The Public in Public Service Media*. Göteborg: Nordicom.

Lowe, G.F. and Bardoel, J. (eds) (2007). *From Public Service Broadcasting to Public Service Media*. Göteborg: Nordicom.

Moe, H. (2008). Between supranational competition and national culture? Emerging EU policy and public broadcasters' online services. In I. Bondebjerg and P. Madsen (eds), *Media, Democracy and European Culture* (pp. 215–239). Bristol: Intellect.

Murdock, G. (2005). Building the digital commons: Public broadcasting in the age of the Internet. In G.F. Lowe and P. Jauert (eds), *Cultural Dilemmas in Public Service Broadcasting* (pp. 213–230). Göteborg: Nordicom.

Pickard, V. (2019). *Democracy Without Journalism*. Oxford: Oxford University Press.

Price, M. and Raboy, M. (eds) (2003). *Public Service Broadcasting in Transition: A Documentary Reader*. The Hague: Kluwer Law International.

Raats, T. (2013). *And now for something completely different? De rol en positie van de publieke omroep in een genetwerkte samenleving; onderzoek naar de publieke omroepopdracht en – organisatie aan de hand van een comparatieve analyse van de culturele missie* (Unpublished Ph.D. thesis). Vrije Universiteit Brussel, Brussels. [*And now for something completely different? The role and position of the public broadcaster in a networked society: A comparative analysis of the public service remit and organisation in the cultural domain*].

Raboy, M. (ed.) (1995). *Public Broadcasting for the 21st Century*. Luton: University of Luton Press.

Ramsey, P. (2018). It could redefine public service broadcasting in the digital age: Assessing the rationale for moving BBC Three online. *Convergence, 24*(2), 152-167.

Sibeon, R. (1996). *Contemporary Sociology and Policy Analysis: The New Sociology of Public Policy*. Eastham: Tudor Business Publishing.

Steemers, J. (2003). Public Service Broadcasting is not dead yet: Strategies in the 21st century. In G.F. Lowe and T. Hujanen (eds), *Broadcasting and Convergence: New Articulations of the Public Service Remit* (pp. 123–136). Göteborg: Nordicom.

Syvertsen, T., Enli, G., Mjøs, O.M. and Moe, H. (2014). *The Media Welfare State: Nordic Media in the Digital Era*. Ann Arbor: University of Michigan Press.

Taylor-Gooby, P. (2001). The politics of welfare in Europe. In P. Taylor-Gooby (ed.), *Welfare States Under Pressure* (pp. 1–28). London: Sage.

Terzis, G. (ed.) (2007). *European Media Governance: National and Regional Dimensions*. Bristol: Intellect.

Tracey, M. (1998). *The Decline and Fall of Public Service Broadcasting*. Oxford: Clarendon.

Van den Bulck, H. and Moe, H. (2012). To test or not to test: Comparing the development of ex ante public service media assessments in Flanders and Norway. *International Journal of Media and Cultural Politics, 8*(1), 32–50.

Vennesson, P. (2008). Case studies and process tracing. In D. Della Porta and M. Keating (eds), *Approaches and Methodologies in the Social Sciences* (pp. 223-239). Cambridge: Cambridge University Press.

Vladisavljević, N. (2016). Competitive authoritarianism and popular protest: Evidence from Serbia under Milošević. *International Political Science Review, 37*(1), 36–50.

Part I

Theory

2 Public Service Media in a digitised and international media market

Is there a spontaneous achievement of public interest objectives in a digitised and internationalised media landscape?

Media, media usage and the media industry are in flux. Fast technological, social, economic and cultural, evolutions provoke heated debates on the power of technology (see Holmes, 2005; Fuchs, 2017; Van Dijck et al., 2018; Hjorth and Hinton, 2019; a.o. Isin and Ruppert, 2020). Changes occur at an exponentially increasing pace. Linear consumption of audiovisual content is declining, youngsters turn to vlogs, online news of mainstream media is slowly recovering, the success of non-journalist made media is increasing, artificial intelligence results in more far-going personalisation and allows for virtual reality, augmented reality and chat bot applications that will be fairly similar to what was depicted in sci-fi not so long ago, social media have become the main gateway to news for several groups in society, and so on.

While many things change, there are also some constant factors that can be observed. The political economy of media is rather stable in most European countries. Media concentration is a remaining point of concern for scholars inside and outside Europe. In fact, scholars point at a further intensification not only in audiovisual production, broadcasting, distribution or the newspaper industry, but also, and increasingly so, across the borders of media content, electronic communications and Internet sectors of economic activity (Evens and Donders, 2018). The sheer size of merger and acquisition strategies of companies such as Amazon, Facebook and Google puts media concentration in perspective. Not that the integration of ownership structures in media content sectors has become irrelevant, but rather the platformisation we observe today is a warning that the worst is yet to come when talking about media concentration (see several contributions in Moore and Tambini, 2018; Mansell and Steinmueller, 2020).

Moreover, consumers still have a preference for local content. There seems to be a paradox here between the internationalisation of the media sector on the one hand and the importance of cultural proximity on the other hand. 'Think global, act local' strategies have been researched by many scholars (e.g.,

Straubhaar, 1991; Cho and Chung, 2009; Thussu, 2018) as the means to over-come the tension between the achievement of economies of scale and scope and consumers' attachment to content they can identify with. The interactions between the local, the national and the transnational are, according to an increasing amount of scholars, highly complex though. Language, landscape, narrative, and so on, all play a role in allowing for some sort of identification with content (see, for example, Weissmann, 2018).

It is crucial to have a deeper look into all of these changes which impact public broadcasters deeply. Largely, visions can be divided between boom and doom perspectives (for a more granular discussion on notions of media power and views of change, see Freedman, 2014). The positive, boom views focus on the process of creative destruction. Economic growth and innovation bring more choice at a lower cost to consumers. The 'old' media are considered dinosaurs, incapable of renewing themselves and act defensively against pro-active, innovation-driven market entrants. Politicians are too much focused on protecting the interests of legacy media instead of allowing markets to play and handing control to consumers. The new Internet age is considered to come with global citizenship, democratic control via social media, and even revolutions as a consequence of this. On the other side, there is the more pessimist doom vision related to technological change. Inequality in power structures remains. Consumers have an illusion of control, but are in fact commodified further, not in the least on the basis of their data. Policy focuses mainly on economic growth of some and neglects communication rights. Such rights are diverse and concern citizens' right to access information and different interpretative frameworks. They relate to the need for deliberative fora where these interpret-ative frameworks are discussed and evaluated. All opinions must be represented in the public sphere and citizens should not be conceived as mere recipients, but also as active participants and even performers. Graham Murdock (2004: 5-7) advocates for a 'digital commons' as a non-commercial space where citizens can fully enjoy, utilise and benefit from their communication rights. Public broadcasters were to be hubs of the digital commons. It seems that his ideas, first presented in 2004, were visionary. Authors such as Phil Napoli (2019) and Victor Pickard (2019) have added to these ideas on the extension, not shrinking of public service in media and communication. Mina Aslama and Phil Napoli even call for media scholars' activism to bring this about (2011).

Of course, both the doom and boom perspective – while seeming com-pletely antagonist at first sight – are to some extent true. There is change. At the same time, there is more of the same. There is agency. At the same time, structures can be very resistant. Digitisation and internationalisation are two trends that have been widely discussed and, as hinted at above, while scholars agree on the relevance of these phenomena, they do not see eye to eye on what their impact will be on economics, society, politics, culture, and so on. Some will consider these trends as possibilities to break free from the past and to change, often implicitly assumed to the benefit of the consumer. Others will consider these trends as a reinforcement of the existing capitalist society: from an industrial, to a service, to a completely weightless economy (Webster, 2002).

Needless to say that it is very difficult to pin down what exactly the impact of these trends on public broadcasters will be. The aim of this chapter is not to provide for an exhaustive definition, analysis and evaluation of digitisation and internationalisation. Rather, I want to pinpoint how these trends are discussed in literature on Public Service Media and how they are increasingly being seen as justifications for a stronger public broadcaster presence in media markets and society at large. My main argument is that digitisation and internationalisation are essentially antagonists of Public Service Media and public broadcasters. Public Service Broadcasting was, and it is likely (yet, not necessarily desirable) that Public Service Media will remain for both practical and ideological reasons, the playground of nation states. Public broadcasters are because of the latter, but also because of historical reasons mainly a radio and broadcast organisation and, as much as other traditional media organisations, face difficulties to adapt to the new out-of-control environment. Having said that, digitisation and internationalisation put pressure on a lot of public interest related values public broadcasters are supposed to safeguard. In that sense, a stronger case can be made for a public broadcaster active across platforms and devices and this in strong relation with 'the local', provided that public broadcasters are not captured by political control and/or commercial imperatives. Some (e.g., Sørensen and Hutchinson, 2017; Bonini, 2019) have in this respect argued for the creation of Public Service Media platforms, public service infrastructures, or even algorithmic Public Service Media: proposals I will discuss more in detail at the end of this chapter.

Digitisation: thinking beyond convergence

Digitisation and convergence have been buzzwords of communications research from the 1970s until the 1990s. The promise of digitising content was seen as a possibility to produce more content, distribute it more widely and invest in new services not imaginable at the time. Digital was also related quite immediately to convergence, being the coming together of media content, telecommunications and information and communications technology (ICT) industries (Street, 1988; Castells, 1996).

Analogue is death, long live digital

The analogue environment was a place of scarcity. Until the 1980s, for some countries the end of the 1990s, citizens were faced with the dullness of Public Service Broadcasting monopolies. Indeed, programmes of value were made. But, to a large extent, producers were focused on their own motivations and relatively certain of delivery to an audience that was in many cases not terribly fascinated with the emancipating content delivered to them (Donders, 2012).

In telecommunications, there was a monopoly too. And the large-scale penetration of the Internet was not there yet.

The advent of cable and satellite technology, the liberalisation of both broadcasting and telecommunications networks, and a more general ideological turn to neoliberal ideology changed all that. State intervention was looked at from a negative angle and the near-consensus on the existence of public broadcasting and telecommunications monopolies dissolved. Some countries took this very/too far, which made Nicholas Garnham (1990: 127-128) conclude that there was a 'loss of faith in the Statist solution'.

While often frowned upon in academic literature for its consumerist turn (e.g., Dyson, 1985), most media users were rather content with the arrival of commercial television. Admittedly, the Reithian ethos 'to inform, to educate and to entertain' had resulted in far-going paternalism and 'worthy, but ultimately dull programmes, which alienated sections of the audience, with their refusal to recognise the demands of a culturally divided society' (Hughes, 1988: 53-54). Public broadcasters in the end benefited from some pressure of commercial counterparts and more quality in production could be observed.

The Internet added to the situation of more competition, more quality, more commercialism, more ... In work of, among others, Amstrond and Weeds (2007) and Elstein et al. (2004) the emergence of the Internet, more competition, increased content services online and lower market entry barriers were used as the basis for a plea for less Public Service Broadcasting. In the meantime, these trends came with a reality check on what markets actually deliver and even more so where they fail. The excesses and structural failures in converged media markets (e.g., Fuchs, 2020; Mansell and Steinmueller, 2020) have indeed provided fertile ground for arguing in favour of Public Service Media. One can observe the marked difficulty of sustainable and profitable business models for digital journalism (Krumsvik, 2012; Pickard, 2019), the increased commercialisation of audiovisual content in areas such as children's television (Ene, 2017), unethical treatment of data (Sevignani, 2016; Mansell and Steinmueller, 2020), and the concerns that algorithms drive personalisation at the detriment of pluralism, diversity and serendipity (Reviglio, 2017; Spohr, 2017; Nechushtai and Lewis, 2019). Several scholars have demonstrated that concerns on filter bubbles are exaggerated, online news consumption is rather diverse and emerging local or community-based media initiatives can add to diversity (Foth et al., 2016; Haim, Graefe, and Brosius, 2017; Møller et al., 2018). Fake news and deep fakes are dangerous, but effects are difficult to foretell and of a more complex nature than some might have anticipated (e.g., Dobber et al., 2020). Nonetheless, public broadcasters have responded to some of the threats posed by the digital environment. In response to platforms such as Facebook and Netflix shaping British youth culture, the BBC announced in 2017 to up its investments in children's content dramatically (Furness, 2017). In their mapping of public broadcasters' personalisation strategies, Van den Bulck and Moe (2018) find that most of the researched public broadcasters are conscious about pitfalls of personalisation, developing strategies related to privacy, diversity, universality, and so on.

At the same time, several public broadcasters also fail to adequately balance commercial interests when developing targeted advertising, analysing user behaviour, and manufacturing personalised recommendations. In making use of third-party data and servers they participate 'in the exposure economy increasingly managed by international companies', often if not always without the knowledge of users (Sørensen and Van den Bulck, 2020). Besides, scholars such as Tom Mills (2016) have also counterargued that public broadcasters such as the BBC have in fact become part of the elite, exposing a clear liberal bias. Des Freedman (2019: 214) has reached a similar, yet more nuanced and layered conclusion, arguing that the BBC 'represents the strategic interests of powerful elites far more than it does the disparate and messy views of domestic audiences'. The issue of public broadcasters becoming captured and institutionalised within hegemony are taken up again in Chapters 4 and 5.

Long live digital, long live Public Service Media

Essentially, I see three big challenges for public broadcasters that can be related to digitisation. First, in a digital environment there is more competition for the time of media users. On the positive side, there is more choice. Also from players (e.g., YouTube) and types of services (e.g., memes) that were completely absent from popular culture two decades ago (Burgess and Green, 2018). On the negative side, there is more triviality and repetitiveness in what is on offer. 'Churnalism', that is, taking over news from same sources (often PR, spokes persons), has, for example, been a growing concern in research (e.g., Jackson and Moloney, 2016; Saridou, Spyridou and Veglis, 2017). Regardless the normative appreciation of what is happening, public broadcasters need to work harder to reach audiences. That is particularly true for youngsters who are more online, engaged with fast food media consumption, and notorious fans of YouTube and the various vloggers active on the platform. But, research of, among others, Ofcom (2019), also shows that age categories below 45 have an increasingly on-demand consumption patterns, using services such as Netflix to watch content ATAWAD, at any time, anywhere on any device. We also know that people with a migration background and refugees consume less domestic media, have more appetite for international news and information on their country of origin (Christiansen, 2004; Gillespie, 2006; Metykova, 2010). And some groups disconnect from classic media content altogether, opting for immersiveness in online worlds or gaming (Domahidi and Quandt, 2014). Whereas the user was the almost natural endpoint of the media value chain two decades ago, competition has become fiercer and it is not per se the quality of the offer, but also the way you get it to the end consumer that determines success (Donders, Raats and Tintel, 2020).

Second, connecting with citizens does not only become more difficult because of the enormous amount of content available, but also because user interfaces are no longer controlled by public broadcasters themselves. User interfaces are increasingly controlled by international platforms. Digital decoders, electronic programming guides, the start screen of your Samsung television set, and so on (Johnson, 2020; Hesmondhalgh and Lotz, 2020; Hesmondhalgh and Lobato, 2019). They have one thing in common: public broadcasters have no or a very limited say in where and how they are to be found. That might change with the approval of the 2018 Audiovisual Media Services Directive. The directive indeed allows Member States to impose rules on due prominence of content. Countries such as Germany, the United Kingdom and Belgium (both language communities) are exploring how they can safeguard the findability and prominence of European works, also through recommender systems (Van Nieuwenhuyze, Picone and Donders, 2020).

Third, digitisation is not only a challenge from the outside, but also on the inside. Public broadcasters not only need to adjust to the digital, they have to become the digital. Public Service Media as a concept refers to public service delivery across media and platforms. For many public broadcasters, even though embracing the concept at the rhetorical level, this transition appears to be extremely difficult (Donders, 2019). There is organisational resistance to really break through the boundaries of radio and television. The focus, also of management, is habitually still on massive reach. While the latter is definitely important to ensure relevance of public broadcasters for a big group in society, that does not necessarily mean the point to multi-point model of broadcasting needs to be stuck to. Instead, the opportunities of audience engagement, of dialogue and of co-creation with audiences should be explored. This should not be done in a purely experimental setting or be treated as an accessory activity of Public Service Media. It, on the contrary, ought to be at the heart of Public Service Media (Vanhaeght, 2019). I will study at both the theoretical, legal and practical level where, why and how the transition from Public Service Broadcasting into a 'digital-adapted' version poses issues (see Chapters 3, 9 and 12).

Internationalisation: The limits and possibilities of nation state intervention

Digitisation has gone hand in hand with internationalisation: another buzz word of communications research from the 1970s up until today. For the purpose of this book, internationalisation is approached mainly from an economic angle. It concerns issues such as transnationalisation, audiovisual contents flows, cross-media ownership, platformisation, and so on. Identified as a trend from the 1980s onwards (Doyle, 2013), internationalisation has taken gigantic proportions with companies such as Apple, Facebook, Amazon and Google dictating the very functioning of global e-markets (Evens and Donders, 2018; Mansell and Steinmueller, 2020). That does not mean though that smaller, local initiatives do not exist. Several European countries are blessed with broadcasters, newspapers and distributors that invest in local content creation. Admittedly, also those are scaling up. Or several, notably local media players, are going out of business. New entrants, sometimes referred to as emerging media organisations (Badran, 2020), can have a profound impact on journalism culture and have a legitimate place in the world of media entrepreneurship as Mark Deuze and Tamara Witschge (2020) so convincingly argue in *Beyond Journalism.*

From forecast to reality

While internationalisation of media has been a fact already since the 1980s, 'the internationalised media market' as a phenomenon, no longer a trend, is of a more recent nature (Enli et al., 2019). As already hinted at before, media and communication conglomerates are active across borders and in many cases dictate the overall performance of media ecosystems (Kostovska et al., 2020). So-called multi-layered platforms have become gatekeepers, centres of accumulated intermediation nodes and thus economic power. They also target domestic audiences (Hoelck and Ballon, 2016) and are in that sense on top of the value chain. Winseck (2020) disagrees, saying that more traditional media and telecommunications companies still call the shots when looking at distinct markets such as the Canadian market. The claims on platforms' destructive impact on journalism and the media industries do not stand up to scrutiny, he says. Subscription and direct purchases are the most important revenue basis for media industries, not advertising. While his analysis holds merit and demystifies a lot of the hype on platforms, it still sets out from separate media, telecommunications and platform industries while platformisation as a phenomenon cuts across these previously separate industry branches. Structural collaborations and joint ventures between companies such as Netflix and Telefonica are a sign of that.

The internationalisation of media markets is a good example of how different parts of the world and economy are becoming increasingly interconnected. Some would argue that such increased interconnectedness comes with a strengthening of capitalism and multinationals on the one hand, a weakening power of nation states to enforce policies and an increased homogenisation and commercialisation of culture on the other hand (De Bens, 2007: 17). Admittedly, internationalisation and digitisation have resulted in a market where a multitude of domestic media companies (whether legacy or new emerging players) seem to be more out of control and a limited number of conglomerates (whether legacy media or platforms) are increasingly in control. The latter have a pre-set interest in homogenisation as a cost-efficient, relative guarantee for commercial success (see Esser, 2013).

Public broadcasters from the centre to the periphery

How is internationalisation affecting public broadcasters specifically? First, internationalisation comes with more competitors (Evens and Donders, 2018). These are often not legacy media such as broadcasters and newspaper publishers. Platform players such as Netflix, Google, Facebook and Spotify are companies public broadcasters compete with for audience attention. Especially in younger age groups (up to 35) these platform players are increasingly popular. Recently, the BBC admitted it faced intense competition from Netflix. The market share of its iPlayer service dropped considerably and quite synchronically with the rise of Netflix's share. The iPlayer is a free service, but apparently the legal limitations on the period the BBC can offer content (30 days) makes iPlayer less appealing compared to the library content of Netflix. Some scholars have criticised the BBC's collaboration with Netflix in this regard, not only for strategic reasons, but also arguing the value proposition of Netflix is a commercial one and conflicts with the public service agenda of the BBC (Ramsey, 2018).

Second, and related, the internationalisation of media markets is usually connected to intensified merger and acquisition activity (Evens and Donders, 2016; 2018). Scaling up intra-chain, but also inter-chain can be observed. The take over of Time Warner by AT&T has created a colossus that is active in mobile, broadband, television distribution, broadcasting, production, premium rights, OTT, and so on. Liberty Global is buying cable infrastructure, software companies, broadcasters, production companies, and so on across Europe. There are joint ventures between the American multinational of John Malone and Vodafone in the Netherlands and Germany and with Discovery Communications in the UK market. Telefonica works together with Netflix on a structural basis, offering Netflix's SVOD service in its bundles to users. Some production companies such as All3Media, Endemol Shine Group and Red Arrow have become bigger entities than broadcasters. Private broadcasters in countries such as Germany and Belgium are part of bigger groups also active in radio, newspapers, online classifieds, and so on (see company profiles in the European Audiovisual Observatory's database MAVISE). Leaving the BBC and ARD aside, most European public broadcasters will thus, comparably speaking, become smaller and lose their status as market leader. They will be less able to determine the terms of trade deals with production companies and are definitely already not doing this when working together with Spotify, YouTube, Netflix and the likes. Somewhat in contradiction to that, governments across Europe are asking public broadcasters to intensify collaborations with other media companies to protect domestic 'media ecosystems' (Donders, Raats and Tintel, 2020).

Third, findability of public service content will be less evident in an internationalised market place with big and more competitors. During monopoly, audiences had access to public service content only. That was not per se a good thing. Public broadcasters became overly paternalist and programme makers were usually more concerned with their own wishes, than the wants and needs of the audience (Hughes, 1988). In the dual broadcasting market, public broadcasters competed for viewers and listeners with commercial broadcasters. However, choice for consumers was still limited to 'traditional' linear television and radio. In that sense, content of public broadcasters could be easily discovered and when consumers were fond of it, they listened or watched. Otherwise, they zapped to alternative programmes. Competition could be fierce and, according to some, resulted in commercialisation of public broadcasters' offers and convergence between television schedules of the generalist channels in particular (Hultén and Brants, 1992; Donders, 2012). Nowadays, the findability of public service content has become less evident than was the case during monopoly and the subsequent dual broadcasting market. Interfaces such as the electronic program guide (EPG), the on-demand catalogue of television distributors, the apps interface on a smart television set and the YouTube or Netflix start screen do not per se put local or public service content in a very visible position. We know that the placing of content is crucial, though, in terms of consumption level. That could mean that less advantageous placing of public service content reduces its discoverability, its actual consumption and thus also its societal relevance (see Ofcom, 2018; Van Nieuwenhuyze et al., 2020).

While internationalisation comes with threats of public broadcasters and the commercialisation often related to it might be considered at odds with the fundamental values underlying Public Service Media, it also offers a continued justification for the project. Indeed, regardless the internationalisation of media markets, public broadcasters have remained the biggest investors in local content (EBU, 2019). That is a first important reason to sustain Public Service Media. Moreover, internationalisation is also said to result in a lower sovereignty of countries over their cultural policies. That makes the presence of a public broadcaster as part of the so-called 'cultural policy toolkit' (Grant and Wood, 2004; Gibbons and Humphreys, 2012; Donders and Raats, 2015) more, not less, important.

Some indeed argue that nation states have no power over media anymore. Some politicians share this idea, believing that they can no longer do something meaningful to stimulate public interest objectives in media and communications. The latter has been criticised by Evens and Donders (2018) as a cowardly 'laissez-faire' policy that can be observed notably in the field of platform policies but also manifests itself in the continuous relaxation of media ownership rules across Europe. Admittedly, the use of political power is more challenging in a digital and converged media environment. Competencies are also shared between nation states and supranational organisations such as the World Trade Organization (WTO) and the European Union. Such institutions are largely inspired by an economic and free market-driven policy agenda (Harcourt, 2005). The persistent conflicts between the EU and Member States on the funding of public broadcasters shows that policy agendas are indeed not always easy to align between different levels.

Others show that internationalisation has given rise to more complex and multi-layered interactions and interdependencies (Thompson, 1995: 149) in which nation states still hold considerable power to intervene. Sinclair (2004: 79), for example, stresses that the struggle with supranational organisations does not mean that nation states have become obsolete regulatory authorities. Especially in the media sector with its mixed economic and cultural importance, one can still observe significant activity from national governments. That is not in the least the case for negative types of intervention like censorship. Governments can also take justifiable decisions protecting their domestic industries that work through for many years and even decades to come, as is illustrated in research of Lowe, Berg and Nissen (2011), Nordahl Svendsen (2011), Syvertsen, Enli, Ole and Moe (2014) and Raats, Evens, Vanhaeght and Ruelens (2015).

In any case, public broadcasters do not have that many commercial allies in an international media market. Audiovisual content production companies of course are still in need of public broadcasters commissioning content with them, but besides, public broadcasters do risk to end up as a fairly isolated actor in a highly integrated value networked based media market. That makes collaborations between public broadcasters such as the BBC and Flemish VRT on the one hand with international platforms such as Netflix not per se a wise undertaking (Ramsey, 2018). It might bring in money in the short term, but in the longer term it can potentially add to the commercialisation of Public Service Media, as pointed out in earlier research by Donders and Van den Bulck (2016) and Ramsey (2018). Moreover, it could very well undermine public broadcasters' appeal to audiences. Smaller public broadcasters such as Flemish public broadcaster VRT put in considerable amounts of money in drama productions. When Netflix adds to that investment, even in a minor way, it insists on a drama series to be a 'Netflix Original' and the brand of the public broadcaster that invests heavily is being removed. That also results in youngsters saying the public broadcaster should make more interesting Flemish drama series, like Netflix is doing. This is a rather invisible power play, often overlooked in the United Kingdom where Netflix actively pursues the inclusion of the BBC brand on Netflix series, basically because it is an international power brand.

Digitisation and internationalisation combined: how platformisation strengthens the case for Public Service Media

As already hinted at before the platformisation of media markets is adding to the pressure on public broadcasters. But it also creates a case for stronger Public Service Media (organisations). Two reasons account for this. In the article 'User data as public resource: Implications for social media regulation', Philip Napoli says that data breaches, abuse of dominance by platform companies, disinformation issues, and so on, have resulted in policy debates on user data and privacy on the one hand and content moderation and curation on the other hand. While 'platforms emerged and evolved outside of the traditional public interest governance frameworks that have traditionally applied to media' (Napoli, 2019: 3), there is a growing awareness of a need to regulate platforms, but also to ensure alternatives to the highly commercialised ecosystems that some of the biggest platforms have built. Indeed, local journalism (Pickard, 2019), investigative journalism and domestic content (Raats, 2020) are having a hard time in platform land.

Those observations have led some scholars to argue for Public Service Media platforms or new public interest-oriented initiatives. Until five years ago, the focus of scholars was mainly on public broadcasters being active across platforms (Enli, 2008; Bennet and Strange, 2008; Debrett, 2009; Suarez-Candel, 2012; Bennet and Medrado, 2013; Klein-Shagrit and Keinonen, 2014; Donders, 2019). That focus has shifted to public broadcasters becoming Public Service Media platforms (Bonini, 2019). Such thinking is still in an embryonic state, but is based on the fertile ground of communication rights research. Public Service Media platforms could be argued to safeguard access, availability, competence, dialogical and privacy rights of citizens.

> Access is about citizens' equal access to information, orientation, entertainment, and other rights-related content. Availability indicates that relevant content (as to information, orientation and entertainment, among others) should be equally available to citizens. Competence means that citizens should be educated in the skills and abilities that enable them to use the means and information available to them according to their own needs and desires. Dialogical rights go beyond the right to create content. They involve making public spaces available that enable citizens to publicly share information, experiences, views, and opinions on common issues, and the right to be heard by those in power. Finally, privacy indicates two different things: first, everybody's private life has to be protected from unwanted publicity, unless its exposure is in the public interest or a person decides to make it public; and second, protection of personal data means that all information gathered by authorities or businesses must be treated as confidential.
>
> (Horowitz and Nieminen, 2017: 107)

In a similar vein, Phil Napoli (2019) has criticised the completely commodified platform architecture that controls media and communication today. In *Social Media and the Public Interest: Media Regulation in the Disinformation Age*, Napoli advocates for a revival of the public interest in media governance and a public utilities approach to platforms. Victor Pickard (2019) makes a similar plea. Observing commercial imperatives driving the information infrastructure of the US and even 'market fundamentalism', he pushes for a public media system that has (local) journalism at its core and that can act independently from the platforms and conglomerates that dominate media markets these days.

Of course, these views need to be developed further. What they have in common though is, first, a rejection of a complete market-controlled digital infrastructure; second, a public interest and communication rights-inspired model of media production and delivery; and third, a call for transparency and citizen empowerment in all of this. Admittedly, these ideas are US-focused and set out from the idea that a BBC-style public broadcasting organisation is a superior organisation model and might be the perfect starting point for a Public Service Media platform. While the idea of a Public Service Media platform is highly interesting at the theoretical level, it risks not being an improvement in practice in case we rely on heavily politicised public/state broadcasters such as Polish TVP, on public broadcasters such as VRT that insufficiently distinguish their data processes with those of commercial media and platform companies (Sørensen and Van den Bulck, 2020) or on the BBC that is, regardless of its value for society at the same time, also embodying and representing elites and elite structures (Freedman, 2019).

The intrinsic incongruity between digitisation, internationalisation and Public Service Media

The whole idea of Public Service Media sets out from the premise that public broadcasters have to become active across platforms, on multiple devices, with programmes and other media content services. That is of course far from an easy task. While most scholars would indeed agree that Public Service Media is the next and semi-natural step for Public Service Broadcasting, there is less agreement about the current position of public broadcasters in this transition. We can distinguish between five phases of development. First, there is the experimental phase. In this phase, public broadcasters realise that the Internet offers possibilities to distribute content in a different manner. It also allows for interactivity, co-creation, app development, and so on. Public broadcasters experiment in order to see what works and what can be improved. Pilots such as combined television-online formats that are co-created with the audience (for example: TV Lab in France, Carte Blanche in Belgium and BNN University in the Netherlands) (Donders, 2019) are typical of this phase. Second, there is the panic phase, when public broadcasters realise that other companies or even some private individuals are more successful than they are at attracting audience attention online. This tends to result in directionless strategies, aimed largely at channelling audiences to their websites. To some extent, this is comparable with the period when public broadcasters were first confronted with competition from commercial broadcasters and wanted to see 'bottoms on seats' (Nossiter, 1991). This is also reflected in the third phase: the expansionist phase, in which the public broadcasters aim to maximise their presence online, placing more value on this than on their public service mission (Donders, 2012). During the fourth consolidation phase, public broadcasters prioritise what is important and what is not. Repeatedly confronted with budget cuts, they critically evaluate what they need to do to satisfy the public interest in media. Interestingly, this phase results in a greater focus on distribution, which is characterised by the offer of quality on-demand services, while at the same time seeking to avoiding stringent regulation on the delivery of these services across digital platforms. This, in turn, leads on to internal reorganisation through the shifting of budget away from the linear to the non-linear distribution of services (Raats, 2013: 128). The fifth and final phase is the maturity phase, when public broadcasters have managed to develop an online strategy that focuses on the public service proposition of each of their brands, combined with a solid view of how to connect

with the audience. By this stage, public broadcasters have become more conscious of the need for competitive trade-offs with, for example, Netflix, YouTube
or Twitter. Of course, this does not mean that their content and the related
distribution strategies are uniformly coherent. Digital evolution is still far from
complete: in this sense, it is still a moving target (Ramsey, 2018). Moreover, this
stage-based perspective should not be seen as a purely linear model. It is perfectly
possible for public broadcasters to show elements of the maturity phase, while
also providing good examples of panic behaviour.[1]

In the transition to Public Service Media, public broadcasters have few
natural allies. Media markets are becoming highly concentrated, international
in scope and platform-based in nature (Evens and Donders, 2018). Activities
are developed in line with a highly commercial logic, one in which public
broadcasters such as the BBC participate (Donders and Van den Bulck,
2016). That commercial logic is most of the time at odds with what public
broadcasters are supposed to do, being the universal provision of services in
the public interest irrespective of people's willingness-to-pay, capability-to-
pay or attractiveness for advertisers. Moreover, service delivery is more and
more dependent on companies that are vastly bigger than public broadcasting
organisations. Cable, social media, search engines, video-on-demand
platforms, and so on, are owned by big conglomerates that decide increasingly on how content is being displayed and what content is actually reaching
the user. This might lead to a situation where more diversity at the supply
side could, because of algorithms and subsequent personalisation, eventually
result in less diversity at the consumption side. A final complicating factor is,
as pointed at above and developed further in this book, public broadcasters'
own organisations. They struggle to adapt to the digital environment, stuck
not only in radio and television land, but often also in a bureaucratic, inflex-
ible and resistant administration.

An additional stage that could, in light of the commercialising and
internationalising platform environment, be added to the evolution from Public
Service Broadcasting to Public Service Media is the emancipation of Public
Service Media into Public Service Media platforms. That conceptualisation is
theoretically challenging though and difficult to transpose into practice.

Note

1 This paragraph draws from an earlier publication in *Media Culture & Society* (see
Donders, 2019).

References

Armstrong, M. and Weeds, H. (2007). Public service broadcasting in the digital
world. In P. Seabright and J. von Hagen (eds), *The Economic Regulation of
Broadcasting Markets: Evolving Technology and Challenges for Policy* (pp. 81–149).
Cambridge: Cambridge University Press.

Aslama, M. and Napoli, P. (2011). Introduction. In P. Napoli and M. Aslama (eds), *Communications Research in Action* (pp. 1-6). New York: Fordham University Press.

Badran,Y. (2020). Strategies and (survival) tactics: The case of Syrian oppositional media in Turkey. *Journal of Alternative & Community Media*, *5*(1), 69-85.

Bennett, J. and Medrado, A. (2013). The business of multi-platform public service: Online and at a profit. *Media International Australia*, *146*(1), 103–113.

Bennett, J. and Strange, N. (2008). The BBC's second-shift aesthetics: Interactive television, multi-platform projects and public service content for a digital era. *Media International Australia*, *126*(1), 106–119.

Bonini, T. (2019). Public Service Media (PSM) in the Age of Platform Society: From PSM to 'Convivial' Public Service Platforms. Paper presented at the IAMCR Conference 'Communication, Technology and Human Dignity: Disputed Rights, Contested Truths', 7-11 July, Madrid.

Burgess, J. and Green, J. (2018). *YouTube: Online Video and Participatory Culture*. Malden, MA: Polity Press.

Castells, M. (1996). *The Rise of the Network Society*. Oxford: Blackwell Publishers.

Cho, S. and Chung, J.G. (2009). We want our MTV: Glocalisation of cable content in China, Korea and Japan. *Critical Arts, South-North Cultural and Media Studies*, *23*(3), 321–341.

Christiansen, C.C. (2004). News media consumption among immigrants in Europe: The relevance of diaspora. *Ethnicities*, *4*(2), 185-207.

De Bens, E. (2007). Media between culture and commerce, an introduction. In E. De Bens (ed.), *The media between culture and commerce* (pp. 9-24). Bristol: Intellect.

Debrett, M. (2009). Riding the wave: Public service television in the multi-platform era. *Media, Culture & Society*, *31*(5), 807–827.

Deuze, M. and Witschge, T. (2020). *Beyond Journalism*. Cambridge: Polity.

Dobber, T, Metoui, N, Trilling, D, Helberger, N. and de Vreese, C. (2020). Do (microtargeted) deepfakes have real effects on political attitudes? *The International Journal of Press/Politics*, 26(1), 69-91.

Domahidi, E. and Quandt, T. (2014). Living in a virtual world? An excessive gamer typology. In T. Quandt and S. Kröger (eds), *Multiplayer: The Social Aspects of Digital Gaming* (pp. 202–212). London, New York: Routledge.

Donders, K. (2012). *Public Service Media and Policy in Europe*. Basingstoke: Palgrave Macmillan.

Donders, K. (2019). Public service media beyond the digital hype: Distribution strategies in a platform era. *Media Culture & Society*, *41*(7), 1011-1028.

Donders, K. and Raats, T. (2015). From public service media organisations to decentralised public service for the media sector: A comparative analysis of opportunities and disadvantages. *Javnost – The Public*, *22*(2), 145-163.

Donders, K. and Van den Bulck, H. (2016). Decline and fall of public service media values in the international content acquisition market: An analysis of small public broadcasters acquiring BBC Worldwide content. *European Journal of Communication*, *31*(3), 299–316.

Donders, K., Raats, T. and Tintel, S. (2020). (Re)defining public service media from an economic perspective: Damned if they do, damned if they don't. In B. Van Rimscha and S. Kienzler (eds), *Management and Economics of Communication* (pp. 203-222). Berlin: Mouton De Gruyter.

Doyle, G. (2013). Re-invention and survival: Newspapers in the era of digital multiplatform delivery. *Journal of Media Business Studies*, *10*(4), 1-20.

Dyson, K. (1985). The politics of cable and satellite broadcasting: Some West European comparisons. In R. Kuhn (ed.), *Broadcasting and Politics in Western Europe* (pp. 152–171). London: Routledge.

EBU (2019). Investing in European Content and Culture. Retrieved from www.ebu.ch/news/2019/01/investing-in-european-content-and-culture (accessed October 2020).

Elstein, D., Cox, D., Donoghue, B., Graham, D. and Metzger, G. (2004). *Beyond the Charter: the BBC after 2006*. London: The Broadcasting Policy Group.

Ene, L. (2017). *Media Ownership: Children's TV Channels in Europe – Who Are the Key Players?* Strasbourg: European Audiovisual Observatory.

Enli, G.S. (2008). Redefining public service broadcasting: Multi-platform participation. *Convergence: The International Journal of Research into New Media Technologies, 14*(1), 105-120.

Enli, G.S., Raats, T., Syvertsen, T. and Donders, K. (2019). Media policy for private media in the age of digital platforms. *European Journal of Communication, 34*(4), 395-409.

Esser, A. (2013). Format is king: Television formats and commercialisation. In K. Donders, C. Pauwels and J. Loisen (eds), *Private television in Western Europe: Content, Markets, Policies* (pp. 151-168). Basingstoke: Palgrave Macmillan.

Evens, T. and Donders, K. (2016). Mergers and acquisitions in TV broadcasting and distribution: Challenges for competition, industrial and media policy. *Informatics and Telematics* (special issue on "Television distribution: Economic dimensions, emerging policies"), *33*(2), 674-682.

Evens, T. and Donders, K. (2018). *Platform Power and Policy in Transforming Television Markets*. New York and Basingstoke: Palgrave MacMillan.

Foth, M., Tomitsch, M., Forlano, L., Haeusler, M.H. and Satchell, C. (2016). Citizens breaking out of filter bubbles: Urban screens as civic media. *Proceedings of the 5th ACM International Symposium on Pervasive Displays (PerDis'16)*, 140–147.

Freedman, D. (2014). *The Contradictions of Media Power*. New York: Bloomsbury.

Freedman D. (2019). 'Public Service' and the journalism crisis: Is the BBC the answer? *Television & New Media, 20*(3), 203–218.

Fuchs, C. (2017). *Social Media: A Critical Introduction* (2nd ed.). London: Sage.

Fuchs, C. (2020). *Communication and Capitalism: A Critical Theory*. London: University of Westminster Press.

Furness, H. (2017). Britain's youth culture is being shaped by American tech giants like Facebook and Netflix, BBC warns. Retrieved from www.telegraph.co.uk/news/2017/07/03/bbc-reinvent-childrens-tv-amid-fears-britains-youth-shaped-american/ (accessed October 2020).

Garnham, N. (1990). *Capitalism and Communication: Global Culture and the Economics of Information*. London: Sage.

Gibbons, T. and Humphreys, P. (2012). *Audiovisual Regulation Under Pressure: Comparative Cases from North America and Europe*. New York: Routledge.

Gillespie, M. (2006). Transnational television audiences after September 11. *Journal of Ethnic and Migration Studies, 32*(6), 903–921.

Grant, P.S. and Wood, C. (2004). *Blockbusters and Trade Wars: Popular Culture in a Globalized World*. Vancouver: Douglas & McIntyre.

Haim, M., Graefe, A. and Brosius, H.-B. (2017). Burst of the filter bubble? *Digital Journalism, 6*(3), 330–343.

Harcourt, A. (2005). *The European Union and the Regulation of Media Markets*. Manchester: Manchester University Press.

Hesmondhalgh, D. and Lobato, R. (2019). Television device ecologies, prominence and datafication: The neglected importance of the set-top box. *Media, Culture & Society*, *41*(7), 958–974.

Hesmondhalgh, D. and Lotz, A. (2020). Video screen interfaces as new sites of media circulation power. *International Journal of Communication*, *14*, 386–409. Retrieved from https://ijoc.org/index.php/ijoc/article/view/13261/2913 (accessed October 2020).

Hjorth, L. and Hinton, S. (2019). *Understanding Social Media*. London: Sage.

Hoelck, K. and Ballon, P. (2016). Broadcasting in the Internet Age: Survival of the Fittest? Paper presented at the 12th World Media Economics and Management Conference, 2-6 May, New York.

Holmes, D. (2005). *Communication Theory: Media, Technology and Society*. London: Sage.

Horowitz, M.A. and Nieminen, H. (2017). Diversity and rights: Connecting media reform and public service media. *Revista Científica de Información y Comunicación*, *14*, 99-119.

Hughes, R. (1988). Satellite broadcasting: the regulatory issues in Europe. In R. Negrine (ed.), *Satellite broadcasting: the politics and implications of the new media* (pp. 49-74). London: Routledge.

Hulten, O. and Brants, K. (1992). Public service broadcasting: Reactions to competition. In K. Siune and W. Truetzschler (eds), *Dynamics of Media Politics: Broadcast and Electronic Media in Western Europe* (pp. 116-128). London: Sage.

Isin, E. and Ruppert, E. (2020). *Being Digital Citizens*. London: Rowman & Littlefield International.

Jackson, D. and Moloney, K. (2016). Inside churnalism. *Journalism Studies*, *17*(6), 763–780.

Johnson, C. (2020). The appisation of television: TV apps, discoverability and the software, device and platform ecologies of the internet era. *Critical Studies in Television*, *15*(2), 165–182.

Klein-Shagrir, O. and Keinonen, H. (2014). Public service television in a multi-platform environment: A comparative study in Finland and Israel. *VIEW Journal of European Television History and Culture*, *3*(6), 14–23.

Kostovska, I., Raats, T., Donders, K. and Ballon, P. (2020). Going beyond the hype: Conceptualising 'media ecosystem' for media management research. *Journal of Media Business Studies*, *18*(1), 6–26.

Krumsvik, A.H. (2012). Why old media will be funding journalism in the future. *Journalism Studies*, *13*(5–6), 729-741.

Lowe, G.F., Berg, C. and Nissen, C.S. (2011). Size matters for TV broadcasting policy. In G.F Lowe and C.S. Nissen (eds), *Small among Giants: Television Broadcasting in Smaller Countries* (pp. 21-41). Nordicom: Göteborg.

Mansell, R. and Steinmueller, E. (2020). *Advanced Introduction to Platform Economics*. London: Edward Elgar.

Metykova, M. (2010). Only a mouse click away from home: Transnational practices of Eastern European migrants in the United Kingdom. *Social Identities*, *16*(3), 325-338.

Mills, T. (2016). *The BBC: Myth of a Public Service*. London: Verso.

Möller, J., Trilling, D., Helberger, N. and van Es, B. (2018). Do not blame it on the algorithm: An empirical assessment of multiple recommender systems and their impact on content diversity. *Information, Communication & Society*, *21*(7), 959–977.

Moore, M. and Tambini, D. (2018). *Digital Dominance: The Power of Google, Amazon, Facebook, and Apple*. Oxford: Oxford University Press.

Murdock, G. (2004). Building the Digital Commons: Public Broadcasting in the Age of the Internet. Paper presented at the 2004 Spry Memorial Lecture, 22 November, Montreal.

Napoli, P.M. (2019). *Social Media and the Public Interest: Media Regulation in the Disinformation Age*. New York: Columbia University Press.

Nechushtai, E. and Lewis, S.C. (2019). What kind of news gatekeepers do we want machines to be? Filter bubbles, fragmentation, and the normative dimensions of algorithmic recommendations. *Computers in Human Behavior, 90,* 298-307.

Nordahl Svendsen, E. (2011). From sovereignty to liberalization: Media policy in small European countries. In G.F. Lowe and C.S. Nissen (eds), *Small among Giants: Television Broadcasting in Smaller Countries*. Nordicom: Göteborg.

Nossiter, T.J. (1991). British television: A mixed economy. In J.G., Blumler and T.J. Nossiter (eds), *Broadcasting Finance in Transition: A Comparative Handbook* (pp. 95-143). New York: Oxford University Press.

Ofcom (2018). Review of prominence for public service broadcasting. Retrieved from www.ofcom.org.uk/__data/assets/pdf_file/0021/154461/recommendations-for-new-legislative-framework-for-psb-prominence.pdf (accessed October 2020).

Ofcom. (2019). The Communications Market Report – Interactive data. Retrieved from www.ofcom.org.uk/research-and-data/multi-sector-research/cmr/interactive-data (accessed October 2020).

Pickard, V. (2019). *Democracy without Journalism: Confronting the Misinformation Society*. Oxford: Oxford University Press.

Raats, T. (2013). *And now for something completely different? De rol en positie van de publieke omroep in een genetwerkte samenleving: onderzoek naar de publieke omroepopdracht en – organisatie aan de hand van een comparatieve analyse van de culturele missie* (Unpublished Ph.D. thesis). Vrije Universiteit Brussel, Brussels. [*And now for something completely different? The role and position of the public broadcaster in a networked society: A comparative analysis of the public service remit and organisation in the cultural domain*].

Raats, T. (2020). Sustaining small television ecosystems: Lessons from policy-driven research in Flanders. In U. Rohn and T. Evens (eds), *Media Management Matters: Challenges and Opportunities for Bridging Theory and Practice* (pp. 138-154). London: Routledge.

Raats, T., Evens, T., Vanhaeght A.-S. and Ruelens, S. (2015). *Stakeholderbevraging ter voorbereiding van de nieuwe beheersovereenkomst van de VRT met de Vlaamse Regering*. Brussels: SMIT, VUB.

Ramsey, P. (2018). The BBC Ideas Service: The Corporation's Search for Universalism Online. Paper presented at the 2018 RIPE Conference 'Universalism and PSM', 18–20 October, Madrid.

Reviglio, U. (2017). Serendipity by design? How to turn from diversity exposure to diversity experience to face filter bubbles in social media. In I. Kompatsiaris, J. Cave, A. Satsiou, G. Carle, A. Passani, E. Kontopoulos, S. Diplaris and D. McMillan (eds), *Internet Science. INSCI 2017. Lecture Notes in Computer Science* (pp. 281–300). Cham: Springer.

Saridou, T., Spyridou, L.-P. and Veglis, A. (2017). Churnalism on the rise? *Digital Journalism, 5*(8), 1006–1024.

Sevignani, S. (2016). *Privacy and Capitalism in the Age of Social Media*. New York: Routledge.

Sinclair, J. (2004). Globalization, supranational institutions and media. In J.D.H. Downing (ed.), *The Sage Handbook of Media Studies* (pp. 65-82). London: Sage.

Sørensen, J.K. and Hutchinson, J. (2017). Algorithms and public service media. In G.F. Lowe, H. Van den Bulck and K. Donders (eds), *Public Service Media in the Networked Society* (pp. 91–106). Göteborg: Nordicom.

Sørensen, J.K. and Van den Bulck, H. (2020). Public service media online, advertising and the third-party user data business: A trade versus trust dilemma? *Convergence*, 26(2), 421–447.

Spohr, D. (2017). Fake news and ideological polarization. *Business Information Review*, 34(3), 150–160.

Straubhaar, J.D. (1991). Beyond media imperialism: Asymmetrical interdependence and cultural proximity. *Critical Studies in Mass Communication*, 8(1), 39–59.

Street, J. (1988). Taking control? Some aspects of the relationship between information technology, government policy and democracy. In R. Plant, F. Gregory and A. Brier (eds), *Information Technology: The Public Issues (Fullbright papers)* (pp. 1-20). Manchester: Manchester University Press.

Suarez-Candel, R. (2012). Adapting Public Service to the Multiplatform Scenario: Challenges, Opportunities and Risks. Working papers of the Hans Bredow Institute, No. 25. Hamburg: Hans Bredow Institute.

Syvertsen, T., Enli, G., Mjøs, O.M. and Moe, H. (2014). *The Media Welfare State: Nordic Media in the Digital Era*. Ann Arbor: University of Michigan Press.

Thompson, J. (1995). The globalisation of communication. In J. Thompson (ed.), *The Media and Modernity: A Social Theory of the Media* (pp. 149-173). London: Blackwell.

Thussu, D. (2018). *International Communication: Continuity and Change*. New York: Bloomsbury.

Van den Bulck, H. (2016). *Publieke omroep: Maatschappelijke meerwaarde en individuele impact*. Antwerp: University of Antwerp. [*Public service broadcasting: Added societal value and individual impact*].

Van den Bulck, H. and Moe, H. (2018). Public service media, universality and personalisation through algorithms: Mapping strategies and exploring dilemmas. *Media, Culture & Society*, 40(6), 875–892.

Van Dijck, J., Poell, T. and de Waal, M. (2018). *The Platform Society: Public Values in a Connective World*. Oxford: Oxford University Press.

Van Nieuwenhuyze, J., Picone, I. and Donders, K. (2020). *Vind ik het of vind ik het niet? Impactanalyse van Plaatsing van Programma's en Aanbevelingssystemen in On-Demand Audiovisuele Omgevingen*. Brussels: imec-SMIT. [*Can I find it or not? Impact analysis of the positioning of content in recommender systems of audiovisual on-demand environments*].

Vanhaeght, A.-S. (2019). The need for not more, but more socially relevant audience participation in public service media. *Media, Culture & Society*, 41(1), 120–137.

Webster, F. (2002). *Theories of the Information Society* (2nd ed.) London: Routledge.

Weissmann, E. (2018). Local, National, Transnational. In K. Toft Hansen, S. Peacock and S. Turnbull (eds), *European Television Crime Drama and Beyond* (pp. 119–138). Switzerland: Palgrave Macmillan.

Winseck, D. (2020) Vampire squids, the broken internet and platform regulation. *Journal of Digital Media and Policy*, 11(3), 241-279.

3   From Public Service Broadcasting to public service anything

The gaps in Public Service Media theory

Introduction

Regardless the development of Public Service Broadcasting theory, public broadcasters are seizing some of the opportunities of a digital media environment. Public broadcasters such as BBC, German ARD, Finnish YLE and Spanish RTVE offer services on online platforms. In so doing, public broadcasters are no longer active only in radio and television broadcasting markets. They become multi-media enterprises. This evolution is not without controversy. Some scholars find that public broadcasters are rather directionless in the online realm, offering services without a genuine and thought-through public service logic. They argue for a stronger public interest rationale, among others through strengthening collaboration between public broadcasters and other public institutions. Together, these comprise a so-called 'digital commons' (Murdock, 2004). The first and most important *raison d'être* of such a commons is the prioritisation of public service delivery over commercial objectives (Jakubowicz, 2007). Bardoel and Lowe (2007) emphasise the need for a stronger connection with citizens. These are no longer part of a fairly anonymous mass audience, but can actively participate in the creation of public service content. Moreover, parts of the audience no longer identify with the venerable core values of Public Service Broadcasting. Research of Just, Büchi and Latzer (2017) shows that media users younger than 40 identify values for Public Service Media that are currently not included in the mission statements of public broadcasters nor in most scholarly work, such as self-direction, which one could argue is more related to civic, individual rights.

Next to criticism from scholars that are actually in favour of Public Service Media and public broadcasters in charge of it, we can observe disapproval of the continuation and expansion of Public Service Broadcasting with a small group of researchers. They set out from a market failure perspective (Appelman et al., 2005; Armstrong and Weeds, 2007). Public broadcasters should deliver only these services that are not delivered by commercial media companies. Their activities have to be limited to certain niche services such as documentaries, investigative journalism and local news. Moreover, these areas are said to shrink in a digital age in which abundance instead of scarcity of content is the rule

(Elstein et al., 2004). Emphasis is put on the possibly market-distortive effects of comprehensive Public Service Media systems and the need to regulate public broadcasters' online activities.

These two visions divide policy-makers. To some extent, plenty of European politicians would defend the idea of a public broadcaster that is active on a variety of platforms offering a variety of services. On the other hand, a lot of them also advocate for a free flow of goods and services and minimal levels of government intervention in markets. As a consequence, legal frameworks remain stuck in the linear broadcasting age. They are only adapted superficially. There is a failure to fundamentally reconsider the case for Public Service Broadcasting. That observation, so I argue, does not only pertain to politicians. Researchers have also refrained from studying whether public broadcasters are still the best tool to achieve the delivery of the public interest in media in a context of fragmenting audiences, social media determining talk value of news, clicks driving journalism, renewed polarisation in politics, and so on. The main ambition of this book is exactly this: to confront theory with the law and practice of Public Service Media respectively and this with an eye on, cautiously, attempting to provide an updated set of values for achieving the public interest in media and the best tools for this.

Many will argue that a plethora of new approaches to the role of public broadcasters and the bigger project of Public Service Broadcasting in the digital age has been launched, within and outside academia. Public Service Media (Dahlgren, 2001; Bardoel and Lowe, 2007; Council of Europe, 2007), public service content (Lilley, 2008), public service communication (Tambini and Cowling, 2004; Iosifidis, 2010), Public Service Publisher (Ofcom, 2007), public service light (Broeders and Verhoeven, 2005; Armstrong and Weeds, 2007), public service platform (Bonini, 2019) … These are but a few concepts that pop up. I will discuss several of these concepts below.

My main argument is that these mushrooming concepts give the impression that Public Service Media is everything and nothing at the same time. The question is whether one, from a theoretical perspective, can move beyond public service 'anything' and come to a shared story and set of values and rules for Public Service Media in the digital age. That question is at the core of the final chapter in Part I of this book. The subsequent question, addressed in Parts 2 and 3 of this book, is whether such a new set of values can subsequently be aligned with legal frameworks and with public broadcasters' functioning in practice.

Public Service Broadcasting

From its inception in the 1920s until the 1970s, Public Service Broadcasting was – albeit firmly rooted in a project of political power maximisation (Noam, 1991; Hoffmann-Riem, 1995, p. 82ff) – concerned with emancipation. Media policy, and Public Service Broadcasting as its core element, was a citizen emancipation project. The media ought to be 'a ladder which people could steadily climb, moving from the lowest rungs of packaged commercial entertainment to the highest rungs of consecrated cultural artefacts' (Murdock, 2005: 178). Following the idea of empowerment and firmly believing in the fundamental role of Public Service Broadcasting in contributing to a democratic public sphere (Habermas, 1991), pluralism and universality were central elements in this. Public broadcasters were entrusted with the realisation of the task to educate, inform and entertain the audience (Price and Raboy, 2003). Despite pressure on both the idea of Public Service Broadcasting and its organisation through public broadcasters in the 1980s – largely due to the upsurge of neo-liberalism (Dyson and Humphreys, 1988; Garnham, 1990: 127-128; Blumler, 1991) – the public broadcaster 'axis' remained firmly rooted in most Western and Northern European countries. Admittedly, the distinctiveness of public broadcasters' offers versus commercial media services became more important.

From the 1930s onwards a series of shared values that underpinned the essence of Public Service Broadcasting (Donders and Pauwels, 2012; Donders and Van den Bulck, 2016) has been placed central in policy frameworks and have steered – at least in theory – the functioning of public broadcasters across Europe.

- Universality: Public broadcasters' content should be accessible to all citizens, regardless their geographical location, their ability/willingness-to-pay, their gender, ethnical background, etc. (Garnham, 1990).
- Quality and distinctiveness: Public broadcasters should distinguish themselves through the quality of their services; they should be distinctive from what others offer. Although commercial media companies, some policy-makers and a few scholars advocate for a complementary, gap-filling role for public broadcasters, most scholars agree on the need for a holistic, full-portfolio approach (Bardoel and d'Haenens, 2008: 344).
- Identity construction and diversity: The identity-building aspect of Public Service Broadcasting largely refers to a process of unification around a nation, language and/or culture (Van den Bulck, 2001), while the diversity aspect is concerned with reflecting the growing cultural and ethnic fragmentation occurring within national boundaries, with catering to minority interests, and with celebrating the diversity of cultures on a global scale (Horsti and Hultén, 2011).
- Creativity and innovation: Public broadcasters should offer creative services, provide a safe harbour for experiment and engage in innovation in service and technology (Cunningham, 2009: 85), particularly in internationalising media markets where innovation is under pressure (Cunningham, 2015).
- Accountability: Editorial independence is key to public broadcasters' functioning (Council of Europe, 2009), so is accountability to citizens and legislators. Accountability relates both to the existence of formal control (through independent monitoring bodies or self-regulatory agencies) and to an attitude of transparency and responsiveness to society (Baldi, 2007: 17-19).

All of the abovementioned values continue to dominate discussions on Public Service Media (see below). They nevertheless stem from a radio- and television-dominated period. Mass audiences, linear broadcasting schedules, limited choice for consumers and nation-based competition are key characteristics of that period. In addition, these values are not to be situated at the same level. Whereas quality is a means to realise informed citizenship and thus contributes to democracy, universality and accountability are rather necessary conditions to make the system as such work. Identity, social cohesion and diversity could be seen as societal values. I will come back to this later.

Several trends have put the Public Service Broadcasting *acquis* under pressure. First, late modernity questions the emancipatory and, some would say, paternalist project of Public Service Broadcasting itself. The core values of Public Service Broadcasting do not necessarily correspond with a post-welfare state society model. Second, some remain convinced that, especially in a digital era, the free market can deliver public value to citizens in a more efficient manner than public broadcasters (Elstein, 2008). This argument essentially relates to the trends of internationalisation and digitisation discussed in the previous chapter. Of these I argued that they, on the one hand, indeed put pressure on the idea of Public Service Broadcasting, while, on the other hand, also raising issues that might make the delivery of services in the public interest (regardless the organisational form this takes) more necessary than ever. Third, public broadcasters are imperfect institutions. While scholars defend the institution fiercely, these institutions are legacy players that often lack flexibility, transparency and efficiency required to anticipate market dynamics while still holding true to their core task (Born, 2003; Donders, 2012). Within such a context, several scholars have advanced adapted versions of Public Service Broadcasting and/or of the organisational form through which the project should be realised. The main concepts I discuss below are Public Service Media, being most commonly used now in Public Service Broadcasting research, public service communication and public service content. Whereas Public Service Media should be situated within a democracy-centric perspective on media and the role they perform in society, public service communication and content do not necessary set out from such a view and can, in the work of some scholars, be related with a market failure perspective on the future of Public Service Broadcasting. Public Service Publisher and public service light are notions to be situated within the market failure perspective entirely. In previous work, I also talked about social responsibility vs. market failure perspectives (Donders, 2012). I would argue that the use of 'democracy-centric' is more accurate. The social responsibility paradigm was described by Fred Siebert, Theodore Peterson and Wilbur Schramm (1956) in their well-known work *Four Theories of the Press*. The authors explain how this paradigm emerged and culminated in the conclusions of the Commission on the Freedom of the Press on the state of American journalism in 1949. While still arguing for a free press in a free market place of ideas, the Commission acknowledged that public intervention to the benefit of all and, preferably, self-regulation were necessary to rectify some perversions of the free market. It opposed the libertarian ideas that were so dominant in the US at the time and, one could argue, still today. Corporate responsibility was thought to further ethical, high-quality and professional journalism, and to counter sensationalism and commercialisation. Importantly, the (dis)functioning of markets is the basis of this paradigm. That is not the case for scholarly thinking that puts Public Service Broadcasting or, more recently, Public Service Media at the centre of the wellbeing of society and democracy.

Public Service Media

Most scholars in Public Service Broadcasting research agree on the use of the concept Public Service Media. It is an extended, technology neutral version of Public Service Broadcasting. Interestingly, these scholars most often consider Public Service Media and the institutions in charge of it as one and the same. In other words: many texts referring to Public Service Media actually refer to Public Service Media providers.

The Public Service Media concept rests on a couple of assumptions. First, it is assumed that Public Service Broadcasting is at the core of democracy and the fulfilment of democratic values. Following from that, the justification for Public Service Broadcasting lies not in market failure, but in 'its super-iority to the market as a means of providing all citizens, whatever wealth or geographical location, equal access to a wide range of high-quality enter-tainment, information and education' (Garnham, 1990: 120). Public Service Broadcasting is neither connected to consumer sovereignty as, again referring to Garnham (1994: 153-154): 'Public Service Broadcasting is based on the idea that broadcasting is not merely a series of individual consumer choices'. Second, technological evolutions do not invalidate the legitimacy of Public Service Broadcasting. Spectrum scarcity was not the sole, nor most important reason for having public broadcasters (Hoffmann-Riem, 1995: 82). Hence, its decline is no reason for less Public Service Broadcasting (Donders, 2012: 10; Levy, 1999: 12). This second assumption, even though powerful in its rejection of technological determinism, is destabilised by the frequently observed technological optimism of those defending Public Service Media. When technological evolutions do not end the legitimacy of Public Service Broadcasting, they can equally not be used as a vehicle to argue for more Public Service Broadcasting and a develop-ment into Public Service Media. Rather, the evolutions related to digitisation (discussed in the previous chapter) such as clicks increasingly driving jour-nalism might provide us with more convincing arguments on the increased need for the delivery of media services in the public interest. Third, defenders of Public Service Broadcasting are often also defenders of public broadcasting institutions. They refuse to disconnect Public Service Broadcasting and public broadcasting organisations, claiming the choice of an institution in charge of Public Service Broadcasting has, even though not always optimally, delivered value to citizens. In that sense, one chooses to be pragmatic, refusing to go for more market-oriented options that are at best unproven (Barnett, 2006). Public

Service Media and the institutions delivering it are in this opinion one and the same.

What then are the action points to go from Public Service Broadcasting to Public Service Media? What distinguishes the second from the first concept? The most significant difference (at first sight at least) is the replacement of the B of *broadcasting* for the M of *media*. The concept relates public service provision to all media and no longer exclusively to radio and television. That has more far-reaching and potentially sweeping effects, as most aspects of life and society become mediated. That does not only apply to media and communication, but also to domains as diverse as health, mobility, tourism, retail, and so on. Human bodies themselves become part of this mediatisation evolution through, for example, the technologies of carriables, wearables and ingestibles. There is definitely hype in policies and research on smart media, smart industries, smart cities, smart … Regardless there is evidence of people evolving into 'smart-selves', with all the ethical and societal questions that come along (Murray, 2016). Does this mean that Public Service Media is a concept without limits? Few scholars conclusively answer this question. Most of them seem to assume that everything public broadcasters do is Public Service Media (Moe, 2008; Burri, 2015). An 'as big as necessary' scenario would be more reasonable and practicable (Donders, 2012). Otherwise, one risks Public Service Media being a concept without boundaries and thus useless from a legal and policy point of view. Furthermore, accepting that Public Service Media is about more than radio and television is one thing. Achieving Public Service Media, as many of the subsequent chapters will show, is another.

A second feature of Public Service Media as described in literature is its increased emphasis on the 'service' aspect, meaning public broadcasters should be more service oriented, taking into account the needs and wants of their audiences. They should accept that audiences are, more so than with Public Service Broadcasting, an integral part of Public Service Media. This means using the opportunities of the digital world, to cater for minority interests better and adopting a more inclusive approach towards, for example, urban and migrant audiences (Horsti and Hultén, 2011). Concepts such as co-creation, participation and interaction are often used when talking about improving the service aspect of Public Service Media (Enli, 2008; Bakker, 2011). The inclusion of audiences in the activities of Public Service Media institutions relates to the initial emancipation aspirations of the Public Service Broadcasting project and is, taking a democracy theory point of view, a highly valuable objective. However, there is a risk that action from the audience is considered a goal instead of a means to achieve the objective of fuller inclusion and autonomy in society.

A third aspect concerns the converged nature of Public Service Media. The project is not necessarily about offering services across media devices and technologies, but should embody convergence. This is often related to making content independent from package. The former embodies the public service nature of the offer, the latter the means through which the audience is reached. This aspect has been studied mainly in the field of news and information. The ideal of the 'integrated newsroom' is an epithet of it. Regardless the fact that convergence and the integration of media devices and technologies to the benefit of public service content is heralded by both scholars and public broadcasters, the latter face difficulties in changing their organisation to meet this ideal. Larrondo et al. (2016: 296) compellingly show how professional identities, anxiety and organisational resilience have slowed down newsroom integration plans. Moreover, while many public broadcasters have innovation departments, these are not always connected to the work floor. There seems to be a disconnect to the 'playground' of the tech people and those making television, radio and online services.

A final, and perhaps most important feature, is Public Service Media's remaining dedication to 'public service', providing services to the public regardless their appeal to advertisers or their willingness-to-pay. Not just service delivery for the sake of it, but services in the public interest, that is, contributing to the realisation of socially beneficial goals such as the strengthening of cultural identity and diversity, social cohesion, media literacy, emancipation, informed citizenship, and so on (Donders, 2012). As elaborated upon by Ramsey in his case study of BBC Ideas (a co-creation based online offer of short videos), 'being both popular and good to society' remains key to the realisation of Public Service Media. The main distinguishing feature of Public Service Media from Public Service Broadcasting might not be its multi-platform nature or the fact that it allows for interaction, participation or even co-creation of content. It might be its genuinely public service driven agenda in a world of clickbait, untransparent algorithm-driven personalisation, datafication, and so on. It might be public broadcasters' strategy to offer services that have 'an intrinsically different focus to that which the market provides' (Ramsey, 2018: 13). That is a point that stands the test of the conclusions reached in Chapter 1 dealing with the combined impact of digitisation and internationalisation on the delivery of media services in the public interest.

Remarkably, few scholars deal with the transposition of Public Service Media into law. Politicians are more often than not seen as adversaries of Public Service Media. Although there is an acknowledgement indeed of the necessity to adapt Public Service Broadcasting regulation to the new era (Steemers, 2003; Moe, 2008), instruments like the public value test are rarely embraced (Wheeler, 2010; Bardoel and Vochteloo, 2012), nor are many other options for improving regulation put forward. Exceptions to this are monographs of Donders (2012) and Burri (2015).

In earlier work on European policies regarding Public Service Broadcasting (Donders, 2012), I indeed identified some core elements of sustainable and future-proof legal frameworks for public broadcasters. There were six basic elements, all of which were briefly elaborated upon:

- Cross-media: public broadcasters must offer content on all platforms.
- Core: all public services must be linked to core values, meaning they should contribute to the delivery of the public interest in media instead of online services being linked to existing radio or television services.

- Cost: a sustainable funding base balancing public and commercial revenues is desirable to ensure independence of the Public Service Media project.
- Clarity: the financial and structural organisation of the public broadcaster should be transparent in a Public Service Media scenario as to ensure accountability towards audiences.
- Control and command: one should strive after effective and consistent control ensuring accountability, while at the same time protecting public broadcasters' editorial independence.
- Checks and balances: public broadcasters must play their role while not damaging the competitive position of other players and collaboration to further pluralism and diversity in local media markets as a whole should be a task of public broadcasters as well.

In this model, I also assumed that Public Service Media as a project was the prerogative of public broadcasters. The model, even if basic, tried to reconcile aspirational ideas on Public Service Media as an essential part of democracy with regulatory needs in terms of clarity and minimising market distortion.

In her 2015 monograph *Public Service Broadcasting 3.0: Legal design for the digital present*, Mira Burri sets out from, among others, this framework to identify the legal principles that should underlie Public Service Broadcasting 3.0 or Public Service Media. Essentially, she emphasises that the 'Public Service Media toolkit' should

> make good use of the potential of digital media and adequately reflect the changed and changing reality of media production, distribution, access and consumption in a space where the PSB [public broadcaster] is but one of the content suppliers and many of the noted processes are more complex and multi-directional.
>
> (Burri, 2015: 165)

At the level of objectives, Burri stresses the goal of exposure diversity as one of the key features of a Public Service Media project of the future. The functions she deems essential in the digital age are: public broadcasters as producers of high-quality news and journalism, as navigators of the enormous public space the Internet is (in part), and as memory institutions, digitising, archiving and disclosing content on a wide scale (Burri, 2015: 195ff). These functions, all of which are elaborated upon in Chapter 4 of this book, are still best performed by one institution. Reach and impact are among some of the reasons briefly addressed to justify that choice (Burri, 2015: 224).

Interestingly, Burri (2015: 52) emphasises how much of the scholarly work on Public Service Media focuses too much on the 'micro-picture of Public Service Broadcasting, often quarrelling about "minor" details related to the structure of media organisations or funding schemes, and sometimes ignoring the "bigger picture" developments in technology, culture and society'. She continues that there seems to be a trade-off in this sense between getting too close to the Public Service Broadcasting institution, which certainly permits a finer-grained analysis but is also associated with the danger of being influenced by its legacy and of missing out developments outside the immediate Public Service Broadcasting context.

That observation, from which also her monograph does not entirely escape (as the toolkit she identifies is without extensive elaboration entrusted to centralised public broadcasting organisations, see above), is also one of the starting points of this contribution – even though it would be presumptuous to claim that I entirely escape this pitfall.

Public service communication, public service content

Next to Public Service Media, also the concepts of public service communication and public service content innovated the Public Service Broadcasting concept. Nevertheless, they got less traction. This can largely be explained by the relation between these notions and the Public Service Publisher idea (see next section) of Ofcom. The British media and electronic communications regulator suggested top-slicing part of the BBC's license fee and using it to subsidise a fund for public service content or communication. Essentially, all types of organisations could apply for money provided the proposed service was meeting the public interest and preferably in an innovative manner. Consequently, the notions of public service communication and public service content were contaminated with a politically controversial and market failure inspired idea, that is, the Public Service Publisher (Donders, 2012). That is somewhat regrettable as there are several interesting ideas to be found in discussions on public service communication and public service content.

In 2004 Tambini and Cowling (2004: 4) broadened the debate on the future of Public Service Broadcasting, talking about the ongoing role and increased relevance for public service in communications. Arguing that 'the current debates remain rooted in vested interests and dogma' and that the framework for public service communications must meet the challenges of the 21st century instead of the 1920s, they make a plea for a reconceptualisation of what public service in the media and communications realm should actually be. While Tambini and Cowling do not engage with such a reconceptualisation themselves and none of the contributors to their edited collection offers a consistent attempt in that direction, they make clear that bringing people together in a shared public communication space is and should remain one of the essential features of any public service project in the future. To some extent, one could argue that they take a fundamental rights perspective on this issue. In so doing, they relate to a non-Public Service Broadcasting research tradition on communication rights. Scholars such as Cammaerts (2007: 5) have argued that communication rights as fundamental rights are a 'counter-hegemonic reaction against the commodification of communication and informational tools'. These

rights concern access to infrastructure, skills and content; real diversity and pluralism; pluralistic public spheres in which difference of opinion and minority
interests are respected; independent journalism; providing information to citizens regardless the extent to which these can be commodified from an advertising or payment angle; participation in media; and so on. Whereas Tambini and
Cowling relate public service communication still largely to public broadcasters,
their very basic definition of the concept relates much more to the diverse
features scholars attribute to communication rights outside the institutionalised
setting of public broadcasters and legacy media in general.

Admittedly, public service content is a concept that relates less to theoretical and ideological discussions on the provision of public services in media
and communication environments. It is more practical and even instrumental
in nature. The concept concerns the funding of content that is of a public service nature, whether that content is provided by public broadcasters or not. It
is actually this concept that is most often used in relation to the Public Service
Publisher idea put forward by Ofcom and discussed below. Public service content is content that needs to be funded with an eye on the achievement of
public interest objectives. It is about nurturing creativity outside the commercial realm. In that sense, one could argue that the concept relates also to some
sort of market failure perspective on media provision. However, the concept
sets out more from government or regulatory failure to ensure a media environment that delivers value for citizens. Its most important concern is thus of a
public interest, rather than an economic nature. The concept, moreover, has a
feature in common with the Public Service Media notion. Both set out from
a media neutral approach, abandoning broadcasting as the exclusive terrain for
public service provision. On the contrary, as is the case with Public Service
Media, the argument for delivery of media services across devices and technologies is made (Redmond, 2004).

Public Service Publisher, public service light

As already said the notion of public service content is also used in discussions
on the so-called Public Service Publisher. Setting out from the idea that public
broadcasters are too conservative and centralised organisations to be drivers of
innovative media services, Ofcom argued to take part of the BBC's license fee
and grant it on a competitive basis to smaller media undertakings or non-profit
organisations with an eye on furthering experiments with new formats and
services. The Public Service Publisher was said to be a new model of Public
Service Broadcasting equipped for the digital, rather than the analogue world.
The proposed project went hand in hand with the plan to create an institution
that would commission content and services and would thus be in charge of
organising and supervising the competitive process whereby organisations apply
for money. That could in fact be an existing institution, assigned with certain
responsibilities after a first competitive tender procedure (Ofcom, 2004: 80).
The insistence on introducing competition in every single stage of the Public

Service Publisher is in fact what connects the idea the most with more economic and market failure-oriented perspectives on the future of Public Service
Broadcasting. The belief is that introducing market forces into the provision of
public service delivery will benefit society the most. Ofcom did not invent the
wheel with its Public Service Publisher proposal. In fact, the notorious Peacock
Committee already in 1986 put forward the idea of a Public Broadcasting
Authority (Elstein, 2008: 68ff). That Authority seems to have been the blueprint
for the Public Service Publisher, albeit that the former was still conceptualised
against the background of a dual, public and commercial, broadcasting order.
Importantly, Ofcom's proposal was not to replace the BBC but to complement
it with the Public Service Publisher system (Gardam, 2008: 11ff). Ofcom's plans
were never put into practice. They were incredibly controversial because of
the underlying funding arrangement. No additional funds would be foreseen.
Rather, part of the BBC's license fee would be used for it. That rallied considerable support for the BBC. The, at that time, Director General of the BBC Mark
Thompson warned that top-slicing would endanger 'the independence and the
ability of the BBC to deliver its services to the public'. He criticised Ofcom,
saying that 'there has been a small group of people', inside Ofcom 'who have
been ideologically focused more on the principle of getting a wedge into the
license fee and trying to prove a point about the principle of top-slicing, rather
than having a particular urgent need' (quoted in Holmwood, 2009). Scholars
supported this position, arguing that top-slicing would not only mean the end
of the BBC but also of the provision of media services in the public interest
in general (see Iosifidis, 2010). Others disagreed, saying that the principles of
the Public Service Publisher merit careful reflection and should not have been
abandoned so quickly because of the self-protection interests of an institution
(Elstein, 2008: 46).

The Public Service Publisher discussion presents us with a dilemma. As Des
Freedman (2008: 18) convincingly shows, those in favour of the Public Service
Publisher 'are precisely those commercial groups – broadcasters, ISPs, online
content producers – who have most to gain from media systems in which non-
market actors and objectives are marginalised'. As Raats and I (2015: 157) have
argued elsewhere, the 'aggressors' or defenders of new organisational forms of
Public Service Broadcasting are indeed mainly commercial players, but also cultural organisations and other public institutions that are keen on finding new
revenues in times of austerity. All of these (ab)use the very powerful market
failure ideology out of strategic reasons. While this observation still holds
true today, it has prevented academics from researching whether there is an
intrinsic value to the Public Service Publisher plans and, even more importantly, the notion of public service content which has both a public interest/
democracy-centric and market failure component. One could argue that the
Public Service Publisher can have merit, notably when not falling under nation
states' authority in EU Member States where that has shown to be problematic.
Its decentralised nature makes it much more difficult to control all providers of
media services in the public interest. The Council of Europe, a fierce proponent

of independent public broadcasters, could organise such a system. At the same time, the decentralised nature and the lack of scale of subsidised projects would most likely undermine the effectiveness of such initiatives in terms of contributing to a shared communicative space in a democratic society. Scaling up through the integration and further professionalisation of existing alternative media or emerging media organisations might be able to overcome this issue, albeit only partly.

In parallel with or regardless of discussions on Public Service Publisher, the idea of a public service 'light' was and remains vivid. It concerns the limitation of Public Service Broadcasting as a project and/or institution to these services that are not provided by the market. Market failure should be the basis of government intervention. Governments should intervene only in these areas where the market is under-providing services with positive externalities (e.g., information and historical documentaries) and government failure is lower than market failure. Davies (2005: 131) says that there is market failure if 'there is an under-provision of Reithian broadcasting services under free market conditions, relative to the socially optimum level'. Market failure in that sense refers to a situation in which the market is not performing in an optimal or efficient manner and certain services are not provided or under-provided to the detriment of the achievement of desirable interests of society (Doyle, 2002: 64; Whiters, 2003: 106).

The notion of market failure is often linked with the so-called public good characteristics of broadcasting. Public goods are goods or services that are non-rivalry and non-excludable. Consumption by one consumer does not prevent other consumers from consumption. Excluding consumers from consumption is also difficult (Collins and Murroni, 1996: 7; Barrowclough, 1999: 435ff; Doyle, 2002: 64-65; Hoskins, McFadyen and Finn, 2004: 196-197; Helm, 2005: 7; Ward, 2006: 54-55). Because of these economic features, undertakings are less prone to deliver these kind of goods even if they have so-called positive externalities for society. In contrast, one can often observe that goods with negative externalities (e.g., violent or pornographic content) are over-provided. Hence, markets fail. Public broadcasters are a practical solution to this and funded to make up for the under-provision of public goods with positive externalities and the over-provision of services with negative externalities. They should, moreover, not only provide services with positive externalities but focus specifically on merit goods, that is, goods that are valuable for society, but of which the 'value exceeds the estimation an individual might place on it' (Cox, 2004: 58; see also, Ward, 2006: 55, 61). In other words, merit goods are those goods and services for which the idea of consumer sovereignty does not apply.

Those advocating for a public service light or niche scenario hold that technological and resulting economic evolutions have narrowed the scope of the market failure argument. The market is providing more and more services, catering also for minority interests (see discussions by Heath and Levy, 2005; Ward, 2006). Scarcity, used in the 1930s, to advocate for government monopolies in broadcasting does no longer exist. As a consequence, public broadcasters should offer less and less services (Booth, 2004). It is important to stress that already in the 1940s, Coase criticised the idea that spectrum scarcity validated the existence of broadcasting monopolies. In a 1966 article in the *American Economic Review* he argued for the free exchange of spectrum, allocating this resource to the highest bidders. Such a process would be far more efficient that government-controlled licensing. Moreover, programming policies had to be determined by undertakings' desire for profit making. This was not something to be afraid of. It would, besides, prevent governments from intervening in the so-called market place of ideas to a societally undesirable instead of desirable extent (see Coase, 1947; 1948; 1966; 1974).

While the launch of digital television and the emergence of the Internet in the 1980s and 1990s gave rise to very optimistic accounts on a to be expected abundance of diversity, pluralism and creativity of content (see Peacock, 1986; 2004) and market failure ideas have retained traction in policy circles, we know that the reality of media contributing to the public interest in society is less upbeat than we might have hoped. Specific types of content (e.g., domestic drama, children's programming, investigative journalism, local media services) continue to be economically fragile. Moreover, the processes underlying media production and consumption are increasingly commodified in a data-driven media landscape where clicks are a driver of more clicks.

Public service platforms and public service algorithms

A new addition to literature talks about public service platforms and public service algorithms. The focus is indeed no longer on distribution content across platforms (Bennet and Strange, 2008; Enli, 2008; Debrett, 2009; Candel, 2012; Bennet and Medrado, 2013; Klein-Shagrit and Keinonen, 2014; Donders, 2019). It now is on how that content is being gathered, aggregated and distributed. The criticism on the practices of platforms such as Google, Facebook, Amazon and Apple has revivified debates on the public interest in media infrastructures. The observation that personalisation by commercial media is not per se enhancing agency of users (Monzer et al., 2020) adds to this.

Profit-driven platforms need to be complemented with Public Service Media platforms (Bonini, 2019). The public utilities approach to platforms, advocated for by Napoli (2019) is related to this idea, as is Victor Pickard's (2019) rejection of market fundamentalism in our information infrastructures and his push for a public media system that invests in local journalism and that can act independently from the platforms and conglomerates that dominate media markets these days.

A midway solution to the structural issues that provoked the Public Service Media platform idea is 'public service algorithm'. What algorithms will public broadcasters and possibly also other companies within and outside the media sector use to position and recommend content and services to users? Algorithms that lack transparency to users, drive them towards more consumption, and do not take diversity and pluralism to heart? Or the exact opposite? That opposite is considered a public service algorithm. The European Broadcasting Union, for example, has developed such an algorithm called PEACH. Sørensen and Hutchinson (2017: 99) explain how it 'combines classic recommender algorithms (content-based filtering to find similar content and collaborative filtering to find similar users) with a novel mechanism to recommend diverse content'. The whole idea is 'to implement Public Service Media-specific editorial values in an algorithm'. Flemish public broadcaster VRT has adapted the PEACH algorithm and has reported on its success in terms of increasing people's consumption of cultural or informational content when making use of its video player *VRT NU* (Hellemans, 2020). Also the BBC is investing in public service algorithms. Essentially, so several BBC strategists argue, the whole idea of a public service algorithm is to operationalise the Reithian ethos 'to inform, educate and entertain' in an on-demand environment.

> In the domain of recommender systems the Reithian view of Public Service Media commits to providing content which fulfils the public's need for diverse and balanced information, entertainment, and education in a manner which is unexpected or surprising – best expressed by Reith's assertion that 'the best way to give the public what it wants is to reject the express policy of giving the public what it wants'. Notions of public service inevitably vary across different geo-political and cultural contexts and a one size fits all model is likely to be unsatisfactory but it is clear that the Public Service Media remit has implications for how we design and evaluate recommenders to ensure principles such as exposure diversity and surprise are maintained.
>
> (Fields, Jones and Cowlishaw, 2018)

At the core of the public service algorithm concept is the rejection of consumption and engagement-driven recommender systems, on the one hand, and the aspiration to expose users to something new, to open new horizons and to achieve a public service remit close to domestic societies and identities, on the other (Helberger, 2015; Verdegem and Lievens, 2016). Mira Buri (2015) initially called this 'public service navigator'.

Nonetheless, the essential element of transparency towards users often remains absent with most existing public broadcasters' algorithms. They might be beneficial in terms of both exposure and consumption diversity, but users are largely unaware of the deployment of such algorithms. That is an issue public broadcasters need to look into. Research by Harambam, Helberger and van Hoboken (2018), though focused on people's own agency in relation to algorithms, might assist public broadcasters in that quest. They define four ways to increase agency of users: alternation, awareness, adjustment and obfuscation. Public broadcasters can in particular work with awareness and adjustment. First, people's awareness of their exposure to algorithms should be increased. Second, users should be enabled to adjust algorithms. Further experimentation with this is needed and worked on by public broadcasters such as Flemish VRT, Dutch NPO and British BBC.

Why this tectonic field between democracy-centric and market failure perspectives?

Evolving ideas on Public Service Broadcasting all add to theorising public broadcasters' value for society. The continued opposing position of democracy-centric and market failure protagonists have dominated quite some academic and policy discussions on Public Service Broadcasting and its future. Market failure protagonists (see Elstein et al., 2004) have insisted that an omnipresent public broadcaster is not necessary in a market that is adequately functioning. Scholars taking a democracy-centric point of view have counterargued that such an observation is, first, irrelevant and, second, not true. Ian Kearns (quoted in Cielen 2005: 27), for example, insists that 'market failure has little or nothing to do with the thought process that came up with the Reithian principles of educate, inform and entertain'. As stated earlier, Nicholas Garnham (1990: 120) even argues that Public Service Broadcasting is a model superior to market forces. Newer concepts such as public service platform or public service algorithm actually set out from the same idea of superiority over market-driven models. Steven Barnett (quoted in Fairbairn, 2004: 62) agrees, saying market failure advocates look at Public Service Broadcasting 'through the wrong end of the telescope'. He (Barnett, 2002: 43-44) holds that we 'make a collective decision as a society that the benefits to citizens and the quality of our cultural and democratic life outweigh any loss to the private sector'.

Barnett's argument provides solid ground for the continuation of a public broadcasting organisation as the cornerstone of Public Service Media policy. It is indeed a democratic and collective decision of society to have a public broadcaster like the BBC, even if this is perhaps not the economically most optimal or efficient instrument.

Do market failure believers dismiss this altogether? Neither David Elstein nor Allan Peacock would argue that there is no value in what the BBC or any other public broadcaster offer. However, there is a conflict at a fundamental level between the democracy-centric and market failure perspectives on Public Service Media. According to Peacock (2004: 36), government intervention 'must be derived from the wishes of individuals and that the "guardians" of the public interest are there to implement those wishes if, for some reason, they are not satisfied in the broadcasting market'. Governments should not impose their own preferences upon sovereign consumers. Peacock acknowledges that this assumption, that is in fact the starting point of the entire analysis in the Peacock Committee Report, is a value judgement, which is not intrinsically better than other value judgements (1986: 36). Having said that, the value proposition of the market failure perspective is completely at odds with the assumption that a society can collectively make a decision for public broadcasters delivering media services in the public interest. There is a tectonic tension between these two perspectives, that is bigger than making the argument in favour or against Public Service Media. It is about more than technology. It is a tension that relates to 'the values and principles governing society and social life – in short, about the kind of society we want to live in' (Jakubowicz, 2007: 115).

So, even if scholars setting out from a democracy-centric perspective on Public Service Media, dismiss market failure ideas, they will at the legal, policy and practical level be confronted with those ideas again. The democracy-centric and market failure perspectives are part of a tectonic field on which Public Service Media law, policy, strategy and practices have to navigate. This is one of the reasons why I have argued in earlier work that a more pragmatic approach between the democracy-centric and market failure perspectives was necessary. Stevenson and Rashid (2020) have called this the 'socio-market pragmatism' perspective, being a dialectic synthesis between the two other perspectives. Admittedly, this pragmatic approach is somewhat naïve on the possibility to combine two, essentially, antagonist standpoints.

The fierce opposition between democracy-centric and market failure ideas on the future of Public Service Broadcasting makes it necessary to move beyond the public service 'anything' status of 'Public Service Media'. While it is useful that a majority of scholars and public broadcasters unite around it, it is not sufficiently clear on what it is, on what it is not, on how it relates to other schools of thought and how it relates to the actual organisations in charge of Public Service Media.

The question is whether one can move from Public Service Broadcasting over public service 'anything', to a Public Service Media concept that is based on a common set of values and goals. I will make an attempt in the subsequent chapters to clarify some of these aspects, while acknowledging this is but one step in a process many scholars have been and will continue to be engaged with.[1]

Note

1 Parts of this chapter are based on an earlier publication in *International Journal of Media and Cultural Politics* (see Donders, Pauwels and Loisen, 2012).

References

Appelman, M., van Dijk, M., Nahuis, R., Vollaard, B. and Waagmeester, D. (2005). Een economisch vooronderzoek ten behoeve van het rapport van de WRR over de media. In W.B.H.J. van de Donk, D.W.J. Broeders and F.J.P.M. Hoefnagel (eds), *Trends in het medialandschap: vier verkenningen* (pp. 11-66). Amsterdam: WRR & Amsterdam University Press. [*An economic analysis for the WRR report on the media – Trends in the media landscape: four explorations*].

Armstrong, M. and Weeds, H. (2007). Public service broadcasting in the digital world. In P. Seabright and J. von Hagen (eds), *The Economic Regulation of Broadcasting Markets: Evolving Technology and Challenges for Policy* (pp. 81–149). Cambridge: Cambridge University Press.

Bakker, P. (2011). Expectations, experiences & exceptions: Promises and realities of participation on websites. In G.F. Lowe and J. Steemers (eds), *Regaining the Initiative for PSM* (pp. 237–251). Göteborg: Nordicom.

Baldi, P. (2007). Media accountability in Europe: A fragmented picture. In P. Baldi and U. Hasebrink (eds), *Broadcasters and Citizens in Europe: Trends in Media Accountability and Viewer Participation* (pp. 17–32). Bristol: Intellect.

Bardoel, J. and d'Haenens, L. (2008). Reinventing public service broadcasting in Europe: Prospects, promises and problems. *Media, Culture & Society, 30*(3), 337–355.

Bardoel, J. and Lowe, G.F. (2007). From public service broadcasting to public service media: The core challenge. In G.F. Lowe and J. Bardoel (eds), *From Public Service Broadcasting to Public Service Media* (pp. 9–28). Göteborg: Nordicom.

Bardoel, J. and Vochteloo, M. (2012). Conditional access for public service broadcasting to new media platforms: EU state aid policy vis-à-vis public service broadcasting – the Dutch case. In N. Just and M. Puppis (eds), *Trends in Communication Policy Research: New Theories, Methods & Subjects* (pp. 301–315). Bristol: Intellect.

Barnett, S. (2002). Which end of the telescope? From market failure to cultural value. In J. Cowling and D. Tambini (eds), *From Public Service Broadcasting to Public Service Communications* (pp. 34–45). London: IPPR.

Barnett, S. (2006). Public Service Broadcasting: A Manifesto for Survival in the Multimedia Age (A Case Study of the BBC's New Charter). Paper presented at the RIPE (Re-Visionary Interpretations of the Public Enterprise) Conference 'Public Service Broadcasting in a Multimedia Environment: Programmes and Platforms', 15-18 November, Amsterdam.

Barrowclough, D. (1999). Lighthouses, television and the theory of public goods. In P. Kriesler and C. Sardoni (eds), *Themes in Post-Keynesian Economics: Essays in Honour of Geoff Harcourt* (pp. 433–449). London: Routledge.

Bennett, J. and Medrado, A. (2013). The business of multi-platform public service: Online and at a profit. *Media International Australia, 146*(1), 103–113.

Bennett, J. and Strange, N. (2008). The BBC's second-shift aesthetics: Interactive Television, multi-platform projects and public service content for a digital era. *Media International Australia, 126*(1), 106–119.

Blumler, J.G. (1991). *Broadcasting Finance in Transition: A Comparative Handbook.* Oxford: Oxford University Press.

Booth, P. (2004). Introduction. In A. Peacock (ed.), *Public Service Broadcasting Without the BBC?* (pp. 17–32). London: The Institute of Economic Affairs.

Born, G. (2003). From Reithian ethic to managerial discourse: Accountability and audit at the BBC. *Javnost – The Public, 10*(2), 63–80.

Broeders, D. and Verhoeven, I. (2005). Kiezen uit overvloed: social-culturele ontwikkelingen in vraag en aanbod in het medialandschap. In W.B.H.J. Van de Donk, D.W.J. Broeders and F.J.P.M. Hoefnagel (eds), *Trends in de medialandschap: vier verkenningen* (pp. 67–122). Amsterdam: WRR and Amsterdam University Press. [*Choosing from abundance: socio-cultural developments in demand and offer in the media landscape – Trends in the media landscape: four explorations*].

Burri, M. (2015). Contemplating a 'public service navigator': In search of new (and better) functioning Public Service Media. *International Journal of Communication, 9*, 1341–1359. Cammaerts, B. (2007). Citizenship, the public sphere and media. In N. Carpentier and B. Cammaerts (eds), *Reclaiming the Media* (pp. 1–8). Bristol: Intellect.

Cielen, S. (2005). *Are we being served? Een kritische analyse van The Big Read and Restoration als cultuurparticipatieverhogende televisieprojecten in een context van digitalisering*

(Unpublished master's thesis).Vrije Universiteit Brussel, Brussels. [*Are we being served? A critical analysis of The Big Read and Restoration as television projects that enhance participation in culture in a context of digitisation*]

Coase, R.H. (1947). The origin of the monopoly of broadcasting in Great Britain. *Economica, 14*(55), 189–210.

Coase, R.H. (1948). Wire broadcasting in Great Britain. *Economica, 15*(59), 194–220.

Coase, R.H. (1966). The economics of broadcasting and government policy. *The American Economic Review, 56*(1–2), 440–447.

Coase, R.H. (1974). The market for goods and the market for ideas. *The American Economic Review, 64*(2), 384–391.

Collins, R. and Murroni, C. (1996). *New Media, New Policies: Media and Communications Strategy for the Future.* Cambridge: Polity Press.

Council of Europe (2007). *Recommendation (2007)3 on the Remit of Public Service Media in the Information Society.*

Council of Europe (2009). *Recommendation 1878 on The Funding of Public Service Broadcasting.*

Cox, B. (2004). *Free for All? Public Service Television in the Digital Age.* London: Demos.

Cunningham, S. (2009). Reinventing television: The work of the "innovation" unit. In G. Turner and J. Tay (eds), *Television Studies After TV: Understanding Television in the Post-Broadcast Era* (pp. 83–92). London: Routledge.

Cunningham, S. (2015). Repositioning the innovation rationale for public service media. *International Journal of Digital Television, 6*(2), 203–220.

Dahlgren, P. (2001). Public service media, old and new: Vitalizing a civic culture? *Canadian Journal of Communication, 24*(4), 1–19.

Davies, G. (2005). The BBC and public value. In T. Little and D. Helm (eds), *Can the Market Deliver? Funding Public Service Television in the Digital Age?* (pp. 129–150). Eastleigh: John Libbey Publishing.

Debrett, M. (2009). Riding the wave: Public service television in the multi-platform era. *Media, Culture & Society, 31*(5), 807–827.

Donders, K. (2012). *Public Service Media and Policy in Europe.* Basingstoke: Palgrave Macmillan.

Donders, K. (2019). Public service media beyond the digital hype: Distribution strategies in a platform era. *Media Culture & Society, 41*(7), 1011-1028.

Donders, K. and Pauwels, C. (2012). Ex ante tests: A means to an end or the end for public service media? In G.F. Lowe and J. Steemers (eds), *Regaining the Initiative for Public Service Media* (pp. 79–96). Göteborg: Nordicom.

Donders, K. and Raats, T. (2015). From public service media organisations to decentralised public service for the media sector: A comparative analysis of opportunities and disadvantages. *Javnost – The Public, 22*(2), 145-163.

Donders, K. and Van den Bulck, H. (2016). Decline and fall of public service media values in the international content acquisition market: An analysis of small public broadcasters acquiring BBC Worldwide content. *European Journal of Communication, 31*(3), 299–316.

Donders, K., Pauwels, C. and Loisen, J. (2012). Introduction: All or nothing? From public service broadcasting to public service media, to public service 'anything'? *International Journal of Media and Cultural Politics, 8*(1), 3–12.

Doyle, G. (2002). *Understanding: Media Economics.* London: Sage Publications.

Dyson, K. and Humphreys, P. (1988). The context of new media politics in Western Europe. In K. Dyson and P. Humphreys, with R. Negrine and J.-P. Simon, *Broadcasting and New Media Policies in Western Europe* (pp. 1–61). London: Routledge.

Elstein, D. (2008). How to fund public service content in the digital age. In T. Gardam and D.A.L. Levy (eds), *The Price of Plurality: Choice, Diversity and Broadcasting Institutions in the Digital Age* (pp. 86–90). Oxford: Reuters Institute for the Study of Journalism.

Elstein, D., Cox, D., Donoghue, B., Graham, D. and Metzger, G. (2004). *Beyond the Charter: The BBC After 2006*. London: The Broadcasting Policy Group.

Enli, G.S. (2008). Redefining public service broadcasting: Multi-platform participation. *Convergence: The International Journal of Research into New media Technologies*, *14*(1), 105-120.

Fairbairn, C. (2004). Commentary: Why broadcasting is still special. In A. Peacock (ed.), *Public Service Broadcasting Without the BBC?* (pp. 58-70). London: Institute for European Affairs.

Fields, B., Jones, R. and Cowlishaw, T. (2018). The case for public service recommender algorithms. Retrieved from https://piret.gitlab.io/fatrec2018/program/fatrec2018-fields.pdf (accessed on October 2020).

Freedman, D. (2008). *The Rise and Fall of the PSP*. London: Goldsmith University Research Online. Retrieved from http://research.gold.ac.uk/7080/1/PSParticle.pdf (accessed October 2020).

Gardam, T. (2008). The purpose of reality. In T. Gardam and D.A. Levy (eds), *The Price of Plurality: Choice, Diversity and Broadcasting Institutions in the Digital Age* (pp. 11-22). Oxford: Reuters Institute for the Study of Journalism.

Garnham, N. (1990). *Capitalism and Communication: Global Culture and the Economics of Information*. London: Sage.

Garnham, N. (1994). The broadcasting market and the future of the BBC. *The Political Quarterly*, *65*(1), 11–19.

Habermas, J. (1991). *The Structural Transformation of the Public Sphere: An Inquiry into a Category of Bourgeois Society*. Cambridge: MIT Press.

Harambam, J., Helberger, N. and van Hoboken, J. (2018). Democratizing algorithmic news recommenders: How to materialize voice in a technologically saturated media ecosystem. *Philosophical Transactions of the Royal Society A: Mathematical, Physical and Engineering Sciences*, *376*(2133).

Heath, J. and Levy, D. (2005). *Can the Market Deliver? Funding Public Service Television in the Digital Age*. Eastleigh: John Libbey Publishing.

Helberger, N. (2015). Merely facilitating or actively stimulating diverse media choices? Public Service Media at the crossroad. *International Journal of Communication*, *9*, 1324–1340.

Hellemans, L. (2020). Visie op de nieuwe beheersovereenkomst. Brussels: Vlaams Parlement. [*Vision on the new management contract*].

Helm, D. (2005). Consumers, citizens and members: Public service broadcasting and the BBC. In J. Heath and D. Levy (eds), *Can the Market Deliver? Funding Public Service Television in the Digital Age?* (pp. 1–21). Eastleigh: John Libbey Publishing.

Hoffmann-Riem, W. (1995). Germany: The regulation of broadcasting. In M. Raboy (ed.), *Public Broadcasting for the 21st Century* (pp. 64–86). London: John Libbey.

Holmwood, L. (2009). BBC's Mark Thompson attacks plans to 'top-slice' licence fee. Retrieved from www.theguardian.com/media/2009/jun/24/bbc-mark-thompson-top-slice (accessed October 2020).

Horsti, K. and Hultén, G. (2011). Directing diversity: Managing cultural diversity media policies in Finnish and Swedish public service broadcasting. *International Journal of Cultural Studies*, *14*(2), 209–227.

Hoskins, C., McFadyen, S. and Finn, A. (2004). *Media Economics: Applying Economics to New and Traditional Media*. London: Sage.

Iosifidis, P. (2010). Pluralism and funding of public service broadcasting across Europe. In P. Iosifidis (ed.), *Reinventing Public Service Communication: European Broadcasters and Beyond* (pp. 23–35). Basingstoke: Palgrave Macmillan.

Jakubowicz, K. (2007). Public service broadcasting in the 21st century. What chance for a new beginning? In G.F. Lowe and J. Bardoel (eds), *From Public Service Broadcasting to Public Service Media* (pp. 29-50). Göteborg: Nordicom.

Just, N., Büchi, M. and Latzer, M. (2017). A blind spot in public broadcasters' discovery of the public: How the public values public service. *International Journal of Communication, 11*, 992–1011.

Klein-Shagrir, O. and Keinonen, H. (2014). Public service television in a multi-platform environment: A comparative study in Finland and Israel. *VIEW Journal of European Television History and Culture, 3*(6), 14–23.

Larrondo, A., Domingo, D., Erdal, I.J., Masip, P. and Van den Bulck, H. (2016). Opportunities and limitations of newsroom convergence. *Journalism Studies, 17*(3), 277–300.

Levy, D. (1999). *Europe's Digital Revolution: Broadcasting Revolution, the EU and the Nation State*. London: Routledge.

Lilley, A. (2008). The fertile fallacy: New opportunities for public service content. In T. Gardam and D.A. Levy (eds), *The Price of Plurality: Choice, Diversity and Broadcasting Institutions in the Digital Age* (pp. 95–100). Oxford: Reuters Institute for the Study of Journalism.

Moe, H. (2008). Between supranational competition and national culture? Emerging EU policy and public broadcasters' online services. In I. Bondebjerg and P. Madsen (eds), *Media, Democracy and European Culture* (pp. 215–239). Bristol: Intellect.

Monzer, C., Moeller, J., Helberger, N. and Eskens, S. (2020). User perspectives on the news personalisation process: Agency, Trust and utility as building blocks, *Digital Journalism*, 8(9), 1142-1162.

Murdock, G. (2004). Building the Digital Commons: Public Broadcasting in the Age of the Internet. Paper presented at the 2004 Spry Memorial Lecture, 22 November, Montreal.

Murdock, G. (2005). Building the digital commons: Public broadcasting in the age of the Internet. In G.F. Lowe and P. Jauert (eds), *Cultural Dilemmas in Public Service Broadcasting* (pp. 213–230). Göteborg: Nordicom.

Murray, S. (2016). *Get Smarter: The Wearables, Carriables, and Shareables of Digital Self-Actualization*. Madison: University of Wisconsin Press.

Napoli, P.M. (2019). *Social Media and the Public Interest: Media Regulation in the Disinformation Age*. New York: Columbia University Press.

Noam, E. (1991). *Television in Europe*. New York: Oxford University Press.

Peacock, A. (ed.) (1986). *Report of the Committee on Financing the BBC*. London: Her Majesty's Stationary Office.

Peacock, A. (2004). Public service broadcasting without the BBC? In A. Peacock (ed.), *Public Service Broadcasting Without the BBC?* (pp. 33–53). London: Institute for Economic Affairs.

Pickard, V. (2019). *Democracy Without Journalism*. Oxford: Oxford University Press.

Price, M. and Raboy, M. (eds)(2003). *Public Service Broadcasting in Transition: A Documentary Reader*. The Hague: Kluwer Law International.

Ramsey, P. (2018). The BBC Ideas Service: The Corporation's Search for Universalism Online. Paper presented at the 2018 RIPE Conference 'Universalism and PSM', 18–20 October, Madrid.

Redmond, J. (2004). *Balancing on the Wire: The Art of Managing Media Organizations* (2nd ed.). Cincinnati: Atomic Dog.

Siebert, F., Peterson, T.B. and Schramm, W. (1956). *Four Theories of the Press. The Authoritarian, Libertarian, Social Responsibility, and Soviet Communist Concepts of What the Press Should Be and Do.* Urbana: University of Illinois Press.

Sørensen, J.K. and Hutchinson, J. (2017). Algorithms and public service media. In G.F. Lowe, H. Van den Bulck and K. Donders (eds), *Public Service Media in the Networked Society* (pp. 91–106). Göteborg: Nordicom.

Steemers, J. (2003). Public service broadcasting is not dead yet: Strategies in the 21st century. In G.F. Lowe and T. Hujanen (eds), *Broadcasting and Convergence: New Articulations of the Public Service Remit* (pp. 123–136). Göteborg: Nordicom.

Stevenson, N. and Rashid, I. (2020). Bringing the politics back into public service media policy: Three political case-making perspectives in the UK Communications Act Review 2012. Retrieved from www.academia.edu/4518722/Bringing_the_politics_back_into_public_service_media_policy (accessed October 2020).

Suarez-Candel, R. (2012). Adapting Public Service to the Multiplatform Scenario: Challenges, Opportunities and Risks. Working papers of the Hans Bredow Institute, No. 25. Hamburg: Hans Bredow Institute.

Tambini, D. and Cowling, J. (2004). Introduction: Redefining public service broadcasting for the 21st century. In D. Tambini and J. Cowling (eds), *From Public Service Broadcasting to Public Service Communications* (pp. 1–4). Oxford: Institute for Public Policy Research.

Van den Bulck, H. (2001). Public service television and national identity as a project of modernity: The example of Flemish television. *Media, Culture & Society*, 23(1), 53–69.

Verdegem, P. and Lievens, E. (2016). Towards a Public Service Algorithm that Promotes News Diversity. Paper presented at the 6th European Communication Conference 'Mediating Discontinuities: Contesting Pasts, Presents and Futures', 9-12 November, Prague.

Ward, D. (2006). Can the market provide? Public service media, market failure and public goods. In C. Nissen (ed.), *Making a Difference: Public Service Broadcasting in the European Landscape* (pp. 51–64). Eastleigh: John Libbey.

Wheeler, M. (2010). The EU's competition directorate: State aids and public service broadcasting. In P. Iosifidis (ed.), *Reinventing Public Service Communication: European Broadcasters and Beyond* (pp. 49–62). New York: Palgrave Macmillan.

Withers, G. (2003). Broadcasting. In R. Towse (ed.), *A Handbook of Cultural Economics* (pp. 102-113). Cheltenham: Edward Elgar.

4 Public Service Media as a democracy- and citizenship-centric project

Introduction

From its inception in the 1920s until the 1970s, Public Service Broadcasting was – albeit firmly rooted in a project of political power maximisation (Noam, 1991; Hoffmann-Riem, 1995: 82ff) – concerned with emancipation. Media policy, and Public Service Broadcasting as its core element, was a citizen emancipation project. The media ought to be 'a ladder which people could steadily climb, moving from the lowest rungs of packaged commercial entertainment to the highest rungs of consecrated cultural artefacts' (Murdock, 2005: 178). Following the idea of empowerment and firmly believing in the fundamental role of Public Service Broadcasting in contributing to a democratic public sphere (Habermas, 1991), pluralism and universality were central elements in this. Public broadcasters were entrusted with the realisation of the task to educate, inform and entertain the audience (Price and Raboy, 2003). Despite pressure on both the idea of Public Service Broadcasting and its organisation through public broadcasters in the 1980s – largely due to the upsurge of neoliberalism (Dyson and Humphreys, 1988; Garnham, 1990: 127–128; Blumler, 1991) – the public broadcaster 'axis' remained firmly rooted in most Western and Northern European countries. Admittedly, the distinctiveness of public broadcasters' offers versus commercial media services became more important after the abolishment of public broadcast monopolies in the 1980s and 1990s throughout Europe. Ever since, scholars have emphasised the importance of public broadcasters addressing audiences primarily as citizens and not so much as consumers (Hesmondhalgh, 2019: 152). Their independence from both politics and commercial pressures is key in this (Freedman, 2019: 203). Public Service Media is in that sense a project focused on citizenship and a 'responsibility for the health of the political process and for the quality of public discourse generated with it' (Blumler quoted in Hesmondhalgh, 2019: 152).

It is this notion of citizenship that I will take as the core of defining the values and objectives of a 'modern' Public Service Media project. Starting from contributions on Public Service Broadcasting and Public Service Media from Monroe Price and Marc Raboy (2003), Karol Jakubowicz (2007), Gregory Ferrell Lowe and Jo Bardoel (2007) and Wolfgang Hoffmann-Riem (2000;

2002), I will define the project of Public Service Media not in relation to platforms or devices, but more so in relation to its potentially transformative powers in a society and market in transition. I make a distinction between Public Service Media and its relation to political, cultural and social citizenship, whereby I argue that specifically the contribution of public broadcasters to the latter aspect of citizenship will increase in importance in line with the transformations described in Chapter 2 on digitisation and internationalisation.

Public Service Media as a project to serve democracy

There is no unique, universal and conclusive definition of what exactly Public Service Media is, nor of what the organisations delivering it should do precisely. However, setting out from a broad societal perspective and the importance of Public Service Media for democracy, various scholars have put forward goals like pluralism, diversity, social cohesion, quality, universal service delivery, and so on, as at the core of public service communication policies and institutions (see, among others, Brown 1996; Tracey 1998; Price and Raboy 2003; Aslama and Syvertsen 2007).

While I agree with most of what these scholars have written about Public Service Broadcasting and, later on, Public Service Media, it is for reasons of analytical clarity and theorisation, important to make a distinction between the following aspects of Public Service Media theory:

- Values: What is the normative construct Public Service Broadcasting and Public Service Media are built on?
- Objectives: What is the essential contribution Public Service Media as a project should make? And have these objectives remained the same in a society that is from a technological, economic and social perspective in transition?
- Means and principles: What are the means and principles to achieve the project of Public Service Media?
- Necessary conditions: What is needed to make all of this happen? In other words: what has the power to make or break Public Service Media?

The values and objectives are discussed in this chapter; an elaboration of means, principles and necessary conditions follows in the subsequent chapter.

The values that underpin Public Service Broadcasting and Public Service Media theories so far are strongly related to representative democracy and the Enlightenment. Public Service Media serves democracy and the 'good society', that is, a society where government, while accepting that there are limits to what it can do, assumes some level of responsibility over the economic and social wellbeing of people (Galbraith, 1996: 2-3). The aim is to contribute via information, education and entertainment to the overall wellbeing of society and all citizens therein. Society is believed to function in a way that is beneficial for all when people are free, equal and part of a community. That is basically what the values *liberté, fraternité* and *égalité* stand for. This *credo* of the French Revolution sets out from the conviction that more people would be happy in the broadest meaning of the word possible when societies would invest in the values of freedom, brotherhood and equality. That is not easy to test empirically, and explorative studies into the issue are somewhat undecided on what causal relation exists between, for example, equality and happiness (Veenhoven, 2000). Of course these values are also interpreted in diverging ways by different political ideologies. Liberals will place more emphasis on freedom, while socialists will focus more on equality.

Especially, there is a different weight attached to values and that weight can, moreover, vary according to circumstances. Andreea Ernst-Vintila and Irina Macovei (2016) show a compelling attachment to the value of freedom of speech after the Charlie Hebdo events in Paris in January 2015. Terrorists killed several journalists of the satirical magazine. The event, as they show on the basis of analysing 840,000 people's online responses, strengthened the importance average citizens placed on the fundamental right to hold opinions and express them via any means possible if they wanted to. However, in the same research the scholars concluded that public support for the victims from an attack on a kosher supermarket in Paris in the same month was less outspoken and in some cases even absent. One event was accompanied by a different reaction than another. Many reasons, that will not be dived deeper in here, explain for this.

There is often also a trade-off to be observed between the values of freedom, brotherhood and equality. For example, striving after equality will inevitably limit freedom and vice versa. Discussions on universal health care are ultimately about the level of accessibility for all citizens regardless of income to health care vs. the individual freedom to decide on whether one wants health care insurance at all. Similarly, a license fee for public broadcasters is a contribution that ensures free-at-the-point-of-use media access to citizens even if people are not really into public broadcasters' content or when they would be willing to pay more. Most license fees are flat fees. While some would say this is in line with the idea of equality, others can argue that a single mother with three children will probably have more difficulties paying this than a business man who has inherited a family fortune. There is also a friction between freedom and the idea of solidarity or being part of a community that is embodied by the *fraternité* idea. Former Prime Minister of the United Kingdom (1979-1990), Margaret Thatcher, once said that there is no such thing as a society (O'Sullivan, 1993: 223). Neoliberals would indeed argue that the world is driven by individual and rational consumer choices. The whole liberalisation of media markets is firmly set on the idea that the free movement and expression of ideas within a free market place of ideas is a better guarantee to pluralism, diversity and quality than government intervention will ever be (Bromley, 2002: 219). However, most nationalists would argue that the construction of society around a unified identity is key to making the myth or social imaginary (Lee and LiPuma, 2002) of a nation state work. In fact, in *Sapiens: A Brief History of Humankind*, Yuval Noah Harari (2011) advocates that the construction of society around a unified identity is key to keeping in place most 'myths', including capitalism. So, in making reference to the values underlying Public Service Media, I do not claim that these values are at the level of interpretation stable, indivisible and undisputed. But, they serve as high-level and agreed-upon values of a Public Service Media system in European democracies. This is reflected in the Amsterdam Protocol's (see Chapter 7) assertion that Public Service Broadcasting is there to contribute to the continued and sustainable achievement of democratic societies. It is shown most explicitly in the German system that constitutionally protects Public Service Media as an essential feature of liberal democracy (Hoffmann-Riem, 1991: 21; Humphreys, 1994: 128; Schüller-Keber, 2009: 67). Commercial media's existence is dependent on the public broadcasting system, not the other way around. A democracy-centric approach is adhered to sternly and even passionately by the Constitutional Court in Germany (Hoffmann-Riem, 2002; Donders, 2012: 128).

While public broadcasters are obliged to report objectively, independently from economic, political or other forces in society, and impartially, they are not neutral in the absolute sense of that word (Price and Raboy, 2003; note that objectivity of journalism is from the outset an unachievable goal as reporting equals selection, see McChesney, 2003: 304). It is key to understand that Public Service Broadcasting and Public Service Media as concepts set out from liberal democracy as the best form to organise society.

Contributing to political, social, cultural and civic citizenship

The main objective of Public Service Media is thus to contribute to the well-being of people, society and democracy at large. The concept of citizenship is key in this. As Bart Cammaerts (2007: 1) explains, citizenship is the basis upon which we structure democratic societies. It can be related to civic, political and social rights. Civic rights concern an individual's personal freedom; political rights relate to people's exercise of political power, be it through voting, debating, taking up a political mandate themselves, and so on; and social rights as the widest set of rights. They relate to citizens' economic wellbeing, their security, sharing in social heritage, their affinity with a community, and so on.

That is why I prefer to discuss the objectives of Public Service Media in relation to the achievement of different types of citizenship. Inspired by Hilde Van den Bulck's (2016; see also Dahlgren, 1995; Marshall, 2006) work on this issue, I make a distinction between four types of citizenship: political, social, cultural and civil citizenship. While one could argue that cultural citizenship is a part of social citizenship, it is in a work on Public Service Media analytically more clear to talk about those separately.

Political citizenship

Most public broadcasters emphasise that information is at the core of their remit. This relates to the expected contribution of Public Service Media to the strengthening of political citizenship. Murdock (2004: 5-7) talks about several associated rights, including information rights, knowledge rights, deliberative rights, representation rights and participation rights. Political citizenship is not only about being informed, but also about having access to different interpretative frameworks and deliberative fora where these are discussed and evaluated. Political citizenship requires pluralism, which is not the same as abundance of content (Barber, 2004). Structural pluralism, so Beata Klimkiwiecz (2010: 907) says, 'refers to a condition where diverse, independent media entities exist within a system and are arranged together in a particular way'. It 'is one of the basic conditions for public sphere formation in contemporary democratic societies' (Klimkiwiecz, 2005: 1). Allen, Connolly and Hargreaves Heap (2017: 47) see media pluralism as 'an essential pillar in the right to information and freedom of expression'. It requires the representation of all relevant opinions and the possibility for citizens to engage in a debate, not as mere spectators or formatted in ways that determines what can and cannot be said. Citizens should be part of a process of interaction and of genuine dialogue within some sort of public sphere (Habermas, 1991) and this should not be eroded into consumption (Scannell, 1995: 23-24; see also McQuail, 1998: 140). As maintained by Picard and Pickard (2018: 16), 'a healthy democracy requires opportunities for citizens to deliberate in public spaces that are largely independent from state and market forces'. The European understanding of media pluralism as a necessary condition for political citizenship goes beyond rejecting government control over media; it extends to avoiding commercial interests from becoming so overly dominant that they can inhibit a free, pluralistic exchange of media services (Czepek, Hellwig and Novak, 2009). That opinion diverges significantly from the US model where the freedom of individual media owners is placed above the equality of all citizens to receive information as well as to express their opinions (Humphreys, 1996). While the free market place of ideas has not delivered (McChesney, 2015) – look for example at the low voter turnouts – also several EU Member States are adopting media policies that are inspired by libertarian ideas (for a further elaboration of media policy trends in Europe, see Chapter 6).

While there is a consensus on Public Service Media being a project that should contribute to political citizenship, there is less agreement on whether public broadcasting organisations are doing their jobs in this respect. Some argue that public broadcasters have 'contributed modestly to a public sphere of debate and critical discourse' (Herman, 1993: 86). Others are more enthusiastic about public broadcasters' dedicated approach to news and current affairs programming. Research indeed shows higher levels of current affairs knowledge with citizens in strong public broadcasting systems. People watching public broadcasters learn more about domestic and international affairs than those watching commercial news. Factors such as independence, adequate public funding and audience share are relevant factors in determining levels of hard news in particular (Cushion, 2012).

Some scholars have been more critical, pointing at public broadcasters investing less or insufficiently in investigative journalism (Cordell, 2009), being insufficiently critical of the ruling party/parties largely because of funding issues and/or institutional weakness (Stetka and Örnebring, 2013), reporting in overly dramatic manners without adequate attention for historical context on serious issues such as the financial crisis in 2008/2009 (Berry, 2016), or being straightforward mouthpieces of government. Public broadcasters, some research shows, have gone along with polarisation of public discourse, not critically questioning statements made by politicians (e.g., related to the Brexit referendum, Cushion and Lewis, 2017) or failing to represent all opinions in society, specifically those of ethnic minorities (Panis, Paulussen and Dhoest, 2019). Some also argue that the emphasis has been too much on a one-directional transfer of knowledge (Bardoel and Lowe, 2007) instead of a two-way understanding of political processes, current affairs and events in society. Several of these distinct elements of critique can be related to Des Freedman's analysis of the BBC's contribution to pluralistic information provision. While in principle in favour of a public interest-driven media system, Freedman (2019: 206) demonstrates the gap between theory and practice. He points at structural and institutional elements that limit the BBC's 'truth-telling, democracy-enhancing' potential.

> Far from retaining its independence from all vested interests, and delivering a critical and robust public interest journalism, the BBC is a compromised version of a potentially noble ideal: far too implicated in and attached to existing elite networks of power to be able to offer an effective challenge to them.

Freedman (2019: 211) admits that it is unrealistic, in fact a mission impossible, to expect public broadcasters to exist fully independent from society. However, the BBC's staff composition and manifest failure to adequately represent women and ethnic minorities, the acceptance of the 'prevailing neoliberal consensus' as middle-ground (or a given) in its news reporting and its coverage of disagreement within the establishment's borders are a threat to its independence and undermine the BBC to live up to its fullest potential.

As literature shows and is affirmed by our case study research, it is difficult to reach conclusions on public broadcasters' contribution to political citizenship for all public broadcasters in all countries in all given circumstances for the last 100 years. A contextual approach is necessary here. Such an approach should, however, not result in easy conclusions whereby Central Eastern European countries are 'scoring' poorly and Western European countries are superior. That is one of the things that should be taken on board on the basis of Freedman's work.

Social citizenship

Next to political citizenship, Public Service Media is a societal project. It is about connecting people to public life (Scannell, 1990). It is 'a form of speaking to, and engaging with, viewers as citizens' (Van Dijck and Poell, 2015: 149).

Setting out from the assumption that mediated communication creates a public sphere (Habermas, 1991; Garnham, 2000), Public Service Media is about ensuring a level of 'mediated publicness' in a commercial and commodified media landscape (Lowe and Jauert, 2005: 25). Its main aim is to contribute to citizenship and not consumerism within a given society. That goes beyond political citizenship, even if overlapping with it, but is a purposeful project to create a sense of belonging to society. Social citizenship and social capital are intricately linked. Coleman (1988) argues that social capital is a concept that unites two at first sight opposed views of society. The first view sees people as socialised and their actions as being governed by social norms, rules and obligations. Social context explains actions. The second view sees people as individuals that make completely self-interested decisions. They aim to maximise their own utility. Societal norms do not explain for that at all. Coleman rejects both perspectives, defining social capital as the productive force that comes about 'through changes in the relations among persons that facilitate action'. Trust is the glue in social capital. When people trust structures, they will become more productive and happier. A notion of 'we' emerges, which becomes 'the object of future identifications' (Lee and LiPuma, 2002: 200) and social imaginaries allowing people to 'imagine their social existence, how they fit together with others, how things go on between them and their fellows, the expectations that are normally met, and the deeper normative notions and images that underlie these expectations' (Taylor, 2002: 106).

Lowe and Jauert (2005: 29) identify four key elements of social citizenship-building by Public Service Media. All of these are in line with Coleman's view on social capital. First, public broadcasters should be a socialising agent.

> Socialising with others and being associated in shared ways of life, is the muscle that builds social capital. In a social context where everything is increasingly individualistic, investment in shared communication infrastructure is an essential driver. Where it has been entrusted to commercial media to handle, one finds a correlated weakening of participation in community and public affairs.

As said earlier, social capital is usually being related to trust in the organisation of society and social connectedness. Higher levels of social capital are considered to result in higher levels of civic engagement (cf. infra) (Putnam, 1995). That is why most scholars hold that Public Service Media has to be holistic or full-portfolio in its service offering. Some entertainment or sports programming can have a high impact in terms of socialising people into society. Some creative documentaries might have a smaller short-term impact, but can work through in the long run, fragments being used in a daily news broadcast or talk show.

Second, Public Service Media ought to be a discursive medium for the 'act of witnessing' and the process of working through history, events, what they mean and their effects. Public broadcasters do not only report, they should explain and help people to make sense of things (Livémont, Donders and Pauwels,

2017). Documentaries, drama, sitcoms and satirical programmes can contribute to that. Showing diversity of views as well as cross-levelling across differences is key in this regard (Lowe and Jauert, 2005).

Third, the interest of citizens should be at the heart of what public broadcasters do. Public Service Media is a civil society project. It is not about markets, nor about governments. The goal of public broadcasters should therefore be to 'facilitate trust, reciprocity, fairness, and all the other attributes that figure in the quality of life' (Lowe and Jauert, 2005: 30). It is not per se about interacting with audiences, even thought that might be a manner to connect better with the needs of citizens (Enli, 2008).

Fourth, public broadcasters should mediate inter-cultural communication. Giddens, Lowe and Jauert (2005: 30) put forward that public broadcasters should offer a democratic mediated space for reconciliation between individuals that have their personal freedom (see section on civic citizenship below) depending on the same rights for all. That comes with language policies as well. Moreover, several nations have multiple languages spoken by their population. Some of these languages are official. Language is a key component in forming a collective identity, in nation-building. It is a sensitive, political issue. While some public broadcasters in Europe and North America have embraced language differences and do an effort to serve their audiences in the languages they speak, this has been a big issue for others that have focused, for economic or political reasons, on one language only. Some public broadcasters take a middle-ground position, focussing on one language, but also engaging in language competencies of audiences that do not speak the domestic language at an advanced level (Wilkinson, 2005). Inter-cultural communication also refers to mediating dialogue between different communities in a given country. Highly complex and perhaps unrealistic, some would argue. Castelló's (2015) analysis of Spanish national and regional public television's coverage of the Catalan struggle for independence is a case in point. Both the national public broadcaster and the regional ones only selectively covered the event. They failed to provide context and historical perspective, and largely focused on political strategy. In so doing, they mediated mass demonstrations in a way 'that neglected the political expression of the citizens in favour of emphasising the role of political leaders, their political party tactics, and other extra-political arguments'. They did not contribute to more understanding among citizens, often holding opposed views, and in fact weakened social capital, nation-building and social citizenship at large.

Creating a sense of belonging to society is complicated and clearly related to levels of political and especially cultural citizenship. Socio-economic and cultural differences divide people. Online media, at some point seen as a democratic meeting place for all, seem to have added to polarisation, fast food consumption of news and current affairs, and disinformation. A study on Facebook usage of 2,844 US users showed that reality is more complicated as Facebook de-activation decreased both factual news knowledge and political polarisation at the same time (Allcott, Gentzkow and Yu, 2019).

Cultural citizenship

Social and cultural citizenship are very much intertwined. Whereas social citizenship deals with togetherness and trust in society, cultural citizenship might be considered to function as the glue of attachment to a specific society. There are two main aspects of cultural citizenship. The first relates to the aspect of nation-building around a shared identity, values and language. The second concerns the offer of services that guide people from *culture* to *Culture*, meaning the arts, theatre, classical music, ballet, and so on. Both *culture* and *Culture* can contribute to the first aspect of cultural citizenship. While the second function was already omnipresent when public broadcasting monopolies in radio emerged in the 1920s and 1930s, the 'bigger' issue of creating cultural citizenship around a nation became more important post World War II and was, in countries such as Finland, Belgium and Germany, firmly related to the creation of inter-cultural harmony (Lowe and Jauert, 2005: 13; Donders, 2012). Both aspects essentially consider Public Service Media an emancipation project, even when permeated with basic political aspirations (Garnham, 2000: 6). Scholars, policy-makers and many public broadcasting practitioners saw and still see the project as a means to open new horizons for the less privileged. They, as already said in the introduction of this chapter, want public broadcasters to push/ nudge people from *culture* to *Culture* (Murdock, 2005: 178).

The aspect of nation-building is admittedly highly complex. Because what connects people around a nation? Why do people feel Belgian, Dutch, Polish or French and is it important that they identify with a nation? Relating back to the goal of social citizenship and the importance of trust in the order of society, identification with a nation state or other governmentally steered community makes sense (see Lowe and Jauert, 2005: 14). Public broadcasters have played an important role is this regard. Hilde Van den Bulck (2001) has demonstrated that public broadcaster VRT added to the materialisation of a Flemish, 'national' identity. At the same time, public broadcaster RTBF can be said to have contributed to the persistence of a Belgian, unified identity in the French-speaking part of Belgium (Donders, Van den Bulck and Raats, 2019b). When we see the Polish Government's determination to broadcast documentaries and films on Poland's heroic history on public broadcaster TVP, it is clear that their objective – also in Polish education at large – is to 'arouse patriotic emotions, cultivate love for homeland and strengthen bonds with the national community' (Bacia, 2019).

At the same time, there are also trends of disintegration of society that public broadcasters face difficulties to address. How to represent a growing diversity in the population? How to connect with people that do not per se relate to a domestic culture? While not agreeing with notions of *Leitkultur* (Pautz, 2005) and a supposed 'clash of civilisations' (Huntington, 1996), there is obviously a level of moral panic about migration and integration, on the one hand, and an apparent disconnect from parts of the population with public broadcasting offers, on the other. Turkish and Moroccans communities in several EU

Member States watch television channels from Turkey and Morocco more so than they watch German, Belgian or French television. Setting out from the idea that Public Service Media is about strengthening citizenship and democracy, one can hardly deny that that is not a problem. Regarding moral panics, public broadcasters take different routes. First, some public broadcasters such as the Canadian and Australian public broadcasters aim to create empathy for people from other cultural backgrounds. In its successful programme *Little Mosque on the Prairie* about Muslims in a fictional small town in Saskatchewan, the Canadian Broadcasting Corporation CBC aimed to overcome stereotypes about Muslims. Created by a Muslim film-maker, the comedy show included plots that appealed to Muslim and non-Muslim viewers. Issues such as learning to swim by a female instructor were addressed, but also the wishes of Muslim teenagers to engage with Halloween or the employment of an imam born in Canada. The idea thereof was to effectively address Canadians' concerns about Muslim integration in Canada, and to appeal to interests of Canadian Muslims at the same time. The programme was very successful and spanned over six seasons. Conway (2014) concludes it can inspire 'other national broadcasters attempting to improve the representation of diversity on television'. That 'requires creative strategies that open a space for producers to operate, even if that space is circumscribed'. Risk-taking is thus crucial. A more controversial example of a public broadcaster dealing with a contested issue such as migration is Australian public broadcaster's SBS *Go back to where you came from* reality documentary. Six ordinary Australians, and in a second season six celebrities, were sent on a reversed asylum-seeker journey. The objective was not to convince people of more lenient asylum policies, but rather to increase understanding and empathy for the complexities and human struggle underlying migration as a phenomenon. SBS itself communicated that the goal was 'to get the nation talking' (Sauter and Bruns, 2014: 3). A subsequent Twitter analysis indeed showed that the nation was talking, but largely opposite views remained and there was no genuine dialogue (Sauter and Bruns, 2014). While some public broadcasters take the risk to allow for open discussions on issues that divide 'the nation' (these issues can also be the environment, religion, ethical issues, etc.), which sometimes fail and at times succeed, others prefer – voluntarily or mandatory – to represent one unified national identity. In Hungary and Poland, both public broadcasters put forward an exclusive identity for native Hungarians and Polish people. LGBTQ+ communities, migrants and foreigners in general are excluded from this. The idea is to promote one joint understanding of problems and one, inescapable solution. That approach to cultural citizenship, however, goes against notions of civic citizenship and the encouragement of participation in democracy (cf. infra). It is embedded in what some would call *Leitkultur* though. Anna Borgos (2007) compellingly demonstrates the rooted homophobia in Hungarian society. That engrained normative judgement against 'the other' is instrumentalised by political leaders and sustained by the public broadcaster. The opposite can be found in Flanders where Vanlee, Dhaenens and Van Bauwel (2018) demonstrate 'queer normality' in the public broadcaster's programming. While at the theoretical level, there is thus an understanding of what Public Service Media ought to be in relation to cultural citizenship and there are plenty examples of public broadcasters being aspirational in line with theoretical assertions, multiple public broadcasters are doing exactly the opposite. The same applies to Public Service Media being a project for all. While public broadcasters should reach all citizens, practice shows other things.

That brings us, second, to public broadcasters' difficulty to connect with parts of the audience; in terms of reach of migrant populations, and in terms of immigrants and also more conservative parts of the citizenry feeling represented. Horsti, Hultén and Titley (2014) have argued that public broadcasters need to support the integration of immigrants in society and bring about social cohesion, bringing both ethnic majority and minorities into society. Multiple studies have shown that the tenacious under-representation of minorities, stereotyping, one-sided negative images of certain minorities and polarisation around these issues made that a mission impossible so far (for an overview, see Panis, Paulussen and Dhoest, 2019). At the same time, populists politicians have argued that some public broadcasters are imposing diversity on 'normal people' in society. And indeed, an increasing amount of people feel that also they are not being represented by 'their' public broadcasters. Elite media oppose the will of the people (Mazzoleni, 2003: ff). Disappearance of party-affiliated or ideologically aligned press has added to this feeling of not being heard and reflected. That growing discontent with part of the population is, so Ford and Goodwin (2017: 17; see also Calhoun, 2016) contend in an analysis of Brexit, 'a symptom of longer-term social changes that have quietly been reshaping public opinion, political behaviour, and party competition in Britain as well as in other Western democracies'. These social changes relate to the decreased size of the normal working class, a liberal leftist stance on ethical issues and the multiculturalism in society. Diversity was seen as a strength and discrimination as a social evil. Individual freedoms were put above communal values. To some extent, civic citizenship (cf. infra) trumped cultural and subsequently social citizenship (Ford and Goodwin, 2017: 18ff). Growing parts in society felt that the political system became non-responsive to their needs and relate this also to public broadcasters.

Also public broadcasters' offer of culture as well as *Culture* is a place of contestation, both at the theoretical and practical level. Some scholars have critiqued the over-emphasis on *Culture* and the reproach of public broadcasters for failing to live up to high expectations in bringing people closer to the arts. They argue that national identity is formed on the basis of everyday culture. Lowe and Jauert (2005: 14) refer to Bourdieu's *habitus* to explain that 'phenomena which are hard to describe precisely or to comprehensively grasp, but in general deal with widely shared social experiences' can contribute more to nation-building through public broadcasters' radio, television and online services than *Cultural* services. Keeping the former paragraphs in mind, that makes sense. However, the relevance of culture should not be too easily abused by public broadcasters to fail in their duties regarding *Culture*. Indeed, when the market is effectively failing in this areas (see Livémont, Donders and Pauwels, 2017; Ali, 2016;

Steemers, 2017), who else is there to deliver media services to the public that document society, that reflect what *Cultural* life has to offer, that are diverse at the level of origin, genre and ideas?

Essentially, cultural citizenship is an inherently conflicting concept. It presumes unity and yet also diversity and this at the level of aims and means. Culture as a concept presumes some level of uniformity, coherence, social homogeneity, and collectivity. At the same time, differentiation, fragmentation, unequal distribution of cultural power and individualism also exist (Rathje, 2009). Public Service Media as a concept and public broadcasters as an institution feel more at ease with the former and less so with the latter.

Civic citizenship

A final component of citizenship is civic citizenship, referring to civic rights, civic duties and civic virtues. Civic rights concern each citizen' rights to freedom, freedom of expression, ownership, and so on. They essentially protect citizens from far-going control by governments, corporate elites and other organisations in society. At the same time, they allow citizens to participate in public life without discrimination, coercion or oppression (Heater, 2003: 221ff). Civic duties are the responsibilities to be involved in economic and political life. Citizens should obey the law, pay taxes and – when required – vote. Active involvement in political debate, being knowledgeable about current affairs and educated in the broad sense, and holding strong democratic values are all civic virtues (Theiss-Morse and Hibbing, 2005: 227).

There are diverging views on civic citizenship and specifically on how to strengthen it. Political sciences have focused most on civic participation and engagement for the good of democracy. Increasing citizen participation in politics or at least political debate is seen as a corner stone of that ambition. Quite some media and communication scholars have consistently held though that 'citizenship is practised as much through everyday life, leisure, critical consumption and popular entertainment as it is through debate and engagement with capital "P" politics' (Burgess, Foth and Klaebe, 2006: 1). Building civic citizenship thus not only happens in some sort of rational, Habermasian, public sphere, but also through small acts of engagement (Picone et al., 2019). Everyday agency helps us to overcome the often pessimist conclusions on citizens' willingness to participate in and through media on the one hand and public broadcasters' eagerness to allow citizens in their kitchens on the other hand (Vanhaeght, 2019). It also puts too optimist accounts on citizen journalism, blurring boundaries between producers and consumers, and self-publication in perspective (Picone et al., 2019).

Public broadcasters have struggled with civic citizenship. While they have, as already shown, contributed to knowledge of news and current affairs, there is no evidence that public broadcasters strengthen civic rights or virtues at least when taking the democracy angle. In several Southern, Central and Eastern European countries there is an ongoing alienation from civic citizenship (see

Chapter 6). But also in Western and Northern European countries, stimulating civic citizenship is by no means evident and certainly not a 'natural' goal for public broadcasters. Flemish public broadcaster VRT investigated new voters' attachment to democracy. Twenty-six per cent of youngsters aged between 18 and 23, who never voted before, said that they would prefer an authoritarian leader over democracy; in lower educated groups that went up to 50 per cent. A large majority had no idea about who was ruling the country, Flanders or its biggest city, Antwerp. Even bigger numbers could not tell which other parties, besides the leading party, were in the multi-party governments that characterise the Belgian political system (De Vadder and Callebaut, 2020). Mary Debrett's (2015) investigation of ABC's political talk show, *Q&A*, that aimed to integrate citizens in political debate, shows that stimulating civic engagement is far from evident. She concludes that the valuable initiative came with controversy, but that power imbalances between elites and other citizens remained. Moreover, while controversy is often related to popularity, it can also adversely impact trust. The latter is a corner stone of credible Public Service Media organisations in society.

Now, also when looking at small acts of engagement, the relationship between media users and public broadcasters is not an easy one. While several public broadcasting brands, notably radio brands, are good to interact with users, their sociological notion of participation (Couldry, Livingstone and Markham, 2010; Jenkins and Carpentier, 2013) that indeed values participation over its societal meaning, might have rendered participation meaningless.

Anne-Sofie Vanhaeght's (2019) research shows that public broadcasters' apparent failure to contribute to civic citizenship and engagement can be explained by their exclusive focus on the sociological notion of participation in some cases and on participation in the political sense in other cases. The former celebrates participation as such, whereas the latter only values 'meaningful' participation: actions that have an impact on democratic societies. A combination of the two perspectives across types of content and brands is thus needed.

Civic citizenship is a more individualistic notion, while political, social and cultural citizenship set out from collectivity. In fact, all these subforms of citizenship cannot exist without the other. Taras Kuzio (2002: 24) says that 'without a cultural legacy there will be no shared consent to live together', there would be no notion of 'a community set apart from and using the state as a means of self-government'. In that sense, Public Service Media is a project that ought to contribute to citizenship from both an individualistic and collective point of view.

Does the public recognise public broadcasters' contribution to citizenship and liberal democracy? That seems to be a key question, specifically from a civil citizenship point of view. Research points in different directions. In countries such as Switzerland and Belgium, citizens support the existence of public broadcasters, even if their own consumption of Public Service Media is rather low. In other countries, such as Spain or Poland support is considerably lower. To date, there is no comparative research on the matter, but case-specific studies exist. Just, Büchi and Latzer (2017) show why Swiss public broadcaster SRG survived a referendum on its future. Over 70 per cent of the Swiss population voted for the public broadcaster in the so-called *No Bilag* (no license fee) referendum in March 2018. The research of Natasha Just, Moritz Büchi and Michael Latzer (2017: 1000) found that 67 per cent of their representative sample of the Swiss population indeed agreed with the importance of public service. Less than half of the respondents (43.8 per cent) was of the opinion that SRG did a good job though. Very few were of the opinion that they did a poor job, so many were somewhat in the middle on this. Having said that, the Swiss population could make abstraction of their own gratification on the one hand and the importance of Public Service Media on the other. The two did correlate highly. In other words: the higher your personal satisfaction, the more likely a sentiment pro-Public Service Media became. Similar findings in Flanders (the Northern part of Belgium) where about 60 to 65 per cent of the audience values both the task and execution of the public task by VRT. The latter should, according to the respondents, reach as many people as possible, offer a full-portfolio service and focus on information at the same time (Paulussen et al., 2015). At the same time, other public broadcasters face smaller levels of audience support. The closure, undone after four years, of the Valencian public broadcaster provoked little reaction from the audience. Employees of *à punt media* protested and disclosed wrongdoings, political meddling and even straightforward cases of censorship. They did so after they lost their job though. The broadcaster was perceived as a part of the political system and, ultimately, not worthy of the audience's trust. Similar sentiments can be found in Poland where a small fraction of the population actually pays the license fee, government after government engages in management and journalist personnel changes (Jaskiernia and Pokorna-Ignatowicz, 2017) and where most of the experts I talked to advocated for a smaller public broadcaster with an eye on minimising damaging effects in case of government capture (see Chapter 14). This could lead to the conclusion that higher levels of independence come with more support for public broadcasters. That is not necessarily true as illustrated by the big street protests against the closure of Greek public broadcaster ERT in 2013 (Iosifidis and Katsirea, 2015). ERT could and can hardly be considered an independent and accountable public broadcaster. My main point is though that citizens can make abstraction of their own consumption behaviour and think normatively about society and policy projects such as Public Service Media.

How to serve the public interest in media

Essentially, Public Service Media is a project focused on serving democracy. When analysing the concept, one cannot but observe that its underlying assumption is that liberal democracy, how it is conceived in theory, is a good thing. Democracy should not only be understood in light of politics. It is about more than discussions in Parliament, political fights on Twitter, the re-form of

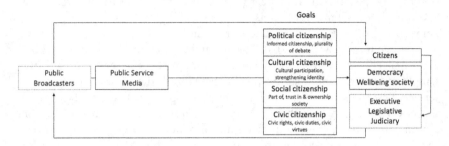

Figure 4.1 Public Service Media as a democracy- and citizenship-centric project

taxes or health care, and so on. It is about the wellbeing of a society that rests on the firm belief and will that all people are free, equal and part of a community: *liberté, fraternité* and *égalité*. Even if these values of the French revolution seem to contradict each other and are interpreted differently and are assigned a different weight by political ideologies, they are the basis of the European integration project and democracy in EU Member States. The idea of a Public Service Media project is that it contributes to the continued and sustainable achievement of this democratic project (see Figure 4.1). Public broadcasters – and most scholars would agree with that – contend that centralised and publicly funded institutions are the best means of taking up this role.

One of the main questions in the subsequent chapters is whether that is indeed the case. Are public broadcasters effectively contributing to stronger levels of political, cultural, social and civic citizenship as has been suggested by some of the literature discussed so far? The continued existence of public broadcasters rests, according to the argument I develop, on the role they play in society and not the perceived or actual distinctiveness of their offers compared to commercial media. That is why the framework in Figure 4.1, that will be developed further in the following chapter, is firmly rooted in a democracy-centric conceptualisation of Public Service Media and not in a market failure paradigm. It does not make it a 'public service anything' (see previous chapter) though as the means and goals of this project are clear, even if high-level, and firmly grounded in a citizenship- and democracy-centric approach to Public Service Media. For sake of clarity and repeating what has already been mentioned more implicitly, citizenship does not relate to a legal status of human beings in society. When I talk about citizenship, I mean all people regardless of them having legal citizenship or being *stateless*. I refer to citizenship as the corner stone of democratic culture, as something that relates to the political, the social, the cultural and the individual and never so with an exclusive focus on consumerism (see also Dahlgren, 1995: 141ff, who admittedly takes a more *étatiste* perspective). Citizenship throughout this book is thus not a controlling notion, but an 'empowering institution' (Isin, 2009: 369).

Hesmondhalgh (2019:154) says that scholars in the 1980s and 1990s were not massively researching the quality of public broadcasting during these decades. Their point was 'not necessarily to defend Public Service Broadcasting as it was, but as it could be'. That reflects one of the core points of this book: that Public Service Media theory is more about what we want it to be than about what it is. That has obvious value, but more work, also outside the field of news and current affairs, is needed on how public broadcasters manage or fail to contribute to political, cultural, social and civic citizenship.

The model sets out from the idea that Public Service Media contributes to liberal democracy and that citizens and polity are beneficiaries of this. This kind of modernist thinking is obviously under pressure in contemporary societies where the very foundations of our liberal democracy are being debated not only beyond the Western hemisphere, but within fortress Europe.

References

Ali, C. (2016). The merits of merit goods: Local journalism and public policy in a time of austerity. *Journal of Information Policy*, *6*, 105–128.

Allcott, H., Gentzkow, M. and Yu, C. (2019). Trends in the diffusion of misinformation on social media. *Research & Politics*. Retrieved from doi:10.1177/2053168019848554 (accessed October 2020).

Allen, H., Connolly, S. and Hargreaves Heap, S.P. (2017). Media pluralism: What matters for governance and regulation? *Journal of Media Economics*, *30*(2), 47–64.

Aslama, M. and Syvertsen, T. (2007). Public service broadcasting and new technologies: Marginalisation or re-monopolisation. In E. De Bens (ed.), *Media Between Culture and Commerce* (pp. 167–179). Bristol: Intellect.

Bacia, E. (2019). The phenomenon of banished soldiers in Polish schools as an example of the politics of memory. *Journal of Social Science Education*, *18*(1), 13–31.

Barber, B.R. (2004). Which technology and which democracy? In H. Jenkins and D. Thorburn (eds), *Democracy and New Media* (pp. 33–48). Cambridge: MIT Press.

Bardoel, J. and Lowe, G.F. (2007). From public service broadcasting to public service media. The core challenge. In G.F. Lowe and J. Bardoel (eds), *From Public Service Broadcasting to Public Service Media* (pp. 9–28). Göteborg: Nordicom.

Berry M. (2016). The UK press and the deficit debate. *Sociology*, *50*(3), 542–559.

Blumler, J.G. (1991). *Broadcasting Finance in Transition: A Comparative Handbook*. Oxford: Oxford University Press.

Borgos, A. (2007). Getting to know gays and lesbians in Hungary: Lessons from a Gender-Informed educational program. In J. Sempruch, K. Willems and L. Shook (eds), *Multiple Marginalities: An Intercultural Dialogue on Gender in Education* (pp. 425–436). Königstein/Taunus: Ulrike Helmer Verlag.

Bromley, M. (2002). The media. In J. Hollowell (ed.), *Britain since 1945: Making contemporary Britain* (pp. 211–238). London: Wiley-Blackwell.

Brown, A. (1996). Economics, public service broadcasting, and social values. *The Journal of Media Economics*, *9*(1), 3–15.

Burgess, J., Foth, M. and Klaebe, H. (2006). Everyday creativity as civic engagement: A cultural citizenship view of new media. In F. Papandrea (eds), *Proceedings 2006 Communications Policy & Research Forum* (pp. 1–16). Australia: Network Insight Institute.

76   *Theory*

Calhoun, C. (2016). Brexit is a mutiny against the Cosmopolitan elite. *New Perspectives Quarterly, 33*(3), 50–58.

Cammaerts, B. (2007). Citizenship, the public sphere and media. In N. Carpentier and B. Cammaerts (eds), *Reclaiming the Media* (pp. 1–8). Bristol: Intellect.

Castelló, E. (2015). Masking political engagement: Television coverage of a mass demonstration in Barcelona. *Television & New Media, 16*(6), 521–537.

Coleman, J.S. (1988). Social capital in the creation of human capital. *The American Journal of Sociology, 94*, 95–120.

Conway, K. (2014). Little Mosque, small screen: Multicultural broadcasting policy and Muslims on television. *Television & New Media, 15*(7), 648–663.

Cordell, M. (2009). What is happening to investigative journalism? A pilot study of ABC's Four Corners. *Pacific Journalism Review, 15*(2), 118–131.

Couldry, N., Livingstone, S. and Markham, T. (2010). *Media Consumption and Public Engagement: Beyond the Presumption of Attention.* Basingstoke: Palgrave Macmillan.

Cushion, S. (2012). *The Democratic Value of News: Why Public Service Media Matter.* Basingstoke: Palgrave Macmillan.

Cushion, S. and Lewis, J. (2017). Impartiality, statistical titforthats and the construction of balance: UK television news reporting of the 2016 EU referendum campaign. *European Journal of Communication, 32*(2), 208–223.

Czepek, A., Hellwig, M. and Novak, E. (2009). Introduction: Structural inhibition of media freedom and plurality across Europe. In A. Czepek, M. Hellwig and E. Novak (eds), *Press Freedom and Pluralism in Europe: Concepts and Conditions* (pp. 9–22). London: Intellect.

Dahlgren, P. (1995). *Television and the Public Sphere.* London: Sage.

De Vadder, I. and Callebaut, J. (2020). Het DNA van Vlaanderen: Wat willen de Vlamingen echt? Antwerpen: Uitgeverij Vrijdag. [*Flanders' DNA: What do Flemings truly want?*].

Debrett, M. (2015). 'Tools for Citizenship?' Public Service Media as a Site for Civic Engagement: An Australian Case Study. *Television & New Media, 16*(6), 557–575.

Donders, K. (2012). *Public Service Media and Policy in Europe.* Basingstoke: Palgrave Macmillan.

Donders, K., Van den Bulck, H. and Raats, T. (2019). Public service media in a divided country: governance and functioning of public broadcasters in Belgium. In E. Połońska and C. Beckett (eds), *Public Service Broadcasting and Media Systems in Troubled European Democracies.* Basingstoke: Palgrave Macmillan.

Dyson, K. and Humphreys, P. (1988). The context of new media politics in Western Europe. In K. Dyson and P. Humphreys, with R. Negrine and J.-P. Simon, *Broadcasting and New Media Policies in Western Europe* (pp. 1–61). London: Routledge.

Enli, G.S. (2008). Redefining public service broadcasting: Multi-platform participation. *Convergence: The International Journal of Research into New media Technologies, 14*(1), 105–120.

Ernst-Vintila, A. and Macovei, I. (2016). "Je suis Charlie" La liberté au-delà de l'égalité et la fraternité? Interprétation collective des attaches terroristes de janvier 2015 en France et expression online d'un nexus. *Psihologia Sociala, 38*(2), 111–123. [*'Je suis Charlie' Freedom beyond equality and fraternity? Collective interpretations of the terrorist ties of January 2015 in France and online expression of a nexus*].

Ford, R. and Goodwin, M. (2017). Britain after Brexit: A nation divided. *Journal of Democracy, 28*(1), 17–30.

Freedman D. (2019). "Public Service" and the journalism crisis: Is the BBC the answer? *Television & New Media, 20*(3), 203–218.

Galbraith, J.K. (1996). *The Good Society: The Humane Agenda.* New York: Mariner Books.

Garnham, N. (1990). *Capitalism and Communication: Global Culture and the Economics of Information.* London: Sage.

Garnham, N. (2000). *Emancipation, the Media, and Modernity: Arguments About the Media and Social Theory.* Oxford: Oxford University Press.

Habermas, J. (1991). *The Structural Transformation of the Public Sphere: An Inquiry into a Category of Bourgeois Society.* Cambridge: MIT Press.

Harari, Y.N. (2011). *Sapiens: A Brief History of Humankind.* London: Vintage UK.

Heater, D. (2003). *A History of Education for Citizenship.* London: Routledge.

Herman, E.S. (1993). The externalities effects of commercial and public broadcasting. In K. Nordenstreng and H.I. Schiller (eds), *Beyond National Sovereignty: International Communication in the 1990s* (pp. 85-115). New York: Ablex.

Hesmondhalgh, D. (2019). *The Cultural Industries* (4th ed.). London, Thousand Oaks, New Delhi, Singapore: Sage.

Hoffmann-Riem, W. (1991). Rundfunk als public service – ein überaltertes Konzept. In R. Weiss (ed.), *Aufgaben und Perspektiven des öffentlich-rechtlichen Fersnsehens* (pp. 21–47). Hamburg: Nomos. [*Broadcasting as a public service – An outdated concept. Tasks of and perspectives on public television*].

Hoffmann-Riem, W. (1995). Germany: The regulation of broadcasting. In M. Raboy (ed.), *Public Broadcasting for the 21st Century* (pp. 64–86). London: John Libbey.

Hoffmann-Riem, W. (2000). Thesen zur Regulierung der dualen Rundfunkordnung. *Medien & Kommunikationswissenschaft, 48*(1), 7-19. [*Statements about the regulation of the dual broadcasting order*].

Hoffmann-Riem, W. (2002). Medienregulierung als objektiv-rechtlicher Grundrechtsauftrag. *Medien & Kommunikationswissenschaft, 50*(2), 175-194. [*Media regulation as an objective legal constitutional task*].

Horsti, K., Hultén, G. and Titley, G. (2014). Introduction: National conversations: Public service media and cultural diversity in Europe. In K. Horsti, G. Hultén and G. Titley (eds), *National Conversations: Public Service Media and Cultural Diversity in Europe* (pp. 1-20). Bristol: Intellect.

Humphreys, P. (1994). *Media and Media Policy in Germany: The Press and Broadcasting Since 1945.* Oxford: Berg.

Humphreys, P. (1996). *Mass Media and Media Policy in Western Europe.* Manchester: Manchester University Press.

Huntington, S. (1996). *The Clash of Civilizations and the Remaking of World Order.* New York: Simon & Schuster.

Iosifidis, P. and Katsirea, I. (2015). Public Service Broadcasting in Greece: Back to the future or point of no return? *GMJ: Mediterranean Edition, 10*(1), 1-12.

Isin, E. (2009). Citizenship in flux: The figure of the activist citizen. *Subjectivity, 29*, 367-388.

Jakubowicz, K. (2007). Public service broadcasting: a new beginning, or the beginning of the end. Retrieved from www.knowledgepolitics.org.uk (accessed October 2020).

Jaskiernia, A. and Pokorna-Ignatowicz, K. (2017). Public service media vs. sovereign national media. In M. Głowacki and A. Jaskiernia (eds), *Public Service Media Renewal. Adaptation to Digital Network Challenges* (pp. 171–192). Frankfurt am Main: Peter Lang.

Jenkins, H. and Carpentier, N. (2013). Theorizing participatory intensities: A conversation about participation and politics. *Convergence, 19*(3), 265–286.

Just, N., Büchi, M. and Latzer, M. (2017). A blind spot in public broadcasters' discovery of the public: How the public values public service. *International Journal of Communication, 11*, 992–1011.

Klimkiwiecz, B. (2005). Media pluralism: European regulatory policies and the case of Central Europe. Retrieved from http://cadmus.eui.eu/bitstream/handle/1814/3368/05_19.pdf?sequence=1 (accessed October 2020).

Klimkiwiecz, B. (2010). Introduction: Structural media pluralism. *International Journal of Communication, 4*, 906–913.Lee, B. and LiPuma, E. (2002). Cultures of circulation: The imaginations of modernity. *Public Culture, 14*(1), 191–213.

Livémont, E., Donders, K. and Pauwels, C. (2017). De documentaire als merit good op de publieke omroep: Theorie, beleid en praktijk in Vlaanderen. *Tijdschrift voor Communicatiewetenschap, 45*(4), 286–303. [*Documentary as merit good in public broadcasting: Theory, policy and practice in Flanders*].

Lowe, G.F. and Jauert, P. (2005). Public service broadcasting for social and cultural citizenship: Renewing the Enlightenment mission. In G.F Lowe and P. Jauert (eds), *Cultural Dilemmas in Public Service Broadcasting* (pp. 13–33). Göteborg: Nordicom.

Marshall, T.H. (2006). Citizenship and social class. In C. Pierson and F.G. Castles (eds), *The Welfare State Reader* (pp. 30–39). Cambridge: Polity Press.

McChesney, R. (2003). The problem of journalism: A political economic contribution to an explanation of the crisis in contemporary US journalism. *Journalism Studies, 4*(3), 299–329.

McChesney, R. (2015). *Rich Media, Poor Democracy: Communication Politics in Dubious Times*. New York: The New Press.

McQuail, D. (1998). Media and sociocultural change. In D. McQuail and K. Siune (eds). *Media Policy: Convergence, Concentration and Commerce* (pp. 107–179). London: Sage.

Murdock, G. (2004). Building the Digital Commons: Public Broadcasting in the Age of the Internet. Paper presented at the 2004 Spry Memorial Lecture, 22 November, Montreal.

Murdock, G. (2005). Building the digital commons: Public broadcasting in the age of the Internet. In G.F. Lowe and P. Jauert (eds), *Cultural Dilemmas in Public Service Broadcasting* (pp. 213–230). Göteborg: Nordicom.

Noam, E. (1991). *Television in Europe*. New York: Oxford University Press.

O'Sullivan, S. (1993). No such thing as society: Television and the Apocalypse. In L.D. Friedman (ed.), *Fires Were Started: British Cinema and Thatcherism* (pp. 223–242). Minneapolis: University of Minnesota Press.

Panis, K., Paulussen, S. and Dhoest, A. (2019). Managing super-diversity on television: The representation of ethnic minorities in Flemish non-fiction programmes. *Media and Communication, 7*(1), 13–21.

Paulussen, S., Panis, K., Dhoest, A., Van den Bulck, H. and Vandebosch, H. (2015). *De Vlaming over de VRT: Publieksbevraging 2015*. Antwerpen: UA. [*Flemish citizens on the VRT: Consultation of the audience 2015*].

Pautz, H. (2005). The politics of identity in Germany: The Leitkultur debate. *Race & Class, 46*(4), 39–52.

Picard, R. and Pickard, V. (2018). Essential Principles for Contemporary Media and Communications Policymaking. Oxford: Reuters Institute for Journalism.

Picone, I., Kleut, J., Pavlíčková, T., Romic, B., Møller Hartley, J. and De Ridder, S. (2019). Small acts of engagement; Reconnecting productive audience practices with everyday agency. *New Media & Society, 21*(9), 2010-2028.

Price, M. and Raboy, M. (eds)(2003). *Public Service Broadcasting in Transition: A Documentary Reader.* The Hague: Kluwer Law International.

Putnam, R.D. (1995). Bowling alone: America's Declining Social Capital. *Journal of Democracy, 6*(1), 65-78.

Rathje, S. (2009). The definition of culture: n application-oriented overhaul. *Interculture Journal: Online-Zeitschrift für interkulturelle Studien, 8*(8), 35-58.

Sauter, T. and Bruns, A. (2014). Tweeting the TV event, creating 'public sphericules': ad hoc engagement with SBS's Go Back to Where You Came From – season two. *Media International Australia, 152*(1), 5-15.

Scannell, P. (1990). Public service broadcasting: The history of concept. In A. Goodwin and G. Whannel (eds), *Understanding Television* (pp. 11-29). London: Routledge.

Scannell, P. (1995). Britain: public service broadcasting, from national culture to multi-culturalism. In M. Raboy (ed.), *Public Broadcasting for the 21st Century* (pp. 23–41). Luton: John Libbey Publishing.

Schüller-Keber, V. (2009). Die Kommunikationsfreiheiten in der Verfassung. In D. Dörr, J. Kreile and M.D. Cole (eds), *Handbuch Medienrecht: Recht der elektronischen Massenmedien* (pp. 63-82). Frankfurt am Main: Verlag Recht und Wirtschaft. [*The freedoms of communication in the Constitution – Handbook of media law: electronic mass media law*].

Steemers, J. (2017). Public service broadcasting, children's television, and market failure: The case of the United Kingdom. *International Journal on Media Management, 19*(4), 298-314.

Stetka, V. and Örnebring, H. (2013). Investigative journalism in Central and Eastern Europe: Autonomy, business models, and democratic roles. *The International Journal of Press/Politics, 18*(4), 413-435.

Taras, K. (2002). The myth of the civic state: A critical survey of Hans Kohn's framework for understanding nationalism. *Ethnic and Racial Studies, 25*(1), 20-39.

Taylor, C. (2002). Modern social imaginaries. *Public Culture, 14*(1), 91-124.

Theiss-Morse, E. and Hibbing, J.R. (2005). Citizenship and civic engagement. *Annual Review of Political Science, 8*, 227-249.

Tracey, M. (1998). *The Decline and Fall of Public Service Broadcasting.* Oxford: Clarendon Press.

Van den Bulck, H. (2001). Public service television and national identity as a project of modernity: The example of Flemish television. *Media, Culture & Society, 23*(1), 53–69.

Van den Bulck, H. (2016). *Publieke omroep: Maatschappelijke meerwaarde en individuele impact.* Antwerp: University of Antwerp. [*Public service broadcasting: Added societal value and individual impact*].

van Dijck, J. and Poell, T. (2015). Making public television social? Public Service Broadcasting and the challenges of social media. *Television & New Media, 16*(2), 148-164.

Vanhaeght, A.-S. (2019). The need for not more, but more socially relevant audience participation in public service media. *Media, Culture & Society, 41*(1), 120–137.

Vanlee, F., Dhaenens, F. and Van Bauwel, S. (2018). Understanding queer normality: LGBT+ Representations in millennial Flemish television fiction. *Television &
New Media, 19*(7), 610-625.

Veenhoven, R. (2000). Freedom and happiness: A comparative study in 46 nations in
the early 1990s. In E. Diener and E.M. Suh (eds), *Culture and Subjective Wellbeing* (pp.
257-288). Cambridge: MIT Press.

Wilkinson, K.T. (2005). Language, economics, and policy: Challenges to PSB in North
America and the European Union. In G.F. Lowe and P. Jauert (eds), *Cultural Dilemmas
In Public Service Broadcasting* (pp. 239-316). Göteborg: Nordicom.

5 Making Public Service Media work through institutions

Introduction

The previous chapter focused on the normative argument that Public Service Media is about strengthening citizenship and, in so doing, serving liberal democracy. This chapter clarifies what means, principles and necessary conditions are required to transform the democracy- and citizenship-centric notion of Public Service Media into reality. The insights from the literature discussed below will be added to the framework of Public Service Media presented at the end of the previous chapter and will serve as an analytical tool for the empirical chapters that are to follow.

The sections below go further into what is needed to make public broadcasters live up to the ideal of Public Service Media. I base the chapter on the work of well-known scholars in the field and also on a more comprehensive analysis (with a focus on means and conditions) of all web-of-science articles that were published over the last six years (2012-2020) containing the words 'Public Service Broadcasting' or 'Public Service Media' in the title. From this sample I removed seven articles that were not concerned with Public Service Broadcasting at their core or that were book reviews. Eighty-four articles related to Public Service Broadcasting were studied. This is not an exhaustive meta-analysis of all literature on Public Service Media related topics. It is a discussion structured around those elements that other scholars and I find important in terms of the means, principles and necessary conditions of the Public Service Media project.

How can public broadcasters achieve the tasks assigned to them? There are certain means for public broadcasters to achieve political, social, cultural and civic citizenship; and a number of conditions that need to be met to make this happen. These conditions are not only government-, but also public broadcaster-dependent.

Means and principles

In order for Public Service Media to reach the goal of increased political, social, cultural and civic citizenship, several high-level means need to be deployed.

Several of these are well known and sometimes also treated as values of Public Service Media (see, among others, Price and Raboy, 2003; EBU, 2013): universality, quality, creativity, and so on. Other means are of a more recent nature as they concern the increased difficulty of connecting between Public Service Media and the audience: multi-platform presence, innovation, dialogue, fact-checking, and so on. I discuss several of the essential means below, clustering them around 'access', 'content' and 'connection'. Innovation cuts across those three.

Access

From the early origins of Public Service Broadcasting, access to public broadcasters' public service delivery was of fundamental importance. Universality has been the key determining concept here. Public broadcasters' content should be accessible to all citizens, regardless of their geographical location, their ability/willingness-to-pay, their gender, ethnical background, and so on. (Garnham, 1990). Universality is a layered concept, including geographical, program, audience and socio-economic universality. It does not only refer to the requirement that public broadcasters' services should be free at the point of use, they should also appeal to many different interests and needs in society, and be understandable to all, also those that have not pursued university studies.

Ensuring access has admittedly become more difficult in a digitised, internationalised landscape where platforms act not only as intermediators but also as gatekeepers to content. This requires (more) strategic action and institutional reform from public broadcasters (Lim, Bali and Moo, 2019).

Content

The aspect of content has been elaborated upon the most in Public Service Media literature. Scholars advocate for a holistic remit covering a variety of content types and genres, including information, culture, education, documentary (Livémont, Donders and Pauwels, 2017), drama (Hoschscherf, 2019; Raats and Jensen, 2020), entertainment, sports (Smith, 2017; Taylor and Thomass, 2017), children's television (D'Arma and Labio, 2017; Steemers, 2017), and so on. Public broadcasters should, first, distinguish themselves through the quality of their services; they should be distinctive from what others offer. Both quality and distinctiveness are concepts that are quite difficult to measure and are hence relentlessly part of discussions on the performance of public broadcasters and the wider validity of the Public Service Media project in an alleged era of abundance. Distinctiveness is almost always used in relation to the offer of commercial media, also and increasingly so online. Sjøvaag, Pedersen and Owren (2019) show that public broadcasters' offer online is in fact very different from commercial news media. The latter's offers are more similar to each other than to public broadcasters' news websites. Offering high-quality and being distinctive does not mean, however, that public broadcasters ought to be niche players. Most scholars agree on the need for a holistic, full-portfolio approach, albeit that commercial media companies, some policy-makers, and also some scholars advocate for a complementary, gap-filling role for Public Service Media instead of the comprehensive approach (Bardoel and D'Haenens, 2008: 344). The inclusion of entertainment, also online, will remain necessary in case public broadcasters want to achieve a relevant reach. Vermeer et al. (2020) convincingly show how news websites consumption shows a strong preference for entertainment news.

Second, and related most to the aims of social and cultural citizenship strengthening, identity construction and diversity are part of what public broadcasters ought to do. Identity-building largely refers to a process of unification around a nation, language and/or culture (Van den Bulck, 2001). There is an 'on-purpose' element to that as public broadcasters across Europe show more local and non-American content (De Bens and De Smaele, 2001), but research for some time now also shows that audiences have a preference for content that is close to them. Linguistic and cultural proximity matters (Biltereyst, 1992; Manias-Munoz and Martori Muntsant, 2017). Use of 'standard language' is usually held to high esteem by governments across Europe and, even if public broadcasters are more flexible in this domain in formats such as comedy and drama, they do play a role here (Van Hoof, 2018). Identity is increasingly connected with the economic objective of strengthening local audiovisual production (Ballon et al., 2018). Diversity is concerned with reflecting the growing cultural and ethnic fragmentation occurring within national boundaries, with catering to minority interests, with celebrating the diversity of cultures on a global scale (Horsti and Hultén, 2011), and ensuring diversity of media producers as well (e.g., Madsen, 2017). Identity and diversity might, in that sense, be considered to be somewhat antagonistic (see Donders and Raats, 2015). Nevertheless, both are important tasks of public broadcasters. In reality, as already hinted at before (cf. supra), public broadcasters can go about them in very different ways. That also relates to the views of public broadcasters and politicians on identity.

Third, public broadcasters should offer creative services and provide a safe harbour for experiment (Cunningham, 2009: 85), particularly in internationalising media markets where innovation is under pressure (Cunningham, 2015). Also, this aspect of Public Service Media is difficult to live up to on all occasions. For budgetary or audience retention reasons, public broadcasters have not always allowed for creativity and risk-taking. The BBC's reliance on income from international export has, for example, led to the conclusion that plot writing and production are increasingly determined by the demands of the international market and adapted to tastes of the Asian, American and European audiences (Donders and Van den Bulck, 2016).

Fourth, and most disputed, is the element of impartiality. Public broadcasters are required to report as objectively, neutrally and impartially on current affairs and other issues as possible. That is largely understood as reporting free from political and commercial interests, in a balanced manner and showing the diverse views in society. For public broadcasters such as the BBC, impartiality has become some sort of a corporate norm that should convince audiences of the public broadcaster's trustworthiness after repeated scandals on government meddling with the editorial line (Bélair-Gagnon, 2013). Regardless of concrete breaches of the impartiality principle, Flood et al. (2010) have pointed out that the civic values of liberal democracy that the BBC sets out from *a priori* make a difficult, theoretical, alignment between impartiality and ideology.

> The values implicit in the Public Purposes are constituents of the ideology of modern, democratic liberalism in its British variant. They presuppose, *inter alia*, individual reason, personal liberty and autonomy, the existence and necessity of civil society, with an informed citizenry, civic responsibility, parliamentary representation, ethnic, cultural and religious pluralism, and public debate.
>
> (Flood et al., 2010: 225)

Freedman (2019) has reached similar conclusions (see also the previous chapter). And also research in other countries shows that public broadcasters struggle with the notion of impartiality. Not because they are biased towards the left, as is often alleged, but – in line with Freedman's and Flood et al.'s research on the BBC – because they conform to the status quo too much. Otto et al. (2020) demonstrate that the coverage of the Greek financial debt crisis in information programmes of the German public broadcasters was partial, from the outset biased against the Greek Government and conforming to the opinion of the German authorities.

Connection

Access to qualitative, creative and impartial content used to be the most important part of public broadcasters' activities. After the liberalisation of broadcasting markets in the 1980s, it became, in the face of competition, more important to connect with audiences. Brand and marketing strategies to build a relationship between public broadcasters and audiences emerged. Full-portfolio strategies to ensure people were interested in what public broadcasters had on offer were deployed. Sometimes that resulted in a convergence between public and commercial broadcasters' offerings and thus in a declining distinctiveness (Nossiter, 1991; Donders, 2012). The arrival of the Internet and the increasing internationalisation and convergence in media markets comes with challenges of a different size. In such markets, the connection with audiences is not a given or merely an issue of broadcasters and newspapers, it is contested by a multitude of professional and non-professional media services and intermediated by conglomerates with little or no concern for the protected position of public broadcasters in nation states (Donders, 2019; Hesmondalgh, 2019; Lobato, 2019).

The evolution from the Public Service Broadcasting to Public Service Media concept essentially expresses the necessity to adopt a multi-platform and multi-device strategy. While that is a principle embraced by scholars (see several contributions in Lowe, Van den Bulck and Donders, 2018) and public broadcasters, the latter struggle in that environment to connect with audiences. Their online strategies are often directionless, even non-existing (Raats, 2013; Ramsey, 2018a) or inspired by the need for budget cuts or techno-optimism (e.g., moving BBC Three online, see Ramsey, 2018b). Connection is still focused on mechanics, on rather superficial interaction and, in case of more ambitious participation and engagement goals, not structurally embedded in offers and the organisation (Vanhaeght, 2019). Nonetheless, research shows that there are significant opportunities for increasing, among others, political participation, also through online means and that public broadcasters are an excellent site for this (Vaccari and Valeriani, 2018). There is indeed a correlation between the existence of public broadcasters and respect for the political views that others hold (Castro-Herrero, Nir and Skovsgaard, 2018). Public broadcasters seem to mitigate political selective exposure (Bos, Kruikemeier and de Vreese, 2016). Participation should be meaningful. Public broadcasters should not accommodate 'para-interactivity', high superficial acts of engagement. They should stimulate societal participation (Keinonen and Shagrir, 2017) or meaningful participation (Vanhaeght, 2019) that also strengthens citizens within society.

Moreover, even in the case of (emerging) mature multi-platform strategies (see Doyle, 2010), interfaces that connect content with consumers are (see Chapter 2) most often not in the hands of public broadcasters. Over-the-top providers of on-demand audiovisual media services, cable operators, Internet giants, and so on, determine the terms of trade under which public broadcasters' content is offered to citizens. Indeed, BBC content is branded as such to Netflix users. The BBC is a global brand and hence commercially useful to the over-the-top player. Smaller public broadcasters all too often give up on that right for the OTT player to contribute 5 to 10 per cent of a production budget though. Scholars such as Lobato (2019) have, for that reason, suggested extending must-carry obligations into the online environment, also coined as ensuring 'due prominence' of valuable content (Ofcom, 2018). Others have critically investigated how public broadcasters deal with platforms, especially when incorporating them in their own service proposition. Burkart and Leijonhufvud (2019: 9) talk about the Spotification of Public Service Media in this regard, referring to 'public media institutions capitalising on new opportunities but at the expense of a social democratic model of cultural policy'. Even when public broadcasters control interfaces, many challenges surface. How to ensure that people consume not only drama and entertainment, but more diverse genres? How to deal with citizens' data in a privacy-friendly manner? And how to deploy personalisation to the benefit of the individual as well as society and cohesion therein? Research shows that most public broadcasters struggle with these questions (e.g., Van den Bulck and Moe, 2018; Kennedy, Steedman and Jones, 2020; Sørensen and Van den Bulck, 2020).

Innovation

While innovation as a goal is usually related to the transition from Public Service Broadcasting to Public Service Media, public broadcasters have had a longstanding innovation task. That was in most countries technology-inspired and related to big projects such as digital terrestrial television, high definition television and digital audio broadcasting (Donders, Pauwels and Loisen, 2012). Innovation in the broader sense is connected to the entire transformation of a broadcast to a multi-media organisation (Flew, 2011; Gomez-Dominguez, 2018). It concerns the 'new possibilities for producing, aggregating, distributing and accessing content' (Direito, forthcoming) and, moreover, for engaging with audiences as part of their mission and with respect for ethical consider-ations such as privacy (Martin, 2002;Van den Bulck and Moe, 2018;Vanhaeght, 2019). Public Service Media is about more than adding platforms. It concerns rethinking what public broadcasters can and should do in an increasingly cor-porate context, how they can engage in a more complex and dialogue-based relationship with their audiences, how they can service citizenship and whether that is possible without alienating part of the audience (Debrett, 2010).

Direito (forthcoming) makes a distinction between technological innov-ation, innovation at the level of content development (e.g., Ibrus, Rohn and d' Nani, 2019), connecting with audiences and organisational improvements. In all of these areas scholars assign public broadcasters with tasks to perform. That is far from easy given institutional inertia, policy limitations and budgetary cuts though. There is on top of that also organisational resistance to embrace the digital (Yilmaz and Matthes, 2019) or, at minimum, a tension between process and product innovation (Evans, 2016). As said by Van Dijck and Poell (2015: 150), a 'duality of suspicion and attraction would market Public Service Broadcasting's institutional embrace of social media for the years to come'. Similarly, in earlier work (Donders, 2019) I have shown that public broadcasters do not always want to leave the safe and predictable ground of television and radio where they have been market leaders for decades to move boldly into a new terrain where they are often entrants at a competitive disadvantage to others.

The area where public broadcasters have evolved mostly towards digital players is news. Converged, integrated newsrooms (also physically) exist in sev-eral European countries. Of course, the level of implementation and success varies (Sehl et al., 2018; Larrondo et al., 2016). In addition, focal areas of innovation can also be different between public broadcasters. Zaragoza-Fuster and Garcia-Aviles (2020), for example, demonstrate that the BBC's innov-ation strategies have focused more on processes (e.g., facilitating journalists work through speech-to-text software) while Spanish RTVE has been more concerned with content innovation (e.g., multi-media narratives). An area of innovation that receives quite some attention is interactivity with users, but also there it is apparent that lots of initiatives are still rather experimental and not structurally embedded within the organisation (López-Cepeda, López-Golán and Rodríguez-Castro, 2019b).

Admittedly, public broadcasters' capacity to innovate is not only in their own hands, but determined also by the extent to which legislative frameworks allow them to innovate. Mechanisms such as the notorious public value tests can be a strength in terms of analysing and legitimising new services. They can, however, also discourage public broadcasters from innovating or result in outcomes that legally inhibit new services, even if those expose convincing value to the public (Donders and Van den Bulck, 2020). Legal limitations of public broadcasters' remit are discussed in Chapter 9. They are often the result of private sector lobbying, even though emotional perceptions on crowding out private initiative because of strong online presence from public broadcasters have been shown to be unjustified (Sehl et al., 2020a).

All of these means essentially relate to the vision you take on Public Service Media and public broadcasters. Taking a market failure perspective, you might in principle agree with most of the above, but probably interpret all of it in a more narrow, 'smallish' manner than when taking a democracy-centric view on Public Service Media (see Chapter 3). Taking the latter perspective, you would not be content with filling gaps that commercial companies leave. You would want to make sure that quality and creative content, that is pluralistic and diverse in nature, reaches all people, abiding by their preferences or in spite of those, and regardless of the ways of working together or competing against each other in an international and converged media market.

Necessary conditions

I already referred to research that shows the success, but also the imperfectness of public broadcasters in living up to the ideal of Public Service Media. One could argue that these failures are due to high expectations, unachievable objectives (see e.g., Ciaglia, 2017) and a considerable amount of intervening factors such as education, wealth and political stability. While all of that is valid, the main causes of success or not are related to a number of issues closer to each national system of Public Service Media. These can be seen as the 'necessary conditions' for public broadcasters achieving Public Service Media. Some of these concern politicians' behaviour, other elements are to be situated within public broadcasting organisations. Most are relational, existing, evolving and adapting between public broadcasters and the political class.

Independence and professional governance

First and foremost, independence from both commercial and political forces is tantamount to the functioning of public broadcasters. If they want to achieve Public Service Media, they need to act in the public interest and not in the interest of market or state. Acting in the public interest fundamentally means doing things with an eye on strengthening citizenship and democracy. While commercial media can also do this, their purpose is not to serve the public interest, but profit-making. Internationalisation and convergence (see Chapter 2) have added to that motivation (Meier and Trappel, 1992; Croteau and Hoynes, 2006: 38-39). Good things can come out of this, bad things too. That is why scholars have argued for a combination of both public and commercial media (Bogart, 2017). They have pushed for something more than a mere reliance on 'the marketplace of ideas', in which elements of economic theory such as efficiency, consumer welfare and competition have been combined with democratic theory's attachment to civic virtues and informed citizenship, and in which laissez-faire views on government seem to have gained the upper hand over government intervention (Entman and Wildman, 1992). Having said that, this book does not take the view that commercial media cannot further public interest objectives: 'profit-seeking and public service are not either-or propositions' (Croteau and Hoynes, 2006: 33). However, some system to ensure the public interest in media comes first and that is not a derivative of buyer-seller relations is paramount to democracy (Syvertsen et al., 2019). That also implies that public broadcasters' independence from economic forces is paramount to its sustainability as a policy project. The tendency for some public broadcasters, often stimulated by government, to adopt a more economic rationale in terms of supporting ecosystems is in that sense a slippery slope (Donders, Raats and Tintel, 2020) and the trend has been criticised by scholars such as Alessandro D'Arma (2018) in his work on BBC Studios.

Dependency on the state can effectively undermine and even completely erode public broadcasters' contribution to the public interest up to the point that there is no policy project of Public Service Media in place. Indeed, when serving a political agenda, a public broadcaster is no longer adding to citizenship, but to compliance with the views of a ruling elite or party. Independence is an issue extensively elaborated upon by Chris Hanretty (2011) in his book *Public Broadcasting and Political Interference*. Hanretty explains not only why independence matters, but also why some public broadcasters have been more successful in withstanding political interference, whereas others have not. Legal safeguards, the existence of professional journalistic standards, the size of a market and economic development, the polarisation of the party political system, and so on, are all explanatory factors, but cultural and historical context matter too (see also Hallin and Mancini, 2004). These factors clarify why even in the presence of legal safeguards some public broadcasters have to be seen as parts of the state, rather as an outside actor to hold those in power to account and defend the public's interest in so doing. In that regard, some public broadcasters share features with the political system they are embedded in. For example, countries with party-politicised bureaucracies will likely have party-politicised public broadcasters (Hanretty, 2009: 81). While governments have an obvious interest in controlling public broadcasters, politicisation comes with a decline in trust as 'there is a natural intuition that government intervention is likely to be self-serving' (Allen, Connolly and Hargreaves Heap,

2017: 3). Fraga and Hermann (2019), in a similar vein, argue, focussing on public service broadcasting in Brazil, that there is a manifest contradiction between many public service mandates and the actual internal organisation of public broadcasters whereby governance structures can result in effective political control over editorial processes.

Hanretty (2009: 76) differentiates between *de jure* and *de facto* independence. Legal independence refers to those legal safeguards that protect political interference with editorial strategies of public broadcasters, while *de facto* independence means

> the degree to which Public Service Broadcasting employees take day-to-day decisions about their output or the output of their subordinates, without receiving and acting on the basis of instructions, threats or other inducement from politicians, or the anticipation therefor, or considering whether the interests of those politicians would be harmed by particular choices.

Independence of public broadcasters is fragile in Europe. Western and Northern European public broadcasters all faced a transition from politicisation to fairly high levels of independence from the 1980s until the new millennium (Hanretty, 2011). In several Central, Eastern and Southern European countries (e.g., Pavani, 2017) we witnessed an evolution from state to public broadcaster after fascism or communism collapsed. In a majority of European countries far-going forms of political interference can still be observed and, in some cases, meddling from politics is intensifying again. I will discuss these trends further in Chapter 6.

In any case, independence is not an absolute state of being, but rather to be situated on a continuum from as independent as possible to state mouth piece. The question is where on that continuum a public broadcaster is still independent enough to fit within the theoretical idea of Public Service Media and to strengthen citizenship for democracy. Independence is moreover very much tied to governance. If governance focused on oversight and strategic reflection, when it functions independently from government, this will enhance public broadcasters' performance. When governance is part of political capture of public broadcasters, fragile states of independence towards government will be reinforced (e.g., López-Cepeda, Soengas-Pérez and Campos-Freire, 2019a) from West to East, from North to South in Europe. Transparency and involvement of stakeholders, including civil society and the audience, are related to this and definitely not common place across Europe (Ploch, 2017).

Adequate funding

While a lot of research mentions the pressure on public broadcasters' funding (Donders, 2012; Bonini and Pais, 2017; Enli, 2008) and the European Broadcasting Union publishes reports on the funding of its members on an annual basis, it remains difficult to define what adequate funding is and what type of funding is to be preferred from a public interest perspective.

What is adequate funding? From a European Commission perspective, that is the amount of money needed to fulfil the public service remit (European Commission, 2009a; Donders, 2015). In several of its State aid decisions, notably those dealing with funding of public broadcasters in the South of Europe, the European Commission has regularly concluded that there was undercompensation of the public service remit, meaning public broadcasters such as RTP did not get sufficient funds (European Commission, 2003; 2006). That did not result in more money flowing from the involved governments to the public broadcasters though. The European Commission is only competent when too much money has been granted. Scholars such as Karol Jakubowicz (2007: 41–42) have stressed that the extension of Public Service Broadcasting to Public Service Media requires additional and sustainable means for public broadcasters. We have, however, witnessed declining revenues of public broadcasters in most EU Member States (Ballon et al., 2018; EBU, 2018). In some Member States of the EU that has resulted in declining investments in domestic content, in the abolishment of channels (Ramsey, 2018a), the laying off of staff, and so on. In other countries, not that many visible consequences of budget cuts can be observed.

Overall, funding arrangements that create a direct link between public broadcasters and their audience are considered best for public support, civic engagement and accountability (Benson and Powers, 2011: 4). The license fee is such a system, used in a number of EU Member States as a means to ensure funding of public broadcasters at an arm's length basis from government. Over the last two decades, numerous countries have decided to replace the license fee system with a subsidy system, encapsulating the funding of public broadcasters in overall state budgets (Berg and Lund, 2015). Most Nordic countries, the United Kingdom, Italy, Germany, and so on, still use a license fee system though, albeit that it is no longer dependent in all of those countries on the ownership of a radio or television set (Westcott, 2019). In the case of device-independent systems, preference goes to terms such as household charge. The move away from license fee to subsidy-based systems has been criticised for increasing public broadcasters' vulnerability to government changes and the use of money to control public broadcasters, perhaps more effectively than direct censorship could do.

Most studies focus on budget cuts (e.g., Juanatey-Boga, Martínez-Fernández and Rodríguez-Castro, 2018) and efficiency measures with public broadcasters. Fewer studies concern new types of funding such as crowdfunding. The actual relationship between type and amount of funding on the one hand and the performance of public broadcasters on the other hand is definitely less clear. Better funded public broadcasters usually attract higher market shares, but that is of course only one indicator of success and not necessarily always the case (Ballon et al., 2018; Saurwein, Eberwein and Karmasin, 2019). Nevertheless, type and amount of funding are relevant to consider, not only from the perspective of audience share as more generous public income also correlates with the relevance of public broadcasters as a source of information and a greater trust with audiences in the independence of their public broadcaster from political pressure (Saurwein, 2018). The American Public Service Media model is a good example as it deviates rather significantly from established European practices in terms of funding. Camille Reyes (2013) criticises that only 15 per cent of revenues for PBS comes from tax payers. That according to Reyes, has forced 'PBS to aggressively seek alternative business models that bear striking resemblances to the very system for which they (public broadcasters) were designed to be an alternative.' She continues that besides Sesame Street, most programming is 'an elitist slate of British imports and so-called high culture programmes designed for an upper-middle class audience' (2013: 3). Lack of funding, but also the type of funding, whereby PBS largely relies on income from philanthropy, has resulted in PBS not reaching everyone and specifically not connecting with all audiences and all audience preferences (see also Hoynes, 2007).

Preferably there is a low reliance on commercial revenues as to ensure the public interest outplays institutional interests (Lanara, 2002: 106-108). Restrictions on commercial communication in France, Spain (Biggam, 2009; European Commission, 2009b); Kuhn, 2010; Donders and Lamensch, 2010 and the Netherlands show political sensitivity to that concern, be it more oriented at commercial media's complaints and not so much acting from a public interest perspective. Several countries even prohibit most commercial activities altogether (Latzer et al., 2010). Some 'new' media and content distribution strategies of public broadcasters such as the BBC are also criticised by scholars for being too much focused on earning money and too little on contributing to citizenship, not only within but also outside the nation. Ramsey (2018a) questions the BBC's collaboration with Netflix, saying such cooperation aims to combine two essentially different logics with the risk of sacrificing a public service logic for commercial gain-seeking reasoning. Earlier, Donders and Van den Bulck (2016) already concluded that the BBC's export strategies were undermining the task of public broadcasters in smaller media markets for profit. Given these shared concerns of commercial media, politicians and scholars, one would expect more public money going to public broadcasters, but the opposite is true. Regardless some exceptions, most public broadcasters have faced budget cuts over the last five to 15 years, also resulting in serious staff reductions. Admittedly, efficiency improvements could and can be made (see elaboration on funding of public broadcasters in Portugal, Spain and France in Donders, 2012). But again, what is the essential funding mix? Whereas most scientific research sets out from the presumption that more money is necessarily better, I prefer to argue for a device-independent license fee system that is based on a rational cost calculation of public service delivery. It ensures an arm's length relationship from government, a more stable financing, less pressure to engage in all kinds of commercial experimental adventures (see Leurdijk, 2007 for example) and public trust. Whereas others have argued for new means of funding public broadcasters such as crowdfunding part of the money, giving audiences the choice to pay (part of) the license fee and decide on where part of the money will be spent (Bonini and Pais, 2017), such an approach introduces consumerism into Public Service Media and is, for that reason, at odds with the citizenship-centric approach that is presented here. Having said that, some level of co-decision and involvement of the public in the management of public broadcasters might actually strengthen the public 'serviceness' of those broadcasters that are subject to far-going government intervention.

For similar reasons, I oppose the so-called top-slicing of license fees to fund commercial media or non-profit initiatives that want to offer services in the public interest (O'Hagan and Jennings, 2003). This idea was expressed most forcefully when Ofcom proposed to top-slice part of the BBC's license fee for the creation of a 'Public Service Publisher', a fund that would grant money to specifically digital and online media projects that aimed to strengthen public interest objectives (Ofcom, 2007). Of course, the BBC was not very much in favour of that proposal. In the end, there was no transposition into practice. Many attributed this to the fierce lobbying of the BBC and some to Ofcom's own ambitions as a regulator to make a mark, but not necessarily pursue such provocative and visible plans further (see Donders and Raats, 2015). Des Freedman (2008b) essentially criticised the market-driven logic underlying Ofcom's plans and also the lack of evidence on such a system contributing more to strengthening of citizenship and democracy than the one in place. That does not mean that more money for alternative public interest-driven initiatives is not warranted. Contestability among public institutions, on the one hand, and between them and commercial enterprises, on the other, will probably not be the best system to enable that.

Accountability and professionalism

Finally, any Public Service Media system – in Europe usually taken up by public broadcasters – should be accountable to the audience. According to social responsibility theory that emerged in the mid-20th century in the US, media cannot work according to free market laws exclusively. There needs to be some sort of social responsibility towards the audience and society at large (Siebert, Peterson and Schramm, 1956; Loisen and Joye, 2017). The US Hutchins Commission said

> an overall social responsibility for the quality of press service to the citizen cannot be escaped; the community cannot wholly delegate to any other agency the ultimate responsibility for a function in which its own existence as a free society may be at stake.
>
> (Quoted in Bardoel and D'Haenens, 2004: 6)

Media should thus be accountable for the responsibility we as a society entrust on them to act in our public interest. Media should be answerable to democracy (de Haan and Bardoel, 2011: 231).

While applying to media in general, this idea of responsibility has particularly affected the governance of public broadcasters in Europe and this since the 1980s and the gradual liberalisation of media markets across Member States of the European Union. After the end of public broadcast monopolies, governments had to recognise the necessity of public broadcasters being more independent from the state and adaptable to face competition. At the same time, public broadcasters had 'to accept accountability mechanisms which ensure the responsible exercise of their mandates' (Raboy, 1995: 11). Such accountability mechanisms could be self-imposed or not (McQuail, 2003).

Accountability mechanisms had to ensure, first and foremost, that public broadcasters would behave in a professional and cost-efficient manner. An internal culture of professionalism had to be developed post-liberalisation, without falling in the trap of managerialism at the same time (Bardoel and D'Haenens, 2004). An increasing number of sophisticated tools for a better understanding of audience needs, control by independent monitoring bodies, regular audits, extensive lists with key performance indicators, and so on, are all means to measure whether such professional and cost-efficient behaviour indeed exists (Baldi, 2007: 17-19). Admittedly, the explosion of accountability mechanisms has not *per se* increased accountability, nor professionalism. There are many examples of public broadcasters that face issues to transcend bureaucratic culture, even in the presence of multiple accountability mechanisms. The presence of the latter does also not ensure lower government intervention (see several contributions in Połońska and Beckett, 2019). Being accountable requires transparency of organisational structures and money flows. In the absence of such transparency, public broadcasters cannot show they spend money in a responsible manner (Bardoel, 2003; Buckley et al., 2008: 193ff).

Importantly, there are two ways of looking at accountability. Jo Bardoel and Leen D'Haenens (2004) differentiate, in line with work of Denis McQuail (2003), between liability and answerability. A liability model of accountability is used in defensive ways, when governments believe that media are capable of causing harm to people or democracy. Answerability is a more positive approach to accountability and assumes responsiveness of media organisations to legitimate questions from the audience, stakeholders and government. It means being willing to explain actions, to defend editorial choices, to justify strategic routes taken or to come back from any of those when legitimate.

There are several problems related to accountability and professionalism. First, it is unclear how much accountability mechanisms are needed to satisfy political demand for accountability and professionalism. Second, the rise of multi-stakeholderism as a particular aspect of Public Service Media making is said to increase accountability and transparency to stakeholders, but seems to have reinforced the position of commercial lobbying against public broadcasters (Donders, Van den Bulck and Raats, 2019). That lobbying is particularly strong and can result in commercial capture of Public Service Media regulation (e.g., Masduki, 2017), even though some authors have held that a peaceful coexistence of public and commercial media is possible and in fact desirable (Donders, 2012; Ciaglia, 2016). Third, within public broadcasters there is not necessarily a culture of being accountable, but usually a feeling of being overly transparent and continuously under attack. A real understanding of professionalism, accountability and transparency 'sentiments' within public broadcasters would require ethnographic research, which has not been carried out that much.

On a final note, the necessary conditions for Public Service Media to succeed in practice are not exclusively related to government. These conditions are continuously negotiated between governments and public broadcasters. In some cases there is mutual trust in the ideal of Public Service Media and perhaps even in a basic commitment of each of the parties to make this happen. In a lot of countries, that trust is absent. Lack of trust can relate to under-performance of public broadcasters, scandals involving public broadcasters and/or government, electoral competition, low citizen appreciation and also rather hostile neoliberal or extreme *étatist* views on Public Service Media (Erdemir, 2017; Gifreu, 2017; Pavani, 2017; Cushion, 2019). Can one achieve public interest in media in cases where there is no belief in the project?

Additionally, there is the element of adaptivity that is mostly discussed in relation to innovation (cf. supra) and digital media consumption as well as platformisation and internationalisation of media at large. Adaptivity is not to be interpreted in light of the New Public Management doctrine that emerged in the 1980s and 1990s and which

> introduced entrepreneurial management styles and a business-like orientation to public sector management and governance, describing the public as a client (rather than a citizen), celebrating competition as an absolute good, cultivating marketisation and encouraging outsourcing.
>
> (Van den Bulck, 2015: nn)

Adaptivity concerns a post-bureaucracy mentality to respond to change within public broadcasters. That adaptivity is crucial to remain sustainable and should – when looking at the crucial role public broadcasters have in strengthening political, cultural, social and civic citizenship – also be oriented at dealing with changing societies without an exclusive focus on digitisation. Adaptivity in public service transformation has been researched extensively and related to factors such as strong leadership and commitment from management, a shared perception on the need for change within the organisation, the existence of a plan for implementing and 'routinising' change, internal as well as external support for change, the necessary resources to bring about change (see among others Fernandez and Rainey, 2006), and even culture as a moderating variable. Needless to say that all of these elements come with challenges for most public broadcasters across Europe, some of them caused by others such as politicians and commercial media, others ingrained in the organisation itself.

Achieving Public Service Media

Several of the questions raised throughout this chapter and the previous one will be taken up in the empirical chapters. Have public broadcasters contributed to citizenship and democracy? Have they been able to implement and uphold effective access, content and connection strategies? And are they doing this accountable to society, in a professional way, on the basis of adequate funding and as independently from State and market as possible? In case one or more of these three questions are answered negatively and this for several decades in a row, there is a need to rethink Public Service Media, if necessary outside the box of the existing public broadcaster organisation. Hence, the continued existence of public broadcasters rests on the role they play in society and not the perceived or actual distinctiveness of their offers compared to commercial media. In a similar vein, interactive content, digital tricks, participation for the sake of participation and other emerging services in themselves do not and cannot legitimise Public Service Media (as is sometimes put forward in rather technological optimist accounts of Public Service Broadcasting's evolution to Public Service Media, cf. supra). It is in the combination of means and goals, supported by both an enabling not constraining policy framework and organisation, that Public Service Media will be achieved or not.

That is why this framework is still firmly rooted in a democracy-centric conceptualisation of Public Service Media and not in a market failure paradigm. It does not make it a 'public service anything' (see Chapter 3) though as the means and goals of this project are clear, even if high-level, and firmly grounded in a citizenship-based and democracy-centric approach to Public Service Media (see Figure 5.1).

Importantly, Public Service Media needs to be 'made', not only by public broadcasters, but also enabled by the executive, legislative and judiciary powers

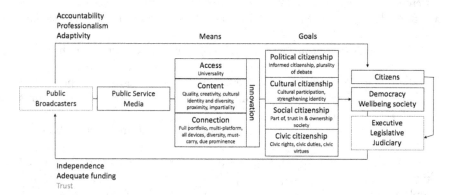

Figure 5.1 Public Service Media as a citizenship- and democracy-centric project: goals, means and necessary conditions

in society. Government should ensure adequate funding, control the professionalism adhered to when realising objectives and refrain from meddling with access, content and connection strategies. Parliament should adopt laws that provide for a transparent framework within which public broadcasters can do their job. And the judiciary is there to protect the independence and adequate funding of public broadcasters when needed. Specifically, when there are deficiencies at both the side of the public broadcaster and the three estates, alternative models for the achievement of Public Service Media should be contemplated.

If the necessary condition of accountability towards government and independence from government cannot be ensured, one could assume that there is no context for a modernist version of public broadcasters delivering services in the public interest. As Barbie Zelizer (2013: 465) argues, journalism scholarship, driven by US scholarship, 'assumed conditions that were not part of the default settings elsewhere in the world'. Interestingly, we, also in relation to Public Service Media, have to reconsider these assumptions because our own setting of liberal democracy is being questioned on a daily basis. The rise of populism is directly related to this. Populists, so Abts and Rummens (2007: 407) put it, 'offer simplistic solutions to complex political problems in a very direct language, appealing to the common sense of the people and denouncing the intellectualism of the established elites'. It rejects plurality of debate and sees political consensus as something that is not pure, not acceptable and not desirable (Cushion, 2019). Cas Mudde (2014: 543) defines populism as 'an ideology that considers society to be ultimately separated into two homogenous and antagonistic groups, "the pure people" versus "the corrupt elite", and which argues that politics should be an expression of the *volonté général* (general will) of the people'. Populism and pluralism are thus different perspectives on what the political and societal debate should be. Pluralism, so Mudde (2014: 544) puts it, 'rejects the homogeneity of both populism and elitism, seeing society as a heterogeneous collection of groups and individuals with often fundamentally different views and wishes'. While often associated with nationalism, populism as a thin-ideology can be integrated with other ideologies such as socialism and ecologism very well (2014: 544).

Public broadcasters, for obvious reasons, struggle to deal with populism.

> the role of PSM in creating a shared national conversation by representing diversity of society has also come under siege from right-wing populists who oppose these ideals.
>
> (Sehl, Fletcher, and Picard, 2020b: 3)

Populism stands at odds with public broadcasters' aim to contribute to informed citizenship, to stimulate people's empathy for 'the other', to bring together people around a shared but intrinsically diverse identity, and so on. Often, public broadcasters provide a platform for populism to thrive, not only by allowing populist politicians in their programmes, but more so by failing to live up to some of the abovementioned public interest objectives. Self-censorship as a process that limits free speech while not being the result of 'an external, coercive and repressive practice by authoratative social actors' and, probably more so, undecidedness on how to deal with the 'post-factual' era (Mortensen, 2018: 1960) account for that While populism can be seen as a means to identify and correct the flaws of representative democracy (Abts and Rummens, 2007: 405), one could argue that informing people about the phenomenon and relevant events is part of public broadcasters' task; providing a platform to liars has nothing to do with the 'moral' task of public broadcasters in liberal democracy, however.

While some would argue this model of Public Service Media results in a limited applicability of the concept, my argument is that talking about Public Service Media in a context that is *not* liberal democracy does not make sense; there is limited explanatory power there. The political situation in which public broadcasters operate is in that sense not only a contextual factor, but co-determining whether public broadcasters can realise the public interest in media and whether Public Service Media as a concept can offer value at all. That is why we in the next chapter elaborate on the different political ideologies and systems in which Public Service Media is organised today. We will confront the findings of our empirical research with the model elaborated above. Of course, that confrontation will not offer binary insights, but rather show that the ideal of Public Service Media does not exist and that the distance from practice to the ideal can be different in varying geographical, political, social and historical contexts.

References

Abts, K. and Rummens, S. (2007). Populism versus democracy. *Political Studies*, *55*(2), 405–424.

Allen, H., Connolly, S. and Hargreaves Heap, S.P. (2017). Media pluralism: What matters for governance and regulation? *Journal of Media Economics*, *30*(2), 47-64.

Baldi, P. (2007). Media accountability in Europe: A fragmented picture. In P. Baldi and U. Hasebrink (eds), *Broadcasters and Citizens in Europe: Trends in Media Accountability and Viewer Participation* (pp. 17–32). Bristol: Intellect.

Ballon, P., Van Looy, B., Raats, T., Wauters, D. and Tintel, S. (2018). *De economische meerwaarde van de VRT: Een onderzoek in opdracht van de VRT*. Brussels: VUB & KU Leuven. [*The added economic value of the VRT: An analysis on behalf of the VRT*].

Bardoel, J. (2003). Back to the public? Assessing public broadcasting in the Netherlands. *Javnost – The Public*, *10*(3), 81–96.

Bardoel, J. and d'Haenens, L. (2004). Media responsibility and accountability: New conceptualizations and practices. *Communications: The European Journal of Communication Research*, *29*(1), 5-25.

Bardoel, J. and d'Haenens, L. (2008). Reinventing public service broadcasting in Europe: Prospects, promises and problems. *Media, Culture & Society*, *30*(3), 337–355.

Bélair-Gagnon, V. (2013). Revisiting impartiality: Social media and journalism at the BBC. *Symbolic Interaction*, *36*(4), 478–492.

Benson, R. and Powers, M. (2011). *Public Media and Political Independence: Public Policy Report*. Washington, DC: Free Press.

Berg, C.E. and Brink Lund, A. (2015). Financing public service broadcasting: A comparative perspective. *Journal of Media Business Studies, 9*(1), 7–21.

Biggam, R. (2009). Public broadcasting and State aid in the new media environment. In C. Pauwels, H. Kalimo, K. Donders and B. Van Rompuy (eds), *Rethinking European Media and Communications Policy* (pp. 165–187). Brussels: VUBPRESS.

Biltereyst, D. (1992). Language and culture as ultimate barriers? An analysis of the circulation, consumption and popularity of fiction in small European countries. *European Journal of Communication, 7*(4), 517–540.

Bogart, L. (2017). *Commercial Culture: The Media System and the Public Interest.* New York: Routledge.

Bos, L., Kruikemeier, S. and de Vreese C. (2016). Nation Binding: How Public Service Broadcasting Mitigates Political Selective Exposure. *PLoS ONE, 11*(5). Retrieved from https://doi.org/10.1371/journal.pone.0155112 (accessed October 2020).

Buckley, S., Mendel, T., Duer, K. and Siochrú, S.Ó. (2008). *Broadcasting, Voice, and Accountability: A Public Interest Approach to Policy, Law, and Regulation.* Michigan: University of Michigan Press.

Burkart, P. and Leijonhufvud, S. (2019). The Spotification of public service media. *The Information Society, 35*(4), 173–183.

Castro-Herrero, L., Nir, L. and Skovsgaard, M. (2018). Bridging gaps in cross-cutting media exposure: The role of public service broadcasting. *Political Communication, 35*(4), 542–565.

Ciaglia, A. (2016). Democratising public service broadcasting: The South African Broadcasting Corporation – between politicisation and commercialization. *African Journalism Studies, 37*(2), 95–115.

Ciaglia, A. (2017). Explaining public service broadcasting entrenched politicisation: The case of South Africa's SABC. *Journalism, 18*(7), 817–834.

Croteau, D. and Hoynes, W. (2006). *The Business of Media: Corporate Media and the Public Interest.* London: Pine Forge Press.

Cunningham, S. (2009). Reinventing television: The work of the 'innovation' unit. In G. Turner and J. Tay (eds), *Television Studies After TV: Understanding Television in the Post-Broadcast Era* (pp. 83–92). London: Routledge.

Cunningham, S. (2015). Repositioning the innovation rationale for public service media. *International Journal of Digital Television, 6*(2), 203–220.

Cushion, S. (2019). PSM contribution to democracy: News, Editorial standards and informed citizenship. In E. Połońska and C. Beckett (eds), *Public Service Broadcasting and Media Systems in Troubled European Democracies* (pp. 23–39). Basingstoke: Palgrave Macmillan.

D'Arma A. (2018). The hollowing out of public service media: a constructivist institutionalist analysis of the commercialisation of BBC's in-house production. *Media, Culture & Society, 40*(3), 432–448.

D'Arma, A. and Labio, A. (2017). Making a difference? Public service broadcasting, distinctiveness and children's provision in Italy and Spain. *International Journal of Television, 8*(2), 183–199.

De Bens, E. and de Smaele, H. (2001). The inflow of American television fiction on European broadcasting channels revisited. *European Journal of Communication, 16*(1), 51–76.

De Haan, Y. and Bardoel, J. (2011). From trust to accountability: Negotiating media performance in the Netherlands, 1987–2007. *European Journal of Communication, 26*(3), 230–246.

Debrett, M. (2010). *Reinventing Public Service Television for the Digital Future*. Bristol: Intellect.

Direito, S. (forthcoming). Public service media as drivers of innovation: A case study analysis of policies and strategies in Spain, Ireland and Belgium. Submitted for publication.

Donders, K. (2012). *Public service media and policy in Europe*. Basingstoke: Palgrave Macmillan.

Donders, K. (2015). State aid to public service media: European Commission decisional practice before and after the 2009 Broadcasting Communication. *European State aid Law Quarterly, 1*(15), 68–87.

Donders, K. (2019). Public service media beyond the digital hype: Distribution strategies in a platform era. *Media Culture & Society, 41*(7), 1011–1028.

Donders, K. and Lamensch, M. (2010). The introduction of a tax-and-fund system to subsidise public television in France: Cultural revolution or legal swamp? *Journal of Media Law, 2*(2), 227–244.

Donders, K. and Raats, T. (2015). From public service media organisations to decentralised public service for the media sector: A comparative analysis of opportunities and disadvantages. *Javnost – The Public, 22*(2), 145–163.

Donders, K. and Van den Bulck, H. (2016). Decline and fall of public service media values in the international content acquisition market: An analysis of small public broadcasters acquiring BBC Worldwide content. *European Journal of Communication, 31*(3), 299–316.

Donders, K. and Van den Bulck, H. (2020). Universality of public service media and pre-school audiences: The choice against a dedicated children's channel in Flanders. In P. Savage, M. Medina and G.F. Lowe (eds), *Universalism in Public Service Media* (pp. 49–68). Göteborg: Nordicom.

Donders, K., Pauwels, C. and Loisen, J. (2012). Introduction: All or nothing? From public service broadcasting to public service media, to public service 'anything'? *International Journal of Media and Cultural Politics, 8*(1), 3–12.

Donders, K., Van den Bulck, H. and Raats, T. (2019). The politics of pleasing: A critical analysis of multistakeholderism in public service media policies in Flanders. *Media, Culture & Society, 41*(3), 347–66.

Donders, K., Raats, T. and Tintel, S. (2020). (Re)defining public service media from an economic perspective: Damned if they do, damned if they don't. In B. Van Rimscha and S. Kienzler (eds), *Management and Economics of Communication* (pp. 203–222). Berlin: Mouton De Gruyter.

Doyle, G. (2010). From television to multi-platform: less from more or more for less? *Convergence, 16*(4), 431–449.

EBU (2013). *Empowering Society: A Declaration on the Core Values of Public Service Media*. Geneva: EBU.

EBU (2018). *Funding of Public Service Media*. Geneva: EBU.

Enli, G.S. (2008). Redefining public service broadcasting: Multi-platform participation. *Convergence: The International Journal of Research into New media Technologies, 14*(1), 105–120.

Entman, R.M. and Wildman, S.S. (1992). Reconciling economic and non-economic perspectives on media policy: Transcending the 'marketplace of ideas'. *Journal of Communication, 42*(1), 5–19.

Erdemir, G. (2017). The effects of neo-liberal policies on public service broadcasting and the example of TRT. *Amme Idaresi Dergisi, 50*(2), 73–104.

European Commission (2003). Decision of 15 October 2003 on *Ad hoc funds implemented by Portugal for RTP.*

European Commission (2006). Decision of 22 March 2006 on *Compensation payments from Portugal for RTP.*

European Commission (2009a). Communication of 2 July 2009 on the *application of the State aid rules to Public Service Broadcasting.*

European Commission (2009b). Decision of 1 September 2009 on *Capital injections for France Télévisions.*

Evans, S.K. (2016). Making sense of innovation: Process, product and storytelling innovation in public service broadcasting organisations. *Journalism Studies, 19*(1), 4-24.

Fernandez, S. and Rainey, H.G. (2006). Managing successful organizational change in the public sector. *Public administration Review, 66*(2), 168-176.

Flew, T. (2011). Rethinking public service media and citizenship: Digital strategies for news and current affairs at Australia's Special Broadcasting Service (SBS). *International Journal of Communication,* 5, 215-232.

Flood, C., Hutchings, S., Miazhevich, G. and Nickels, H. (2010). Between impartiality and ideology: The BBC's paradoxical remit and the case of Islam-related television news. *Journalism Studies, 12*(2), 221-238.

Freedman, D. (2008b). *The Rise and Fall of the PSP.* London: Goldsmith University Research Online. Retrieved from http://research.gold.ac.uk/7080/1/PSParticle.pdf (accessed October 2020).

Freedman, D. (2019). 'Public service' and the journalism crisis: Is the BBC the answer? *Television & New Media, 20*(3), 203–218.

Garnham, N. (1990). *Capitalism and Communication: Global Culture and the Economics of Information.* London: Sage.

Gifreu, J. (2017). The battle for the BBC: An approach to the political debate on public service broadcasting in the UK (2014-2016). *Comunicació: Revista de Recerca i d'Anàlisi [Societat Catalana de Comunicació], 34*(1), 9-26.

Goddard, P. (2017). 'Distinctiveness' and the BBC: A new battleground for public service television? *Media, Culture & Society, 39*(7), 1089-1099.

Gomez-Dominguez, P. (2018). A methodological approach to the challenges of the CCMA (Catalan Public Service Media Corporation) to adapt to the digital and social environment. Proposal of indicators to measure consumption, professional processes and digital management. *Comunicació: Revista de Recerca i d'Anàlisi [Societat Catalana de Comunicació], 35*(1), 67-93.

Hallin, D.C. and Mancini, P. (2004). *Comparing Media Systems: Three Models of Media and Politics.* Cambridge: Cambridge University Press.

Hanretty, C. (2009). *The Political Independence of Public Service Broadcasters* (unpublished Ph.D. thesis). European University Institute, Florence.

Hanretty, C. (2011). *Public Broadcasting and Political Interference.* New York: Routledge.

Hesmondhalgh, D. (2019). *The Cultural Industries* (4th ed.). London, Thousand Oaks, New Delhi, Singapore: Sage.

Horsti, K. and Hultén, G. (2011). Directing diversity: Managing cultural diversity media policies in Finnish and Swedish public service broadcasting. *International Journal of Cultural Studies, 14*(2), 209–227.

Hoschscherf, T. (2019). Narrative complexity and cultural relevance in the name of public service broadcasting: The cases of Borgen and Herrens Veje. *European Journal of Scandinavian Studies, 49*(1), 156-177.

Hoynes, W. (2007). Public broadcasting for the 21st century: Notes on an agenda for reform. *Critical Studies in Media Communication, 24*(4), 370–376.

Ibrus, I., Rohn, U.A. and d' Nani, A. (2019). Searching for public value in innovation coordination: How the Eurovision Song Contest was used to innovate the public service media model in Estonia. *International Journal of Cultural Studies, 22*(3), 367–382.

Jakubowicz, K. (2007). Public service broadcasting in the 21st century: What chance for a new beginning? In G.F. Lowe and J. Bardoel (eds), *From Public Service Broadcasting to Public Service Media* (pp. 29–50). Göteborg: Nordicom.

Juanatey-Boga, O., Martínez-Fernández, V.A. and Rodríguez-Castro, M. (2018). The two-speed Europe reflected in Public Service Media funding: A budget based analysis. *Revista Latin a de Comunicación Social, 73*, 1054–1071.

Keinonen, H. and Shagrir, O.K. (2017). From public service broadcasting to soci(et)al TV: Producers' perceptions of interactivity and audience participation in Finland and Israel. *Nordicom Review, 38*(1), 65–79.

Kennedy, H., Steedman, R. and Jones, R. (2020). Approaching public perceptions of datafication through the lens of inequality: A case study in public service media. *Information, Communication and Society.* Retrieved from https://doi.org/10.1080/1369118X.2020.1736122 (accessed October 2020).

Kuhn, R. (2010). France: Presidential assault on the public service. In P. Iosifidis (ed.), *Reinventing Public Service Communication: European Broadcasters and Beyond* (pp. 158–170). New York: Palgrave Macmillan.

Lanara, Z. (2002). *Public Service Broadcasting: New Challenges for a New Age.* Brussels: UNI-MEI.

Larrondo, A., Domingo, D., Erdal, I.J., Masip, P. and Van den Bulck, H. (2016). Opportunities and limitations of newsroom convergence. *Journalism Studies, 17*(3), 277–300.

Latzer, M., Braendle, A., Just, N. and Saurwein, F. (2010). Public-service broadcasting online: Assessing compliance with regulatory requirements. *International Telecommunications Policy Review, 17*(2), 1–25.

Leurdijk, A. (2007). Will public broadcasters survive in the online and digital domain? In P. Cesar, K. Chorianopoulos and J.F. Jensen (eds), *European Conference on Interactive Television* (pp. 86–95). The Netherlands: Amsterdam.

Lim, T., Bali, A. and Moo, M. (2019). New digital realities and old public service broadcasting models: The case of public access and participation in Singapore's televisual landscape. *Media International Australia, 170*(1), 100–114.

Livémont, E., Donders, K. and Pauwels, C. (2017). De documentaire als merit good op de publieke omroep: Theorie, beleid en praktijk in Vlaanderen. *Tijdschrift voor Communicatiewetenschap, 45*(4), 286–303. [*Documentary as merit good in public broadcasting: Theory, policy and practice in Flanders*].

Lobato, R. (2019). *Netflix Nations: The Geography of Digital Distribution.* New York: NYU Press.

Loisen, J. and Joye, S. (2017). *On Media & Communication: An Introduction to Communication Sciences: Theory and Research.* Leuven: Acco.

López-Cepeda, A.M., Soengas-Pérez, X. and Campos-Freire, F. (2019a). Gobernanza de las radiotelevisiones públicas europeas: poder estructural centralizado y politizado. *Revista internacional de Información y Comunicación, 28*(6). Retrieved from https://doi.org/10.3145/epi.2019.nov.18 (accessed October 2020).

López-Cepeda, A.M., López-Golán, M. and Rodríguez-Castro, M. (2019b). Participatory audiences in the European public service media: Content production and copyright. *Comunicar*, *27*(60), 93-102.

Lowe, G.F., Van den Bulck, H. and Donders, K. (eds) (2018). *Public Service Media in the Networked Society RIPE@2017*. Göteborg: Nordicom

Madsen, V. (2017). Innovation, women's work and the documentary impulse: Pioneering moments and stalled opportunities in public service broadcasting in Australia and Britain. *Media International Australia*, *162*(1), 19-32.

Manias-Munoz, M. and Martori Muntsant, M. (2017). BBC Alba: Public Service Broadcasting and Gaelic representation in Scotland. *Historia y Comunicacion Social*, *22*(1), 191-206.

Martin, F. (2002). Beyond Public Service Broadcasting? ABC online and the user/citizen [online]. *Southern Review: Communication, Politics & Culture*, *35*(1), 42-62.

Masduki (2017). Public service broadcasting (PSB) regulation in Indonesia: Between market and public interest. In B. Mohamad and H. Abu Bakar (eds), *International Conference on Communication and Media: An International Communication Association Regional Conference (i-COME'16), Volume 33*. Kuala Lumpur: SHS.

McQuail, D. (2003). Public service broadcasting: Both free and accountable. *The Public*, *1*(3), 13-23.

Meier, W.A. and Trappel, J. (1992). Small states in the shadow of giants. In K. Siune and W. Truetzschler (eds), *Dynamics of Media Politics: Broadcast and Electronic Media in Western Europe* (pp. 129-142). London: Sage.

Mortensen, M. (2018). The self-censorship dilemma: Media coverage of terrorists in the post-factual era. *Journalism Studies*, *19*(13), 1957-1968.

Mudde, C. (2014). Fighting the system? Populist radical right parties and party system change. *Party Politics*, *20*(2), 217–226.

Nossiter, T.J. (1991). British television: a mixed economy. In J.G Blumler and T.J. Nossiter (eds), *Broadcasting Finance in Transition: A Comparative Handbook* (pp. 95-143). New York: Oxford University Press.

O'Hagan, J. and Jennings, M. (2003). Public broadcasting in Europe: Rationale, licence fee and other issues. *Journal of Cultural Economics*, *27*, 31-56.

Otto, K., Degen, M., Olgemöller, M. and Kohler, A. (2020). News coverage of the Greek sovereign debt crisis in German public service broadcasting: A case study analysis in Tagesschau, Heute, Brennpunkt and ZDF Spezial. *Journalism Practice*. Retrieved from https://doi.org/10.1080/17512786.2020.1760729 (accessed October 2020).

Pavani, G. (2017). Anomalies of the Italian Public Service Broadcasting despite the Law 220 of 2015. *European Public Law*, *23*(3), 507-524.

Ploch, M. (2017). An integrated model for public service media governance based on participatory governance and actor-centered institutionalism: Initial application to the independence of the Polish public broadcaster TVP S.A. *Central European Journal of Communication*, *2*, 193-209.

Połońska, E. and Beckett, C. (2019). Introduction. In E. Połońska and C. Beckett (eds), *Public Service Broadcasting and Media Systems in Troubled European Democracies* (pp. 1-20). Basingstoke: Palgrave Macmillan.

Price, M. and Raboy, M. (eds) (2003). *Public Service Broadcasting in Transition: A Documentary Reader*. The Hague: Kluwer Law International.

Raats, T. (2013). *And now for something completely different? De rol en positie van de publieke omroep in een genetwerkte samenleving: onderzoek naar de publieke omroepopdracht* en—*organisatie aan de hand van een comparatieve analyse van de culturele missie* (Unpublished Ph.D. thesis). Vrije Universiteit Brussel, Brussels. [*And now for something completely different? The role and position of the public broadcaster in a networked society: A comparative analysis of the public service remit and organisation in the cultural domain*].

Raats, T. and Jensen, P.M. (2020). The Role of Public Service Media in Sustaining TV Drama in Small Markets. *Television & New Media*. Retrieved from doi:10.1177/1527476420913398 (accessed October 2020).

Raboy, M. (ed.) (1995). *Public Broadcasting for the 21st Century*. Luton: University of Luton Press.

Ramsey, P. (2018a). The BBC Ideas Service: The Corporation's Search for Universalism Online. Paper presented at the 2018 RIPE Conference 'Universalism and PSM', 18–20 October, Madrid.

Ramsey, P. (2018b). It could redefine public service broadcasting in the digital age: Assessing the rationale for moving BBC Three online. *Convergence, 24*(2), 152-167.

Saurwein, F., Eberwein, T. and Karmasin, M. (2019). Public service media in Europe: Exploring the relationship between funding and audience performance. *Javnost – The Public, 26*(3), 291-308.

Sehl, A., Cornia, A., Graves, L. and Nielsen, R.K. (2018). Newsroom integration as an organisational challenge: Approaches of European PSM from a comparative perspective. *Journalism Studies, 20*(9), 1238-1259.

Sehl, A., Fletcher, R. and Picard, R. (2020a). Crowding out: Is there evidence that public service media harm markets? A cross-national comparative analysis of commercial television and online news providers. *European Journal of Communication*. Retrieved from https://doi.org/10.1177/0267323120903688 (accessed October 2020).

Sehl, A., Simon, F.M. and Schroeder, R. (2020b). The populist campaigns against European public service media: Hot air or existential threat. *International Communication Gazette*. Retrieved from https://doi.org/10.1177/1748048520939868 (accessed October 2020).

Siebert, F., Peterson, T.B. and Schramm, W. (1956). *Four Theories of the Press: The Authoritarian, Libertarian, Social Responsibility, and Soviet Communist Concepts of What the Press Should Be and Do*. Urbana: University of Illinois Press.

Sjøvaag, H., Pedersen, T.A. and Owren, T. (2019). Is public service broadcasting a threat to commercial media?. *Media, Culture & Society, 41*(6), 808-827.

Smith, P. (2017). Playing under pressure: Sport, public service broadcasting and the British Broadcasting Corporation. *International Communication Gazette, 79*(2), 203–216.

Sørensen, J.K. and Van den Bulck, H. (2020). Public service media online, advertising and the third-party user data business: A trade versus trust dilemma? *Convergence, 26*(2), 421–447.

Steemers, J. (2017). Public service broadcasting, children's television, and market failure: The case of the United Kingdom. *International Journal on Media Management, 19*(4), 298-314.

Syvertsen, T., Donders, K., Enli, G. and Raats, T. (2019). Media disruption and the public interest: How private media managers talk about responsibility to society in an era of turmoil. *Nordic Journal of Media Studies, 1*, 11-28.

Taylor, G. and Thomass, B. (2017). Sports rights and public service media/public broadcasting: Case studies on economic and political implications. *International Communication Gazette, 79*(2), 111-119.

Vaccari, C. and Valeriani, A. (2018). Dual screening, public service broadcasting, and political participation in eight western democracies. *The International Journal of Press / Politics*, *23*(3), 367–388.

Van den Bulck, H. (2001). Public service television and national identity as a project of modernity: The example of Flemish television. *Media, Culture & Society*, *23*(1), 53–69.

Van den Bulck, H. (2015). PSM accountability in recent decades: A progressive shift from state to market. In K. Arriaza Ibarra, E. Nowak and R. Kuhn (eds), *PSM in Europe: A Comparative Approach* (pp. 73–88). London: Routledge.

Van den Bulck, H. and Moe, H. (2018). Public service media, universality and personalisation through algorithms: Mapping strategies and exploring dilemmas. *Media, Culture & Society*, *40*(6), 875–892.

van Dijck, J. and Poell, T. (2015). Making public television social? Public service broadcasting and the challenges of social media. *Television & New Media*, *16*(2), 148–164.

Van Hoof, S. (2018). Civilization versus commerce: On the sociolinguistic effects of the deregulation of the TV market on Flemish public service broadcasting. *Language Policy*, *17*, 199–216.

Vanhaeght, A.-S. (2019). The need for not more, but more socially relevant audience participation in public service media. *Media, Culture & Society*, *41*(1), 120–137.

Vermeer, S., Trilling, D., Kruikemeier, S. and de Vreese, C. (2020). Online news user journeys: The role of social media, news websites, and topics, *Digital Journalism*, 8(9), 1114–1141.

Westcott, T. (2019). The future of public broadcasting: Funding strategies from around the world. Retrieved from https://entertainment.report/Resources/Whitepapers/a1d7f13b-97a3-4cfe-aebc-871456e46a69_miptv-mipcom-ihs-public-broadcasting-white-paper.pdf (accessed October 2020).

Yilmaz, F. and Matthes, F. (2019). Investigating the Challenges of European Public Service Media Companies from an Enterprise Architecture Point of View. Paper presented at the *2019 IEEE 23rd International Enterprise Distributed Object Computing Workshop*, Paris.

Zaragoza-Fuster, M.T. and Garcia-Aviles, J.A. (2020). The role of innovation labs in advancing the relevance of public service media: The cases of BBC News Labs and RTVE Lab. *Communication & Society*, *33*(1), 45–61.

Zelizer, B. (2013). On the shelf life of democracy in journalism scholarship. *Journalism*, *14*(4), 459–473.

Part II
Law

6 Ideological divisions in national Public Service Media policy

Introduction

Public broadcasters held a monopoly position in most Western and Northern European countries from the 1930s until the 1970s. Their initial status of monopolist in the 1930s can be explained at large by the aspiration of politicians to control the broadcast medium in an era of spectrum scarcity (Burgelman, 1990). Monopoly came to an end throughout the 1970s and 1980s. The United Kingdom and Italy introduced competition in their broadcasting markets already in the 1950s and 1960s; Luxembourg never had a public broadcaster (Iosifidis, 2008, p. 305). In Southern and Central and Eastern Europe public broadcasting became a legal phenomenon only after fascism or communism came to an end. They turned their state broadcasters into public broadcasters throughout the 1980s and 1990s (Terzis, 2007). In practice, we can see that several Member States of the European Union have difficulties embracing the idea of an independent public, instead of a state, broadcaster in practice (Levitsky and Way, 2010).

Whereas Public Service Media is considered a European phenomenon, its transposition varies and is very much intertwined with the political, historical, economic, societal and cultural context in which it is embedded (Katsirea, 2008; Hesmondhalgh, 2019: 152). Before we discuss the national legal frameworks for Public Service Media in the subsequent chapters, the aim of this chapter is to devote some attention to the different political contexts in which public broadcasters work. In some parts of Europe there is an evolution towards a libertarian free market place of ideas ideology, putting pressure on a holistic public broadcaster servicing all groups in society (Donders, 2012). In other parts of Europe, the social democratic or even media welfare state model (Syvertsen et al., 2014) seems to be fairly resistant. In another group of countries, scholars refer to the emergence of competitive authoritarianism, combining the features of neoliberal with authoritarian ideologies (Vladisavljević, 2016). These 'models' in turn cover an even bigger variety of Public Service Media practices in Europe. Public broadcasters relate differently with their audiences, other public institutions, competitors, politicians and with themselves, depending on what EU Member State we are talking about. This chapter mostly aims to illustrate that Public Service Media and public broadcasters are far from a homogeneous thing, but are in fact – for better or worse – a perfect example of the diversity that characterises the EU. It will relate policy models to the democracy-centric and market failure perspectives on Public Service Media. It will become clear though that most political models contain elements from both perspectives.

Hallin and Mancini's media models as starting point

The actual status of Public Service Media organisations in Europe is slightly to very different. It depends strongly on the political economic context of a given Member State. Hanretty (2011) illustrates this very well in his book *Public Broadcasting and Political Interference*. His main thesis in this book is that the independence of public broadcasters is determined by the existence of legal protections on the one hand and the size of the market for news on the other hand.

While Hallin and Mancini's (2004) distinction between three types of European media models has been criticised, it offers a welcome and also a much used starting point for the analysis of media policy, economy and practices. Agreeing with Humphreys (2012) that countries rarely fit entirely with one of the models defined by Hallin and Mancini and with Syvertsen et al. (2014) on the necessity to define more models such as the Scandinavian 'media welfare state', we use the typology as a point of departure for further analysis, looking at the diversity of legal, political, economic, social, cultural and historical variables that have impacted the Public Service Media system in place. Essentially, the idea thereof is to explain why the media are how they are while avoiding media-centric explanations (see Mihelj and Downey, 2012).

The first model in Hallin and Mancini's typology (2004) is the liberal one. Countries such as the US, the United Kingdom, Ireland and Luxembourg are part of it. The model is, in line with the libertarian and also social responsibility theory in Siebert et al.'s work *Four Theories of the Press* (1956), based on free market ideology, assuming competitive markets will deliver most value to consumers. The latter are considered rational human beings, choosing consciously to watch or read a particular broadcaster or newspaper. Intervention from government in the media sector is limited to market failure only.

Second, countries such as Germany, Belgium, Austria, Norway and the Netherlands are part of the democratic corporatist model. There is extensive state intervention, but largely with an eye on safeguarding pluralism and diversity of the media. Independence of the media is constitutionally protected. The historical coexistence of public and commercial media is deemed to be the optimal scenario for diverse and pluralistic media.

Third, countries with weak commercial media and highly politicised Public Service Media organisations are part of the polarised pluralist model. The state takes an active role in both the private and public media sectors, not so much with an eye on furthering some of the values of Public Service Media discussed above, but more so with the aim to instrumentalise the media to further the government's political agenda. Typically, that model can be observed in previously fascist countries such as Portugal and Spain.

Terzis (2007) added a fourth model, being the post-communist countries. Poland and Hungary are members of this group. These states have abolished communist rule and, in principle, embraced democracy. However, Sabina Mihelj and John Downey (2012: 7) point out that the situation in Central and Eastern European countries varies significantly. And 'in many cases continues to display important continuities with the pre-1989 period'. There are several economic, political and socio-cultural reasons for this, including the relative weakness of commercial media markets and the tenacity of behaviour that limits independence of journalists.

Essentially, Hallin and Mancini's typology only recognises one model that embraces Public Service Media as something that is good for society. In the liberal model, despite its different crystallisations in practice, public broadcasters are seen as a tool to remedy market failure. In the polarised pluralist model, they are heavily politicised. Post-communism as a model presents us with challenges as some countries such as Latvia have embraced elements of the liberal media system whereas Poland and Hungary moved back to politicising public broadcasters, considered mouth pieces for the ruling party's ideology.

While the economic status of a country is relevant to each model, the political system seems to be the most important factor in terms of classification. One can legitimately dispute this as research on small media markets has shown that size matters. It makes these markets more vulnerable on the one hand, but often also more combative in the development of media policies to the protection of their own domestic industry (Puppis, 2009; Lowe et al., 2011). Examples of 'controlled liberalisation', whereby markets were opened up to competition – in line with European policies – and, at the same time, significant government intervention through subsidy schemes for audiovisual production, public broadcasters, advertising regulation, and so on, can be observed in several Scandinavian countries, Belgium, Austria and Switzerland to date (Van den Bulck and Donders, 2014). This issue will be taken on board when discussing the Public Service Media models in Europe below.

Caught between neoliberal, social responsibility and social democratic media policies

Models can clarify the main differences between European countries. They are not static though. Most scholars would agree on the convergence between the liberal and democratic corporatist model. As a consequence of the rising popularity of neoliberal ideology and national and European de-regulation policies in the media sector (Noam, 1991), several of the democratic corporatist countries are moving towards the liberal or, more accurately so, a social responsibility model. Self-regulation or co-regulation of media companies is preferred over ex ante regulation by states. Competition law is favoured over sector-specific rules. Moreover, several public interest objectives such as pluralism and diversity are said to be achieved first and foremost by markets, and only secondly by government intervention (Dyson, 1985; Hitchens, 2006).

The convergence between the liberal, social responsibility and social democratic models, with a dominance of liberal ideas, did not happen overnight. The process is ongoing since the 1980s when, according to Garnham (1990: 127-128) there was 'a profound shift in people's attitudes to the State and to the State's proper role in social time'. Dyson and Humphreys (1988) argue that new technologies caused a 'paradigm change' in West European broadcasting. The promise of more services, more diversity and more pluralism was used to re-regulate media sectors, often with an increased reliance on horizontal policy domains such as competition law. The reliance on holistic public broadcasters was seen to contradict the era of abundance and consumer sovereignty.

Having said that, most European countries in the liberal or social democratic models of Hallin and Mancini, have stuck to a strong public broadcaster ever since these pessimist accounts in the 1980s. Luxembourg is an exception. But in Ireland, the United Kingdom, Belgium, the Netherlands, Germany, Switzerland, Denmark, Sweden, and so on, public broadcasters are most often market leader in radio and television (EBU, 2018), frequently also in online news, online video players and websites for children (Donders et al., 2019). In line with the more pessimist predictions about the future of public broadcasters in Europe, Public Service Media and specifically its realisation by public broadcasters is being limited in a number of the abovementioned countries. Public value tests of new media services, the prohibition to deliver specific media services and word limits on text-based news articles are examples of legal constraints imposed on public broadcasters, largely on the basis of liberal ideology. Admittedly, sheer protectionism and political clientelism towards wealthy captains of the media industry can be seen as more rudimentary reasons as well (Donders et al., 2019; cf. infra).

It seems that we have ended up with a mishmash or hodgepodge of the liberal, social responsibility and social democratic models. Policy discourse is characterised mainly by liberal and social responsibility arguments, whereas practices are based on a combination of these and social democratic arguments and economic protectionism. It is crucial to recognise this as the fall and demise of public broadcasters has been announced so many times, that we have to understand that not only liberal, but also the democracy-centric ideas discussed in Chapter 4 and their manifestations can be more resilient than sometimes anticipated.

The relative stability of the polarised pluralist countries

Hallin and Mancini (2004) describe polarised pluralist countries as countries where there is a complex, yet manifest collusion between political and media elites. While the high-level principles of freedom of speech and media are respected at the legal level, several aspects of regulation, but also day-to-day practices in government-media relations show that the fourth estate cannot act to its fullest potential. Spain, Italy, Portugal, France, Malta, Cyprus, and so on, are countries that exhibit these characteristics. They all show high levels of politicisation of the media (Hallin and Mancini, 2004). The countries in the polarised pluralist model share a history of dictatorship or very strong leadership that was not always in full respect of democracy. In the transition to democracy or a more democratic system, notably Spain, Italy and Greece have remained very much attached to political parallelism. France and Portugal, one could argue, have moved beyond this to some extent, reaching also higher levels of journalistic professionalism (Hallin and Mancini, 2004). Essentially, the Mediterranean model has four key characteristics. First, political parallelism between media and politics, sometimes also between media and the Catholic church. Second, there is a weak market development in most Southern European countries (Papathanasopoulos, 2007; see also Arriaza Ibarra and Nord, 2014). Low circulation of newspapers and also television-centric media markets are exemplary of this. Public broadcasters can, but do not always attract high audience shares. Third and related to the former, professional autonomy of journalists is limited. Fourth, high levels of state interventionism can be observed, among others through the arbitrary and non-objectified granting of licenses and subsidies.

Several authors indeed show that the countries within the polarised pluralist model, even if democratic in nature, having some quality media, and knowing governments that have been challenged by and fallen because of investigative journalism, still check three to four of the abovementioned boxes (e.g., Iosifidis and Papathanassopoulos, 2019). Esser and Umbricht (2013: 991) define the Italian and French journalistic tradition as a mix between 'news and views to prioritise opinion over reportage'. Their 'greater dependence on State aid and political favouring, strong press–party ties and the late development of journalism as an independent profession have made scrutinising watchdog reporting (i.e. media initiated negativity) less likely'. While it has been argued that France does not entirely fit the polarised pluralist model, eminent expert on the French media system Raymond Kuhn, emphasises the countries' 'long and chequered relationship with Public Service Media'. He says that 'it was reasonable to talk of state, rather than public, broadcasting' until the 1980s (Kuhn, 2019: 76). Even after that moment, subsequent presidents of the Republic such as Nicolas Sarkozy challenged the freedom of public service television, for example, through a limitation of commercial funds, to the benefits of and specifically asked by be-friended personal friends in the commercial media sector. President Macron has promised to ensure appointment processes of public broadcaster management are independent and less influenced by government. The situation of public broadcasting in Italy is in some ways similar. RAI's television and radio services are, admittedly, more popular. The organisation also contributes significantly to Italian film and television production. However, it too faces political and commercial pressure that has, according to Alessandro D'Arma (2019: 125), 'historically weakened its performance as a Public Service Media organisation'. Personal ties between politics and media are very visible, with of course Berlusconi's empire as its most explicit exponent (Mangani and Tarrini, 2018). While the Renzi government promised more independence of RAI and is also acting against evading payment of the license fee, the substantial decrease of the latter and the initial moves in the area of news are not particularly positive. Greece is another example of the resilience of the polarised pluralist model in the Mediterranean countries. Its public broadcaster is highly politicised and has a small market share (the last years at about 11 per cent for television). Commercial media markets are intertwined with commercial activities in shipping and finances. Subsequent governments treat media as mouthpieces of a specific political and ideological agenda. In 2013, the conservative government abolished public broadcaster ERT. Its employees were fired. And a new public broadcaster NERIT was created with fewer staff, a lower budget and with a less left-wing agenda. The European Broadcasting Union and many colleague public broadcasters protested against the decision of the Greek Government. Also the European Commission, Council of Europe and the European Parliament criticised the abolishment of the public broadcaster, of which the programming continued to be aired via EBU-operated satellites and online. ERT attracted more viewers in this period than before. When Alexis Tsipras of Syriza became prime minister, he, as promised, re-established ERT, re-hired its staff and … made it a propaganda tool of his government. This was, according to Iosifidis and Papathanassopoulos (2019: 149), a missed opportunity and confirms their conclusion that 'Public Service Broadcasting never really existed in Greece'.

Of course, the transition to democracy is a slow and uneven trend (Papathanasopoulos, 2007) one. While the abovementioned countries are democracies that work according to the rule of law, political parallelism persists. It is a very peculiar and particular phenomenon. It relates to economic elites instrumentalising media (ownership) with an eye on influencing politics and politicians using this to exert influence as well. Typical examples are the conglomerates in shipping, construction, finance, and so on, that became active in the media sector throughout the 1980s and remained in the driver's seat in media in France, Greece, Italy, and so on, today still. The close ties between economic and political elites has in many cases resulted in far-going de-regulation of the private sector and a tenacious politicisation of the public broadcaster and regulatory bodies. While there are many examples of reform or at least the intention to reform the Public Service Media system in all of the named countries, it seems hard to leave behind the basic, inveterated structures of governmentalisation of Public Service Media. For example, whereas Spanish national public broadcaster RTVE was subject to different legislative improvements at the end of the 1990s and the beginning of the 21st century – among others because of European Commission intervention on the basis of State aid rules (Donders, 2012) – the rise of the Partido Popular (i.e. the Conservative party that has roots in the Franco regime) came with an increased politicisation again and this, so Fernández Viso and Fernández Alonso (2019: 156) argue, 'apparent societal acceptance of practices of political interference in Public Service Media'. Both scientists are worried about this as there is a remarkable political and media polarisation around issues such as Catalan independence; issues for which a balanced, fair, objective and pluralistic coverage of a or more independent public broadcasters is very much necessary (2019: 170 171). At the same time, they maintain that the changes made before were not in vain and have 'raised the threshold of Spanish democracy's intolerance of political interference in Public Service Media' (2019: 171). The polarised pluralist model cannot too easily be equalled with some of the neo-authoritarian regimes that we see emerging in Eastern Europe though.

The persistence of government capture and the emergence of competitive authoritarianism

Besides the pressure on the democratic corporatist model, several scholars have claimed that not the polarised pluralist, nor the post-communist, post-soviet or neo-soviet model fully capture the complexity of media in and the significant differences between post-communist countries (Castro-Herrero, Nir and Skovsgaard, 2017). Several previously communist countries could be said to have moved towards the democratic corporatist or liberal models. For example, Latvia has adopted a discourse of open markets, liberalisation and digitisation in its policies. Its media market is competitive and, at the same time, shows significant tendencies towards media concentration. It ranks 28th on the World Press Freedom Index (compared to the 71st place for Hungary and the 54th position for Poland). Issues concerning independence of the media relate mainly to the media serving the Russian-speaking community in Latvia. These media are known to be pro-Kremlin. Also Croatia has opened up its markets and is seen as a country with the characteristics of the polarised pluralist model: low levels of newspaper circulation, low professionalisation and unionisation of journalists and political parallelism. Especially personal, and not per se institutional, ties between political and media elites are considered strong (Perusko, 2013). Other countries such as Poland and Hungary have adopted recipes for the media sector that show a marked resemblance with the authoritarian view on media as a tool of government to defend the status quo and to unite people around the ideology of the ruling party (Siebert, Peterson and Schramm, 1956). In Hungary, the media law adopted in 2014 has provoked massive outcry in the country itself and within the European Union. It is said to increase the government's influence over the media, particularly when deciding on the appropriateness of content and on granting licenses to broadcasters. The public broadcaster is considered a state broadcaster by most observers. Its programming policies are reported to be influenced by the lead party in government and tough questioning of its politicians is actively discouraged (Dunai, 2014). In Poland, the government has strengthened its control over the public broadcaster, gaining decision-making power over management appointments. Several scholars (e.g., Levitsky and Way, 2010; Vladisavljević, 2016) have classified such countries in the model of competitive authoritarianism, meaning they have become a part of the EU's internal market and, hence, accepted a capitalist organisation of the media. However, at the same time, the intervention of government in the media has intensified and freedom of speech is being curbed significantly. Some have argued to talk about neo-authoritarianism instead (e.g., Becker, 2014). I opt for competitive authoritarianism though as the European countries we talk about have adopted internal market recipes of liberalisation, fairly open markets and commercial entrepreneurship in media. That element is not sufficiently present in the neo-authoritarianism notion. Essentially, competitive authoritarianism is characterised by two basic features. First, there is a definite trend of marketisation after the collapse of the Soviet Union. Second, there is a far-going state influence over media in general, Public Service Media and journalism, in particular (Dovbysh and Belyuga, 2020). Moreover, there is a perverse relationship between the two, whereby corporate ownership is often closely affiliated with political elites. Also, the dependence of Public Service Media organisations in some of the concerned countries on commercial funding is rather high. Add to this, with some exceptions, relatively low market shares and one can see what the fundamental issues in the competitive authoritarianism model are.

Whereas the trend towards more liberal ideologies puts pressure on public broadcasters' online activities, the crystallisation of competitive authoritarianism presents us with an admittedly more fundamental issue. The essence of independent media as part of European democracies is being questioned. Whereas free media exist from an economic point of view, the same cannot be said from a political, societal and cultural perspective. Not surprisingly, public broadcasters in countries that are moving towards or have adopted a competitive authoritarian view on media and society can better be considered state broadcasters (Hanretty, 2011). The question then is whether in these countries the existence of a public/state broadcaster contributes to the set of common values that is part of theories on Public Service Media. Essentially, one should recognise that the applicability of Western-centric notions of media policy and Public Service Media is restricted in several European countries (as was observed by De Smaele, 1999, in relation to Russia).

The thin blue line between policies and politics across media models

All of the above confirms the thesis of Des Freedman that media policy is highly political in nature. In his seminal work *The Politics of Media Policy*, Freedman is firm when saying that 'media systems are [instead] purposefully created, their characteristics shaped by competing political interests that seek to inscribe their own values and objectives on the possibilities facilitated by a complex combination of technological, economic and social factors'. He continues that there is nothing inevitable about the shape of media sectors in countries, in Europe or internationally (Freedman, 2008: 1). He convincingly illustrates how public broadcasting organisations such as the BBC and PBS in the United States have been subjected to policies that show the politics of neoliberalism and thus a defence of pro-market voices (2008: 169). McChesney (1999: 227) agrees that 'the attack on Public Service Broadcasting is part and parcel of the current attack on all non-commercial public service institutions and values' and a neo-liberal political agenda. Also O'Malley (2009: 11) emphasises that a libertarian political agenda is winning from a more collectivist political appreciation of Public Service Media. Research on the rise of multistakeholderism in Public Service Media policy-making also shows that policy is being captured by pol-itics, even zero-sum games between political parties and a strong market-driven agenda. That agenda is at the level of rhethorics liberal, but in essence protec-tionist towards the commercial interests of a few (certainly not all) media com-panies in a given market (see Donders, Van den Bulck and Raats, 2019). Castells and Arsenault (2008: 491) talk about companies such as Rupert Murdoch's NewsCorp that act as a 'switching point, connecting media, political and eco-nomic networks in the shared project of the company's financial expansion'.

I agree with Freedman, McChesney, O'Malley and others that politics are a determining element in Public Service Media policies and that commercial actors are often successful in instrumentalising power to advance the policy agenda in a certain way. However, there are three aspects of Public Service Media policy-making that are not addressed in this. First, and as already hinted at before, Public Service Media policy and media policy, in general, does not meet the interest of all commercial entities, but usually the interests of spe-cific companies and even individual media elites. One could argue that has to do with collusion of power, personal networks and protectionism, some-times for a very long time and sometimes subject to short-term mutual benefit. Economic liberalism or even neoliberalism is used, but actually not adhered to in practice. Second, public broadcasters – in spite of all of the accounts on their demise – have proven to be extremely resilient, especially in Western and Northern Europe. Yes, they have in many countries faced budget cuts. Yes, they are sometimes not allowed to offer text-based articles online. Yes, they are criticised heavily in parliaments, and so on. But, they still exist, they still receive considerable levels of funding and, most importantly, they still reach a lot of people in society. They are also protected by the Treaty on the Functioning of the European Union (TFEU) and several resolutions of the Council of Europe (see Chapter 5). Also these policy documents result from a political process that, in numerous but certainly not all Member States of the EU, has kept public broadcasters in place as essential, not niche or complementary, providers of media services in the public interest. Third, socio-cultural elements ought to play a more considerable role in theorising Public Service Media. Is there a culture of independence, professional journalism, of free speech or is there another, more state- or elite-driven culture, not only in media, but in all the important parts of society? And is it possible at all to evolve from one cul-ture into something else? Prominent media scholar Karol Jakubowicz (2001) researched that during his entire career and wrote several publications about the issue, including *Rude Awakening: Social and Media Change in Central and Eastern Europe*. His argument was that the state of play of democracy and media are heavily intertwined and that 'the extent of media independence and freedom in the region will be closely related to the extent of democratic consolidation' (Jakubowicz, 2012: 15). He is not saying that free media cannot exist without democracy or that journalism in such a context cannot contribute to society and citizenship. However, the impact of media 'is predicated on the existence of favourable political conditions without which they could not perform that function' (2012: 16). The normative beliefs and values of political elites are crucial in this regard. These elements will receive considerable attention in the subsequent chapters on Public Service Media laws and practice.

The declining legitimacy of public broadcasters as mainstream media

While there has been a lot of criticism on media systems theory and for very legitimate reasons, it is very useful for this book that is focused on the state of play of Public Service Media and public broadcasters in a variety of European countries. The focus of media systems theory on features such as profession-alisation of journalism, political parallelism, autonomy of media, and so on, makes it not only a solid background. It provides a sound basis for the for-mulation of hypotheses (see also Hardy, 2012: 189 on the use of media system classifications). One of the key arguments of this book is that Member States of the EU that do not respect basic values of democracy provide the least fertile ground for public broadcasting organisations acting as Public Service Media. We could in fact wonder whether this model will work in such a context at all. In countries that are democratic, but still show high levels of political paral-lelism, work needs to be done to ensure autonomy, professionalisation of public broadcasters and mutual trust between government and public broadcasting management. In countries that do not show such problems, notably those in Western and Northern Europe, the rise of populism and a disconnect between public broadcasters and a part of their audience might in fact be the big issue to deal with.

Coming back to this later, it is important to stress that regardless of the media model there is definitely a declining legitimacy of public broadcasters to be observed in all European countries. There are various reasons for this.

First, since the 1980s there is an increased political pressure on public broadcasters. On the one hand, a pro-market discourse rejects a democracy-centric approach to Public Service Media. A smaller public broadcaster that rectifies market failure, focuses on specific niches and acts with caution online is argued for. On the other hand, public broadcasters are often considered leftist, representing the interests of a progressive, urban elite and this at a time when many EU Member States witness a move to the right side of the political spectrum (Hanretty, 2011; Sehl, Simon and Schroeder, 2020b). Second, commercial media remain fierce critics of public broadcasters. In the 1990s, commercial broadcasters protested against public broadcasters' activities in entertainment, sports programming and advertising. Nowadays, mainly newspaper publishers challenge public broadcasters' online news services. These are too much text oriented, for free and thus competing with the development of a paid news offer (Donders et al., 2019). It is clear that economic uncertainty intensifies the tensions between public broadcasters and commercial media. Criticism is sometimes incorrect, sometimes justified in light of the public interest objectives achieved, and sometimes – albeit often ignored in scientific literature – reasonable. Some public broadcasters engage in commercial behaviour that is not adding to the realisation of their public remit. It might bring in revenues, but undermines the universality, quality or trustworthiness of their offer and at the same time it harms pluralism and diversity in the rest of the market. Third, public broadcasters struggle with the issue of representation. They have the task to strengthen identity (Van den Bulck, 2001) and reflect the diversity within the nation (Horsti and Hultén, 2011). Admittedly, this is an area of ideological struggle in many, if not most, European countries. While minorities often do not feel represented by the public broadcaster, the 'majority' takes issue with political correctness and a perceived over-representation of certain groups in the population. That does not only concern ethnic minorities, but can also relate to countries with distinct regions that hold political power and exhibit some sort of national(ist) identity on their own (see, among others, Ramsey, 2015 on Northern Ireland). Public broadcasters seem to be between a rock and a hard place here. Even in case they perform well, providing impartial information, explaining the context to complex issues and confronting diverse opinions, this will still be perceived as biased by some groups in society. In case they under-perform, stimulating polarised discussions and refraining from fact-checking (Cushion and Lewis, 2017), they will be perceived as biased still. They are being labelled as 'mainstream media', #msm. In that sense, living up to the aspirations of the Reithian remit might still be the wisest and also most desirable thing to do. Fourth, although Public Service Media stands for public service beyond radio and television broadcasting, the transition to a provider of media in the public interest across platforms and via multiple devices is a difficult one. Keeping up with technological evolutions has become a mission impossible. We will discuss these issues further in Chapters 13 and 14; the issue of technological developments and public broadcasters' strategy in that area are discussed also separately in Chapter 12.

The increasing value of alternative media

Faced with the failure of public broadcasters in many European countries and the perception of a part of the audience that their public broadcaster is actually not theirs, 'not mainstream' or alternative media, including professional non-profit initiatives, community media and activist media projects could be seen as a viable option to achieve the public interest in media. There is a vast amount of literature on these kinds of media. Discussing that field of scholarly work in an exhaustive manner is beyond the scope of this book. However, some consideration of it is interesting also in relation to Public Service Media's key objective to strengthen political, social, cultural and civic citizenship (see Chapter 4).

While it remains difficult to define non-profit or alternative media, there is a wide agreement among scholars that these challenge the concentration of media power. They are counter-hegemonic. They approach people beyond their status as collective publics (Lievrouw, 2011). Atton defines alternative media as media

> that bypass the usual channels of commercial production and distribution, and that are most often organised and produced by 'ordinary' people, local communities and communities of interest. It is primarily interested in social and cultural practices that enable people to participate directly in the organisation, production and distribution of their own media, and how these media are used to construct and represent identity and community, as well as to present forms of information and knowledge that are underrepresented, marginalised or ignored by other, more dominant media.
>
> (Atton, 2015: 1)

The purpose of alternative media is twofold. First, the idea of alternative media is to impact those involved in making, contributing to output or being in a very close relationship to it. Second, it wants to have a wider social and political impact related to 'public-formation, group representation, political deliberation, contestation and social movement formation/mobilisation' (Mowbray, 2015: 22). Community media are a particular manifestation, focussing on the local. UNESCO (2001: iii) defines community radio as 'a medium that gives voice to the voiceless, that serves as the mouthpiece of the marginalised and is at the heart of communication and democratic processes within societies'. It is about empowerment of citizens (Cammaerts, 2009: 636).

Alternative media are not only a reaction against the mainstream (Forde, 2011: 2). Rodríguez, Ferron and Shamas (2014: 151) consider alternative media a superior model compared to mainstream media which 'existed in a universe of advertisers, target audiences, and a continuous commodification of leisure and information'. Parallel, and 'in a separate sphere, social movements and media activists appropriated media technologies, divorced them from their corporate originators, and re-invented technology's uses in ways not intended by the designers'.

While I am not per se sure that alternative media are always superior, they do allow for a 'certain amount of room for manoeuvre for alternative democratic media strategies' (Downey and Fenton, 2003: 186). They are definitely different from mainstream media and in some contexts they might offer an interesting possibility to inform citizens, confront them with a diversity of viewpoints and to create an understanding of society and its complexity (see also Deuze and Wtischge, 2020). The big issue with a lot of initiatives is, usually, the lack of scale to add to informed citizenship, social cohesion, cultural awareness, and so on, at a wider scale. The techniques of alternative media (in terms of inclusiveness, shared ownership, etc.) often take the upper hand, also in scientific literature. Uzelman talks about the 'determinism of technique' whereby 'particular techniques are assumed to have effects (generally positive) independent of the social relations in which they are embedded or the purposes to which they are directed' (quoted in Mowbray, 2015: 22). Moreover, while models of shared ownership are interesting from a theoretical point of view and might work in relatively small initiatives, it can also stand in the way of professionalisation. Finally, there is an issue in terms of sustainable funding. A lot of alternative media initiatives depend on a variety of revenue streams, including advertising, crowdfunding, donations from international organisations or civil society and payment by consumers. In several countries such as Egypt one consciously limits revenue from advertising as especially big advertisers are part of the system of political parallelism (Sakr, 2016). There are close ties between political, media and advertiser elites that alternative media want to escape from. Payment by consumers is often not so evident in countries with a low GDP. Crowd-sourcing and funding from other donors can be rather volatile. In case the European Union can reach a political consensus on the necessity of independent media in each and every Member State of the European, it could be considered to create additional funding and also training possibilities for non-profit initiatives in specific Member States, for example, during and several years after the conclusion of an Article 7 procedure. On the positive side, the digital media environment offers possibilities for alternative media to achieve more impact on society. For example, there has been an increase in citizen journalists (Forde, 2011: 96ff). Lievrouw (2011: 2) says

> websites, mobile telephones, digital photography, video, and audio, blogs, wikis, file-sharing systems, social media, and open-source software all permit social groups with diverse interests to build and sustain communities, gain visibility and voice, present alternative or marginal views, produce and share their own do-it-yourself information sources, and resist, talk back, or otherwise confront dominant media culture, politics, and power.

In this environment, alternative media can grow, but also impact more than before mainstream media (Lievrouw, 2011). Several authors have nuanced this idea, particularly when alternative media are activist. The 'cell phone revolution' or 'Twitter revolution' ideas, according to Rodríguez, Ferron and Shamas (2014: 153), 'erase historical contexts and the passion(s) of politics, as technology becomes equated with political action'. The optimism on technology as a driver of alternative media should be moderated to some extent also when taking into account that citizen journalism and blogging has been captured by market forces too, on the one hand, and the negative side effects of platformisation of media industries at large, on the other (see Chapter 2), there is a definite opportunity to complement or challenge fully commercial media outlets and to contribute to equity and stronger citizenship in society.

In countries that can be classified as competitive authoritarianist or that are showing high levels of political parallelism for decades in a row, one should contemplate on the idea to strengthen alternative media, to professionalise them and lift them up to the level of reach of mass media or at least a reach that is relevant. Building trust on the basis of local initiatives could enable the subsequent coverage of more abstract, nation-wide issues related to politics, economics and society at large. The European Broadcasting Union could in fact play a role here, but cutting loose some members to the benefit of competing alternative media has potential diplomatic, but also financial (membership fee) repercussions.

Conclusions

It would be wrong to assume that media typologies explain fully the state of play of Public Service Media in Europe. Public broadcasters transpose the common values of Public Service Media within the wider context of more stringent policies (whether market-oriented or steered by an increasing desire of governments to control public broadcasters) in a variety of ways. When relating to audiences, other public institutions, competitors, politicians, themselves as an organisation, public broadcasters show vastly different behaviours. For some audience ratings are more important than for others. There is also a noteworthy difference in audience ratings with public broadcasters such as those operating in Iceland, Germany, Finland, the United Kingdom, Norway, Denmark, Italy, Sweden, the Netherlands, and so on, heaving high market shares with over 35 per cent of the audiences watching their TV channels. On the other side are public broadcasters from Lithuania, Bulgaria, Greece, Romania, and so on. These have difficulties to attract 10 per cent of the viewers (EBU, 2017: 5). Most public broadcasters offer online services such as simulcast or catch-up video. However, only 34 per cent of public broadcasters offer full episodes of programmes on YouTube, and a mere 35 per cent is active on radio streaming services such as Spotify. The duration of online offers differs significantly as well. Seventy-four per cent of European public broadcasters offer content online up to one month after initial broadcast. Others go beyond that period (EBU, 2017: 30-31), espe-cially for content types such as culture, historical programming, documentary, and so on. Some public broadcasters are more active when it comes to online media. For example, the BBC is known to invest heavily in its websites and dedicated content for online. In 2017 it announced strengthening its online content offering for children. Other public broadcasters such as the different German, the Swiss, and also the Irish public broadcasters, are more reluctant to enter this area or face more restrictions doing so. The Swiss and German public broadcasters are exemplary cases of how public broadcasters' online expansion can be curbed through the adoption of lists of new media services they cannot offer, a word limit in text articles, the requirement that new services must be related to existing radio and television services, and so on. Whereas in most markets tensions between public broadcasters and commercial media can be quite high, some witness the emergence of collaborations between both parties to further joint interests in an internationalising media landscape. In Belgium, but also in Sweden and even in France, the latter being a rather straightforward example of a polarised pluralism media model, you see the emergence of collaborative initiatives. The joint video-on-demand platform Salto, operated by among others France Télévisions and commercial broadcaster TF1, is a concrete example. Some public broadcasters spend a lot of money on external production. The United Kingdom and Belgium are examples of countries that impose rather ambitious quotas for independent production on their public broadcasters. These invest up to 20 per cent of their programming budget on independent production. In other countries, such as Ireland, Sweden, Denmark and France, this figure does not exceed 10 per cent and most production budgets are spent in-house. In terms of funding, the variety across Europe is enormous with the Scandinavian public broadcasters, the Swiss, the Austrian, British and German ones being funded rather generously. Not surprisingly, Central and Eastern European public broadcasters receive less money from the state (Raats, Van den Bulck and d'Haenens, 2016). This is only a snapshot of what public broadcasters do or don't do, how much money they get, audience ratings, budget expenditure, and so on. An in-depth comparative perspective would show an even greater diversity.

Whereas a shared set of values underlies Public Service Media across Europe, the practice of what public broadcasters do and the context within which they work are in fact very diverse and more diverse than political economy models of media make us believe. That is in itself not problematic as public broadcasters are embedded within a specific historical, economic, political and socio-cultural setting. What might be more challenging is the observation that the highly utopian idea of what public broadcasters ought to be does not necessarily correspond with what is happening in practice. Aspirational goals can in such a case be (ab)used to pretend that all is well with Public Service Media in Europe. As illustrated above that is certainly not the case. At the same time, certain political conditions might from the outset impede the full achievement of Public Service Media. In reality there can be glimpses of contributions to political, social, cultural and civic citizenship in spite of this though.

More European action is needed to strengthen Public Service Media. So far, the European Union's most active role in this area is to be situated in the field of competition law. The European Commission checks whether the State aid (subsidies, license fee) given to public broadcasters by EU Member States is not market distortive. In so doing, the European Commission has asked countries to be more specific about what it is they expect their public broadcasters to do, to install independent monitoring of performance and to ensure funding does not exceed the amount of money necessary to deliver the entrusted services (Donders, 2012). Whereas the role of the European Commission has had positive effects on public broadcasters' governance, its goal is essentially to limit public broadcasters' activities. There is no balancing act from parts in the European Commission that are more concerned with strengthening democracy, journalism that informs citizens and independence of the media in general. One can point at Article 7 procedures that imply the European Commission challenging a specific Member State when it is not adhering to the rule of law, including respect for press freedom. Such a procedure is in place against Poland. However, the procedure is only used in highly exceptional circumstances and moving slowly. That is a major weakness, largely caused by Member States' opposition against European interference in this arena.[1]

Note

1   The sections on media systems are to some extent based on an earlier publication (see Donders, 2019b) in the edited collection *Transnational Media: Concepts and Cases* (published with Wiley Blackwell in 2019, edited by Suman Mishra and Rebbeca Kern-Stone).

References

Ariazza, K.I. and Nord, L.W. (2014). Public service media under pressure: Comparing government policies in Spain and Sweden 2006–2012. *Javnost – The Public*, *21*(1), 71–84.

Atton, C. (2015). Introduction: Problems and positions in alternative and community media. In C. Atton (ed.), *The Routledge Companion to Alternative and Community Media* (pp. 1–18). London: Routledge.

Becker, J. (2014). Russia and the new authoritarians. Retrieved from https://demokratizatsiya.pub/archives/22_2_F1T0164470351334.pdf (accessed October 2020).

Burgelman, J.-C. (1990). *Omroep en politiek in België. Het Belgisch audio-visuele bestel als inzet en resultante van de naoorlogse partijpolitieke machtsstrategieën (1940–1960)*. Brussels: BRT. [*Broadcaster and politics in Belgium. The Belgian audiovisual set-up as the stake and outcome of post-war party political power strategies (1940–1960)*].

Cammaerts, B. (2009). Community radio in the West: A legacy of struggle for survival in a state and capitalist controlled media environment. *International Communication Gazette*, *71*(8), 635–654.

Castells, M. and Arsenault, A.H. (2008). The structure and dynamics of global multimedia business networks. *International Journal of Communication*, *2*, 707–748.

Castro-Herrero, L., Nir, L. and Skovsgaard, M. (2017). Bridging gaps in cross-cutting media exposure: The role of public service broadcasting. *Political Communication*, *35*(4), 542–565.

Cushion, S. and Lewis, J. (2017). Impartiality, statistical titforthats and the construction of balance: UK television news reporting of the 2016 EU referendum campaign. *European Journal of Communication*, *32*(2), 208–223.

D'Arma, A. (2019). Public service media in Italy: Troubled RAI in a troubled country. In E. Połońska and C. Beckett (eds), *Public Service Broadcasting and Media Systems in Troubled Democracies* (pp. 111–128). Basingstoke: Palgrave Macmillan.

De Smaele, H. (1999). The applicability of Western media models on the Russian media system. *European Journal of Communication*, *14*(2), 173–189.

Deuze, M. and Witschge, T. (2020). *Beyond Journalism*. New York: Wiley.

Donders, K. (2012). *Public Service Media and Policy in Europe*. Basingstoke: Palgrave Macmillan.

Donders, K., Van den Bulck, H. and Raats, T. (2019). The politics of pleasing: A critical analysis of multistakeholderism in public service media policies in Flanders. *Media, Culture & Society, 41*(3), 347-366.

Dovbysh, O. and Belyuga, T. (2020). Whose voices and what values? State grants for significant public content in the Russian media model. In P. Savage, M. Medina and G.F. Lowe (eds), *Universalism in Public Service Media: RIPE@2019* (pp. 151-173). Göteborg; Nordicom.

Downey J. and Fenton, N. (2003). New media, counter publicity and the public sphere. *New Media & Society, 5*(2), 185-202.

Dunai, M. (2014). How Hungary's government shaped public media to its mould. Retrieved from www.reuters.com/article/us-hungary-media-insight-idusbrea1i08c20140219 (accessed October 2020).

Dyson, K. (1985). The politics of cable and satellite broadcasting: Some West European comparisons. In R. Kuhn (ed.), *Broadcasting and Politics in Western Europe* (pp. 152–171). London: Routledge.

Dyson, K. and Humphreys, P. (1988). The context of new media politics in Western Europe. In K. Dyson and P. Humphreys, with R. Negrine and J.-P. Simon, *Broadcasting and new Media Policies in Western Europe* (pp. 1–61). London: Routledge.

EBU (2017). *PSM Barometer.* Geneva: EBU.

EBU (2018). *Funding of public service media.* Geneva: EBU.

Esser, F. and Umbricht, A. (2013). Competing models of journalism? Political affairs coverage in US, British, German, Swiss, French and Italian newspapers. *Journalism, 14*(8) 989-1007.

Fernández Viso, A. and Fernández Alonso, I. (2019). Political interference in the Spanish and Catalan public service media: Attempts to reform and resistance to change (2006-2017). In E. Połońska and C. Beckett (eds), *Public Service Broadcasting and Media Systems in Troubled European Democracies* (pp. 155–176). Basingstoke: Palgrave Macmillan.

Forde, S. (2011). *Challenging the News: The Journalism of Alternative and Community media.* Basingstoke: Palgrave Macmillan.

Freedman, D. (2008). *The Politics of Media Policy.* Cambridge: Polity Press.

Garnham, N. (1990). *Capitalism and Communication: Global Culture and the Economics of Information.* London: Sage.

Hallin, D.C. and Mancini, P. (2004). *Comparing Media Systems: Three Models of Media and Politics.* Cambridge: Cambridge University Press.

Hanretty, C. (2011). *Public Broadcasting and Political Interference.* New York: Routledge.

Hardy, J. (2012). Comparing media systems. In F. Esser and T. Hanitzsch (eds), *The Handbook of Comparative Communication Research* (pp. 185-206). London: Routledge.

Hesmondhalgh, D. (2019). *The Cultural Industries* (4th ed.). London, Thousand Oaks, New Delhi, Singapore: Sage.

Hitchens, L. (2006). *Broadcasting Pluralism and Diversity: A Comparative Study of Policy and Regulation.* Oxford: Hart Publishing.

Horsti, K. and Hultén, G. (2011). Directing diversity: Managing cultural diversity media policies in Finnish and Swedish public service broadcasting. *International Journal of Cultural Studies, 14*(2), 209–227.

Humphreys, P. (2012). A political scientist's contribution to the comparative study of media systems in Europe: A response to Hallin and Mancini. In N. Just and M. Puppis (eds), *Trends in Communications Policy Research* (pp. 157–176). Bristol: Intellect.

Iosifidis, P. (2008). Public television policies in Europe:The cases of France and Greece. *International Journal of Media and Cultural Politics*, 4(3), 349–367.

Iosofidis, P. and Papathanassopoulos, S. (2019). Greek ERT: State of public service broadcaster?. In E. Połońska and C. Beckett (eds), *Public Service Broadcasting and Media Systems in Troubled European Democracies* (pp. 129–153). Basingstoke: Palgrave Macmillan.

Jakubowicz, K. (2001). Rude awakening: Social and media change in Central and Eastern Europe. *Javnost – The Public*, 8(4), 59–80.

Jakubowicz, K. (2012). Post-communist political systems and media freedom and independence. In J. Downey and S. Mihelj (eds), *Central and Eastern European Media in Comparative Perspective: Politics, Economy and Culture*. London: Ashgate.

Katsirea, I. (2008). *Public Broadcasting and European Law: A Comparative Examination of Public Service Obligations in Six Member States*. New York: Wolters Kluwer International.

Kuhn, R. (2019). Public service media in France. In E. Połońska and C. Beckett (eds), *Public Service Media in Troubled Democracies* (pp. 69–87). Basingstoke: Palgrave Macmillan.

Levitsky, S. and Way, L. (2010). *Competitive Authoritarianism: Hybrid Regimes after the Cold War*. Cambridge: Cambridge University Press.

Lievrouw, L. (2011). *Alternative and Activist New Media*. London: Polity.

Lowe, G.F., Berg, C. and Nissen, C.S. (2011). Size matters for TV broadcasting policy. In G.F Lowe and C.S. Nissen (eds), *Small Among Giants: Television Broadcasting in Smaller Countries* (pp. 21–41). Nordicom: Göteborg.

Mangani, A. and Tarrini, E. (2018). Social pluralism in public and private television broadcasting. *Javnost – The Public*, 25(3), 282–297.

McChesney, R. (1999). *Rich Media, Poor Democracy*. New York: New Press.

Mihelj, S. and Downey, J. (2012). Introduction: Comparing media systems in Central and Eastern Europe: politics, economics and culture. In J. Downey and S. Mihelj (eds), *Central and Eastern European Media in Comparative Perspective* (pp. 1–14). London: Ashgate.

Mowbray, M. (2015). Alternative logics? Parsing the literature on alternative media. In C. Atton (ed.), *The Routledge Companion to Alternative and Community Media* (pp. 21–31). London: Routledge.

Noam, E. (1991). *Television in Europe*. New York: Oxford University Press.

O'Malley, T. (2009). Introduction. In T. O'Malley and J. Jones (eds), *The Peacock Committee and UK Broadcasting Policy*. Basingstoke: Palgrave Macmillan.

Perusko, Z. (2013). Rediscovering the Mediterranean characteristics of the Croatian media system. *East European Politics & Societies*, 27(4), 709–726.

Puppis, M. (2009). Media regulation in small states. *International Communication Gazette*, 71(1-2), 7–17.

Raats, T., Van den Bulck, H. and d'Haenens, L. (2016). Inleiding. Een VRT voor morgen, of geen VRT meer morgen? In T. Raats, H. Van den Bulck and L. d'Haenens (eds), *Een VRT voor morgen, of geen VRT meer morgen? De publieke omroep tussen politiek, publiek, partners en concurrenten* (pp. 9–26). Kalmthout: Pelckmans.

Ramsey, P. (2015). Broadcasting to reflect 'life and culture as we know it': Media policy, devolution and the case of Northern Ireland. *Media, Culture & Society*, 37(8), 1193–1209.

Rodríguez, C., Ferron, B. and Shamas, K. (2014). Four challenges in the field of alternative, radical and citizens' media research. *Media, Culture & Society*, 36(2), 150–166.

Sakr, N. (2016). Survival or sustainability? Contributions of innovatively managed news ventures to the future of Egyptian journalism. *Journal of Media Business Studies*, 13(1), 45–59.

Sehl, A., Simon, F.M. and Schroeder, R. (2020b). The populist campaigns against European public service media: Hot air or existential threat. *International Communication Gazette*. Retrieved from https://doi.org/10.1177/17480485209 39868 (accessed October 2020).

Siebert, F., Peterson, T.B. and Schramm, W. (1956). *Four Theories of the Press: The Authoritarian, Libertarian, Social Responsibility, and Soviet Communist Concepts of What the Press Should Be and Do*. Urbana: University of Illinois Press.

Syvertsen, T., Enli, G., Mjøs, O.M. and Moe, H. (2014). *The Media Welfare State: Nordic Media in the Digital Era*. Ann Arbor: University of Michigan Press.

Terzis, G. (ed.) (2007). *European Media Governance: National and Regional Dimensions*. Bristol: Intellect.

UNESCO (2001). *Community Radio Handbook*. Paris: UNESCO.

Van den Bulck, H. (2001). Public service television and national identity as a project of modernity: The example of Flemish television. *Media, Culture & Society*, 23(1), 53–69.

Van den Bulck, H. and Donders, K. (2014). Of discourses, stakeholders and advocacy coalitions in media policy: Tracing negotiations towards the new management contract of Flemish public broadcaster VRT. *European Journal of Communication*, 29(1), 83–99.

Vladisavljević, N. (2016). Competitive authoritarianism and popular protest: Evidence from Serbia under Milošević. *International Political Science Review*, 37(1), 36–50.

7   Weak European cultural versus strong economic policies

Market integration as first objective of European policies in media

Until the 1970s, there was no European media market. Most EU Member States kept in place broadcast monopolies and those countries, such as the United Kingdom and Italy, that allowed some level of competition to occur insisted on their sovereignty in this area. Things changed throughout the 1970s and 1980s. Several events ensued. More countries started with the liberalisation of their broadcasting markets. France, rather revolutionarily, even decided to privatise its main public television channel TF1 – to date, it remains one of the biggest commercial broadcasting players in the French market. Technological change allowed cable and satellite as commercially viable services. Neoliberalism as an ideology infiltrated political environments in the US and Europe. And the European Commission itself wanted media to become part of the market integration project (Pauwels and Donders, 2013).

Media as an economic good

In 1974, the European Court of Justice declared television was an economic good and hence subject to the rules of the EU internal market. Answering to a preliminary question of cable operator Guiseppte Sacchi (through a small tribunal court in Biella), the Court ruled that RAI's advertising monopoly at the time was not per se illegitimate, but rejected the claim that television was a non-economic and purely cultural activity (ECJ, 1974). This stance was repeated in the 1980 *Debauve* case where the Court went a step further saying discrimination of broadcasting signals from another Member State because of their original was illegal. In all other subsequent cases, the Court did not accept Member States' claim that their authority in the cultural policy domain made discriminatory measures acceptable. Its main argument was that the pursued policies went beyond the stated objectives of diversity and pluralism. The *Sacchi* case thus marks the official start of European intervention in media on the basis of the internal market project (Harcourt, 2002).

The European Commission took matters forward with the publication of its 1984 'Green Paper on the establishment of the common market for broadcasting, especially by satellite and cable'. Not the Directorate General ('DG') for audiovisual matters, but the DG for the internal market was the responsible author. Essentially, the Green Paper proposed to harmonise fragmented broadcasting policies in the EU and in so doing allow for the emergence of an integrated television market (Michalis, 2007). That was seen as essential to become more competitive, also vis-à-vis other trade blocks such as the US and Japan, as was expressed later on in the 1994 *Bangemann* report on 'Europe and the global information society' and is in fact still a core concern underlying the EU's Digital Single Market policies.

The Television without Frontiers directive and its successors

The Television without Frontiers directive was adopted in 1989 (Council, 1989) and a landmark in the liberalisation of European television markets. Two principles lie at the core of the directive. First, the country of origin principle, which provides that companies delivering television services are captured by the rules in the country of television transmission. That concretely means that a Member State such as Denmark cannot block a television signal coming from Spain even if that signal does not comply with specific Danish rules on advertising. There should thus be a mutual recognition between Member States of the EU that the minimum regulation that they apply in the area of television is sufficient. Reversed discrimination on companies established in the own jurisdiction is allowed, but cannot be used to impose stricter rules on incoming signals. Only in exceptional cases, for example when the protection of minors or issues related to hate speech are at stake, can deviations be accepted. Second, all Member States have to transpose the minimum rules of the directive into their own national legislation. These rules relate to free movement, advertising, protection of minors, quotas for European works and independently produced programmes, and so on. Some rules are largely economic in nature, others are clearly oriented at cultural objectives. Admittedly, the rules related to establishing the internal market are easier to enforce than those dealing with the protection of domestic and European culture. For example, the quotas have to be complied with where practicable and by appropriate means.

Several authors have argued the directive immediately made clear the inherent tension between economic and cultural objectives in audiovisual policy-making, according to most of them to the detriment of the latter set of goals (Pauwels, 1995; Levy, 1999; Harcourt, 2007; Michalis, 2014). *Dirigiste* and liberal approaches conflicted with each other, the former arguing for a more prudent, protectionist and cultural policy, the latter for full-fledged market liberalisation. Moreover, and related to the cultural rationale of European audiovisual policies, there was the disagreement between Member States of the EU and the European Commission on these policies being concerned with the creation of a European identity or with protecting the diversity of distinct national and subnational culture. Wolton (1990: 92, emphasis added) said:

> En réalité, les projets de télévision Européenne sont conçus dans deux perspectives finalement antagonistes et qui renvoient bien à la contradiction dans laquelle se trouve actuellement l'Europe. Ils sont d'une part pensés comme un outil de communication pour rapprocher les différents peoples d'Europe et d'autre part comme le moyen de refléter les différentes cultures. *Mais il faut choisir. Ou la télévision est plutôt un facteur d'intégration sociale et culturelle comme elle l'a presque toujours été dans tous les pays du monde ou elle est un facteur d'expression de différences.* Mais il faur toute la cauistique des eurocrates et des hommes politiques pour dire que les deux sont complémentaires. Cette complémentarité est idéalististe au sens ou tout sépare ces deux dimensions, l'intégration européenne et l'identité culturelle.

These tensions remained in the subsequent revisions of the Television without Frontiers directive in 1999, 2007 and 2018. In 1999, Member States got the right to list a number of major events (societal, cultural, sports) to ensure these would not disappear behind pay walls. Some aspects of the country of origin principle were clarified further. The 2007 revision was more far-going and resulted in the directive being renamed the Audiovisual Media Services Directive. Coping with the technological innovations in the sector, the objective was to subject all 'television-like' services (Sabbach, 2005) to the directive's regulation, including thus linear and non-linear services in so far these were under the editorial responsibility of a provider. For linear services the main rules stayed in place, albeit that advertising rules were relaxed a bit. For non-linear services more lenient rules were in place (Valcke and Lievens, 2009). For example, quotas were replaced by a due prominence requirement for European works in video-on-demand catalogues (Valcke and Ausloos, 2014). The revision was criticised mainly for not being future-proof. Hettich (2008: 1449) says 'these new rules seem still inspired by an old media environment' and 'they hardly try to address phenomena like YouTube or Tudou, YouTube's larger Shanghai clone, and their consequences on the future provision of TV-like services'. He could not have been more right. The, for now, last revision in 2018 included video sharing platforms such as Facebook and YouTube. These are captured by some rules, notably those related to the protection of minors and hate speech. Responding to criticism on the lack of a level playing-field between legacy media and platforms, on the one hand, and the concern about harmful content being published on platforms, on the other, a light-touch regulatory framework for video sharing platforms was added to the directive. Most of the rules will have to be designed further on the basis of self- and co-regulatory action between media regulators, EU Member States and platforms (Council and European Parliament, 2018).

In short, market integration at the European level effectively ended public broadcasting monopolies. It was contested from its very beginning until today, opposing those taking a more interventionist and a liberal approach, those sticking with broadcasting regulation and those arguing for more future-proof policy recipes, and those supporting more Europe versus those defending EU Member States' sovereignty in the cultural policy domain. I will show that these tensions are not only apparent in the area of State aid control of public broadcasters' funding, but also a shaping force of the actual application of the rules by the European Commission.

First attacks on public broadcasters in Europe

The Television without Frontiers and Audiovisual Media Services directives should not be seen in isolation from public broadcasters. The latter also have to comply with these provisions. But also the 1989 Television without Frontiers directive made liberalisation and the related market thinking an unstoppable force throughout Europe. Contrary to what some might believe, that was not a top-down phenomenon. Bigger Member States such as the United Kingdom and Germany were very much in favour it and most EU Member States were rather successful in adopting some sort of controlled liberalisation. They embraced a free market with limits, allowing private broadcasters to grow and reap the benefits of liberalisation in a market that was still rather nationally or even regionally organised. Countries thus combined European market integration policies with national industrial policies. That is a story of developments in Western and Northern Europe mainly (Donders and Van den Bulck, 2016). In Southern Europe the introduction of commercialism in broadcasting was more disruptive, often ill-managed and resulted in even more instead of less politicisation of public broadcasters (Papathanasopoulos, 2007).

After the liberalisation of European media markets, the competition rules became more relevant for public broadcasters across Europe. First, 'attacks' on the position of public broadcasters did not happen within the framework of European State aid rules (cf. infra), but on the basis of anti-trust rules. Indeed, in 1987, Screensport filed a complaint with the European competition authorities, arguing the European Broadcasting Union's joint acquisition of sports rights constituted an unfair collusion. Article 101(1) of the Treaty on the Functioning of the European Union prohibits 'all agreements between undertakings, decisions by associations of undertakings and concerted practices which may affect trade between Member States and which have as their object or effect the prevention, restriction or distortion of competition within the common market'. Satellite company Screensport used this article to argue that the European Broadcasting Union's acquisition of sports rights on behalf of its members amounted to an agreement prohibited by Article 101(1) of the Treaty. Its complaint marked the beginning of the much-researched *EBU/Eurovision* cases, in which the European Commission issued two decisions in 1991 and 2000, both of which were later on rejected by the General Court (1996; 2002; see also Coates and Sauter, 2007: 1505–1510). Simplifying things a lot, the European Commission essentially held that the *Eurovision* system was in line with the internal market rules and moreover also had some public interest considerations at its roots. The General Court disagreed, criticising the European Commission for not sufficiently legitimising how it came to its decisions. After a few years, the case was not pursued further by commercial competitors though. The sports rights market has changed dramatically and it is clear to many companies that the *Eurovision* system has had its best time (Van Rompuy and Donders, 2013).

European State aid control as a friend and foe of Public Service Media

It is only after paving the way under anti-trust law that private companies challenge the competitive position of public broadcasters under State aid law. Telecinco files the first State aid complaint against the dual (i.e. a combination of commercial and public) funding in March 1992 (Court of First Instance, 1998). The company started its activities in 1990. In July 1993, SIC, a Portuguese broadcaster (that started activities in October 1992), raised objections against the funding of Portuguese public broadcaster RTP (Court of First Instance, 2000). Soon after these two complaints, other companies in Italy, France, the United Kingdom and Germany followed.

The illegality and admissibility of State aid under European law

State aid rules determine that the use of subsidies, tax exemptions or benefits, and other types of selective financial gain for undertakings that have an impact on State's budgets are prohibited. Article 107(1) of the Treaty on the Functioning of the European Union reads:

> Save as otherwise provided in this Treaty, any aid granted by a Member State or through State resources in any form whatsoever which distorts of threatens to distort competition by favouring certain undertakings or the production of certain goods shall, insofar as it affects trade between Member States, be incompatible with the common market.

There is thus a negative presumption against the use of State aid (Friederiszick, Röller, and Verouden, 2005: 3; Crocioni, 2006: 90). Measures qualify as State aid provided there is an aid, a selective advantage and a(n) (potential) impact on competition and trade. Related to public broadcasting, particularly elements one and two have been contested. First, in case of license fees one could argue there is no direct impact on government resources and, hence, no use of State resources. The European Commission has consistently dismissed the issue and no Member State has dared to take it to court. Nevertheless, the German Länder insisted in the European Commission's decision on the funding of ARD and ZDF that the amendment to 'the current financing regime for public service broadcasters cannot be understood as having accepted the Commission's qualification of the license fee funding as State aid' (European Commission, 2007: §323). Moreover, several scholars have stressed that direct payment by citizens, organised by independent collecting bodies, does not impact the State's budget in any way (Koenig and Haratsch, 2003; Arhold, 2007: 152; Santa Maria, 2007: 19; Katsirea, 2008: 333f). Others have backed the European Commission's stance though, arguing that government control of 'imputability' to the State is the key element in deciding on the existence of State aid. Second, several countries have argued that the mere compensation of a public task cannot be considered a selective advantage. That argument, while never having been accepted in a public broadcasting case, is supported by a massive amount of case law and found fertile ground in the *Ferring* and *Altmark* cases. In 2001, the General Court said the compensation of a public service task cannot be considered State aid. Later on, in 2003, the Court nuanced this a bit in *Altmark*, saying that certain conditions need to be complied with in order for a measure to be considered a mere compensation of a public service cost. One of these conditions is that the cost has to be made by an efficiently run undertaking, preferably granted with the public service assignment on the basis of a tendering procedure. The European Commission has always ruled that public broadcasters do not comply with this particular condition and can hence not benefit from the exception regime of *Altmark*. This has been criticised for being a too rigid application of the *Altmark* conditions (see Donders, 2012). The idea here is not to go too far in legalistic analyses, but it should be clear from this that the State aid regime is a tough regime and that exceptions are to be interpreted strictly.

When a measure is considered State aid, many exceptions are in place to escape prohibition. For the funding of public broadcasters there are, in principle, two exceptions that could apply. First, the cultural exception of Article 107(3)d of the Treaty on the Functioning of the European Union. Second, the exception for the funding of so-called services of general economics interest (also referred to as 'SGEI') in Article 106(2) of the Treaty. The European Commission interprets the State aid rules in cases concerning public broadcasters on the basis of Article 106(2) (Donders, 2015).

Article 106(2) provides that while competition rules apply to both public and private undertakings entrusted with the delivery of services of general economic interest, the application of these rules cannot obstruct the delivery of services of general economic interest.

> Undertakings entrusted with the operation of services of general economic interest or having the character of a revenue-producing monopoly shall be subject to the rules contained in this Treaty, in particular to the rules on competition, in so far as the application of such rules does not obstruct the performance, in law, or in fact, of the particular tasks assigned to them. The development of trade must not be affected to such an extent as would be contrary to the interests of the Community.

While the Treaty does not contain a definition of these services, they are generally assumed to be important for and open to all consumers (Gromnicka, 2005: 492; Nicolaides, Kekelekis and Buyskes, 2005: 48). The discretion of the European Commission to define what services of general economics are is limited to checking for manifest errors. That means it can only dispute a Member State's definition of such a service when it is abundantly clear a service is by no means contributing to the achievement of some general interest considerations. It is thus essentially up to Member States to decide on the definition of a service of general economic interest (General Court, 2008 in the *Bupa* case). The European Commission, however, in checking for manifest errors is asking for a definition that is as clear as possible, emphasises the need for a proper entrustment of the public tasks to the provider and subjects State aid to a proportionality test (Grespan, 2008). In so doing, it overcomes the 'uneasy' space between State aid to services of general economic interest and the objectives of the European internal market. The delivery of high-quality services of general economic interest, as well as oversight by the European Commission and courts, is ensured (Szyszczak, 2004; Anestis and Drakakis, 2006). In this regard, Buendia Sierra (2006: 543) commented that Article 106(2) does not solve the apparent spread between the continuing delivery of services of general economic interest, on the one hand, and safeguarding fair and government-free competition, on the other. Rather, the article captures 'the main point of contact between two tectonic plates moving in opposite direction'. This general remark will also hold for the application of Article 106(2) to public broadcasting.

Broadcasting Communication 2001 and 2009

While the funding of most services of general economic interest is being dealt with on the basis of a generic Article 106(2) framework, public broadcasters 'benefit' from a special regime. The so-called 'Communication on the application of the State aid rules to Public Service Broadcasting' (original version published in 2001; amended in 2009) is used by the European Commission in State aid cases concerning public broadcasting. It is thus a soft law instrument that clarifies how the European Commission will implement the State aid rules in public broadcasting cases. It is not binding for Member States, but, as I will show later, the Communication has harmonising effects on Member States' Public Service Media regulation.

The Communication, which lists three criteria funding to public broadcasters, has to comply with:

1. 'the service in question must be a service of general economic interest and clearly defined as such by the Member State' (*definition*);
2. 'the undertaking in question must be explicitly entrusted by the Member State with the provision of that service' (*entrustment and control*);
3. 'the application of the competition rules of the Treaty (in this case, the ban on State aid) must not obstruct the performance of particular tasks assigned to the undertaking and the exemption from such rules must not affect the development of trade to an extent that would be contrary to

the interests of the Community' (*proportionality and transparency*) (European Commission, 2001: §29).

To cope with vivid criticism on public broadcasters' expansion to new media markets, the European Commission adopted a revised version of the 2001 Broadcasting Communication on 2 July 2009. The basis of the Communication remains Article 106(2) of the Treaty on the Functioning of the European Union. As mentioned by Held and Kliemann (2012: 38), 'the 2009 Communication to a large extent confirms and clarifies the rules of 2001', particularly with regard to the entrustment and proportionality conditions. However, the most important alteration of the Communication resulted in particularly heated discussions between the European Commission and the Member States. This alteration relates to the introduction of the so-called 'Amsterdam test' (referring to the so-called Amsterdam Protocol on public broadcasting, cf. infra) or public value test.

According to the 2009 Communication, Member States need to assess to what extent significantly new services contribute to the social, cultural and democratic needs of society, on the one hand, and affect competition, on the other. Respecting Member States' near-autonomy to define services of general economic interest, it is up to Member States to define what a significantly new service is. Once a service is deemed significantly new, the Amsterdam or public value test (inspired by the United Kingdom's procedure to evaluate new services of the BBC) should be carried out by an independent regulatory body. It ideally consists of two steps.

1. The public value of the service must be evaluated. Does it contribute to the social, cultural and democratic needs of society? In answering this question, Member States need to take into account the distinctive characteristics of the service and the impact of the service on the diversity of the existing offer of the public broadcaster.
2. The market impact of the service must be assessed. Will the service harm or strengthen competition? Member States should evaluate the counterfactual situation, the existing market situation, remaining possibilities for commercial exploitation, the market position of the public broadcasters and its competitors, the risk for crowding-out effects, and so on (see European Commission, 2009).

From the beginning, the specifications on the test provoked concerns with Member States and public broadcasters, both accusing the European Commission of going against Member States' competencies to define services of general economic interest and, moreover, slowing down innovation through curbing public broadcasters' online activities (see several contributions in Donders and Moe, 2011; Donders, 2012; Donders and Moe, 2014). Already during the drafting process the European Commission counterargued, saying it did 'not challenge the competences of Member States to define the remit' and that it merely wanted that the 'process of defining the remit is transparent and that there is accountability' (Lowe, 2008). I will elaborate on this element of accountability later on as it is key to the citizenship or democracy-centric model of Public Service Media that I defined in Chapter 5.

Amsterdam Protocol

Several Member States also claimed that the Broadcasting Communication 2009 and specifically the demand for an ex ante test of new services went against the Amsterdam Protocol. The Protocol was adopted in 1997. It is part of the Treaty on the Functioning of the European Union and in that capacity should be read together with all the other rules elaborated above. Notably Belgium and France pushed for its inclusion in the Treaty of Amsterdam, hoping it would slow down the European Commission in its application of the State aid rules after the initial complaints filed by private broadcasters in the early 1990s (cf. supra).

The Amsterdam Protocol provides:

> The High Contracting Parties,
>   Considering that the system of public broadcasting in the Member States is directly related to the democratic, social and cultural needs of each society and to the need to preserve media pluralism,
>   Have agreed upon the following interpretive provisions, which shall be annexed to the Treaty on European Union and to the Treaty on the Functioning of the European Union: The provisions of the Treaties shall be without prejudice to the competence of Member States to provide for the funding of Public Service Broadcasting and in so far as such funding is granted to broadcasting organisations for the fulfilment of the public service remit as conferred, defined and organised by each Member State, and in so far as such funding does not affect trading conditions and competition in the Union to an extent which would be contrary to the common interest, while the realisation of the remit of that public service shall be taken into account.

The Protocol thus acknowledges Member States' autonomy in the area of Public Service Broadcasting and in fact it, together with Article 106(2) of the Treaty, serves as the basis of the Broadcasting Communication. Some commentators said the demand for a test of new services was a breach of the Protocol (Bardoel and Vochteloo, 2009) – a claim that might re-surface in the European Commission's decisional practice (see next chapter).

Due to its vague wording, the legal effectiveness of the protocol might seem limited. Nevertheless, it should be considered a firm political statement on behalf of the Member States in terms of emphasising their autonomous right to organise a system of Public Service Broadcasting with a view to fulfilling the democratic, social and cultural needs of society (Nitsche, 2001). To date, Public Service Broadcasting is the only institution with such an explicit protection in the Treaty on the Functioning of the European Union. That shows its relevance for Member States. And is exemplary for the 'lively concern of some mainland Member States that an all-pervasive force of liberalism is about to crush certain important vested interests of mostly state-owned public undertakings' (Duff, 1997: 84).

Procedural aspects

How does the European Commission on the basis of all of the above, such a complex web of rules and exceptions, intervene in the funding of public broadcasters? Also this is prescribed by law. Depending on whether aid is existing or new, the procedures for intervention are different. In case of existing aid, being aid that existed when the State aid rules were adopted in the 1950s, the European Commission can ask for modifications of an aid regime, but it can never ask for reimbursement of aids. In case of new aids such reimbursement from beneficiary to the State can be required, even when the latter has no desire to reclaim the granted benefits. New aids are regimes that were newly created or that are a significant modification of existing aid schemes. Needless to say that it is not always easy to interpret what exactly is a significant alteration of an existing aid. In any case, most State aid to public broadcasters is considered existing aid since most public broadcasters already exist since the 1920s or 1930s and their basic remit has not substantially altered since then. There are examples of new aid though. The creation of new funding schemes for regional music channels would qualify as new aid and a formal, prior notification of a Member State and a subsequent approval of the European Commission is required before such policies can enter into force (Soltesz and Bielesz, 2004).

Usually, State aid procedures are the result of a private sector complaint. These complainants remain unknown until a procedure moves into a formal investigation stage. In a preliminary phase, the European Commission asks questions to Member States. These are usually assisted by 'their' public broadcasters for filling in these rather lengthy questionnaires. Public broadcasters are not a formal party in the procedure. After a preliminary investigation, the European Commission can conclude there is no State aid, the aid is compatible, the Member State should make some modifications, or can decide for a formal investigation procedure. After that phase, the European Commission can come to a positive decision (modifications made), a conditional decision (modifications underway) or a negative decision (the aid scheme is prohibited). In case of a negative decision, Member States usually take matters to Court (see Donders, 2012).

Importantly, as long as the preliminary investigation is ongoing there are no formal, publicly available documents of the State aid inquiry. That also means that when Member States agree to certain modifications in such a phase, there is not official evidence of this that scientists can research. An increasing amount of procedures are dealt with and concluded in this phase, which is worrying for obvious reasons.

An increased attachment to culture and freedom speech

Is there no room for Public Service Media in the European legal order? Of course there is, but – regardless of some scholars' rightful frustration on the limited impact of the culture Articles 107(3)d and 167(4) in the Treaty on the Functioning of the European Union (Harrison and Woods, 2007; Psychiogopoulou, 2006) – that room is to be situated more within the Council of Europe than within the European Union.

The Council of Europe's protective stance on Public Service Media

The Council of Europe has been very active on Public Service Media from the beginning of the 1990s onwards until today. It has repeatedly recognised the importance of Public Service Broadcasting and later on Public Service Media for European democracies. The Council, not surprisingly given its mandate, takes a democracy-centric approach to Public Service Media that is in fact similar to the one presented in Chapter 5 of this book. The Council has stressed three issues related to Public Service Media.

First, it defines public broadcasters' task in light of the organisations' role in democratic societies. In 1994, before the adoption of the Amsterdam Protocol, it agreed on the so-called *Prague Resolution* in which it stressed the importance of public broadcasting and the need for stability of public broadcasters in European democratic societies. In its 2004 recommendation on 'Public Service Broadcasting', the Council considers Public Service Broadcasting 'a vital element of democracy in Europe' (Council of Europe, 2004: §1). In 2009, the Council of Europe published another recommendation on the funding of public broadcasters, essentially arguing for guaranteed and appropriate funding of public broadcasters that fulfil 'the needs of individuals and society' (Council of Europe, 2009a: §6) and embracing a democracy-centric definition of what public broadcasters ought to be for society:

> Public service broadcasters must be an important public source of unbiased information and diverse political opinions; they must function under high editorial standards of objectivity, fairness and independence from party political or economic interference; they should be subject to higher public scrutiny and accountability for their programming than commercial broadcasters; they should contribute decisively to the production of audiovisual works of high quality; they should provide a wide audience with free access to informal educational and cultural programmes; they have the possibility and obligation also to serve minority viewers and people with special needs who would not be served in a purely commercial market; they should therefore support non-commercial objectives, such as social progress, public interest in democratic processes, intercultural understanding and societal integration. When they fulfil these functions, public service

broadcasters constitute an important public asset which should not be diminished or abandoned.

(Council of Europe, 2009a: §5)

It re-emphasises in a recommendation on 'the regulation of audiovisual media services' that the principle of Public Service Media in a changing media landscape must be preserved for the sake of democracy and its wellbeing (Council of Europe, 2009b: §13.3).

Second, the Council of Europe embraces the idea of Public Service Media. Already in 1999, so two years before the first Broadcasting Communication was published by the European Commission in a very broadcast-dominant rationale, the Council adopted a resolution in which the role of public broadcasters in bringing the benefits of new audiovisual and information society services to the audience was addressed. In 2007, the Council no longer spoke of Public Service Broadcasting, but published a 'Recommendation on the remit of Public Service Media in the information society'. Recognising public broadcasters can perform their task 'via diverse platforms and an offer of various services, resulting in the emergence of Public Service Media', the Council seems to implicitly criticise the European Commission for its rather prudent and, some would say (e.g., Bardoel and Vochteloo, 2009), negative stance towards online activities of public broadcasters. Admittedly, the same recommendation also excludes print services from the remit of public broadcasters. In a recommendation on 'Public Service Media governance' in 2012, the plea for Public Service Media was reaffirmed. The Council says 'the development of new information and communication technologies gives Public Service Media an unrivalled opportunity to fulfil their remit in new and more effective ways, allowing them to offer better-targeted and more interactive content and services' (Council of Europe, 2012: §9). Participation, dialogue, co-creation, reach of youngsters, and so on, are named as opportunities digitisation and convergence can bring for public broadcasters.

Third, nearly all resolutions and recommendations of the Council of Europe mention issues to transpose the ideal of Public Service Media into practice. Usually, this refers to the lack of independence of a number of public broadcasters in Member organisations of the Council of Europe. Independence was already named as a core value of Public Service Broadcasting in the Prague resolution of 1994. In a 1996 recommendation, the Council repeated that guaranteeing independence of public broadcasters was an 'essential factor of pluralistic communication'. Independence does, according to the Council not only relate to programming, but also to decisions in terms of hiring staff, making budgets, the functioning of the Board of Directors and Board of Managers, and so on.

There is an explicit concern that the independence of public broadcasters is under threat and continuously challenged by political and economic interests. It should be independent from those interests. That is precisely what, according to the Council, differentiates Public Service Media from other media companies and organisations in society. It is this that enables public broadcasters to enhance 'social, political and culture citizenship' (§2). Interestingly, the Council explicitly criticises its member organisations for failing to live up to protect such a system of Public Service Media as was committed to in the Prague resolution of 1994. Several countries fail to provide adequate financial means, and even more so do not respect their public broadcasters' independence and most of them have no legislation in place to deal with public broadcasters' moving online. The latter issue, as was discussed in preceding sections, has been picked up by the European Commission on the basis of the State aid rules and, hence, from the perspective to limit public broadcasters' presence in the market.

In its resolution 'Indicators for media in a democracy', the Council of Europe (2008: §8.20) again stresses that 'public service broadcasters must be protected against political interference in their daily management and their editorial work'. Public broadcasters must ensure independence of journalists. In a recommendation of 2012 on 'Public Service Media governance' the Council echoes its earlier concerns, saying public broadcasters cannot fulfil their primary mission for democracy if they are not independent. That independence comes with accountability though. Public broadcasters 'should be subject to constant public scrutiny and be accountable and transparent when performing their functions as they have the obligation to serve the public in all its diversity' (Council of Europe, 2012: §4). The challenge, according to the Council of Europe, is to secure independence from the State and at the same time earn the trust of the audience through exercising editorial autonomy. Public broadcasters must work on optimal internal governance structures. They should be accountable to 'a wide range of stakeholders and coupled with a culture that is open to new ideas and which demonstrates high levels of professional integrity' (§10). That challenge is unyielding, particularly for those countries where the transition from state of public broadcaster is not complete yet. Similar messages were repeated at a Council of Europe conference on Public Service Media and democracy organised in Prague in 2018.

All of this is very important and a lot of it corresponds with our own analyses in some of the previous and subsequent chapters. However, the manifold resolutions and recommendations have been shown to lack the power to enforce change when Member organisations or public broadcasters themselves fail to live up to the ideals so eloquently elaborated upon in the Council of Europe's documents. That does not make the Council's role irrelevant as it has moral authority, but we might have arrived at a point where that in itself is not sufficient, if it ever was.

Pressing issues regarding freedom of expression in Europe

On its website the Council of Europe emphasises

> the important role of Public Service Media in upholding the fundamental right to freedom of expression and information, in accordance with Article

10 of the European Convention on Human Rights, enabling people to seek and receive information, and promoting the values of democracy, diversity and social cohesion.[1]

The resolutions and recommendations of the Council explicate that taking up this role is not evident in all its Member organisations. Also other organisations have expressed concern regarding the extent to which Article 10 of the European Convention on Human Rights is being respected (or not). The European Commission has also taken issue with this and that is remarkable.

The European Commission's concern on freedom of expression is not so much focused on Public Service Media. Rather, it is based on a rather fundamental concern about the continued existence of liberal democracy in all the EU's Member States. In Hungary, Poland and Romania there are significant symptoms of authoritarianism undermining the rule of law. Obviously, governments in these countries would argue they have elections and are therefore democratic in nature, perhaps even more so than the European unelected bureaucracy. However, Jan-Werner Müler (2015: 143), points out that 'a political system with regular elections, but clear limits on media freedom, on election campaigning, and on autonomous activity by civil society is not on the road to being an illiberal democracy; it is on the road to not being a democracy at all'.

It is precisely this apparent link between authoritarianism on the one hand and limits on media freedom, political intervention with public broadcasters and politicians buying their way into media (and the other way around), on the other, that is a major concern for the European Commission as it erodes the entire project of European integration at the level of values. The European Commission, or parts of it, starts to recognise that strong public broadcasters can contribute to resilient democracies instead of focusing on Public Service Media from a market distortion angle solely. By contributing to informed, social, cultural and civic citizenship, independent public broadcasters might reverse strong feelings of Euroscepticism in countries such as Poland (Fomina, 2017). That could very well be a too simplistic assumption on the impact of media on citizens and society, but the belief exists.

There are only a few means the European Commission can use to turn the tide, including the so-called Article 7 procedure. Article 7 of the Treaty on the Functioning of the European Union makes it possible to suspend the voting rights of a Member State in the Council and this in case the Member State is breaching fundamental European values in a tenacious and obstinate manner. That, for sake of clarity, does not mean that the European Commission or Council can intervene in a given Member State. Rather, the idea of the Article 7 procedure is to isolate a Member State from the rest of the Union, which could result in that Member State leaving the European Union – even though the Brexit saga shows that is not an evident option at all.

All of this, so Müller (2015) argues, is not sufficient to deal with the serious threats for democracy in Europe. He advocates for a dedicated democracy watchdog, a separate institution that has the mandate to intervene in case democracy is threatened in a EU Member State. That is not easy and it would be enormously contested 'if the Union started prescribing "correct" understandings of democracy to its Member States' (2015: 143-144). Similar concerns were expressed in several of the interviews I carried out, the findings of which will be presented in the case study chapters.

A stronger mandate for European democracy-centric policies in media

To conclude, the EU's market integration policies and the European Commission's State aid rules are not enemies of public broadcasters. They set out from the shared goal among Member States to further a project of free movement of goods and services within the EU, to stimulate that through harmonised rules and to prohibit or at least discourage behaviour from companies and countries that go against that goal.

The democracy-centric model of Public Service Media stands at odds with this at first sight. It is indeed not the market or market failure that act as the basis of what public broadcasters ought to do, but what is needed in terms of strengthening political, social, cultural and civic citizenship.

Having said that, the Treaty on the Functioning of the European Union and several derived documents already foresee a balancing act between market and non-economic objectives of policy, between interventionists and liberals, between Member States and European Commission competencies. In this balancing, market goals so far have had the upper hand (as will be illustrated further in the next chapter).

There is a possibility to opt for a more equitable balance, but that will require more competences in the cultural policy domain for the European Commission – something Member States have so far always opposed. That shows that the dedication of Member States to the cultural policy domain is perhaps of a largely rhetorical nature and triggered by European Commission more so than by their own convictions.

Note

1 www.coe.int/en/web/freedom-expression/public-service-media.

References

Anestis, P. and Drakakis, S. (2006). State aid policy and services of general economic interest: shedding some light on a controversial area. *The European Antitrust Review*, 60-66.

Arhold, C. (2007). The case law of the European Court of Justice and the Court of First Instance on State aids in 2006/2007. *European State Aid Law Quarterly*, 6(2), 151-214.

Bardoel, J. and Vochteloo, M. (2009). Media Policy between Europe and the Nation-State: The Case of the EU Broadcast Communication 2009. Paper presented at the ECREA-CLP Workshop on 'New Directions for Communication Policy Research', 6-7 November, Zürich.

Buendia Sierra, J.L. (2006). An analysis of Article 86(2) EC. In M.S. Rydelski (ed.), *The EC State Aid Regime: Distortive Effects of State Aid on Competition and Trade* (pp. 541-574). London: Cameron May.

Coates, K. and Sauter, W. (2007). Communications In J Faull and A. Nikpay (eds), *The EC Law of Competition* (pp. 1475-1572). New York and Oxford: Oxford University Press.

Council (1989). *Directive 89/552/EEC of 3 October 1989 on the coordination of certain provisions laid down by law, regulation or administrative action in Member States concerning the pursuit of television broadcasting.*

Council and European Parliament (2018). *Directive (EU) 2018/1808 of 14 November 2018 amending Directive 2010/13/EU on the coordination of certain provisions laid down by law, regulation or administrative action in Member States concerning the provision of audiovisual media services (Audiovisual Media Services Directive) in view of changing market realities.*

Council of Europe (2004). *Recommendation 1641 on Public Service Broadcasting.*

Council of Europe (2008). *Resolution 1636 on Indicators for media in a democracy.*

Council of Europe (2009a). *Recommendation 1878 on The Funding of Public Service Broadcasting.*

Council of Europe (2009b). *Recommendation 1855 on The Regulation of Audiovisual Media Services*

Council of Europe (2012). *Recommendation CM/Rec(2012) on Public Service Media Governance.*

Court of First Instance, 10 May 2000, *SIC v Commission,* T-46–97.

Court of First Instance, 15 September 1998, *Telecinco v Commission,* T-95/96.

Crocioni, P. (2006). Can State aid policy become more economic friendly? *World Competition, 29*(1), 89-108.

Donders, K. (2012). *Public Service Media and Policy in Europe.* Basingstoke: Palgrave Macmillan.

Donders, K. (2015). State aid to public service media: European Commission decisional practice before and after the 2009 Broadcasting Communication. *European State aid Law Quarterly, 1*(15), 68-87.

Donders, K. and Moe, H. (eds) (2011). *Exporting the public value test.* Göteborg: Nordicom.

Donders, K. and Moe, H. (2014). European State aid control and public service broadcasting: When the goals of competition policy clash or match (?) with public interest objectives. In K. Donders, C. Pauwels and J. Loisen (eds), *The Palgrave Handbook of European Media Policy* (pp. 426–441). Basingstoke: Palgrave Macmillan.

Donders, K. and Van den Bulck, H. (2016). Decline and fall of public service media values in the international content acquisition market: An analysis of small public broadcasters acquiring BBC Worldwide content. *European Journal of Communication, 31*(3), 299–316.

Duff, A. (1997). *The Treaty of Amsterdam.* London: The Federal Trust.

European Commission (2001). Communication of 15 November 2001 on the *Application of the State Aid Rules to Public Service Broadcasting.*

European Commission (2007). Decision of 24 April 2007 on *The License Fee Funding of ARD and ZDF.*

European Commission (2009). Communication of 2 July 2009 on the *application of the State Aid Rules to Public Service Broadcasting.*

European Court of Justice (1974). Judgment of the Court of 30 April 1974: *Giuseppe Sacchi – Reference for a preliminary ruling: Tribunale civile e penale di Biella - Italy.* Case 155-73.

Fomina, J. (2017). The unlikely Eurosceptics: The undercurrent anti-European attitudes among the young Poles and the role of the domestic context. *Polish Sociological Review* (198), 141–165.

Friederiszick, H.W., Röller, L.-H. and Verouden, V. (2005). European State Aid Control: En economic framework. Retrieved from www.ecares.org/ecare/personal/sapir/europeanstateaid.pdf (accessed October 2020).

General Court (ex Court of First Instance) (1996). 11 July 1996, *Metropole Télévision and others v Commission*, T-528/93, T-542/93, T-543/93 and T-546/93.

General Court (ex Court of First Instance). 8 October 2002, *Metropole Télévision and others v Commission*, T-185/00, T-216/00 and T-299/00.

General Court (ex Court of First Instance). 12 February 2008, *BUPA v Commission*, T-289/03.

Grespan, D. (2008). Services of general economic interest. In W. Mederer, N. Pesaresi and M. Van Hoof (eds), *EU Competition Law: Volume IV – State aid* (pp. 1123–1208). Brussels: Claeys & Casteels.

Gromnicka, E. (2005). Services of general economic interest in the State aids regime: Proceduralisation of political choices? *European Public Law*, *11*(3), 429–461.

Harcourt, A. (2002). Engineering Europeanization: The role of the European institutions in shaping national media regulation. *Journal of European Public Policy*, *9*(5), 736–755.

Harcourt, A. (2007). Institution-driven competition: The regulation of cross-border broadcasting in the EU. *Journal of Public Policy*, *27*(3), 293–317.

Harrison, J. and Woods, L. (2007). *European Broadcasting Law and Policy*. Cambridge: Cambridge University Press.

Held, A. and Kliemann, A. (2012). The 2009 broadcasting communication and the commission's decisional practice two years after its entry into force. *European State Aid Law Quarterly*, *11*(1), 37–47.

Hettich, P. (2008). YouTube to be regulated? The FCC sits tight, while European broadcast regulators make the grab for the Internet. *St. John's Law Review*, *82*, 1447–1508.

Katsirea, I. (2008). *Public Broadcasting and European Law: A Comparative Examination of Public Service Obligations in Six Member States*. New York: Wolters Kluwer International.

Koenig, C. and Haratsch, A. (2003). The licence-fee-based financing of public service broadcasting in Germany after the Altmark Trans judgment. *European State Aid Law Quarterly*, *2*(4), 569–578.

Levy, D. (1999). *Europe's Digital Revolution: Broadcasting Revolution, the EU and the Nation State*. London: Routledge.

Lowe, L. (2008). Participation in the debate, organized by the Vertretung des Landes Rheinland Pfalz in Brüssel and the Mainzer Medieninstitut, 'Brüsseler Mediengespräch: die Rundfunkmitteilung der Kommission auf dem Prufstand', Brussels, 3 December.

Michalis, M. (2007). *Governing European Communications: From Unification to Coordination*. Lanham: Lexington Books.

Michalis, M. (2014). Thirty years of private television in Europe: Trends and key moments. In K. Donders, C. Pauwels and J. Loisen (eds), *Private Television in Western Europe: Content, Markets, Policies* (pp. 37–55). Basingstoke: Palgrave Macmillan.

Müller, J.W. (2015). Should the EU protect democracy and the rule of law inside Member States? *European Law Journal*, *21*(2), 141–160.

Nicolaides, P., Kekelekis, M. and Buyskes, P. (2005). *State Aid Policy in the European Community: A Guide for Practitioners*. The Hague: Kluwer Law International.

Nitsche, I. (2001). *Broadcasting in the European Union: The Role of Public Interest in Competition Analysis.* The Hague: TCM Asser Press.

Papathanassopoulos, S. (2007). The Mediterranean/polarized pluralist media model countries. In G. Terzis (ed.), *European Media Governance: National and Regional Dimensions* (pp. 191–200). Bristol: Intellect.

Pauwels, C. (1995). *Cultuur en economie: de spanningsvelden van het communautair audiovisueel beleid. Een onderzoek naar de grenzen en mogelijkheden van een kwalitatief cultuur en communicatiebeleid in een economisch geïntegreerd Europa. Een kritische analyse en prospectieve evaluatie aan de hand van het gevoerde Europees audiovisueel beleid* (unpublished Ph.D.). Brussels: Vrije Universiteit Brussel. [*Culture and economy: the fields of tensions in the Community's audiovisual policy. An analysis of the limits and possibilities of a qualitative culture and communications policy in an economically integrated Europe*].

Pauwels, C. and Donders, K. (2013). Opening up Europe to private television: Harmonization and liberalization to the benefit of all? In K. Donders, C. Pauwels and J. Loisen (eds), *Private Television in Europe: Content, Markets and Policies* (pp. 20–36). Basingstoke: Palgrave Macmillan.

Psychiogopoulou, E. (2006). EC state aid control and cultural justification. *Legal Issues of Economic Integration, 33*(1), 3–28.

Sabbagh, D. (2005). EU seeks to regulate television on the net. *The Times,* 12 July. Retrieved from www.thetimes.co.uk/article/eu-seeks-to-regulate-television-on-the-net-xlzncczkjwk (accessed October 2020).

Santa Maria, A. (2007). *Competition and State Aid: An Analysis of the EC Practice.* The Hague: Kluwer Law International.

Soltesz, U. and Bielesz, H. (2004). Judicial review of state aid decisions-recent developments. *European Competition Law Review, 25*(3), 133–152.

Szyszczak, E. (2004). Public services in the new economy. In C. Graham and F. Smith (eds), *Competition, Regulation and the New Economy* (pp. 185–206). Portland: Hart Publishing.

Valcke, P. and Ausloos, J. (2014). Audiovisual media services 3.0: (Re)defining the scope of European broadcasting law in a converging and connected media environment. In K. Donders, C. Pauwels and J. Loisen (eds), *The Palgrave Handbook of European Media Policy* (pp. 312–328). Basingstoke: Palgrave Macmillan.

Valcke, P. and Lievens, E. (2009). Rethinking European broadcasting regulation. In C. Pauwels, H. Kalimo, K. Donders and B. Van Rompuy (eds), *Rethinking European Media and Communications Policy* (pp. 127–164). Brussels: VUBPRESS.

Van Rompuy, B. and Donders, K. (2013). The EBU's Eurovision system governing the joint buying of sports broadcasting rights: Unfinished competition business. *Competition Law Review, 9*(1), 7–28.

Wolton, D. (1990). La télévision européenne en question. *Médiaspouvoirs, 20,* 87–95. [*European television in question*].

8 Applying State aid rules in an internationalised and converged media landscape

Public broadcasters' facing European intervention

The relevance of State aid law in the field of Public Service Media cannot be too easily underestimated. Compared to the Council of Europe's resolutions and recommendations, the impact of the European Commission investigating license fee or subsidy schemes and, in several cases, requiring changes to diverse aspects of these schemes, is real. The aim of this chapter is to investigate this impact.

Main questions

There are three main questions that guide this chapter. First, what are the main issues for the European Commission when applying the State aid rules to the funding of public broadcasters? Second, is it sticking to its competence to check for manifest errors only and does it thus leave it up to Member States to define what Public Service Media is and what public broadcasters ought to do? Third, is it, in all of this, showing sensitivity towards the changed media landscape? Indeed, when the funding of public broadcasters was investigated in the early 1990s, they were still at the top of the food chain. Commercial media had just entered the market. This affected public broadcasters as they, for obvious reasons, lost market share, but the fairly stable duopolies that emerged soon after were hardly as disruptive as the media environment described in Chapter 2 of this book. Media markets are not national anymore. The intensification of merger and acquisition activities, the subsequent further internationalisation of markets and the organisation of media markets around fairly closed platform infrastructures owning data of users are all an issue for public broadcasters (for illustrations thereof, see Evens and Donders, 2018). Is the European Commission aware of this or is it still analysing the possibly market-distortive nature of public broadcaster funding in an exclusively national market analysis framework? One would assume the opposite. The Broadcasting Communication 2009 set out from a need to update the rules for State aid to public broadcasters in a changed digital media environment. That is why this chapter differentiates between the application of the State aid rules before and after the 2009 Broadcasting Communication.

Methodology

We analysed European Commission decisions issued between 1996 and 2 July 2009 and from that date onwards until mid-2019. The adoption of the Broadcasting Communication 2009 is our main marker to differentiate between these two periods. Before the adoption of the Broadcasting Communication in 2001, the European Commission adopted only three decisions, dealing with public broadcasters in Portugal, the United Kingdom and Germany. In the Portuguese case, it concluded there was no State aid. This was later on overruled by the General Court. There were only two more instances in which the European Commission came to that same conclusion, on specific digital channels of the BBC (European Commission, 2002b) and on a theme park operated by German public broadcaster ZDF (European Commission, 2002a). It is fair to say that besides the theme park decision, the European Commission would, under present conditions, always consider the funding of a public broadcaster State aid. After the adoption of the 2001 Broadcasting Communication, 20 decisions were issued until 2 July 2009. There was thus an intensification of decisional activity once a framework for interpretation was published and communicated to the EU Member States. This shows that the European involvement 'in disputes between commercial and public service broadcasters marked a rather more reluctant and even more controversial form of intervention' (Levy, 1999: 95). Contrary to the assumption that the European Commission was eager to enforce its 'neoliberal' agenda in Public Service Media, 'the slow response was not simply a case of bureaucratic omission; the delay reflected the Commission's reluctance to make judgements about how to enforce State aid rules in the area of public broadcasting' (Smit, 2001: 230). Eleven more decisions were issued after the adoption of the Broadcasting Communication 2009, which shows a slowing pace of European Commission intervention, even though that should not be exaggerated as an increasing number of cases are being 'solved' in the preliminary research phase. That usually comes with far-going commitments of EU Member States to alter aspects of their legislation, but without a possibility for research since these documents are not publicly available. In total, I analysed 34 decision documents. Some of these amount to over 100 pages; others are limited to eight pages. The more comprehensive the scope of investigation, the longer the decision. In that sense, I make a distinction between 'single issue' and 'whole package' cases. Single issue cases can be focused on ad hoc restructuring of debts (European Commission, 2003b; 2003c; 2003d; 2004a; 2004b; 2006a; 2006b; 2006c; 2007a; 2008c; 2009b; 2011c) or on the funding of specific services, specifically thematic channels (European Commission, 1999; 2002b), regional media (European Commission, 2013), digital services (European Commission, 2003a) or other singular services (European Commission, 2002a; 2011a; 2011b; 2016). Whole package cases concern the funding, definition of the remit, control mechanisms, entrustment, transparency, and so on. There were, based on Table 8.1, ten of these whole package decisions (indicated with an ★). The decisions on the funding of public broadcasters in France, Italy and Spain (European Commission 2005a; 2005b; 2005c) is focused largely on organisational and financial issues

Table 8.1 Overview State aid decisions before and after the Broadcasting Communication 2009

	Affected country	Affected public broadcaster	Decision date	Outcome
Before adoption Broadcasting Communication				
Decision on State aid to RTP	Portugal	RTP	7 November 1996	No State aid
Agreement on Amsterdam Protocol in 1997				
Decision on specialist channels Kinderkanal and Phoenix	Germany	ARD	24 February 1999	Compatible State aid
Decision on specialist channel BBC News 24	United Kingdom	BBC	14 December 1999	Compatible aid
Broadcasting Communication 2001, 15 November				
Decision on ZDF Medienpark	Germany	ZDF	3 April 2002	No State aid
Decision on BBC Digital Channels	United Kingdom	BBC	22 May 2002	No State aid
Decision on BBC Digital Curriculum	United Kingdom	BBC	1 October 2003	Compatible State aid (SGEI general, not Public Service Broadcasting)
Decision on ad hoc funds	Italy	RAI	15 October 2003	Compatible State aid
Decision on ad hoc funds	Portugal	RTP	15 October 2003	Compatible State aid
Decision on ad hoc funds	France	France Télévisions	10 December 2003	Compatible State aid
Decision on ad hoc funds	Denmark	TV2	19 May 2004	Illegal State aid, reimbursement
Decision on recapitalisation	Denmark	TV2	6 October 2004	Compatible State aid
*Decision on annual funding	France	France Télévisions	20 April 2005	Compatible State aid after commitments
*Decision on annual funding	Italy	RAI	20 April 2005	Compatible State aid after commitments

Table 8.1 Cont.

	Affected country	Affected public broadcaster	Decision date	Outcome
★Decision on annual funding	Spain	RTVE	20 April 2005	Compatible State aid after commitments
Decision on funding of France 24	France	France Télévisions	7 June 2005	Compatible State aid
Decision on compensation payments	Portugal	RTP	22 March 2006	Compatible State aid
Decision on ad hoc funds	The Netherlands	NOS	22 June 2006	Illegal State aid, reimbursement
Decision on ad hoc funds	Portugal	RTP	4 July 2006	Compatible State aid
Decision on remedies for the reduction of RTVE's workforce	Spain	RTVE	7 March 2007	Compatible State aid
★Decision on license-fee funding of ARD and ZDF	Germany	ARD and ZDF	24 April 2007	Compatible State aid after commitments
★Decision on funding Flemish public broadcaster VRT	Flanders, Belgium	VRT	27 February 2008	Compatible State aid after commitments
★Decision on funding of Irish public broadcaster RTE	Ireland	RTE	27 February 2008	Compatible State aid after commitments
Decision on capital injections	France	France Télévisions	16 July 2008	Compatible State aid
Broadcasting Communication 2009, 2 July				
Decision on capital injections	France	France Télévisions	1 September 2009	Compatible State aid
★Decision on funding public broadcaster ORF	Austria	ORF	28 October 2009	Compatible State aid after commitments
★Decision on the funding of the Dutch public broadcasters	The Netherlands	NPO and all television broadcasting organisations	26 January 2010	Compatible State aid after commitments

(continued)

Table 8.1 Cont.

	Affected country	Affected public broadcaster	Decision date	Outcome
*Decision on the funding of the Norwegian public broadcaster	Norway (EFTA member)	NRK	3 February 2010	Compatible State aid after commitments
Decision on creation of a local station	France	France Bleu Maine	22 June 2010	Compatible State aid
Decision on creation of 4FM radio station	Denmark	4FM (to be created) DR (getting competition in the public service market)	23 March 2011	Compatible State aid
Decision on support of public service radio programmes	Denmark	All companies that would benefit from such aid	27 October 2011	Compatible State aid under Article 107(3)d for cultural support measures
Decision on financial support to restructure debts of RTP	Portugal	RTP	20 December 2011	Compatible State aid
Decision on financing of local station France Bleu Saint-Étienne Loire	France	Radio France	8 November 2013	Compatible State aid
*Decision on funding public broadcaster RTBF	French speaking community, Belgium	RTBF	7 May 2014	Compatible State aid after commitments
Decision on financing of France Médias Monde	France	France Médias Monde	27 June 2016	Compatible State aid

though and not so much concerned with the definition of the remit, new media services, ex ante tests, and so on. That means that out of 28 EU Member States, only nine Member States and Norway have faced scrutiny of their entire Public Service Media system. That should by no means result in the conclusion that the impact of European Commission intervention is limited though. The next sections will show that.

Our analysis took place in six languages: Dutch, French, English, and to a lesser extent, Spanish, Italian and Portuguese. When possible, we always worked with an official, European Commission authorised, French or English translation.

Document analysis is usually a form of textual analysis (Karppinen and Moe, 2019: 251). We combined aspects of a qualitative content analysis with a thematic analysis approach. On the basis of a set of distinct concepts, I engaged in a 'systematic analysis of qualitative data by way of assigning categories to text material' (Puppis, 2019: 369). That involved coding of all documents. For the documents preceding 2 July 2009, I scanned for concepts and words related to public broadcasters' public task, the entrustment of this task to them, the control by an independent body, the proportionality of funding, transparency of the organisation and finances and market distortion issues. All of these 'categories' were operationalised further. For the decisions issued after 2 July 2009, I did the same. But I added concepts and words that are related to the specific threats for public broadcasters that were identified in Chapter 2 of this book, including 'internationalisation', 'international competition', 'platformisation', 'convergence', 'relevant market', 'fair trading practices', and so on. Every single time I came across one of the codes identified or a related term, I colour coded this in the text. That way I assigned text to categories, adopting an inductive coding method (Puppis, 2019: 375). On the basis of this coding, text material was extracted, which was interpreted on the basis of a thematic analysis. The latter is defined by Herzog, Handke and Hitters (2019) as something similar to qualitative content analysis, but more explicitly focused on interpretation of text. After the initial coding of text and extracting of relevant passages, there is a search for emerging themes. After identification of these themes, we reviewed the themes by evaluating whether all the extracted text fragments fitted within one or more of the identified themes (largely following the subsequent steps of thematic analysis as elaborated upon by Herzog, Handke and Hitters, 2019: 393–394). The presentation of the findings is structured around these themes. The analysis of the documents preceding the Broadcasting Communication 2009 is also in part on earlier research (Donders, 2012; 2015).

Application of the State aid rules before the 2009 Broadcasting Communication

The main elements of the European Commission's decisional practice, once State aid is in place, concern the clarity of the definition of the public service remit, the existence of a formal document that entrusts this remit to the public broadcaster receiving State aid and subsequent control on performance, and the proportionality of the aid. On the basis of the European Commission's decision documents, some key findings on all these elements can be presented.

Balancing Member States' right to define the remit with a manifest error approach

The definition of public broadcasters' task or remit is the most contentious part of European State aid control. Not only because it goes to the heart of Public

Service Media and its crystallisation in the form of public broadcasters in the EU, but also because it is to be situated on a tectonic field between extensive Member State competencies and rather limited room of manoeuvre for the European Commission. The latter has struggled to define a coherent approach to what a clear definition of the public service remit is without going into co-defining itself.

First, at the end of the 1990s, the European Commission takes a rather lenient approach to the launch of thematic channels such as *Kinderkanal* and *Phoenix* in Germany and *BBC News 24* in the United Kingdom. It stresses that the opinion of private sector complainants that such thematic channels are because of their focus on niche content and niche audiences outside the scope of what public broadcasters ought to do, is essentially irrelevant as it is not up to them or to the European Commission to decide on what fits within the scope of public broadcasters' task (European Commission, 2009a: pt.4). It also said that a level of market distortion is an inevitable consequence of the existence of public broadcasters and admissible provided there is general interest that is being served (European Commission, 1999: §93–99). First signs of caution could be observed, though as the European Commission said, the scope of the remit was so wide that it left a lot of, perhaps too much, room for interpretation (1999: §69).

Second, and after the adoption of the 2001 Broadcasting Communication that specified a clear definition was important to ensure compliance with State aid law, the European Commission became a bit more activist in this area from 2003 onwards. In its decision on the educational software service *BBC Digital Curriculum* it said the service was not part of a public broadcasting remit and hence not captured by the Broadcasting Communication, but by the general rules for Services of General Economic Interest (SGEI). While the scheme was accepted under Article 106(2) provisions, the European Commission's claim that *BBC Digital Curriculum* fell outside the remit of the BBC because it lacked a 'close association' with the public broadcaster's other offers (European Commission, 2003a: §36) and was considered in breach of the Amsterdam Protocol as the idea of close association is nowhere to be found in the Treaty, nor in relevant case law. Scholars (e.g., Moe, 2008; Bardoel and Vochteloo, 2009; Brevini, 2013), moreover, feared that the principle would in fact limit public broadcasters' activities to radio and television. Indeed, education has always been a core goal of the BBC; extending that to the online environment might be criticised by competitors and perhaps for valid reasons, but claiming the online nature of a service does not guarantee a close association seems flawed when taking a technology neutrality point of view. The fact that the UK Government approved the service after extensive research and faced with wide support from teachers and pupils in a pilot scheme (Coe et al., 2002) did not receive a lot of attention at the time, but will appear highly relevant for later developments in State aid law and Public Service Media. The European Commission repeated its stance on close association on several subsequent decisions, including its decision on the funding of public broadcaster TV2 in which it said that infor-mation society services and broadcasting were not similar. Some information society services such as video games and chatrooms were considered not to contribute to the social, democratic and culture needs of society (European Commission, 2004a: §90-92). While one can again claim that such an approach goes beyond the European Commission's competencies, the services of DG Competition expressed their concern on Public Service Broadcasting or Public Service Media becoming a 'public service anything' (see Chapter 3). Not everything that public broadcasters do is Public Service Media. That was essentially the European Commission's stance (Ward, 2008: 78) and resulted in several EU Member States, also those that escaped European Commission State aid control, revising their media laws to be more specific on public broadcasters' remit.

Third, in its decision on the license fee funding of German public broadcasters, the European Commission tries to avoid the trap of over-stepping its competencies, largely criticising the German Länder for inadequately defining the remit of ARD and ZDF. The distinction between commercial and public services is not clear (European Commission, 2007: §238-239), the status of pay-services was unspoken of in relevant legislative documents while possibly problematic (§239-240) and there was no clarity on new services that were added *en cours de route*. What 'added value' do services 'that are not programmes in the traditional sense' have? Do these services fit the remit and who checks that (§227)? Coming back to the issue of control later, the European Commission was not willing to accept a 'hands-off approach' of Member States when talking about the expansion of public broadcasters to, at the time, new media markets. It insisted on more clarity in definitions of the remit in its dealings with public broadcasters in Flanders, Belgium (European Commission, 2008a) and Ireland (European Commission, 2008b). Accepting editorial independence as a key value (European Commission, 2008b: §167), it insisted that independence could not be (ab)used to have remits that were not going beyond the Reithian adage to inform, educate and entertain. All of the involved Member States had to commit to changing and mainly specifying their public service remits in law. In some, that resulted also in the inclusion of *negative lists* of services that were considered outside the remit, a practice that was considered undesirable as an educational video game might be considered part of a public broadcaster's task while a purely entertaining game might be outside the scope of activities (Donders, 2012).

The European Commission gradually developed an approach to deal with complaints of private companies concerning public broadcasters' Internet activities. That approach set out from a 'regular' State aid perspective, meaning the starting point was to limit the influence of State aid and thus public broadcasters in (emerging) markets. The issue was and remains sensitive and, in fact, provoked the drafting of the Broadcasting Communication 2009 (cf. infra).

Requiring explicit entrustment and independent control

The second main points of attention in the European Commission's decisions concerns the formal entrustment of a clearly defined remit to the public broadcaster receiving State aid and the subsequent independent control of performance. Entrustment seems an acceptable requirement. Most countries have management contracts in place and those that did not fell in line rather easily. A more difficult issue was the European Commission's question in the German, Flemish and Irish cases (European Commission, 2007; 2008a; 2008b) to update the entrustment or add a specific entrustment document for new services separately. That is where the so-called ex ante test or public value test comes into the picture. According to the European Commission, public broadcasters added new services to their services portfolio without explicit consent of EU Member States. Hence, there was no entrustment of these services to the public broadcaster. Member States counterargued that they entrusted a task and that services are a means to fulfil that task. Nevertheless, the European Commission insisted on a distinct entrustment of new services and this to be preceded by an ex ante evaluation of the public value and market impact of this new service. In this, it was inspired by the United Kingdom's public value test (Biggam, 2011; Donders, 2011) that was invented largely by the BBC as a means to overcome the issues with market players that were observed during and after the *BBC Digital Curriculum* case (cf. supra). In case of positive advice by an independent regulator, the service could be entrusted to the public broadcaster. Otherwise not. Germany, Ireland and Flanders, Belgium agreed to such a test, albeit that the test regimes are very dissimilar. In Germany over 40 'telemedia services' were tested (Donders, 2012) whereas in Flanders only one service was tested, a pre-school children's channel. While in Germany all services were accepted, the one service that was tested in Flanders was rejected by the Flemish Government after the neutral advice of the media regulator. In Germany, market research is commissioned to independent agencies, in Flanders there was no real market impact assessment to speak of (Donders, Van den Bulck and Raats, 2019). That is, only two cases showed similarity in terms of commitments, but differences at the level of implementation, outcome and impact. While several authors have criticised the ex ante test (Bardoel and Vochteloo, 2009; Brevini, 2013), some have also acknowledged its positive aspects. Jeanette Steemers (2003: 133) says the test might help 'to demonstrate both uniqueness and appeal across a broad range of output' to ensure 'the consensus surrounding public funding' will not dissolve. Also Tim Suter (2008: 5) is moderately positive, saying the test might be a necessary evil to justify investments in new means of production and distribution. And I have argued elsewhere that the ex ante test comes with opportunities to pro-actively tackle questions on the position of public broadcasters (Donders, 2012: 111). Admittedly, I have become less optimistic having studied the actual implementation of many tests (see Chapter 9).

The ex ante test, but also other aspects of public broadcasters' functioning should be in the hands of an independent control body. That means a body that is legally separate from the public broadcaster. This rule resulted in the establishment of more professional media regulators in several countries, including Ireland where the Broadcasting Authority Ireland was created in the process of the European Commission's investigation into the funding of RTE (European Commission, 2008b). Also in Flanders, Belgium the media regulator was adapted to pro-actively deal with probable concerns of the European Commission in this regard (European Commission, 2008a). In the German case, the European Commission was considerably more lenient accepting the broadcasting councils, that are internal to the public broadcasters. It asked for Chinese walls between management and Councils, more staff, and more resources (European Commission, 2007b: §256). Nevertheless, it exceptionally did not insist on a legally external body taking into account the careful crafting of the Councils' being and structure after World War II. This again shows that identical rules can result in different decisions, outputs and impacts in EU Member States.

Aiming for good governance

Finally, the European Commission wants EU Member States to give proportional State aid. That means you cannot give more money than needed to fulfil the public service remit. That might seem evident or even naïve given the years of cost-cutting several public broadcasters have gone through, but the reality of it is that most public broadcasters had no professional cost accounting system in place. While the nature of the funding (public, commercial) is determined by Member States of the EU and has no impact on the qualification of a service as public or not (Antoniadis, 2006: 596), it is considered vital that the aid is limited to what is needed. So-called overcompensation is feared to result in public broadcasters outbidding competitors in the market for sports rights and other market-distortive behaviour that is in fact needless to achieve the pre-set public interest objectives. To ensure proportionality, the European Commission has consistently asked Member States of the EU to separate public and commercial revenues streams in the accounting of public broadcasters (Donders and Pauwels, 2008; 2009), to opt for a structural or at least functional separation of commercial activities from public services, to stipulate a limitation of reserves accumulation and earmark reserves, and to have mechanisms in place that make it possible to oversee the finances of the public broadcasters and possible misuse. Essentially, these are principles of good governance and virtually absent in a lot of Member States before the European Commission started to press for this. The multitude of cases dealing with ad hoc funds, the restructuring of debts, recapitalisation, aids to deal with workforce reductions, and so on (European Commission, 2003b; 2003c; 2003d; 2004a; 2004b; 2006a; 2006b; 2006c; 2007a; 2008c; 2009b; etc.), shows that there were issues here. Also the decisions on the annual funding of France Télévision, RTP and RTVE (European Commission, 2005a; 2005b; 2005c) were filled with requirements to reform the public broadcasting organisations and make them more transparent, efficient and accountable. There were several, more concrete, positive consequences of the European Commission's intervention in this area. First, in several countries the European Commission observed repeated undercompensation of the public service task. In decisions on the French and Portuguese public broadcasters (European Commission, 2003c: §189; 2003d: §69) that was made explicit. Although not resulting in immediate increases of public funding, subsequent decisions show an effort was made to remedy historical flaws (European Commission, 2008c; 2009b; 2011c). Second, public broadcasters were required to engage in normal pricing practices. So, no discriminatory prices to the benefit or disadvantage of specific companies (e.g., European Commission, 2005b: §71; 2005c: §60ff). Third, the practice of State guarantees allowing public broadcasters in countries such as Spain to accumulate debts without the possibility of going bankrupt was prohibited. That was a good thing as the increased dependence on government saving RTVE aggravated a situation that was already not great to begin with (European Commission, 2005c).

State aid decisions issued before 2 July 2009 were clearly very diverse. They dealt with thematic channels, online educational services, a theme park, transparency and organisation issues of highly bureaucratic and politicised public broadcasters, the entire funding regimes of several public broadcasters, and so on. Regardless of this diversity, the three main principles of the Broadcasting Communication 2001 are manifestly present in most decisions. The definition of the remit is the most contentious one and requiring the European Commission to stay within its own competencies while still checking for manifest error. The latter is a vague concept though, which also explains why some observers concluded the European Commission did not overstep, while others found the opposite (see Donders, 2012 for a more elaboration evaluation).

Application of the State aid rules after the 2009 Broadcasting Communication

The Broadcasting Communication 2009 stuck with the three main principles of its 2001 predecessor. It mainly added the ex ante test as a best practice, negotiated with the German, Flemish and Irish Governments. The subsequent analysis aims to uncover whether the decisional practice after 2009 significantly changed from the decisions before. It, moreover and more importantly, analyses to what extent the changed international and converged media landscape did not only inspire the 2009 Broadcasting Communication, but also decisional practice itself.

Limited attention for internationalisation and a presumed impact on markets

In all decision documents analysed, there is limited attention for the changed circumstances in which public broadcasters as well as their competitors operate. It would be too easy to blame this on the European Commission. Also Member States themselves do not seem to highlight the international and converged landscape in which public broadcasters are losing the powerful position they once had. For example, the Danish Government created a scheme for the financial support of radio programmes in the Danish language and reflecting Danish culture. The fund is similar to schemes in place for audiovisual drama, film and documentary production. Danish public broadcaster DR cannot benefit from this scheme. It is a 'public service' scheme, but oriented towards commercial media that lack the means to invest in such programming. The Danish Government considers their participation in the domestic media market with the original programming of fundamental importance for diversity and pluralism. Reference is made to the small Danish language area and the limited possibility to economically valorise such content (European Commission, 2011b: §4, §8). Nowhere is this related to the international media markets that put domestic media forms under more pressure. The aid amounted to 500,000 euros on an annual basis (§11). One can wonder what the impact of such a limited amount of money is at all.

Internationalisation is sometimes in the picture though, not so much related to the impact of a changed market on public broadcasters, but more so the latter's impact on the market. Indeed, for State aid to exist there has to be an impact on competition and trade between Member States. In other words: effects should go beyond national territories. Admittedly, that impact is often assumed by the European Commission from the moment there is a selective advantage being granted to an undertaking. The assumptions made in subsequent decisions show an odd understanding of contemporary media markets though.

For example, in its assessment of the Danish 4FM case, the European Commission (2011a: §60) decides that this new channel, receiving license fee money, 'puts the recipient of the aid in a more favourable position compared with other undertakings which are competing in intra-Union trade'. The channel will compete with radio broadcasters with a foreign or international company structure (e.g., SBS Radio was at the time part of the ProSiebenSat1 group) and foreign radio programmes. The beneficiary could, moreover, participate in the international market for the purchase and sale of programme rights (§61). The Danish authorities argued that their support for 4FM, which basically is taking away one broadcasting channel from public broadcaster DR in an attempt to create more diversity in the Danish radio market, was not a selective advantage, but a mere compensation of a public service obligation and hence complying with the *Almark* and thus no State aid. While the Danish Government provided evidence for an extensive open tendering procedure, the European Commission concluded that it was 'not in a position to conclude that this criterion is fulfilled' (§54). It could not be certain there was no State aid. I find that remarkable. It later on concluded that the State aid is compatible though 'while the competitive environment for private services might be affected by 4FM, the freedom to provide services and the functioning of the internal market as such for radio are not affected to an extent contrary to the Union interest' (§113). The whole decision is based on the presumption that the funding of a Danish radio channel in the Danish language is not a mere compensation of a public service task and can affect trade between Member States because international conglomerates are active on the Danish market and the broadcaster itself might buy rights to broadcast an Italian opera for a Danish audience. That seems so far fetched that one should discuss the empirical evidence-based nature of these decisions.

Similar assumptions on the impact of public broadcasters' on trade between Member States are repeated almost identically in other decision documents. In some decisions such as the one dealing with the funding of France Médias Monde (European Commission, 2016) that makes sense, although one could argue that the impact on trade between EU Member States of an organisation with a 242 million euros annual budget that targets mid-Africa is rather limited compared to its international influence.

In other decisions the assumed effect on trade between Member States of the EU is more or less theoretical only (see a.o. European Commission, 2011b: §19). The evaluation of the 2 million euros of funding for France Bleu à Saint-Étienne, a new local radio channel to be part of Radio France, the European Commission (2013: §31) shows this:

> il suffit de noter que l'aide est accordée à l'une des principlaes stations de radio sur le march français et qu'elle aura à l'évidence une influence sur les échanges entre Etats membres en matière d'acquisition et de vente de droits de diffusion, qui se font souvent à l'échelon international.

France Bleu à Saint-Étienne is servicing a local community and aims to ensure linguistic diversity on a radio channel. That is acknowledged by the European Commission (2013: §48), which also accepts that the revenues from advertising of the channel are extremely limited at approximately 50,000 euros per year and that, hence, no commercial operator would be interested in pursuing such an activity (§54). But still, the impact on trade between Member States is assumed.

Also public broadcasters of Member States of the EU that 'suffer' from a big neighbouring market are assumed to impact trade between Member States, specifically because of this same-language neighbouring market. In its decision on the funding of Austrian public broadcaster ORF, the European Commission essentially said that the presence of international groups such as RTL and ProSiebenSat1 in Austria aggravated the potential effect ORF could have on trade within the internal market.

> this applies in particular with regard to the frequently international purchase and sale of programme rights, advertising with cross-border effect, especially in areas near to the border in which the same language is spoken on both sides of the border, and the ownership structure of commercial broadcasters which may extend to more than one Member State. As a result of financing by means of the programme fee, ORF's position is strengthened to that of its private competitors. The services of ORF can be received beyond the borders of Austria. In Austria itself, ORF is in competition with TV broadcasters with a foreign or international company structure (e.g., SAT1, RTL and ProSieben) and foreign public TV broadcasters (in particular, ARD and ZDF). Additionally, ORF also operates throughout Europe with regard to the purchase and sale of programme rights, particularly via the EBU.
>
> (European Commission, 2009c: §119-120)

The idea that Austria/ORF is the inflicting party and competitors from Germany are the impacted actors was repeated in the case on Wallonian public broadcaster RTBF. The European Commission said it was of the opinion that the funding of public broadcasters can usually be regarded as market and trade distortive. It justified that opinion by pointing at the existence of an international market for rights sales and acquisitions and the cross-border effects in advertising markets that are part of same-language neighbouring markets. In such markets, the existence of a public broadcaster can influence groups that are active across European borders such as RTL Group (European Commission, 2014: §108, §111). This assessment of market reality goes against most scholarship on smaller media markets with big language neighbours (see several contributions in Lowe and Nissen, 2011; Puppis, 2009).

Dismissing the reality of an internationalised, converged and platform-based media market

In line with its decisions before the Broadcasting Communication 2009, the European Commission still requires a clear definition of the remit, focussing largely on online activities in this regard. It continues its no-hands-off approach that became apparent in its decisions on the German, Flemish and Irish public broadcasters' funding. The Commission, so it repeats in its decision on public broadcaster of the French-speaking community in Belgium RTBF, accepts a broad and qualitative description of the remit, including references to the democratic, social and cultural needs of society. Digital activities and the distribution of audiovisual services via all distribution platforms can be part of the remit (European Commission, 2014: §172). Regardless of 'the freedom of the Member States to describe the public task, that description must be as clear and precise as possible as to avoid any doubt on whether a certain activity is considered part of the public task by that Member State' (§174). So, the same issue remains. What is clear and precise enough and how far can the European Commission push Member States of the EU to clarify the public service remit?

Several elements can be discerned in the analysed decisions. First, technology neutrality as a principle is limited to the distribution of audiovisual content over different platforms. It thus sets out from radio and television as the norm. Online service delivery is accepted as part of the existing public task in case it concerns the distribution of radio and television services that already exist (European Commission, 2014: §152). A more wide definition of technology neutrality whereby the public broadcaster uses a diversity of services to live up to its qualitative goals is not accepted (European Commission, 2009b: §94). That became apparent also in an informal investigation on the funding of Flemish public broadcaster VRT. Between 2014 and 2018, the Flemish Government and the European Commission discussed revisions to the Public Service Media legislation. While the Flemish Government adapted the applicable laws already in 2008 (European Commission, 2008a), new amendments of the new management contract (2016-2020) between the VRT and the Flemish Government were asked. That management contract stressed that a definition of the remit in the function of radio, television and online was outdated and that a precise remit on the basis of qualitative objectives in the areas of information, education, culture, entertainment and sports would be outlined (see Chapters 9 and 13). That approach was, however, not accepted by the European Commission, saying it had to be clear what specific services were part of the remit and what was not. That standpoint is fairly similar to the decisions issued before the Broadcasting Communication 2009.

While a clear definition is a legitimate question under State aid law and also when taking a media policy perspective, the focus on online as an accessory activity of radio and broadcasting is outdated. Faced with international competitors that are fully converged, the attachment to radio, television and online as separate devices is outdated. Moreover, it is perfectly well possible that some online services contribute more to strengthening political citizenship than some of public broadcasters' radio and television services. Member States seem unable to convince the European Commission of a more modern, therefore not more lenient, approach to look at the remit. That is probably also due to Member States' own failure to update legislative frameworks for the new era (see Chapter 9).

A second action point remains the implementation of an ex ante test for new media services. Such an instrument was adopted in Austria, Wallonia (Belgium) and the Netherlands after the European Commission's intervention. All three countries also accepted creating a list of services that were commercial in nature and hence not captured by the public service remit (see also Donders, 2015). Some of them also made a list of services that were captured by the remit, in so doing subjecting all other services to an ex ante evaluation. ORF made an exhaustive list of services covered by the remit. The transmission of radio and television services over a different platform could not be considered a new service, but essentially everything else not on the list of services mentioned before would be qualified as a new service and hence be subjected to an ex ante test. For example, in case ORF operates an online web platform for seniors and it decides to do something similar for youngsters, such an initiative would amount to a new service. In case the online web platform for seniors is being invested in more, this might induce a test. Indeed, when 2 per cent of ORF's annual budget would be spent on such an existing service it would qualify as significantly new and require an ex ante evaluation. If Austria wants ORF to launch a new dedicated channel for documentaries and investigative journalism, this requires an ex ante test (European Commission, 2009c: §177ff, 198ff). In the case on RTBF, the public broadcaster for the French-speaking community in Belgium, the European Commission also accepted a remit relating to linear, non-linear and social media distribution of audiovisual services (European Commission 2014: §20). Web fiction, web documentaries and multi-platform formats are explicitly mentioned (§24). There is in fact a full list of what services RTBF can deliver online, ranging from pure audiovisual services, to opinion polls, editorials, textual transcriptions of programmes, databases dealing with information, and so on. Text services are acceptable only in case there is a link with a radio or television programme (§27). And similar to Austria, everything that is not included in this list requires an ex ante test. A 3 per cent instead of 2 per cent norm, as in the Austrian case, is proposed by the Walloon government and accepted by the European Commission, meaning a new service that impacts 3 per cent of the budget of RTBF or more requires an ex ante test automatically. Interestingly, the European Commission rejects the proposal of the Walloon government to test only these services that are not included in the management contract that is updated every five years. That would have meant RTBF and the government could agree on the inclusion of new services every five years without those services requiring a test. Something similar had been accepted in the 2008 decision on the Flemish public broadcaster VRT and afterwards it seemed the European Commission had not fully anticipated the implications of that 'rule', which was basically a pragmatic erosion of their demand for an ex ante test of new services (Donders, 2011). The Dutch case was rather peculiar compared to the Austrian and Walloon decisions, because the European Commission accepts a test procedure that is much less evidence based and more or less in the hands of the minister of media who takes a provisional decision on a newly proposed service even before several advisory bodies have provided their recommendations. A final decision is made once that has happened, but can deviate from the advice. That has been criticised for not being an independent procedure. Pilot projects are at the same time interpreted in a more narrow way than in the Flemish case where in fact all services that are said to be temporary can be rolled out under the concept of a pilot project and do not require a test as long they are in a testing phase, even in the target audience is not limited (Donders, 2015).

There thus are similarities and differences between the cases. That does not per se concern cases that were concluded a couple of years before the Broadcasting Communication 2009 and those after. The question of a more clear description of new media services, the introduction of an ex ante test and regulation taking into account the opinion of third-party (market) stakeholders was present in the decisions issued on the German, Flemish and Irish public broadcasters before 2009 and the decisions dealing with the funding of public broadcasters in Austria, Wallonia and the Netherlands after 2009. That is not abnormal as the German, Flemish and Irish decisions were the blueprint for the Broadcasting Communication 2009. There are differences also across cases. Again, the Broadcasting Communication 2009 is not the differentiating factor here, but rather the differences between national Public Service Media systems and the elements highly valued by the politicians negotiating with the European Commission on compliance of their State aid regime with the internal market, ensuring that compliance is thus not only a legal, but very much also a political exercise.

What can be criticised is not per se the request for an ex ante test, but, rather, the European Commission's lack of a decent market analysis that would show that public broadcasters' capacity to distort markets is much smaller than it was 15 to 20 years ago when the digital market really started to develop. That results, second, in suggested conditions for compliance that slow down the much-needed development of public broadcasters into public media organisations, a development that is already difficult given organisation-internal dynamics (see Chapter 12). While ex ante testing can be a good idea for a specific set of services, the process seems to have been captured by political plotting, private sector lobbying and rarely reflects thoroughly on the public value of proposed services.

A third concern of the European Commission that is very much visible in several State aid decisions issued after the Broadcasting Communication 2009 is their fear that public broadcasters would distort markets for the acquisition of sports rights and other premium rights. That has resulted, most visibly, in the requirement to limit the offer of on-demand content for free to a certain duration. As a generic rule of thumb, the Austrian, Walloon and Dutch Governments agreed to time limits of about 24 hours for sports after the initial broadcast, seven days for other content and no limits for historical and cultural programming (e.g., European Commission, 2009c: §185). In the United Kingdom, the BBC managed to get a more lenient regime in 2019 because it could illustrate that these limits, aiming to protect competitors from a too dominant presence of public broadcasters online, in fact harmed their competition with multinationals such as Netflix that have content on offer with no such limits. Related, the European Commission remains concerned about sports rights and public broadcasters. That concern goes back to the early investigations under anti-trust law of the EBU *Eurovision* system (cf. supra) at the end of the 1980s. Particularly, ORF, which has been very active in securing sports rights and has a dedicated sports channel, faced in-depth attention for its activities in this area and had to comply with a number of conditions to make sure it could not empty the market for premium sports rights (§147). While that might have been the case in the past, few scholars will argue that public broadcasters are still in the possibility to outcompete parties such as Al Jazeera, Discovery Communications, Facebook and Eurosport here (Evens et al., 2013).

Also in post-2009 decisions the European Commission, next to insisting on a clear definition and an ex ante test for new services, stuck to its well-known recipes to ensure compliance, including independent oversight (European Commission, 2009c), close scrutiny of capital injections (European Commission, 2011c) and a limitation of reserves accumulation (European Commission, 2009c: §232).

A double-edged sword

European Commission control of funding schemes for public broadcasters is probably one of the most impactful European policies regarding Public Service Media. It sets out from the idea that public money for Services of General Economic Interest can be acceptable in cases where certain conditions are met. While the Amsterdam Protocol emphasises that public broadcasters are needed to contribute to the social, cultural and democratic goals of European societies, the application of the competition rules is to ensure that that contribution happens with a minimal amount of market distortion. One can already criticise that, when taking a citizenship- and democracy-centric approach to Public Service Media. But looking at the European legal order and the supremacy of the internal market project the approach taken by the European Commission so far makes sense from *their point of view.* Admittedly, one can criticise also staying within the legal and even mental framework of State aid control the European Commission for over-stepping its competencies in defining manifest error. That definition, sometimes involving providing examples of public broadcasters' services that would not fit within the public service remit, is in fact the European Commission co-defining the task of an SGEI: something it can absolutely not do as it is a competence of the Member States. Furthermore, if the European Commission wants to be consistent and coherent in adopting more evidence-based policies, it is necessary – especially after the adoption of the Broadcasting Communication 2009 – to become more facts based in assessing the impact of public broadcasters in contemporary media markets. The frame that is used still is one of duopolistic media markets, public broadcasters on one side and commercial media companies on the other side. The side of public broadcasters has, with the advent of platform companies, become considerably smaller. That does not mean public broadcasters should not try to minimise their distortion of markets, not does it mean they never do this. But essentially, the State aid intervention of the European Commission is not necessarily limiting that impact, is largely a formal legalistic exercise and might slow down the development of public broadcasters' digital strategies without making sure these are aimed at the achievement of public interest objectives.

Does that mean all is bad? No. European Commission intervention has had two positive consequences throughout the years of its application. First and foremost, it has resulted in the implementation of good governance principles related to transparency, robust financial accounting mechanisms and independent control. The European Commission could be a bit more active in following up on the implementation of appropriate measures here. Second, the European Commission has forced several EU Member States and public broadcasters alike to think more carefully about what the Public Service Media project should be in a digital age. That thinking is much needed. It should nonetheless not be limited to making lists of services that can and cannot be offered by public broadcasters, deciding on the scope of pilot projects, and carrying out ex ante tests. It should be focused more on how public broadcasters can still contribute to strengthening citizenship in democratic societies, if that is a possibility at all.

References

Antoniadis, A. (2006). The financing of public service broadcasting. In M.S. Rydelski (ed.), *The EC State Aid Regime: Distortive Effects of State Aid on Competition and Trade* (pp. 591–630). London: Cameron May.

Bardoel, J. and Vochteloo, M. (2009). Media Policy between Europe and the Nation-State: The Case of the EU Broadcast Communication 2009. Paper presented at the

162 *Law*

ECREA-CLP Workshop on 'New Directions for Communication Policy Research', 6-7 November, Zürich.

Biggam, R. (2011). Ex ante regulations, the EU and its Member States: Back to Brussels? In K. Donders and H. Moe (eds), *Exporting the Public Value Test: The Regulation of Public Broadcasters' New Media Services Across Europe*. Göteborg: Nordicom.

Brevini, B. (2013). *Public Service Broadcasting Online: A Comparative European Policy Study of PSB 2.0*. New York: Palgrave Macmillan.

Coe, R., Priest, J. and Hutton, D. (2002). *Evaluation of BBC Digital Curriculum: Summary of Findings*. Durham: University of Durham, Educational Evaluation Group.

Donders, K. (2011). The public value test: A reasoned response or panic reaction? In K. Donders and H. Moe (eds), *Ex Ante Tests in Europe: From Diverging Perspectives to Infinite Conclusions* (pp. 29-38). Göteborg: Nordicom.

Donders, K. (2012). *Public Service Media and Policy in Europe*. Basingstoke: Palgrave Macmillan.

Donders, K. (2015). State aid to public service media: European Commission decisional practice before and after the 2009 Broadcasting Communication. *European State aid Law Quarterly*, 1(15), 68-87.

Donders, K. and Pauwels, C. (2008). Does EU policy challenge the digital future of public service broadcasting? An analysis of the Commission's State aid approach to digitization and the public service remit of public broadcasting organizations. *Convergence, The International Journal of Research into New Media Technologies*, 14(3), 295-311.

Donders, K. and Pauwels, C. (2009). European State aid rules and the public service broadcasting remit in the digital age: Analyzing a contentious part of European policy and integration. In I. Garcia-Blanco, S. Van Bauwel and B. Cammaerts (eds), *Media Agoras: Democracy, Diversity and Communication* (pp. 178-197). Cambridge: Cambridge Scholars Publishing.

Donders, K., Van den Bulck, H. and Raats, T. (2019). The politics of pleasing: A critical analysis of multistakeholderism in public service media policies in Flanders. *Media, Culture & Society*, 41(3), 347-366.

European Commission (1999). Decision of 14 December 1999 on *Financing of 24-hour advertising-free news channels out of the license fee by the BBC*.

European Commission (2002a). Communication of 16 February 2002 on *Certain legal aspects relating to cinematographic and other audiovisual works*.

European Commission (2002b). Decision of 3 April 2002 on *ZDF Medienpark*.

European Commission (2003a). Decision of 1 October 2003 on *BBC Digital Curriculum*.

European Commission (2003b). Decision of 15 October 2003 on *Ad hoc funds implemented by Portugal for RTP*.

European Commission (2003c). Decision of 15 October 2003 on *Ad hoc measures implemented by Italy for RAI*.

European Commission (2003d). Decision of 15 October 2003 on *Ad hoc measures implemented by France for France Télévisions*.

European Commission (2004a). Decision of 19 May 2004 on *Measures implemented by Denmark for TV2/Danmark*.

European Commission (2004b). Decision of 6 October 2004 on *Recapitalisation of TV2/Danmark*.

European Commission (2005a). Decision of 20 April on *Annual funding of France for France Télévisions*.

European Commission (2005b). Decision of 20 April on *Annual funding of Portugal for RTP*.

European Commission (2005c). Decision of 20 April on *Annual funding of Spain for RTVE*.

European Commission (2006a). Decision of 22 March 2006 on *Compensation payments from Portugal for RTP*.

European Commission (2006b). Decision of 22 June 2006 on *Ad hoc funds from the Netherlands for NOS*.

European Commission (2006c). Decision of 4 July 2006 on *Ad hoc funds from Portugal for RTP*.

European Commission (2007a). Decision of 7 March 2007 on *Remedies for the reduction of RTVE's workforce*.

European Commission (2007b). Decision of 24 April 2007 on *The License Fee Funding of ARD and ZDF*.

European Commission (2008a). Decision of 27 February 2008 on the *Funding of Flemish public broadcaster VRT*.

European Commission (2008b). Decision of 27 February 2008 on the *Funding of Irish public broadcaster RTE*.

European Commission (2008c). Decision of 16 July 2008 on *Capital injections for France Télévisions*.

European Commission (2009a). Communication of 2 July 2009 on the *Application of the State Aid Rules to Public Service Broadcasting*.

European Commission (2009b). Decision of 1 September 2009 on *Capital injections for France Télévisions*.

European Commission (2009c). Decision of 28 October 2009 on *Funding of Austrian public broadcaster ORF*.

European Commission (2011a). Decision of 23 March 2011 on *The creation of 4FM radio station*.

European Commission (2011b). Decision of 27 October 2011 on *Support of public service radio programs*.

European Commission (2011c). Decision of 20 December 2011 on *Financial support to restructure the debt of RTP*.

European Commission (2013). Decision of 8 November 2013 on *Financing of Local Stations France Blue Saint-Etienne Loire*.

European Commission (2014). Decision of 7 May 2014 on *Funding of Public Broadcaster RTBF*.

European Commission (2016). Decision of 27 June 2016 on *Financing of France Médias Monde*.

Evens, T. and Donders, K. (2018). *Platform Power and Policy in Transforming Television Markets*. New York and Basingstoke: Palgrave Macmillan.

Evens, T., Iosifidis, P. and Smith, P. (2013). *The Political Economy of Sports Rights*. Basingstoke: Palgrave Macmillan.

Herzog, C., Handke, C. and Hitters, E. (2019). Analysing Talk and Text II: Thematic analysis. In H. Van den Bulck, M. Puppis, K. Donders and L. Van Audenhove (eds), *The Palgrave Handbook of Media Policy Research Methods* (pp. 385-401). Basingstoke: Palgrave Macmillan.

Karppinen, K. and Moe, H. (2019). Text as data I: Document analysis. In H. Van den Bulck, M. Puppis, K. Donders and L. Van Audenhove (eds), *The Palgrave Handbook of Media Policy Research Methods* (pp. 249-262). Basingstoke: Palgrave Macmillan.

Levy, D. (1999). *Europe's Digital Revolution: Broadcasting Revolution, the EU and the Nation State*. London: Routledge.

Lowe, G.F. and Nissen, C.S. (eds)(2011). *Small among Giants: Television Broadcasting in Smaller Countries*. Nordicom: Göteborg.

Moe, H. (2008). Between supranational competition and national culture? Emerging EU policy and public broadcasters' online services. In I. Bondebjerg and P. Madsen (eds), *Media, Democracy and European Culture* (pp. 215–239). Bristol: Intellect.

Puppis, M. (2009). Media regulation in small states. *International Communication Gazette*, 71(1-2), 7-17.

Puppis, M. (2019). Analyzing Talk and Text I: Qualitative content analysis. In H. Van den Bulck, M. Puppis, K. Donders and L. Van Audenhove (eds), *Handbook on Media Policy Research Methods* (pp. 367-384). Basingstoke: Palgrave Macmillan.

Smith, M.P. (2001). How adaptable is the European Commission? The case of State aid regulation. *Journal of Public Policy*, 21(3), 219-238.

Steemers, J. (2003). Public service broadcasting is not dead yet: Strategies in the 21st century. In G.F. Lowe and T. Hujanen (eds), *Broadcasting and Convergence: New Articulations of the Public Service Remit* (pp. 123–136). Göteborg: Nordicom.

Suter, T. (2008). Setting public goals, defining public value, securing public support – the challenge for Europe's PSBs. Presentation at the conference on 'Public service media in the digital age', 17 July, Strasbourg.

Ward, D. (2008). The European Commission's state aid regime and PSB. In D. Ward (ed.), *The European Union and the Culture Industries* (pp. 59-80). London: Ashgate.

9 Regulating public broadcasters' moving online

Sensitivities on public broadcasters' expansion online

Public broadcasters' initiatives in the online world have provoked concern with commercial competitors from the end of the 1990s onwards. Commercial broadcasters and, even more so these days, newspapers argue that public broadcasters' delivery of services on the Internet is market distortive and not officially authorised by governments. There is little evidence of the market-distortive impacts of public broadcasters' online services. On the contrary, research by Sjøvaag, Pedersen and Owren (2019) has shown that Norwegian public broadcaster NRK, which is very active and successful in the online news market, 'cannot, however, be accused of being too similar in this news content to commercial operators, who are generally more similar to each other than NRK is to them'.

Scholars such as Jo Bardoel and Marit Vochteloo (2008) and Hallvard Moe (2008) have argued that online services cannot be considered an expansion of public broadcasters' task. They are basically the consequence of technological evolutions that widen the scope of public broadcasters' activities, but not per se the underlying task to inform, educate and entertain. I have argued else-where that such a view disregards too easily that the task of public broadcasters is to inform, educate and entertain, but not per se at the expense of others (Donders, 2012).

Most policy-makers in Western and Northern Europe are sensitive to private sector concerns and have decided to regulate public broadcasters' new media services, whatever that might be as 'new media' is essentially a moving target. The aim of this chapter is not to discuss at length why commercial competitors argue that public broadcasters are behaving in anti-competitive ways. Some of their concerns are addressed sideways in this chapter and more elaborately in the case study chapters in this book. Rather, the objective is to explain how EU Member States have tried to regulate public broadcasters' online ser-vices. Did regulation follow a market failure or a social responsibility logic (see Chapter 3)? What types of online services were targeted? And is the regulation in place making sense at all? I do not provide an exhaustive overview of regu-latory practices in all EU Member States. There are reports of, among others,

Cappello et al. (2015), Gillebaard et al. (2015) and Donders and Moe (2011) that contain such mapping exercises or a wide variety of brief country case studies. I will study specific cases in detail to describe, analyse and evaluate the state of play of rules that regulate public broadcasters' online behaviour. That analysis will also show that the cover of 'public value test' can be the surface of very different, context-specific practices and that the regulation on 'text-based services' can be very specific in some countries and very vague in other Member States.

Methodology

The chapter zooms in on three case studies. First, the public value test of pre-school children's television channel *Ketnet Jr.* in Flanders in 2017. Second, the rules imposed on the BBC iPlayer in 2007. Third, the constraints on the German public broadcasters to offer text-based services in the area of online news, imposed on ARD, its members and ZDF in 2008 in the 12th Interstate Treaty on Broadcasting and Telemedia. In all three case studies, the focus is on uncovering how new media activities of public broadcasters are regulated, on how technology neutral that regulation is, and how the regulation works or fails to work in practice. The selection of the types of regulatory interventions is based on the European Commission's and competitors' concerns in this area. The focus is thus more on regulatory tools that aim to limit public broadcasters' activities in the digital market place and not so much on what they should do in terms of innovation, differentiation and personalisation, interactivity, and so on. These issues are addressed elsewhere in this book, among others in Chapter 12. The choice for Flanders, the United Kingdom and Germany can be criticised for being selective. There are many more countries that have introduced regu-lation to deal with public broadcasters' new media activities. Where relevant, we will make reference to practices in these countries also. The choice for in-depth case studies, even though these concern one event in one part of Europe in a particular point in time, is valuable because it allows us to understand very complex rules and their application within their political, economic and social context (Eisenhardt, 1989; Flyvbjerg, 2006; Vennesson, 2008; Broughton-Micova, 2019;). Most of the work is based on qualitative document analysis, focused on the main concepts, rules and procedures in place. Where possible, insights from relevant secondary literature are added.

From alleged market distortion, over EU intervention, to Member State regulation

Market distortion

Before elaborating on regulatory practices concerning Public Service Media, I briefly elaborate on the concerns that support such added regulatory inter-vention. Indeed, while commercial media largely oppose regulation, they have been very active – sometimes with reason – to argue for a stricter regulation of public broadcasters and, more recently, also of platform companies. Concerns on market distortion are not new though. In 1987, Screensport, a satellite television company, already filed a complaint with the competition authorities of the European Commission. It basically argued that the joint acquisition of sports rights by the European Broadcasting Union was a violation of the European Union's rules on anti-competitive agreements between undertakings. In the early 1990s, a few years later, other complaints followed based on a different strand of competition law, that is, State aid rules (see Chapter 8). A lot of companies have insisted on the need to control public broadcasters' activities better in areas such as entertainment and sports programming, Internet services and commercial communication since the 1990s at the national level, even more ferociously so than at the European level.

Largely, the concerns expressed by companies are threefold. First, they are of the opinion that public broadcasters do things that are not part of their remit. That can be entertainment or sports, but also relate to online news and text in particular. The idea is that those terrains are catered for by the market and thus not the playground of public broadcasters. A market failure ideology inspires this concern (Donders, 2015). Public broadcasters and scholars have counterargued in two ways. First, entertainment and sports are considered part of public broadcasters' service portfolio. These genres are needed to draw audience attention to 'more public service' genres such as information and education. Second, entertainment, sports and online news are genuinely public service. The specificity of public broadcasters' offers ensure, even in case these types of services are also offered by commercial companies, some level of distinctiveness from what is already offered in the market. More fundamentally, public broadcasters guarantee the provision of a diversity of genres and services, regardless of their profitability at a given moment in time. A second concern commercial media have expressed is public broadcasters' funding. Subsidies or a license fee system with as little reliance as possible on commercial revenues are favoured over a reliance on income from advertising. While under State aid law the manner of funding is irrelevant, most scholars will defend a license fee over subsidies as to increase independence from the State (e.g., Jakubowicz, 2007a) and will also argue that too much commercial revenues undermine public broadcasters' non-alignment with market imperatives. Governments, not markets, are responsible for ensuring adequate funding of public broadcasters (Donders, 2012; see also Jakubowicz, 2007b). Third, there is the sentiment that public broadcasters' behaviour is usually not clearly regulated. The qualitative objectives that public broadcasters ought to achieve are too abstract for many commercial media. They prefer to see a clear list of what is allowed and what is not. That perception is not equally vivid in all European countries. A study on commercial media managers' views on the public interest in Flanders and Norway showed that the latter were more accepting of a broad public broadcast regime compared to their Flemish counterparts (Syvertsen et al., 2019).

European intervention and Member State actions

Commercial media have expressed their concerns on Public Service Media ever since commercial broadcasters entered the market. As discussed more elaborately in Chapter 8, these concerns have later on been voiced at the level of the European Union too. Some of the tools Member States of the European Union have implemented to regulate new media services of public broadcasters have been inspired by European Commission State aid decisions on the funding of public broadcasters. It should, in line with the findings in Chapters 7 and 8, not come as a surprise that the Commission's approach in this has been largely oriented at safeguarding the interests of commercial media. While the application of the State aid rules has been more lenient in the field of Public Service Media than in other areas, because of the Amsterdam Protocol, the quest for legal certainty and predictability for commercial media has resulted in regulatory practices that are considered as breaches of autonomy by public broadcasters, on the one hand, and as insufficient by the competitors, on the other (Donders, 2015).

Generalising to some extent, there are three main ways to deal with public broadcasters' evolution to new media organisations. On the one hand, some governments have decided to define public broadcasters' remit in a technology neutral manner, accepting not only that radio and television broadcasting as well as online distribution is what public broadcasters ought to do in a digital age. But, these governments also consider 'online only' content a public service task. In other words, they have embraced the notion of Public Service Media and entrusted the achievement of that ideal to public broadcasters. Norway, Sweden, Finland, Ireland, and so on, largely follow this view. On the other hand, there are governments that see online almost as a necessary evil part of public broadcasters' activities. Public broadcasters can expand service delivery to non-radio and -television domains, but only in so far as these activities are closely related to what public broadcasters have traditionally done. There are in Europe not that many Member States, besides perhaps the Netherlands and Germany, that follow this line of argumentation. Rather, the largest group of countries can be situated in a more pragmatic view on Public Service Media. These countries, such as Austria, Switzerland, the United Kingdom, Denmark, and so on, accept that public broadcasters ought to become Public Service Media organisations. They also think that the task of public broadcasters should be more clearly defined and restricted when necessary to protect competitors. The problem with that view is that it is sometimes inspired by a market failure perspective and that thus the ultimate aim is to confine public broadcasters to a niche actor in media markets. In the other case, being governments that genuinely attempt to balance the public interest with the interests of commercial media, the negotiation of what Public Service Media is and what public broadcasters have to do is a never-ending one. While that creates pressure on public broadcasters, it, at the same time – provided there is no commercial sector capture of politics – ensures a continuous and much-needed dialogue on the place of public service provision in an increasingly commercialised media environment.

Public value tests: far away from evidence-based in Flanders

The public value test is a tool assessing both the public value and market impact of public broadcasters' new services. It was invented in the United Kingdom as a means to assess initiatives such as the BBC's iPlayer. The European Commission picked it up in its 2009 Broadcasting Communication (European Commission, 2009) as a means for all Member States to evaluate in an evidence-based manner whether online services of public broadcasters were captured by their entrusted task or not. Admittedly, the instrument also aimed at overcoming fierce criticism from private media companies on public broadcasters' so-called 'expansion' into the Internet domain (Donders, 2011; Bardoel and Vochteloo, 2009). It has been introduced as a legal principle and practice in several European countries, including Germany, Ireland, Belgium, the Netherlands, Austria and Norway (Donders and Moe, 2011; Gransow, 2017).

Several scholars have criticised the test for segmenting the role of public broadcasters into singular services; hence, being ignorant of the holistic nature of Public Service Media (Moe, 2008; Bardoel and Vochteloo, 2009). Its alleged focus on the market impact assessment to the detriment of the public value evaluation has also been a point of criticism. An aspect less discussed is the evidence-based nature of the test. Indeed, if the idea is to evaluate new services of public broadcasters in a rational manner, does that idea then also translate to practice? Or do we, in the alternative scenario, see that public broadcasting policies are still very much captured by untransparent lobbying processes in which factual information is of secondary importance? To answer these questions, I had a look at the implementation of the first public value test in Flanders. The test dealt with the planned launch of a pre-school children's television channel in the Flemish market of about 6.5 million inhabitants.

A vague regulatory framework

On 27 February 2008, the European Commission decided that the funding of Flemish public broadcaster VRT was compatible with the internal markets provided some regulatory changes were made. One of these changes was the implementation of a public value test. The Flemish media decree provides:

> VRT can offer services or activities that are not covered by the management contract only after explicit approval of the Flemish Government. The Flemish Government asks the advise of the Flemish Regulator for Media. The Flemish Regulator for Media organises an open, public consultation in that respect. In its advise, the Flemish Regulator for Media, analyses the

public value of the proposal taking into account important evolutions in the media market and in technology, the evolving media landscape and the role of VRT therein. Subsequently, the Flemish Regulator for Media weighs the public value of the proposal against the market impact. The Flemish Regulator for Media will deliver its advise within 6 months after receiving a request for advise from the Flemish Government. The Flemish Regulator for Media publishes the advice on its website. The Flemish Government publishes its motivated decision for accepting to rejecting the new services on its website. The Flemish Government will determine additional rules for the implementation of this article.

(Article 18, Flemish media decree)

The decree thus requires a test of both public value and market impact. The responsible actor for this is the Flemish Regulator for Media, an independent regulatory body. A public consultation should be the starting point of the test procedure. There is a time constraint of six months, not after the public broadcaster submits its proposal, but after the Flemish Government asks for an advise. This in principle could result in lengthening the procedure. The advise has to be published. What the Flemish Government has to do with the advise is less clear. It takes a motivated decision, but what role the advise plays in that regard is not made explicit in the media decree. Article 18 mentions that further specifications will be determined. That indeed happened in the management contract between the public broadcaster and the Flemish Government. The management contract 2012-2016 and 2016-2020 contain rules on new media services and the required ex ante test. The management contract 2016-2020 is more elaborate in this regard, upon the request of the European Commission. It contains a section on new media services which elaborates largely on what existing versus new media services are. Existing services are all services and activities covered by the management contract. That leaves considerable room for interpretation as the management contract has a qualitative scope and does not list services. Also considered are existing services: the non-linear offer of existing linear services; the re-branding or re-styling of all VRT brands within the scope of the management contract; the creation of sub-brands that contribute to the achievement of the management contract; the combination of brands into a new brand provided that happens within the contours of the management contract; the adaptation of the mission of a brand within the scope of the management contract; all editorial changes to services; an expansion or decrease of the quantity of services offered (e.g., hours of content); and functional changes of services that aim to increase the quality of such services, accessibility or ease of audience use. Moreover, temporary pilot projects are allowed as well for a period of 18 months maximum and, preferably but not necessarily, for a limited part of the audience. All services that are not captured by this list of existing services are new services. The creation of a new main brand (e.g., a new television channel) will be considered a new service in any case. The introduction of payment for services or the demand for a significant increase of government funding because of a service is also subject to an ex ante test. The management contract 2016-2020 also identifies a category of services that might be new, but of which this is uncertain. In other words: there is a grey zone of services that might be new or existing. For such services, the public broadcaster needs to explain how they contribute to the achievement of the management contract and meeting new audience needs; whether these complement or replace existing services; and the cost and manner of financing. The Flemish Government will determine on the basis of this exploratory analysis of the public broadcaster whether there is indeed a new service and a test is required (Vlaamse Regering and VRT, 2015: 50-51).

It is noteworthy that the list of what is an existing service is considerably longer than what would constitute a significantly new service; an issue that has been criticised by commercial media for making the public value test largely a legal notion, but − until 2017 at least − a non-existing practice in Flanders (Appel, 2011).

The management contract also specifies that the regulator should evaluate the services based on the changes of the market economic situation in the Flemish media landscape, the existing media offers in the Flemish market, the technological evolutions, international trends, the protection and promotion of the Flemish culture and identity and the expectations and needs of the Flemish media users. The management contract also mentions sideways the public broadcaster has to prepare a file on the new service (Vlaamse Regering and VRT, 2015: 50). No other provisions can be found on the procedure, the requirements of the proposal to be made by the public broadcaster and the relation between the regulator's advice and the Flemish Government's decision. That is odd as more information on procedural aspects of the public value test are available for countries such as the United Kingdom and Ireland. The former published a document 'Guidance on the conduct of the public value test' in 2007 (BBC Trust, 2007a). Ireland's Broadcasting Act elaborates on the public value test as well. This has resulted in rather structured ex ante procedures where RTE's proposals are followed by a response from the Broadcasting Authority Ireland, based on a separate public value and market assessment. The Irish Minister for Communications reaches a decision that is explicitly related to all of the preceding documents and notably the advice of the regulator (see, for example, Department of Communications, 2018). It is important to be specific on the scope and procedure of the test. The lack of clarity on the market impact assessment in the Netherlands provoked justified criticism from the news media lobby. Indeed, the Dutch procedure was unclear on whether an independent market impact assessment was required at all. That resulted in a practice whereby the minister for communications took into account the opinions of consulted companies, but there was no independent assessment of their submissions (Donders and Raats, 2012). This has in the meantime been changed because of private sector lobbying (NDP, 2018). Somewhat similar, some countries do not specify whether public broadcasters have a right to respond to stakeholder submissions, for example in case they can evidence that arguments or data are false. The possibility to comment is not foreseen in Flanders (see later), nor in the Netherlands. In Germany, the United Kingdom, Norway, and so on, public broadcasters have and extensively use this possibility (Donders and Pauwels, 2010). Another issue that is not specified is the use of open or closed consultations of stakeholders. Can everybody participate? Is everybody encouraged to participate? Earlier research on stakeholder consultations related to the future of Public Service Media systems as a whole shows that open consultations result in a lower diversity of stakeholders that is being heard. Commercial media participate but civil society organisations are less active, which can be explained by the technical and often legalistic nature of consultation documents and the broader scope of topics these organisations need to cover (Donders and Raats, 2012). My analysis will show that the lack of clarity on the public value test procedure in Flanders became a problem at the end of 2016 when VRT for the first time needed to submit a proposal to the test, over eight years after the legal adoption of the instrument.

Ketnet Jr. *as a significantly new service*

Indeed, at the end of 2016 the Flemish public broadcaster VRT proposed to launch a pre-school children's television channel *Ketnet Jr.* VRT already had a children's channel *Ketnet.* While that channel targets children until 12 years, there was little possibility to differentiate between the needs of pre-schoolers and other children. International brands such as Disney and Nickelodeon offer separate channels, something parents perceived as an asset of these brands. This also showed in Ketnet's declining market share while Nickelodeon and Disney became increasingly successful to attract more viewers. At the time of the test, the public broadcaster's and Nickelodeon market shares were both at approximately 20 per cent, Disney followed with a 10 per cent market share, and commercial television channels *VTMKzoom* and *Kadet*, largely showing American animation, had a market share of approximately 5 per cent each. American animation is usually dubbed with voice actors from the Netherlands; the public broadcaster's foreign animation shows are dubbed with voice actors from Flanders. VRT does not raise commercial communication revenues in this market. It is active in the merchandising business though. The local commercial channels rely largely on advertising revenues and fees they receive for taking care of the advertising sales of international companies. *DPGMedia*, the company behind *VTMKzoom* and *Kadet*, for example, is also selling advertising space on Nickelodeon's channels. This shows the dominance of American companies in European children's television markets at the level of content sales, but also in the domain of advertising. There has been academic concern about the growing dominance of a few players that add to the homogenisation and admittedly also the commercialisation of content for pre-school children in particular (Steemers, 2010; 2013; 2016; Steemers and D'Arma, 2012; Ene, 2017). Most of the mentioned brands do not have extensive online activities. *Ketnet* as well as *Ketnet Jr.* offer audiovisual content online and other types of services such as educational games or even a social media platform on which parental guidance is facilitated. The *Ketnet* brand enjoys a good reputation with parents and also professionals such as educators and children psychologists (VRT, 2016).

Several reasons are identified to support the launch of a pre-school children's channel. While such an idea might seem old-fashioned and out of date with the digital media consumption behaviour of young children, VRT points at figures that show that 25 per cent of children up to six years old do not have regular, quality access to the Internet. Of course, those children can watch *Ketnet* via linear television and some specific *Ketnet Jr.* slots on the Ketnet channel. However, there is no reliable offer for them. The public broadcaster moreover says it is committed to show animation dubbed with Flemish voice actors, but also to broadcast programmes with real people that cover local habits and issues. Its programming strategy is developed by a Ph.D. in children's psychology and tries to cover essential aspects of children's development stages. Furthermore, should the channel be approved, VRT is committed to investing more in the local production of children's content. That is important as commercial media hardly invest in local production (VRT, 2016).

Some VRT managers were actually of the opinion that an ex ante test was not required. Since *Ketnet Jr.* was an already existing subbrand of the *Ketnet* brand and the app for on-demand consumption already existed, the launch of a linear television channel was seen as the technology neutral expansion of the service offer. However, part of the politically appointed Board of Directors of VRT disagreed and asked a public value test. This dispute shows that even the elaborate list of existing services was not sufficient to classify the *Ketnet Jr* television channel as an existing service, even if the argument made sense from a legal point of view. There was political disagreement on that from the outset and the Board of Directors, which is in charge of strategic decision-taking, used the grey zones in the media decree and management contract to re-politicise the issue. That in some way goes against the objective of the European Commission when asking Member States to implement an ex ante test for new media services: to ensure a prior evaluation of new media services in a rational and evidence-based manner (see several contributions in Donders and Moe, 2011).

The chaotic public value test process

VRT's *Ketnet Jr.* proposal was published online. The proposal was about 70 pages and elaborated on both the public value and likely market impact of *Ketnet Jr.* While the public broadcaster estimated a high public value in terms of local content, educational offer, inclusion, and so on, it estimated a negligible market impact taking the introduction of other children channels as cases in point. The public broadcaster mentioned additional investments in local production, but did not provide figures on this. It considered this confidential information. Later on in the process it would disclose more detailed information to the regulator,

Flemish Parliament and other stakeholders. However, this information was not considered admissible. The Flemish Regulator for Media did not provide any details on what VRT's proposal should contain, however. There was not one single document with specifications on the procedure. When VRT asked, no additional information was provided. At the end of January 2017, the regulator opened a public consultation. Stakeholders were left in the dark on what would happen with their submissions. The public was not consulted. Respondents to the regulator's survey could indicate on various elements whether they supported or objected the service. No other option was available. The highly legalistic language of the survey moreover discouraged some stakeholders from submitting a response. On the basis of all submitted responses and its own analysis the regulator finally scored a number of elements from ++, +, 0 to – and – –. There was no explanation on how it came to the final scoring. There was no genuine and independent public value assessment or market impact study. Independent experts could submit their own response, but were not consulted in their capacity of expert. In its analysis the regulator gave far more prominence to commercial stakeholders' opinion, even in parts that had nothing to do with market impact (see Donders and Van den Bulck, 2020). The public broadcaster had no chance to respond to the submissions of stakeholders, some of which contained factual inaccuracies. For example, commercial broadcaster *DPGMedia* argued that the public broadcaster received *Lego* programmes at zero cost. The programme essentially serves as a big commercial for selling *Lego* products. The public broadcaster later on said that this is not the case. It indeed paid for the few *Lego* programmes it is broadcasting, precisely because it does not want to be part of the commercial deals that the toy manufacturer indeed makes with commercial broadcasters. There was no formal way of objecting against the claim, which was taken over by the Flemish Regulator for Media as a factual statement. At the end of the procedure most political parties agreed that there was a need to clarify the entire procedure and ensure a right of reply for VRT. No further specifications have been made to date.

An indecisive regulator and a government 'no' to Ketnet Jr.

The Flemish Regulator for Media said *Ketnet Jr.*'s impact in terms of technical evolutions, international trends and expectations of media users were neutral. That was a bit odd as research evidencing American dominance over the children's television market (cf. supra), studies on digital exclusion, and VRT's own research of parents' expectations were not taken into account in reaching this conclusion. The service's contribution to Flemish culture and identity was evaluated positively. Its market impact, focussing solely on commercial broadcasters' statements and dismissing producers' support of the proposal, was found to be negative. The regulator said it had 'difficulties in accepting that the introduction of an additional, linear children's channel would have no negative impact on the market shares of the other children's channels' (VRM, 2017: 20 – translated by author from Dutch), without providing evidence on how it came to that conclusion. A strong conclusion, especially given the total absence of a market impact analysis. The regulator said it could not weigh the positive contribution to Flemish culture and identity against market impact and put the hot potato on the plate of the Flemish Government. That was surprising to say the least. It showed the weakness of the regulator, but at the same time also the eagerness of the Flemish Government to be in charge of the process. It is indeed difficult to believe that the regulator came to a neutral conclusion with 1+ and 1−, while other elements were clearly positive as well.

The Flemish Government not so surprisingly rejected *Ketnet Jr*. The Christian Democrat party was very much in favour and managed to postpone a decision until after the summer break. However, opposition of the two other government parties, the Flemish nationalists and the liberal party eventually resulted in the service not being approved. In its motivation the government ignored the issues on Flemish culture and market impact, but argued that the service was not needed in a digital age where all children were online (Vlaamse Regering, 2017).

All in all, all of this shows the reluctance of the regulator and political class to use the tool of an ex ante evaluation to independently and rationally assess the public value and market impact of a service most independent scholars supported for being genuinely public service and actually compensating for a manifest market failure in local children's television. Intuitive statements of the regulator that 'even if some production companies assert that revenue increases are possible, it seems not very plausible that the introduction of Ketnet Jr. will have a positive impact on all production companies and facilitary companies' (VRM, 2017: 20 – translated by author from Dutch) are exemplary and can be found in its advice over and over again. The public value test in Flanders thus did not live up to the initial ambitions at the European level to have a rational, evidence-based assessment of new services to see whether these fit the remit, harm competitors or actually strengthen the market. The latter aspect was not considered at all.

Of course, the public value test is not equally flawed in all contexts. In the United Kingdom, the BBC Trust and Ofcom have engaged in comprehensive and more independent assessments of services such as BBC iPlayer and local news videos. The latter service was rejected (BBC Trust, 2009), which also had to do with the very grave situation of British regional newspapers – a situation that has aggravated since and in fact evidences the need of the service many years later. Germany has used extensive input from independent experts, especially for the market impact assessments. About 40 tests have been carried out, with a cost of nearly 10 million euros in total, and not one single service rejected (Digital Fernsehen, 2009; Donders and Pauwels, 2010). That has provoked criticism from private media that question the credibility and effectiveness of the test. They also criticise the use of *Publizistischer Wetbewerb* as a key concept guiding the market impact assessment. The concept indeed refers to competition for quality and thus does not only take economics and substitution as a starting point (Donders, 2012). Scholars have questioned the usefulness of the *Drei-Stufen-Test* as well, saying the cost is not justified by the purpose and that the entire process might in the end infringe on the editorial independence of public broadcasters (see Kops, Sokoll and Bensinger, 2009). In Norway the government decided in 2011 to go against the negative advise of its regulator and accept a new travel and route planner of public broadcaster NRK. The media regulator argued it was not clear how such as service contributed to the achievement of the public service goals of NRK. The competition authority provided input on the market impact assessment and was clear on the negative impact of NRK's proposal on new market initiatives in this area. Nonetheless, the Norwegian Government dismissed these arguments and, in so doing, undermined the position of its media regulator. This shows that even a test that excels in terms of procedural clarity, timing and quality of public value and market assessment (Lilleborge, 2011) has its problems. In spite of the manifold learnings from different national cases, there seems to be little mutual learning so far and sometimes the conditions imposed on services after a test can come with unintended consequences as the example of the BBC iPlayer in the subsequent section will illustrate.

Constraining on-demand offer of audiovisual content in the United Kingdom

The BBC's on-demand service iPlayer was approved after a public value test in 2007. While accepted, several conditions were imposed as to make sure the service would contribute to the on-demand market, deliver public value but not unduly distort competition. In this part I will explain briefly on what conditions the iPlayer was approved, how that fits with other countries' attempts to regulate the on-demand services of public broadcasters, and why this approach – although still popular in quite some EU Member States – has shown to be counterproductive, specifically when considering the resilience and competitiveness of the local media ecosystem versus international streaming services.

Yes to iPlayer, but ...

The BBC proposed the launch of its iPlayer in 2006; a positive decision was issued by the BBC Trust in 2007. The public value test dealing with iPlayer actually dealt with four services: seven-day catch-up television over the Internet, seven-day catch-up service over cable, simulcast television over the Internet and non-digital rights management audio downloads over the Internet (BBC Trust, 2007b). The BBC Trust evaluated whether these services, including thus the iPlayer, contribute to the achievement of the BBC's public purposes. Ofcom is in charge of the market impact assessment, albeit that the design of the test – at that time – had to be decided upon jointly by the BBC Trust, Ofcom and external experts (Woolard, 2008). The BBC Trust eventually concluded that the service was in check with technological trends, allowed license fee payers to use the BBC's audiovisual content in a more flexible manner and the iPlayer could potentially also contribute to a bigger appetite with users for on-demand services. Conditions were imposed to constrain possible negative market effects.

> Ofcom believes that the recommendations above will secure the best balance between enabling the BBC to bring new services to benefit licence fee payers while avoiding the most significant adverse consequences for the development of the market and hence the overall interests of viewers and listeners. It is also important to note that, where our proposals would lead to a reduction in the scope of the proposed services, the BBC would still be free to offer the excluded services on a commercial basis, through BBC Worldwide.
>
> (Ofcom, 2006: 7)

> the BBC's new on-demand services will create significant public value with limited market impact.
>
> (Coyle in BBC Trust, 2007b)

What were the conditions for iPlayer to go through? Some types of audiovisual content could only be streamed and not stored. The aim thereof was to limit negative market impact on companies offering audio books, classical music, and so on. Most importantly, time limits for the storage of other types of on-demand audiovisual content were introduced. For most audiovisual content the duration of storage was kept at 30 days (depending on the content), opposed to the 13 weeks the BBC originally proposed. For cultural and historical content the time window could be longer. For sports it was shorter. Finally, all content on the BBC's iPlayer had to be available for other parties as well and this on a market conforming basis.

While one can criticise the orientation of these conditions for being focused exclusively on the wellbeing of commercial media companies, one should keep in mind that the on-demand market was in full development at the time. A lot of uncertainty surrounded these trends and hence also BBC's plans to innovate in this domain. Flood Page (2015: 139ff) also illustrates how the BBC itself was internally divided on the strategy to follow with the iPlayer. Indeed, BBC Worldwide was of the opinion that iPlayer had tremendous financial potential and should be offered on a commercial basis. The eagerness of the BBC's commercial subsidiary to control iPlayer was moreover not explained solely by Worldwide's assessment of future evolutions in the market, but also by the fear that iPlayer might end the profitable branch of DVD sales – something that also happened, but that can not be attributed to iPlayer as such. There was thus a protectionist, more so than an innovative approach in this regard. That also relates to the time limits imposed on on-demand offers. While these limits are often perceived as meeting private sector demand, that is only part of the story. Also within the BBC, several managers feared that a lengthy window would increase the cost of rights management, also for in-house produced content for which, for example, author contributions were still due.

In spite of the limitations on iPlayer, the service became an immediate success. The audience reach of BBC increased, notably with youngsters. The brand became well known, also outside the United Kingdom. For some, iPlayer signified the BBC taking the lead on innovation in audiovisual markets (Flood Page, 2015: 155).

Similar rules in other EU Member States

Not only the British public value test, but also the test and conditions of iPlayer became guiding for practices in other EU Member States as well. For several countries shorter time periods of seven days were installed, which can largely be explained by the seven-day time frame of catch-up television. In Germany it was decided that on-demand offers of audiovisual content had to be limited to seven days after broadcast, 24 hours for sports (Koehler, 2008: 8). Telemedia services linked to programmes are also captured by this rule. For example, in case the news broadcast shows a ten-second fragment of an interview with Donald Trump, the full interview can be shown for up to seven days online. More lenient rules apply to cultural and historical programming (Dörr, 2011). This standard can be changed into longer time windows provided a service is made subject to a *Drei-Stufen-Test*. A selection of services such as news, radio comedy, radio drama, and so on, could be made available beyond seven days (see also the 12th Interstate Treaty, Article 11d(2)); which is basically what happened for several audiovisual content types, but can vary depending on the member of ARD that is concerned. As I argue elsewhere (Donders, 2012), the choice for the seven-day time limit was rather arbitrarily made. There is no rational argumentation underlying it. The choice was clearly inspired by the English example and focused on meeting private sector concerns. However, in the German case, there was far less worry about the rights implications of longer time windows.

In Wallonia, the French-speaking part of Belgium, a time limit of seven days applies as well (European Commission, 2014: §261). The Austrian public broadcaster ORF is bound by the same rules, again with more flexibility for cultural and historical content (Donders, 2015; Raats, Van den Bulck and d'Haenens, 2015: 66ff): similar examples can be found elsewhere. The Dutch public broadcasters benefit from a more flexible regulatory regime. Viewers can watch all programmes up to seven days after initial broadcast; for programmes where the public broadcasters own the rights that period is often longer and for content such as documentaries less time limits are foreseen. All other content can be watched on-demand via pay-services. This kind of more pragmatic arrangement is considered beneficial for both viewers, public broadcasters and competitors. It meets the demand of viewers to catch up on programmes they missed; most of that behaviour can be observed within seven days after initial broadcast (NPO, 2015b: 28). It limits costs for the public broadcasters and maximises potential for developing business models on on-demand content. However, it does set out from a broadcast-dominant model.

Why these rules do not work in practice

While Richard Collins (2007: 168ff) concluded that the BBC Trust had no intention to 'rubber-stamp' the BBC's new services with the public value test and fairly balanced public value and market impact and I agreed with that assessment ten years ago (see Donders, 2012), the current situation of an on-demand landscape dominated by Netflix and Amazon suggests we as scholars and also the BBC Trust might have missed something (cf. infra). It also shows that the public broadcasters themselves, who have taken their broadcast activities as the starting point for developing on-demand services (see also Chapter 12), might have missed the point about ten years ago.

Already in 2014, Netflix CEO Reed Hastings said that iPlayer has contributed to the success of his own streaming service: 'The iPlayer really blazed the trail. That was long before Netflix and really got people used to this idea of on-demand viewing' (Williams, 2014). That might give a bit too much credit to the BBC. In other countries such as Belgium, on-demand viewing was not popular before Netflix with no significant streaming or other on-demand offers of public broadcasters (Raats, Van den Bulck and d'Haenens, 2015). Nevertheless, Netflix also conquered audiences' hearts and, most importantly, wallets (Van Halewyn and De Marez, 2018). The service appeals to new viewing habits. It offers audiovisual content outside the frame of traditional broadcast television, often tailored to the personal preferences of each individual user (Evens and Donders, 2018; Lobato, 2019). Public broadcasters' own on-demand strategies have failed to follow track of that (r)evolution, in part, but not solely, because of regulation designed to fit the purpose of balancing market power in a dual broadcasting market.

All of this has triggered UK regulator Ofcom to give the BBC permission to extend its 30-day frame to 12 months, to offer full box sets of series and showcase more content from the archive: more broadly, to turn the catch-up service into an audiovisual content destination in its own right. That is necessary, so Ofcom (2019) agrees with the BBC (2019), to ensure that the public broadcasters remain relevant in a highly competitive and international media landscape. Its reach to younger audiences up to age 35 has fallen and should go up again; that also applies to children. These groups are, moreover, twice as likely to watch BBC content on Netflix than via BBC television channels or iPlayer (Ling, 2019; Waterson, 2019). The regulator remains concerned about the possible impact of that measure on commercial broadcasters and new initiatives such as BritBox, of which the BBC is also part. That paid service run by ITV and the BBC will come at a charge of approximately £6 per month. Rumour has it that ITV backed the BBC's plans to extend the time window on iPlayer in exchange for partnering in BritBox. Ofcom will closely monitor audience behaviour as a consequence of its decision, requiring the BBC to disclose data that make such monitoring possible. Another issue has also popped up in the meantime: the compensation of longer screenings on iPlayer for independent producers. Those claim that the BBC abuses its power position to get a 12-month rights deal for roughly the same amount of money that was given in the 30-day limit era (Sweney, 2019).

The discussion on the approved changes to BBC iPlayer will most likely spread to other parts of Europe as well and actually touches upon four related, but different issues. First, should public broadcasters innovate their on-demand offers to ensure they do not lose out to global giants such as Netflix and Amazon? Second, does it make sense to focus on big drama productions such as *Killing Eve* and *Bodyguard* (the most watched programmes on iPlayer in 2018, Krol, 2019), or should public broadcasters focus more on genres that big platform companies are not really investing it? Third, will those strategies harm commercial broadcasters and do we care about that? Fourth, and related to the former, is it desirable that public broadcasters offer all of that content for free, dissimilar to what platform companies and also commercial, free-to-air broadcasters are doing? All of these questions are far from easy to answer. The answers will also differ depending on the paradigm one sets out from. If one sets out from a citizenship-centric approach, a universally accessible offer of public service content in a commodifying market place is preferable, even if it might soon become an anachronism. Following a market logic, this might erode the potential for commercial media to valorise content. More pragmatic elements come into the picture as well. What to do with the increasing costs for streaming and rights in times of serious budget cuts on public broadcasters? What to do with damaging impacts on commercial broadcasters in more fragile, small media ecosystems (Kostovska et al., 2020)? More of these issues are addressed in Chapter 12, confronting the legal and theoretical aspects of Public Service Media with what happens in practice.

No text-based services in Germany

Next to public value tests and rules imposed on on-demand video players, an increasing number of EU Member States also specify that public broadcasters cannot offer text-based services, competing with newspapers online offers. Germany, Switzerland, both language communities in Belgium, and the Netherlands have such rules in place.

A new Interstate Treaty on Broadcasting and Telemedia

Germany was the first to introduce rules on text-based services in 2008 when it adopted the 12th Interstate Treaty on Broadcasting and Telemedia as the outcome of the European Commission investigation into the license fee funding of ARD, its members and ZDF. That State aid procedure resulted in significant changes of the regulation of the German public broadcasters, among others also in the introduction of a public value test for new media services (European Commission, 2007). The Treaty, in line with the Audiovisual Media Services Directive, makes a distinction between linear broadcasting services and telemedia. *Sendungsbezogene* telemedia are related to a concrete radio or television programmes and are hence admissible. Telemedia that are not related to a concrete radio or television programme might be admissible, but usually require ex ante testing. The German ex ante test is a three-step test (*Drei-Stufen-Test*) First, the public value of the service is evaluated. Second, the market impact is scrutinised. However, as already hinted at, the test looks at competition for quality, diversity, pluralism, and so on. It thus has a wider scope than the UK or other countries' market impact assessment. Third, the above is looked upon in light of the cost of the proposed service (Dörr, 2011; Radoslovov and Thomass, 2011). Articles 11b and 11c of the Interstate Treaty on Broadcasting and Telemedia list all services that are currently captured by the remit, including the main television and radio channels of ARD, its members and ZDF. It is important to stress this as few countries include services in their media decree or act, but most such as the Netherlands, Norway, Finland, Ireland and both language communities in Flanders become more specific only in their management contracts. The periodic changes of a management contract are considered a more flexible manner to alter or adapt the remit of public broadcasters.

The new rules on Public Service Media, adopted in 2009, also contain a negative list of services that are from the outset outside the scope of public broadcasters. This list mentions directories, websites offering price comparisons between services and products, route planners, music downloads of commercial services (services of other undertakings than public broadcasters), and contact websites, social networking websites, online games and photo download programmes that are *nicht sendungsbezogene* services. Such a negative list, which can be found among others in Austria and the French-speaking community of Belgium, is considered rather intrusive as it is a rather static catalogue of services that are considered outside public broadcasters' remit. However that remit changes as the market and citizen behaviour changes as well (Donders, 2015).

It is against the background of a more delineated definition of the public service task, that a more strict approach to press-like services needs to be situated.

A partial prohibition of press-like services

The 12th Interstate Treaty on Broadcasting and Telemedia does not only define more precisely what services are captured by the remit of ARD, its members and ZDF, what services require a test and what services are straightforward prohibited. It also contains a more strict regime on press-like services or *presseähnliches Angebot*. That is defined as 'alle journalistisch-redaktionell gestalteten Angebote, die nach Gestaltung und Inhalt Zeitungen oder Zeitschriften entsprechen' (12th Interstate Treaty on Broadcasting and Telemedia, §2(2)(19). Press-like services are allowed only in case they are Sendungsbezogene telemedia. In other words: there has to be a clear link between online text and a radio or television broadcast. Press-like services that fall outside this category are prohibited.

This provision is seen by some as a victory for the newspaper industry that lobbied intensely for it. The rules, so Woldt says (2010: 179), are 'tough and largely reflect the concerns of the print media'. The definition is questionable because it implies a static benchmark of what press-like is. All journalistic offers that resemble what newspapers and magazines are offerings are considered press-like. That changes over time, however, and today also, include video, podcast, and so on. The offer of both public broadcasters and commercial news provider is not stationary. It changes over time and both innovate. Who then decides on what is press-like and what is not? However, one should keep in mind that concepts such as press-like services are rather vaguely defined (Koehler, 2008) and that the proof of the pudding is in the eating. The Flemish management contract is another illustration of how the concept of press-like services is not a water-tight solution to the (perceived) problem of market distortion in online news. The management contract in Flanders reads: 'The audiovisual is the basis of the digital offers, that with an eye on the achievement of the abovementioned ambitions can be supported by graphs, pictures and text' (VRT and Vlaamse Regering, 2015: 19). At the same time the same section also mentions that the public broadcaster 'performs her information task in a technology neutral manner ... News, information and current affairs are accessible on all relevant formats through diverse, creative formats and narrative structures' (VRT and Vlaamse Regering, 2015: 18). That thus leaves considerable room for interpretation. This showed in autumn 2017 when former minister of media Sven Gatz criticised VRT's news website for containing too much text. Several newspaper publishers had raised concerns with politicians as well as with VRT itself. As a consequence VRT agreed, without this being incapsulated in the management contract, to limit text to 50 per cent on its websites. Switzerland is also limiting text services of public broadcasters. For news that has no immediate link to radio or television broadcasts, texts cannot exceed 1,000 characters (Raats, Van den Bulck and d'Haenens, 2015). Austria has been more creative, identifying a number of commercially interesting services such as chats, fora, online games, regional advertising and regional news and is prohibiting or limiting these services. At times when local journalism is under pressure the latter might not be the best choice (Pickard, 2019; Ali, 2016).

Indeed, while these rules indicate a more stringent approach on Public Service Media, one could at the same time argue that the rules reflect the political consensus that the public service remit is not without limits and, in a worst case scenario, are bent by public broadcasters in all kinds of creative manners.

De-publication of websites

The rules on press-like services might be open to interpretation; their effect has been most visible in Germany where ARD and ZDF finished a painful process of *Depublizierung* of approximately 80 per cent of their websites. Those were not captured by the admissible Telemedia concepts or fell outside the seven-day time frame. Of course, not all websites contained press-like services, but a considerable amount of text was removed. ZDF intendant Markus Schächter was far from happy with this, saying *Depublizierung* evidenced that 'Den Interessen von Verlegern und kommerziellen TV-Sendern wurde damit sehr weitgehend Rechnung getragen' while 'die Auswirkungen unserer Angebote auf die Geschäftsmodelle der kommerziellen Veranstalter marginal sind' ('The interests of publishers and commercial TV broadcasters were thus largely taken into account "while" the effects of our offers on the business models of commercial organizers are marginal'). Some also questioned whether the *Depublizierung* was not violating citizen rights; after all those had contributed to offers that were taken online while paid with license fee money (Hesseling, 2016; Piontek, 2017).

Regardless of the *Depublizierung* drama, all German public broadcasters can still inform citizens. More important is the idea that public broadcasters cannot offer services that are similar to what others are offering. Setting out from such an idea is basically exemplifying the abandonment of a citizenship-centric approach to Public Service Media and embracing a market failure rationale. At least to some extent as there is clear market failure in online news (Pickard, 2019). Moreover, what is offered on a commercial basis today might not be tomorrow. In that sense, making the scope of public broadcasters' service delivery dependent on the constantly changing offer of commercial media is volatile. The approach to prohibit or limit press-like services and text – I do not argue here they should be part of the public service remit – also overlooks that there is no evidence on market distortion of public broadcasters in online news. On the contrary. Research evidences that there is no causal relationship between the offer of quality news online for free by a public broadcaster and willingness-to-pay (Fletcher and Kleis Nielsen, 2017). Scholars such as Annika Sehl, Richard Fletcher and Robert Picard (2020) have convincingly demonstrated that there is no crowding-out effect because of freely available Public Service Media news. Willingness-to-pay seems to be impact more by experience-to-pay, for example, for services such as Netflix and Spotify (Fletcher and Kleis Nielsen, 2020).

The necessity of an alternative narrative

In 2011, Richard Collins wrote that the European push for public value tests was to a large extent inspired by a pragmatic market logic and not by the idea to define more clearly what the contours of a Public Service Media project are. The public value test was indeed seen as the golden egg solution for the manifold private sector complaints under State aid law (Donders, 2011). However, as predicted by, among others Jo Bardoel and Marit Vochteloo (2008), the test did not result in less commercial broadcaster and newspaper complaints. In spite of ex ante tests for new services, constraints on online text and regulation on what can and cannot be done in on-demand environments, the frustration with public broadcasters' new media activities remains considerable. In turn public broadcasters are annoyed and discouraged with what they perceive as an unneeded limitation of their scope of activities. While some might think that this tension is dissolving because of bigger issues relating to platformisation, as was suggested by Greg Polad (head of the Association of Commercial Television in Europe), and also makes sense in a highly internationalised and converged media landscape (see Chapter 1), the opposition between public broadcasters and commercial media remains rather twitchy in several countries and regions, including Flanders and Ireland (see Chapters 13 and 14).

My main point though is that this ought not to be a story of public broadcasters versus commercial media, but that media regulation, also the tools discussed above, needs to set out more from public interest considerations and Public Service Media organisations' contributions to strengthening citizenship and democracy. Media regulation is normally determined by three factors: the political, the economic and public interests (see Picard and Pickard, 2018). While scholars agree that the last factor is the most important in developing media policy, the sections above amply illustrate that the regulation of public broadcasters' activities in the online realm is to a large extent inspired by private sector lobbying (see also Donders, Van den Bulck and Raats, 2019). It would be too easy to attribute public value tests, limitations of text services and other types of similar rules to the pursuit of commercial interests only though. First, regulation is needed to make sure public broadcasters spend their money wisely on the services that contribute most to political, social, cultural and civic citizenship. Second, some rules have been provoked by public broadcasters themselves. When online offers mimic what private players are doing and expose little added value, doubts on the legitimacy of public broadcasters' new media services increase. Third, regardless of the lobbying from private media, several of the legal instruments above are inspired by a more economic, often market failure, view on media. There is a caveat here as the assumption that these markets do not show market failure as was the case with radio or television is incorrect. There is a reported under-provision of regional news, investigative journalism, local children's content, and so on. Those warrant more Public Service Media, not less.

Regulating Public Service Media is definitely a tricky thing. There is always a slippery slope between the necessity of editorial independence and innovation capacity, on the one hand, and the political reality of a well-defined task that acts as the basis for accountability, on the other. While several EU Member States are adopting similar recipes for regulating Public Service Media, the above analysis – even if selective in nature – evidences that one can learn most from what is not working. Furthermore, while Gromnicka (2005) puts that the application of European State aid rules in this domain has resulted in a harmonisation of Public Service Media rules at the national level, our analysis shows that contextual factors result in different legislative frameworks that are transposed in a variety of manners. Similar lessons can and will be drawn in the subsequent chapters on the funding and governance of public broadcasters.

References

Ali, C. (2016). The merits of merit goods: Local journalism and public policy in a time of austerity. *Journal of Information Policy, 6,* 105-128.

Appel, B. (2011). Long live the ex ante test: The ex ante test is dead! In K. Donders and H. Moe (eds), *Exporting the Public Value Test: The Regulation of Public Broadcasters' New Media Services Across Europe* (pp. 165-174). Göteborg: Nordicom.

Bardoel, J. and Vochteloo, M. (2008). Squeezing Public Service Broadcasting from the Mainstream to the Margin? EU State Aid Policy vis-à-vis Public Service Broadcasting. Paper presented at the RIPE Conference 'Public Service Media in the 21st Century: Participation, Partnership and Media Development', 8-11 October, Mainz.

Bardoel, J. and Vochteloo, M. (2009). Media policy between Europe and the Nation-State: The Case of the EU Broadcast Communication 2009. Paper presented at the ECREA-CLP Workshop on 'New Directions for Communication Policy Research', 6-7 November, Zürich.

BBC Trust (2007a). *Guidance on the Public Value Test.* London: BBC Trust.

BBC Trust (2007b). *Press Release: BBC Trust Approves BBC's On-demand Proposals.* London: BBC Trust.

BBC Trust (2009). *Local Video: Public Value Test Final Conclusions.* London: BBC Trust.

Broughton-Micova, S. (2019). Case study research. In H. Van den Bulck, M. Puppis, K. Donders and L. Van Audenhove (eds), *Palgrave Handbook of Methods for Media Policy Research* (pp. 71-84). Basingstoke: Palgrave Macmillan.

Cappello, M., Biggam, R., Brink Lund, A., Edelvold Berg, C., Matzneller, P., Neukamm, K., Polyak, G., Radke, K., Schweda, S. and Urban, A. (2015). *Online Activities of Public Service Media: Remit and Financing.* Strasbourg: European Audiovisual Observatory.

Collins, R. (2007). The BBC and 'public value'. *Medien und Kommunikationswissenschaft, 65*(2), 164-184.

Collins, R. (2011). Public value, the BBC and Humpty Dumpty words: Does public value management means what it says? In K. Donders and H. Moe (eds), *Exporting the Public Value Test: The Regulation of Public Broadcasters' New Media Services Across Europe* (pp. 49-57). Göteborg: Nordicom.

Department of Communications (2018). *RTE Enhanced Service Proposal: Results of Analysis and Considerations.* Dublin: Department of Communications.

Digital Fernsehen (2009). Drei-Stufen-Test kosted ARD und ZDF an die zehn Millionen Euro. Retrieved from www.digitalfernsehen.de/news/medien-news/maerkte/drei-stufen-test-kostet-ard-und-zdf-an-die-zehn-millionen-euro-454399/ . (accessed October 2020) [*Three-step-test costs ARD and ZDF 10 million Euro*].

Donders, K. (2011). The public value test: A reasoned response or panic reaction? In K. Donders and H. Moe (eds), *Ex Ante Tests in Europe: From Diverging Perspectives to Infinite Conclusions* (pp. 29-38). Göteborg: Nordicom.

Donders, K. (2012). *Public Service Media and Policy in Europe.* Basingstoke: Palgrave Macmillan.

Donders, K. (2015). State aid to public service media: European Commission decisional practice before and after the 2009 Broadcasting Communication. *European State aid Law Quarterly, 1*(15), 68-87.

Donders, K. and Moe, H. (eds) (2011). *Exporting the Public Value Test.* Göteborg: Nordicom.

Donders, K. and Pauwels, C. (2010). The introduction of an ex ante evaluation for new media services: 'Europe' asks it or public broadcasters need it? *International Journal of Media and Cultural Politics, 4*(2), 133-148.

Donders, K. and Raats, T. (2012). Analyzing national practices after European state aid control: Are multi-stakeholder negotiations beneficial for public service broadcasting? *Media Culture & Society, 34*(2), 162-180.

Donders, K. and Van den Bulck, H. (2020). Universality of public service media and pre-school audiences: The choice against a dedicated children's channel in Flanders. In P. Savage, M. Medina and G.F. Lowe (eds), *Universalism in Public Service Media* (pp. 49-68). Göteborg: Nordicom.

Donders, K., Van den Bulck, H. and Raats, T. (2019). The politics of pleasing: A critical analysis of multistakeholderism in public service media policies in Flanders. *Media, Culture & Society, 41*(3), 347-366.

Dörr, R. (2011). The ZDF three-step-test: A dynamic tool of governance. In K. Donders and H. Moe (eds), *Exporting the Public Value Test* (pp. 69-82). Göteborg: Nordicom.

Eisenhardt, K.M. (1989). Building theories from case study research. *The Academy of Management Review, 14*(4), 532-550.

Ene, L. (2017). *Media Ownership: Children's TV Channels in Europe: Who Are They Key Players?* Strasbourg: European Audiovisual Observatory.

European Commission (2007). Decision of 24 April 2007 on *The License Fee Funding of ARD and ZDF.*

European Commission (2009). Communication of 2 July 2009 on the *Application of the State Aid Rules to Public Service Broadcasting.*

European Commission (2014). Decision of 7 May 2014 on *Funding of Public Broadcaster RTBF.*

Evens, T. and Donders, K. (2018). *Platform Power and Policy in Transforming Television Markets.* New York and Basingstoke: Palgrave Macmillan.

Fletcher, R. and Kleis Nielsen, R. (2017). Paying for Online News. *Digital Journalism, 5*(9), 1173-1191.

Fletcher, R. and Kleis Nielsen, R. (2020). Are Netflix and Spotify subscribers more likely to pay for online news? Comparative analysis of data from six countries. *International Journal of Communication* 14, 3439-3457.

Flood Page, M. (2015). *The Development of BBC On-demand Strategy 2003–2007: The Public Value Test and the iPlayer* (Unpublished Ph.D. thesis). University of Glasgow: Glasgow.

Flyvbjerg, B. (2006). Five misunderstandings about case-study research. *Qualitative Inquiry, 12*(2), 219-245.

Gillebaard, H., Maltha, S., Leurdijk, A., Hermanussen, L., Veldman, J. and Driesse, M. (2015). *Landenvergelijking goedkeuringsprocedure nieuwe aanbodkanalen publieke omroep.* Utrecht: Dialogic. [*Comparative country analysis of ex ante assessments for public broadcasters' new services*].

Gransow, C. (2017). *Public Value-Konzepte im öffentlichen Rundfunk: Eine vergleichende Analyse europäischer Rundfunksysteme.* Wiesbaden: Springer-Verlag. [*The public value concept in public service broadcasting: A comparative analysis of European systems*].

Gromnicka, E. (2005). Services of general economic interest in the State aids regime: Proceduralisation of political choices? *European Public Law, 11*(3), 429-461.

Hesseling, C. (2016). Sieben Tage und Schluss? Mediatheken aufnehmen und Sendungen speichern, retrieved from https://irights.info/artikel/sieben-tage-und-schluss-mediatheken-aufnehmen-und-sendungen-speichern/27520 (accessed October 2020) [*Seven days and that's it? Record media libraries and save programs*].

Jakubowicz, K. (2007a). Public service broadcasting: A new beginning, or the beginning of the end. Retrieved from www.knowledgepolitics.org.uk (accessed October 2020).

Jakubowicz, K. (2007b). Public service broadcasting in the 21st century: What chance for a new beginning? In G.F. Lowe and J. Bardoel (eds), *From Public Service Broadcasting to Public Service Media* (pp. 29-50). Göteborg: Nordicom.

Koehler, L. (2008). Current Challenges for PSBs in Germany and ZDF's Digital Strategies. Paper presented at the RIPE Conference 'Public Service Media in the 21st Century', 8 October, Mainz.

Kops, M., Sokoll, K. and Bensinger, V. (2009). Rahmenbedingungen für die Durchführung des Drei-Stufen-Tests: Gutachten erstellt für den Rundfunkrat des Westdeutschen Rundfunks (Arbeitspapiere, nr. 252). Cologne: Institut für Rundfunkökonomie. [*General conditions for the introduction of the three-step-test*].

Kostovska, I., Raats, T., Donders, K. and Ballon, P. (2020). Going beyond the hype: Conceptualising 'media eocsystem' for media management research. *Journal of Media Business Studies, 18*(1), 6–26.

Krol, C. (2019). License glee! BBC iPlayer can now hosts shows for a whole year. Retrieved from www.nme.com/news/license-glee-bbc-iplayer-can-now-host-shows-for-a-whole-year-2534344 (accessed October 2020).

Lilleborge, M.T. (2011). The public service remit in Norway: What's in and what's out? In K. Donders and H. Moe (eds), *Exporting the Public Value Test* (pp. 95–105). Göteborg: Nordicom.

Ling, T. (2019). BBC under threat in wake of streaming battle, says Ofcom. Retrieved from www.radiotimes.com/news/tv/2019–10–24/bbc-facing-extinction/ (accessed October 2020).

Lobato, R. (2019). Netflix Nations: The Geography of Digital Distribution. New York: NYU Press.

Moe, H. (2008). Between supranational competition and national culture? Emerging EU policy and public broadcasters' online services. In I. Bondebjerg and P. Madsen (eds), *Media, Democracy and European Culture* (pp. 215–239). Bristol: Intellect.

NDP Nieuwsmedia (2018). *Kamervragen over analyseren markteffecten bestaande kanalen NPO*. Retrieved from www.ndpnieuwsmedia.nl/2018/11/05/kamervragen-over-analyseren-markteffecten-bestaande-kanalen-npo/ (accessed October 2020) [*Parliamentary questions on the market impact analysis of existing NPO channels*].

NPO (2015b). *Het Publiek Voorop: Concessiebeleidsplan 2016–2020*. Hilversum: NPO. [*Audience first: Management contract 2016–2020*].

Ofcom (2006). BBC new on-demand proposals: Market impact assessment. Retrieved from www.ofcom.org.uk/research-and-data/tv-radio-and-on-demand/on-demand-research/bbc-on-demand (accessed October 2020).

Ofcom (2019). BBC iPlayer competition assessment: Final determination. Retrieved from www.ofcom.org.uk/__data/assets/pdf_file/0029/159725/statement-bbc-iplayer-final-determination.pdf (accessed October 2020).

Picard, R. and Pickard, V. (2018). *Essential Principles for Contemporary Media and Communications Policymaking*. Oxford: Reuters Institute for Journalism.

Pickard, V. (2019). *Democracy Without Journalism*. Oxford: Oxford University Press.

Piontek, H. (2017). Was macht eigentlich die Depublizierungspflicht? Retrieved from https://netzpolitik.org/2017/was-macht-eigentlich-die-depublizierungspflicht/ (accessed October 2020) [*Why the obligation to de-publish?*].

Raats, T., Van den Bulck, H. and d'Haenens, L. (2015). *Benchmark van de publieke omroep in Europa: een analyse van het aanbod, financiering en publieksbereik*. Brussels: VUB, UA, KUL. [*Benchmark of public service media in Europe: An analysis of the offer, funding and audience reach*].

Radoslavov, S. and Thomass, B. (2011). ZDF's three-step test as a societal debate about the future of public service broadcasting. In K. Donders and H. Moe (eds), *Exporting the Public Value Test* (pp. 83-94). Göteborg: Nordicom.

Sehl, A., Fletcher, R. and Picard, R. (2020). Crowding out: Is there evidence that public service media harm markets? A cross-national comparative analysis of commercial television and online news providers. *European Journal of Communication*. Retrieved from https://doi.org/10.1177/0267323120903688 (accessed October 2020).

Sjøvaag, H., Pedersen, T.A. and Owren, T. (2019). Is public service broadcasting a threat to commercial media? *Media, Culture & Society, 41*(6), 808-827.

Steemers, J. (2010). The 'Canary in the Coalmine': The recession and the crisis in the production of British children's television programming. *Popular Communication: The International Journal of Media and Culture, 8*(3), 213-217.

Steemers, J. (2013). Children's television culture. In D. Lemish (ed.), *The Routledge International Handbook of Children, Adolescents and Media* (pp. 103-110). Abingdon: Routledge.

Steemers, J. and D'Arma, A. (2012). Evaluating and regulating the role of public broadcasters in the children's media ecology: The case of home-grown television content. *International Journal of Media and Cultural Politics, 8*(1), 67-85

Sweney, M. (2019). BBC using strong-arm tactics over iPlayer, say independent producers. In *The Guardian*, 18 August. Retrieved from www.theguardian.com/media/2019/aug/18/bbc-strong-arm-tactics-iplayer-tv-producers-independent (accessed October 2020).

Syvertsen, T., Donders, K., Enli, G. and Raats, T. (2019). Media disruption and the public interest: How private media managers talk about responsibility to society in an era of turmoil. *Nordic Journal of Media Studies, 1*, 11-28.

Van Halewyn, B. and De Marez, L. (2018). *Imec Digimeter 2017*. Gent: imec-Mict.

Vennesson, P. (2008). Case studies and process tracing. In D. Della Porta and M. Keating (eds), *Approaches and Methodologies in the Social Sciences* (pp. 223-239). Cambridge: Cambridge University Press.

Vlaamse Regering (2017). *Beslissing Ketnet Jr.* Brussels: Vlaamse Regering. [*Decision Ketnet Jr.*].

VRM (2017). *Advies aan de Vlaamse Regering betreffende de nieuwe VRT-dienst lineaire televisieomroep Ketnet Jr.* Brussels: VRM. [*Advise to the Flemish Government on the offer of a new lineair television channel Ketnet Jr. by VRT*].

VRT (2016). *Jaarverslag 2015*. Brussels: VRT. [*Annual report 2015*].

VRT and Vlaamse Regering (2015). *Beheersovereenkomst 2016–2020*. [*Public service contract 2016–2020*].

Waterson, J. (2019, October 24). BBC at risk of losing young audiences, according to Ofcom. *The Guardian*. Retrieved from www.theguardian.com/media/2019/oct/24/bbc-at-risk-of-losing-young-audiences-according-to-ofcom (accessed October 2020).

Williams, C. (2014). Netflix chief Reed Hastings takes on telcos, cinemas and global expansion. *The Telegraph*, 5 October. Retrieved from www.telegraph.co.uk/finance/newsbysector/mediatechnologyandtelecoms/media/11141864/Netflix-chief-Reed-Hastings-takes-on-telcos-cinemas-and-global-expansion.html (accessed October 2020).

Woldt, R. (2010). Public service broadcasting in Germany: stumbling blocks on the digital highway. In P. Iosifidis (ed.), *Reinventing Public Service Communication: European Broadcasters and Beyond* (pp. 171-182). New York: Palgrave Macmillan.

Woolard, C. (2008). Background and framework. Presentation at OFCOM's Information Seminar 'Market Impact Assessment of the BBC's new on-demand proposals', 18 September, London.

10 Laws and policy instruments dealing with funding

Money matters

Members of the European Broadcasting Union (EBU) had a total operating revenue of approximately 35 billion of funding in 2018. Looking at nominal, thus real growth, revenues went down with 4.3 per cent. Even though many European countries talk about budget cuts, the EBU reports that GDP in the countries their members are active in grew to over 11 per cent. Essentially that means that public broadcasters, when working towards 'Public Service Media', have to do more with less. The EBU's statistics of course also reveal important differences between countries. One-third of the EBU's members takes most of the budget cuts. Some see their revenues increase and another group can work with stabilising budgets. Public broadcasters such as the BBC and ARD take about a third of all that money. While 62.7 per cent of public broadcasters' revenues comes from license fees, some public broadcasters such as the Finnish or Norwegian public broadcasters YLE and NRK rely on that almost exclusively, whereas other public broadcasters such as the Dutch one have abandoned the license fee altogether. Their funding system is based on subsidies and advertising (good for 15.1 per cent and 9.5 per cent of European public broadcasters' revenues respectively). That is a bit similar to the funding of other small public broadcasters such as Flemish VRT and Irish RTE, but rather atypical for Scandinavian public broadcasters, France Télévisions or RTVE that are absent from or have a minimal presence in advertising markets. For the latter two, that was a decision taken some years ago with the idea to stimulate commercial media. Something that did not crystallise in reality though as that money went out of the domestic market to international platform companies (Donders and Lamensch, 2010).

Funding is relevant because, as shown by the EBU's research, it determines the reach and quality of public broadcasters' services. There is a strong correlation between funding on the one hand and the performance of public broadcasters on the other. That does not mean there are no exceptions to that. The Flemish public broadcaster VRT, for example, has been subject to budget cuts since 2007 and still ranks on top of most comparisons in areas such as reach and investments in audiovisual content (Ballon et al., 2018).

Type of funding (i.e. public or commercial) matters too. Under State aid law the method of funding is irrelevant and has no relation to qualifying an aid as illegal or not, or incompatible with the common market or not (Donders, 2012; 2015). Nevertheless, the choice for a dual funding system has repercussions in terms of the commercialisation of Public Service Media as a project, impacts strategic decision-taking of public broadcasters and results in tensions with commercial media as well. The choice to abolish a license fee has consequences as research shows license fee systems are more stable in terms of revenues. Edelvold Berg and Brink Lund (2012: 8) talk about the so-called 'ebb and flow perspective', which means that 'the license fee is quite a stable revenue stream, while advertising is highly volatile and public grants are open to political influence'. License fees thus create more certainty in comparison to subsidy systems that moreover run the risk to make public broadcasters more dependent on government, while independence is of course a core value of Public Service Media.

This chapter does not per se deal with the evolution of Public Service Media funding across Europe, that is well-documented (e.g., EBU, 2019) and in general has shown pressure on revenues over consecutive years now. It wants to analyse how the system of funding has changed (or not) and whether changing rules concerning funding might impact Public Service Media as a whole. Focus is on three trends. First, the evolution from a license fee to a household fee, making citizen contributions to public broadcasters independent from device ownership (note: resistance against device-independent fees exists as well). Second, the evolution from license fee to subsidy-based system, something that also happens and might increase dependency on government. Finally, the chapter also has a look at how funding can be and is effectively weaponised by governments to control public broadcasters.

Methodology

The chapter zooms in on a variety of national cases, for each of the abovementioned trends. First, when looking at the evolution from a license fee to a household fee, we study approaches in Germany and Finland. At the same time, we confront the legal changes in these two countries with heated discussions on the matter in the United Kingdom and Ireland where a shift towards a household fee has not happened yet. Second, we analyse the change from a license fee to a subsidy system in neighbouring countries Belgium (Flemish community) and the Netherlands. Both changed to a subsidy system in the new millennium and hence offer perfect empirical cases for studying the impact of a systemic change on the actual funding level. Findings are subsequently related to plans in some Nordic countries to abandon the license fee for a subsidy system. Third, we scrutinise how funding can and is effectively being weaponised by governments to control public broadcasters. Our focus of analysis is on events in Poland and other Central and Eastern European countries. The selection of cases we focus on has been inspired mainly by relevant scientific literature on the matter and actual legal changes in countries' public broadcasters' funding schemes. Findings are based on a triangulation of data sources including scientific literature, policy documents, coverage of popular and more specialised press outlets, and a limited amount of complementary interviews with experts (notably for our discussion on the Irish household charge case and the increasing dependency on state subsidies in Poland). Interviewees have been anonomysed.

From license fee to household fee: the Finnish, German, British and Irish experiences

The license fee has for a long time been considered the most optimal financing scheme for public broadcasters. It is observed to be more stable, but also more in line with public broadcasters' task to live up to audience wants as well as needs instead of government agendas (Picard, 2001). Essentially, households pay a flat fee when owning a television and/or radio device. That flat fee is usually collected by an organisation independent from the public broadcaster and the money is in full or in part transferred to the public broadcaster. In some countries such as Italy the license fee is collected through the electric bill (Bonini and Pais, 2017). Refusal to pay is punishable by law, even though not that many countries are actively going after people that do not pay. In some countries, there are groups within the population who are exempt from paying. That can, for example, concern the elderly. People aged over 75 do not have to pay the license fee in the United Kingdom, even though the BBC has announced that this becomes a difficult practice to continue given pressure on its funding (Waterson, 2019).

The license fee system is preferred by scholars because it prevents governments from directly controlling the money going to public broadcasters. The system in itself, because of a lower reliance on license fee-funded public broadcasters on state money (Picard, 2001) as well as advertising (O'Hagan and Jennings, 2003), complements other legal safeguards that protect public broadcasters' independence and also enhances public broadcasters' performance in terms of reach and audience trust (Saurwein, Eberwein and Karmasin, 2019). Research confirms this assumption as license fee systems are less prone to fluctuations in funding (Edelvold Berg and Brink Lund, 2012). Moreover, the system ensures the use of public broadcasters' services is free at the point of use. It thus de-commercialises media services and protects public broadcasting as a public service.

The existence of a flat fee has been criticised at the same time for being unfair towards the poor in society. It is a point of criticism expressed by, among others, Cammaerts (2020), who argues that discussions on the reform of the license fee to a household levy and the de-criminalisation of non-payment ignore the unfairness of a flat tax for all:

> This means that the very poorest of our society pay exactly the same rate as the billionaires, to put it in stark terms. In contrast, the fee hurts the wallet of a poor household much harder than it does the billionaire's, or

middle-class family's wallets for that matter. Inequality is thus reflected in those that don't or cannot pay, as well as in their repression and prosecution, which is disproportionately skewed towards the poor, those on benefits and single women, who all tend to be less able (or willing) to pay the fee, and to be at home during the times that inspectors do their visits.

Scholars have advocated for the transition of a license fee to a household fee system (e.g., Ramsey, 2018b; Weeds, 2016; Engblom, 2013). The latter disconnects the payment of a fee and ownership of an electronic device that allows you to receive media. Indeed, faced with near-full penetration of electronic devices such as television sets, radios, smartphones, and so on, the chance that people do not have any means of access to public broadcasters' services has become minimal in Western and Northern European countries. There are not that many countries that have completed the transition to a household fee. Germany and Finland are among those countries, next to Iceland, that replaced a device-based fee with an individual tax in 2009 already (Engblom, 2013: 93). Finland and Germany switched to a device-independent levy in January 2013 (Herzog and Karppinen, 2014). The United Kingdom and Ireland are still debating such a transition.

From a license fee to an individual tax in Finland

Finland originally had a device-dependent license fee. Payment relied on ownership of a radio device. Later on, that model was abandoned and payment was made dependent on ownership of a television set. That approach has been criticised as some people might own a radio, but not a television. Others perhaps own a smartphone, but not a radio or television (Ala-Fossi, 2012).

It took Finland four years to end fierce debates on the reform. While Parliament and most political parties were in favour of the reform after a dedicated committee came to a set of solid recommendations on the reform of the Finnish funding system in 2009, the private media sector and public opposition was immense. Protests by (parts of) the audience were triggered by a coordinated campaign of the private media sector, which spread rumours on the new system being a flat fee and on the need to re-evaluate the broad remit of YLE. Several newspapers organised polls in which a majority of people voted against a reform, also because the reform was potentially linked to an increase of the fee (Hujanen, 2009: 177). In fact, heavy lobbying from private media to opt for a subsidy-based system (more susceptible to fluctuations) resulted in politicians actually considering abandoning the practice of a fee, whether the old license fee or the new device-independent fee. While the committee dealing with the reform of YLE's funding accepted some arguments from the private media sector on the more even fairness of a tax-based system towards citizens, the committee also highlighted the threat of decreasing the political independence of YLE from government and a bigger susceptibility to political fights and crises (Hujanen, 2009). Ala-Fossi (2012) asserts that the discussions on the license fee reform found solid ground not in the technicality of a device-dependent or device-independent fee but in the changed social status of television and even more so in a changed societal appreciation of television and media and a public service.

> It would be more correct to argue tat the TV fee system is becoming socially obsolete rather than technologically obsolete. ... The increasing supply and consumption of TV content is deteriorating the social contract justifying the TV fee system. ... It is clear that the current crisis about the TV fee is fundamentally more related to the social and political development of European societies during the last 30 years than to the development of technology.
>
> (Ala-Fossi, 2012: 43-44)

Herzog and Karppinen (2014: 426) reach similar conclusions when analysing the transition from a license fee to an individual tax in Finland from a public policy perspective. 'The fate of the Public Service Media reform was not just a matter of technocratic problem-solving', so they argue. 'Instead', the authors say, 'it became entangled with broadcaster macro-political developments, in Kingdon's terms the political stream, including electoral tactics, interest groups campaigns and changes in public opinion'.

The device-independent levy that was nonetheless introduced in Finland in 2013 is quite remarkable as it abandons the idea of a flat tax. The Finnish system is an income-linked, personal and earmarked tax. People with a very low income do not have to pay while people with a high income will pay more. Smaller businesses pay less than big businesses. More specifically, citizens pay 0.68 per cent of their annual income, up to a maximum of 143 euros per annum. People with earnings below 10,000 euros per year are exempted from the tax. Corporations pay between 140 and 3,000 euros (Karppinen and Ala-Fossi, 2018: 109). Polls showed that post-introduction of the tax, 62 per cent of people supported the new system (Ala-Fossi, 2012: 45).

From a license fee to a household fee in Germany

Germany's license fee system is admittedly more complicated than the Finnish one. The competence for settling the license fee lies with the Länder, in spite of ARD and ZDF operating at a national level, while ARD indeed has regional member organisations. Taking into account Germany's WWII history, it made sense to assign the competencies over broadcasting, a powerful mass medium, to the Länder. The idea of de-centralisation is to ensure the distance between the State and public broadcasters, often referred to also as *Staatsferne* (Humphreys, 1994; Hesse, 2003: 1-7; Schüller-Keber, 2009: 67). So as to avoid endless discussion about the level of the license fee, that competence was gradually transferred to an independent commission, the *Komission zur Überprüfung under Ermittlung des Finanzbedarfs der Rundfunkanstalten* (KEF). The KEF is also in charge of controlling the budget of the public broadcasters. The *Gebühreneinzugszentrale* (GEZ) is in charge of the actual collection of the license fee (Dörr, 2009; Donders, 2012).

The basis of license fee payment has evolved from radio, over radio or television, to radio, television or new media equipment. Notably the extension to cover new media equipment from 1 January 2007 was rather controversial and received lots of media attention in newspapers or news sites such as *Spiegel Online* (e.g., Lischka, 2007), *Zeit Online* (e.g., Renner, 2007) and *FAZ. NET* (e.g., Hanfeld, 2006). In a way, this extension to new media equipment was an intermediary solution to compensate for license fee evasion in some parts of Germany and a possible deficit as a consequence thereof (Herzog and Karppinen, 2014: 423). A working group on the future of the license fee got the task to investigate more sustainable solutions. This working group identified eight possible scenarios, several of which were practically, politically or logically not preferred. The household fee was the winning scenario, requiring each household and business to contribute to the funding of the German public broadcasters. Herzog and Karppinen (2014: 425) demonstrate how the 2009/2010 discussions on the reform were isolated among a small selection of stakeholders, largely ignorant of private media positions as well as audience opinions – the idea thereof to avoid a torpedo undermining the entire process. Households pay 17.50 euros per month, regardless of the amount or types of device the household has. Because of the Covid-19 pandemic, the German public broadcasters have asked for an increase of 0.86 cents per month on the license fee. While the minister presidents of the Länder approved this increase, several parliaments do not agree. The proposal of ARD, its regional members and ZDF have provoked tremendous opposition from political parties as well as citizens (Hartung, 2020). Nonetheless, it is likely that the proposed increase will be accepted by parliaments in autumn as previous rejections of KEF proposals have been cast off by the German Constitutional Court as unlawful (Von Blazekovic, 2020).

While the German system is an example in terms of independence from government, a rational cost calculation of the amount of money required to fund the public broadcasting system, the device-independent nature of the household fee, and so on, it will not be possible or desirable to ignore public opinion on and de-politicise funding altogether. The German public broadcasters are by far the best-funded public broadcasters in the world. There is no doubt they deliver value. Whether they deliver value for all that money is less clear. Whether the audience actually thinks they do is even less clear. Klimkiwiecz's (2017: 113) evaluation of funding regimes in light of a dynamic relationship between autonomy and accountability underlines exactly that point: whereas the license fee scores high on autonomy, it scores low on accountability towards citizens, specifically in settings such as Germany where the Constitutional Court for just reasons protects the Public Service Media regime, but might take that protection too far. This is also *the* reason for repeated questions for more transparency regarding the expenditure of ARD, its regional members and ZDF.

Each person and business paying the Public Service Media fee has a right to know how funds are spent, which programmes and audiovisual contents are bought and produced, and at what price. These demands, however, remained largely ineffective and were not implemented by either the Federal Government or the Länder governments. Furthermore, the Federal Constitutional Court, the most influential actor in German post-war media policy-making, had repeatedly called for more transparency in its jurisdiction of broadcasting freedom but, until recently, no major action was taken … ARD and ZDF have for a long time seen the Public Service Media governance boards as the only bodies to whom they are accountable. At last, the boards are composed of members of socially rele-vant groups and, in turn, represent the public. This notion, however, as the Federal Constitutional Court has outlined, is merely one side of the coin. The other side is direct accountability vis-à-vis the public.

(Herzog et al., 2018: 5-6)

It is thus important to realise that funding is not only a matter of governments and public broadcasters only, but that also citizens are part of the story or at least should be part of it.

Heated discussions and no reform (yet) in Ireland

Not only in Finland and Germany, but also in several other European coun-tries discussions on replacing the license fee with a household fee are heated. The principle of letting go of a license on a device might seem logical in a digital era. However, it has provoked heated debates among others the United Kingdom and Ireland. We will focus on Ireland, where public broadcaster RTE is dually funded, relying almost evenly on license fee revenue and commercial funding.

A license fee is about 160 euros per annum for each household that has a television set. The postal service collects the license fee. Eighty-five per cent of the collected money goes to RTE. Since 2008, when Ireland as a 'Celtic Tiger' faced the hardship of the financial crisis, revenues from the license fee decreased by 10 per cent. Moreover, 14 per cent of the people that are obliged to pay the license fee, avoid payment. Given the downward pressure on the commercial revenues of RTE, the budgetary situation of Ireland's main public broadcasters is quite precarious. Former RTE CEO Noel Curran (now EBU director general) has argued that the 'lack of license fee reform now represents the most significant risk to RTE's, and the indigenous independent produc-tion sector's long-term sustainability and growth potential' (quoted in Ramsey, 2018a: 9). Plans for a 'Public Service Broadcasting Charge' were supposed to overcome these issues, but were abandoned in 2016. The minority coalition government concluded it could not find a majority in Parliament to go along with a Public Service Broadcasting charge instead of a license fee (Ramsey, 2018b: 85).

Plans for reforming funding were picked up again in 2018 though, when another government-commissioned working group on the funding of Public Service Media concluded that the license fee 'should be replaced by a device-independent charge to support public service content on a sustainable basis' (Department of Communications, 2019: n.p.). The revivification of the debate has not resulted in an actual reform to date.

The debate on the household charge seems to have been contaminated (Respondent F, Ireland) with two other issues. First, do people want to pay for public broadcaster RTE at all? Second, it shows a tension between some people's, notably politicians', support for high-quality drama, investigative journalism, domestic programming, and so on, on the one hand, while not following through on that when money is at stake, on the other. Then, a neoliberal discourse becomes prevalent.

When it comes to payment for RTE, several online polls (e.g., McCrave, 2019) indicate that Irish citizens are not willing to switch the license fee for a household charge, even though such a system is not necessarily more expensive. That shows, in the first instance, limited knowledge of what the discussion is about and perhaps also a failed communication strategy of RTE (Respondent C, Ireland). It, more importantly, demonstrates that part of the audience – admittedly over-represented in polls that lack scientific grounding and social media as well (Respondent G, Ireland) – is against paying for RTE as such. A citizen responding to the poll, for example, said:

> Many people today, myself included, do not watch/listen to RTE, why should we pay a tax to support massive payrolls for people we do not watch? Also we already pay tax on the devices at point of sale and on internet/tv service provider. RTE has ad revenue, if they can't stay afloat with that, shut them down.
>
> (Chat response to McCrave, 2019)

> Barely even watch RTE on the tv let alone multiple devices. Maybe a better way to increase their income would be making watchable content?
>
> (Chat response to McCrave, 2019)

Regarding the tension between the theoretical commitment to Public Service Media on the one hand and ignorance of adequate funding on the other hand, Pat Stacey said in *The Independent*:

> How ironic that, barely a fortnight later, some of the very same people who were lauding RTE for this were now demanding it be either turned into a monthly paid subscription service or dissolved altogether. The trigger was the government's announcement that the licence fee is to be scrapped and replaced with a 'device independent broadcasting charge'. Ultimately, this will require every household in the country, even those without a television, to pay for RTE. It doesn't matter if you never watch RTE; if you

own any electronic device capable of streaming TV programmes – any broadcaster's TV programmes – then you're liable for the charge. Personally, I think it's a bit early to be getting worked up about a still vague plan that won't take effect for another five years. It really is an argument for another day. The bigger question is whether we honestly want to live in a country without Public Service Broadcasting. RTÉ, at present, is a mess and there are many things I loathe about it.

(Stacey, 2019)

Indeed, there are discussions about the quality that RTE delivers. Some of the interviewees I talked to said that there is, given the dependence on commercial funding, an increasingly commercial strategy of RTE in the market. That, but also its critical and excellent news reporting, is a thorn in the flesh of politicians (Respondent A, Ireland). A lack of consistency or transparency about what policy-makers really want can be observed here. One interviewee said: 'we either as a country have to decide that we're going to generate content in the public realm for Public Service Broadcasting, or not'. He continued: 'If we decide that we do, that has to be funded and commissioned' (Respondent E, Ireland).

The political and public debate on the household charge has taken away attention on the amount of money that is needed to ensure Public Service Media to its fullest potential. One interviewee said that the focus should be on how funding can ensure that RTE 'can one, continue to meet the needs of Irish audiences and two, evolve'. The public broadcaster was said to face tremendous complexities and challenges regarding the digital transition, among others in bringing younger people back on board with Public Service Media. Funding is needed to make that transition, regardless of its source (Respondent B, Ireland). It is difficult to tell how things will evolve as one struggles 'to see the political will to ever do what is necessary' (Respondent C, Ireland). The unpopularity of a measure to increase the license fee or change it into a household charge indicates that 'the government or main opposition are not prepared to do anything about the major financial crisis which RTE is currently going through' (Respondent D, Ireland).

From license fee to subsidy-based system: Flanders and the Netherlands taking a similar approach

In several European countries the license fee has been abolished and replaced with a subsidy-based system. In 2002 and 2000 respectively, Flanders and its neighbouring country, the Netherlands, decided to get rid of the license fee.

Socialists abolishing the license fee in Flanders

In Flanders the decision to fund VRT on the basis of government subsidies was taken together with the transition of competencies over the collection of the license fee from the federal government level to the Dutch-speaking community. Indeed, until 2001 the license fee was a Belgian, federal competence – even though its collection happened by the language communities from 1999 onwards. Until 2001, the level of the license fee was set by the Belgian state. The language communities received a part of the collected sum to distribute to their public broadcaster, with Flanders receiving in absolute figures more but in comparison with the number of inhabitants a bit less than the French-speaking community. The total amount of money collected for all three language communities was 712.6 million in 2001: 447.8 million euros for the Dutch-speaking community, 259.7 for the French-speaking community, and 5.1 million for the German-speaking community. It is important to stress that public broadcaster VRT received a little bit more than half of the sum collected. The remainder was spent on other aspects of cultural policy-making.

From 2002 onwards the license fee became a competence in its entirety (laws, collection, distribution) of the language communities. The socialist party already argued for an abolishment of the license fee in 2001. Christian democrats argued against as the abolishment of the license fee would essentially be a new cost in the budget of the Flemish Government. The dispute resulted in the license fee being put at the level of 0 euros per household, rendering it meaningless even before the competence of the existence of the instruments was transferred to the Dutch-speaking community as well. The whole operation should be framed against the background of a socialist party that argued for free education, free public transport, free television, and so on.

In 2002, the Flemish Government opted for a grant of 229 million euros. The Flemish Government and VRT agreed on an annual growth rate of 4 per cent. That system has been left behind altogether (Vlaamse Regering and VRT, 2001). In 2025 VRT will receive an annual government of approximately 260 million euros. In real terms the government grant of VRT has decreased by over 25 per cent since 2002, with consecutive cuts between 2007 and 2020. These cuts largely coincide with financial decision of newly elected governments, indeed demonstrating the volatility of subsidy-based systems. More budget cuts have been announced (Vlaamse Regering, 2019). Staff has decreased with 600 people since 2007.

The French-speaking community abolished the license fee for the public broadcaster RTBF only in 2018. Again, a socialist initiative resulting in a 100 euros cheque for all households in the Southern part of Belgium.

Several scholars have argued that the abolishment of the license fee was more than the mere practical measure that was presented by politicians. It made the funding arrangements of VRT more volatile and left the Flemish public broadcaster essentially more vulnerable to changing governments. It is interesting to note that the socialist party, not in government for two governments in a row, strongly objects against the budgets on public broadcaster VRT. It has been criticising the Flemish Government for not walking the talk: in principle defending the uniqueness of Public Service Media, in practice not putting the money where their mouth is. Ironically, the decision of the socialist party in 2002 enabled (not caused!) the contemporary financial situation of VRT.

From abolishment of the license fee to re-instalment in the Netherlands?

The Netherlands might have inspired the Flemish socialist party to abolish the license fee. In 2000, the Dutch changed their media law: no more license fee (Europese Commissie, 2010: §86). Until 2000, Dutch households paid a license fee. Households that owned a radio and television device paid 194 gulden, or not even 5 euros per annum; for the possession of a radio set only, the amount due was set at 56 gulden or 1.5 euros per year (Beekmans, 1999).

Discussions preceding the abolishment of the license fee in Parliament were not blind to the possible consequences thereof. Members of Parliament indicated that the 'fiscalisation' of the money for the public broadcasting organisations have the advantage of fairness: that is, the flat tax that the license fee was (not necessarily should be) replaced by a system that every citizen contributes to depending on his or her income. The downside of the system, so debates in Dutch Parliament notice, is the possibility of a decline of political independence as one can imagine that this Parliament will have yearly discussions on the amount of money that should go from the overall means of the state to the public broadcaster. Independence and pluriformity, so one member of Parliament contends, are the most important characteristics of the public broadcaster. Those should not be eroded. In case one cuts the financial tie between the public broadcasters and citizens, the system will inevitably evolve from a public to a state broadcaster. The same member of Parliament complained that the ruling majority is silent on the possible consequences of the abolishment of the license fee, even though the outcomes are predictable.

In the Netherlands, the abolishment had the usual impact: a decline of funding for the Dutch public broadcasting organisations. When in 2017 yet another minister of media, Arie Slob, announced budget cuts or, rather, the non-compensation of a 60 million euro loss in advertising revenues, Taco Zimmerman (CEO of production company Tuvala Media) (2017) reminded him in a furious editorial that one of his predecessors said in 1999 when opting for a subsidy-based system: 'The public broadcaster has a right to predictable revenues … The independent functioning of the public broadcaster is a core principle that deserves unrelenting attention.'

The declining government revenues and continuous meddling from politics has put the license fee back on the political agenda – at least that is what public broadcaster NPO has attempted to do. Since 2013 NPO CEO Henk Hagoort has argued for the re-instalment of the license fee, arguing the public broadcasting organisations – NPO included – are too dependent on politics. The public broadcasting organisations have continued their plea ever since, without success so far.

How financing is being weaponised by governments in Spain, Portugal and Poland

Funding can be and has been a weapon of governments to control public broadcasters. The substitution of license fees for government grants in Flanders and the Netherlands are cases in point. That does not mean that enhancing efficiency of public broadcasters or budget cuts in general are always missiles to destroy Public Service Media. However, there are manifold examples of a negative instrumentalisation of funding to increase government control over public broadcasters.

The not-so-objectivity of austerity measures on Public Service Media in Spain and Portugal

Costa e Silva and Diaz-Gonzalez (2020) studied the impact of austerity measures on the funding of Public Service Media in Spain and Portugal. The focus of their analysis was on the period 2010-2015, hence after the financial crisis of 2008-2009. For both countries, revenues, costs, debts and audience reach were measured. Funding of Portuguese public broadcaster RTP – which was already found to be under-compensated by the European Commission in several State aid decisions between 2003 and 2010 (Donders, 2012) – decreased by 31 per cent. License fee funding went up, but direct government subsidies went down dramatically, as did commercial revenues. All of this resulted in lay-offs. Personnel cost was reduced by 31 per cent, showing that media are a people's business. Budget cuts had an impact on audience ratings. RTP lost 40 per cent of its audience in prime time. Similar findings occurred in Spain where direct government contributions to RTVE fell by nearly 50 per cent. The required contributions from private broadcasters and telecommunications players also decreased because of their lower income during the financial crisis. Also RTVE cut costs, largely externally as it already reduced its staff by 40 per cent before the financial crisis and had engaged afterwards in a job stability pact with the unions. Audience ratings decreased in Spain as well, albeit not as drastically as in Portugal. RTVE lost its leadership position in the news. E Silva and Diaz-Gonzalez (2020) included public interventions of policy-makers in their analysis. Their findings are that a discourse of neoliberalism, rationalisation and de-institutionalisation of Public Service Media got intertwined with the actual need to cut costs across government and institutions because of the financial crisis. Politicians focused on the 'wastefulness' of public broadcasters RTP and RTVE and the need for more efficiency, perhaps rightly so. But nowhere this was connected to performance regarding independent news, culture, high-quality drama, and so on. Cuts were 'blind' according to the authors. There was a lot of talk about value for money, but nothing mentioned on value for democracy. One can even doubt whether a neoliberal agenda was indeed at the core of Portuguese and Spanish policy-makers as 'in spite of the measures taken in relation to formal independence (either financial or editorial), governments do maintain mechanisms of pressure over the Public Service Media operators, which negatively impacts the perceived image of editorial and programming independence' (Costa e Silva and Diaz-Gonzalez, 2020: 21).

Massive license fee evasion in Poland and an active subsidy policy from the PiS government

A similar, but yet also different story in Poland. Polish public broadcaster TVP's income relies on a combination of the license fee, ad hoc state subsidies and advertising revenue. There is high license fee evasion, which means that a mere 20 per cent of TVP's income today can be attributed to the license fee. But in fact, over the last 25 years, license fee revenues accounted for 17 to 30 per cent of TVP's income. This shows the collection of the license fee is a structural issue (Klimkiewicz, 2017). While government is not actively pursuing non-payment, the ruling PiS party is quite generous in compensating for deficits. After several sums had already been awarded to TVP in 2017, 2018 and 2019 (Gipson, 2019), another grant of 470 million euros for TVP was agreed upon in Parliament in early 2020. Most of the time these money transfers followed legal changes regarding Public Service Media, including the 'Small Media Act' of 2015 and the 'Big Media Act' of 2016, both of which on paper expressed the PiS government's dedication to support a 'real' Public Service Media project.

> The Public Service Media ignore their mission towards the national com-munity. They promote ideological and moral fashions that are not accepted by a societal majority. The journalists, instead of creating media exposure to Polish raison d'etre, often sympathise with unfavorable opinions regarding Poland. For the good of the national community, this should be changed as soon as possible.
>
> (Elzbieta Kruk, Member of Parliament for PiS, quoted in Klimkiewicz, 2017: 199)

Several scholars (Połońska, 2019; Respondents A, H, I, Poland) as well as civil society members (Respondent C, Poland) have argued the financial depend-ency of TVP shows in its programming that it is conservative, nationalist and pro-PiS or, PiS would argue, 'for the good of the national community'. A 2019 study of the pre-election campaigns, shows TVP covered the PiS party signifi-cantly more than other parties, but also in a highly positive manner whereas, for example, the pro-EU party was depicted negatively almost all of the time (Fundacja Batorego, 2019).

While viewership remains high with a market share of approximately 24 per cent for TVP, public trust is low. That also shows in the dropping figures of TVP's news bulletin *Wiadomosci*, going from an unimpressive 17.4 per cent in 2018 to 15.1 per cent in 2019. The news broadcasters from commercial broadcasters TVN and Polsat reach higher audience figures. When researching brand trust specifically, TVP comes in at an eleventh place (Makarenko, 2019).

The Polish Government is also known to spend considerable amounts of money on state advertising, which also increases its say over commercial media and demonstrates how money talks, not only for public broadcasters, but for private sector initiatives too.

Does that mean that there is a need to strengthen the license fee regime? One of the interviewees I talked to does not think so. He called the license fee system 'broken'. The fact that the vast majority of Polish citizens have not paid for the license fee or they were exempted from payment by law for 25 years makes it a near mission impossible to restore the system. Some sort of tax on commercial television's revenues would make for a better instrument in the Polish context, he argued. If the market goes up, that is good for TVP. If the market goes down, TVP will also feel this. This of course goes against the principle of adequate and predictable funding, but is still to be preferred over the contemporary situation that gives too much room for political capture over TVP (Respondent G, Poland). The Polish case shows how difficult it is to transform from a state to a Public Service Broadcasting regime, but also how Western-centric Public Service Media recipes might not always work in the context of Central and Eastern Europe.

When a democracy-centric and market failure view on Public Service Media clash

Our analysis of changes in funding systems highlights how these legal–financial arrangements are discussed in a contentious political setting in which arguments on the need for a changing format of funding or for more funding easily get conflated with the role of public broadcasters in delivering Public Service Media. The need for a different funding type or a higher amount of money going to a public broadcaster is approached from the angle that public broadcasters are delivering Public Service Media and no longer Public Service Broadcasting; hence the need for a device-independent fee or in light of digital challenges the need for more money. The discussion surrounding the actual reform and the options to go for in several countries is captured by a neoliberal or *étatiste* desire to curb public broadcasters. One can blame politicians and private media for that, but to some extent also public broadcasters have failed to be transparent and accountable to citizens on what they are doing and why that is important for individuals as well as society. That is also the issue with projects such as the European Broadcasting Union's 'Contribution to Society':[1] they focus on legitimising public broadcasters' role in delivering Public Service Media to politicians instead of to citizens.

Thus, while we talked about weaponising public broadcasters' funding only in the final section of this chapter, it comes to mind that in fact also the reform of license fees into household charges or individual taxes and the abolishment of license fees for subsidy-based systems are in fact examples of funding being instrumentalised to gain political control of public broadcasters and Public Service Media as a policy project.

Note

1 www.ebu.ch/Public Service Media-contribution-society.

References

Ala-Fossi, M. (2012). Social obsolescence of the TV fee and the financial crisis of Finnish Public Service Media. *Journal of Media Business Studies, 9*(1), 33–54.

Ballon, P., Van Looy, B., Raats, T., Wauters, D. and Tintel, S. (2018). *De economische meerwaarde van de VRT: Een onderzoek in opdracht van de VRT*. Brussels: VUB & KU Leuven. [*The added economic value of the VRT: An analysis on behalf of the VRT*].

Beekmans, M. (1999). Omroepbijdrage wordt afgeschaft, Trouw, 20 November. Retrieved from www.trouw.nl/nieuws/omroepbijdrage-wordt-afgeschaft~be44532e/?referrer =https%3A%2F%2Fwww.google.com%2F (accessed October 2020) [*License fee gets abolished*].

Bonini, T. and Pais, I. (2017). Hacking public service media funding: A scenario for rethinking the license fee as a form of civic crowdfunding. *International Journal on Media Management, 19*(2), 123–143.

Cammaerts, B. (2020). The decriminalisation of non-payment of the license fee is the wrong debate. Retrieved from https://blogs.lse.ac.uk/medialse/2020/04/06/the-decriminalisation-of-non-payment-of-the-license-fee-is-the-wrong-debate/ (accessed October 2020).

Costa e Silva, E. and Diaz-Gonzalez, M.-J. (2020). Public broadcasting service under austerity: Cross-comparison between Portugal and Spain. *International Communication Gazette*. Retrieved from https://doi.org/10.1177/1748048520915669 (accessed October 2020).

Department of Communications (2019). *Climate Action and Environment*. Dublin: Department of Communications.

Donders, K. (2012). *Public Service Media and Policy in Europe*. Basingstoke: Palgrave Macmillan.

Donders, K. (2015). State aid to public service media: European Commission decisional practice before and after the 2009 Broadcasting Communication. *European State aid Law Quarterly, 1*(15), 68–87.

Donders, K. and Lamensch, M. (2010). The introduction of a tax-and-fund system to subsidise public television in France: Cultural revolution or legal swamp? *Journal of Media Law, 2*(2), 227–244.

Dörr, D. (2009). Grundsätze der Medienregulierung. In D. Dörr, J. Kreile and M.D. Cole (eds), *Handbuch Medienrecht: Recht der elektronischen Massenmedien* (pp. 133–184). Frankfurt am Main: Verlag Recht und Wirtschaft. [*The principles of media regulation – Handbook media law: electronic mass media law*].

EBU (2019). Investing in European Content and Culture. Retrieved from www.ebu.ch/news/2019/01/investing-in-european-content-and-culture (accessed October 2020).

Edelvold Berg, C. and Brink Lund, A. (2012). Financing public service broadcasting: A comparative perspective. *Journal of Media Business Studies, 9*(1), 7–21.

Engblom, L.-Å. (2013). Public service financing in the Nordic countries. In U. Carlsson (ed.), *Public Service Media from a Nordic Horizon: Politics, Markets, Programming and Users* (pp. 93–106). Göteborg: Nordicom.

European Commission (2010). Decision of 26 January on *Funding of the Dutch public broadcasters*.

Fundacja Batorego (2019). Monitoring of the 2019 European Parliament election campaign in the main news programme of Polish public TV. Retrieved from www.batory. org.pl/upload/files/Programy%20operacyjne/Masz%20Glos/RaportTDEnglFin_ June%2010N.pdf (accessed October 2020).

Gipson, A. (2019). New report: Poland's public media serve as propaganda tool. Retrieved from https://ipi.media/new-report-polands-public-media-serve-as-propaganda-tool/ (accessed October 2020).

Hanfeld, M. (2006). 5.52 Euro – die PC-Gebühr ist beschlossen. Retrieved from www.faz.net/IN/INtemplates/faznet/default.asp?tpl=common/zwischenseite. asp&dox={157D32F2–06E1–0DB7–8B71–7BAEB66287A4}&rub={E2C6E0BC-C2F0–4DD7–87CD-C274993E94C1} (accessed October 2020) [5.*52 Euro – The decision on the household fee has been taken*].

Hartung, H. (2020). Die Reform kommt schon. *Frankfurter Algemeine*, 11 March 2020. Retrieved from www.faz.net/aktuell/feuilleton/medien/die-medienstaatssekretaerin-heike-raab-zur-reform-von-ard-und-zdf-16672889.html (accessed October 2020) [*Reform will come*].

Herzog, C. and Karppinen, K. (2014). Policy streams and public service media funding reforms in Germany and Finland. *European Journal of Communication*, *29*(4), 416–432.

Herzog, C., Hilker, H., Novy, L. and Torun, O. (2018). Transparency and funding of public service media in Germany, the Western world and beyond. In C. Herzog, H. Hilker, L. Novy and O. Torun (eds), *Transparency and Funding of Public Service Media: Die deutsche Debatte im internationalen Kontext* (pp. 3–17). Berlin: Springer.

Hesse, A. (2003). *Rundfunk Recht* (3rd ed.). München: Verlag Vahlen. [*Broadcasting law*].

Hujanen, T (2009). Public service media fee to substitute television fee in Finland. *Central European Journal of Communication*, *3*, 173-179.

Humphreys, P. (1994). *Media and Media Policy in Germany: The Press and Broadcasting Since 1945*. Oxford: Berg.

Karppinen K. and Ala-Fossi M. (2018) Finland: Maintaining the Fragile Consensus. In C. Herzog, H. Hilker, L. Novy and O. Torun (eds), *Transparency and Funding of Public Service Media: Die deutsche Debatte im internationalen Kontext* (pp. 107-117). Wiesbaden: Springer.

Klimkiwiecz, B. (2017). State, media and pluralism: Tracing roots and consequences of media policy change in Poland. *Publizistik*, *62*, 197-213.

Lischka, K. (2007). Gebühren-Eintreiber wollen Meinungsäußerung verbieten. *Der Spiegel*, 13 September. Retrieved from www.spiegel.de/netzwelt/web/ 0,1518,505564,00.html (accessed October 2020) [*Licence fee collectors want to prohibit freedom of expression*].

Makarenko, V. (2019). *Poland. Reuters Institute Digital News Report 2019*. Retrieved from www.digitalnewsreport.org/survey/2019/poland-2019/ (accessed October 2020).

McCrave, C. (2019). Poll: Would you support switching to a 'device charge' to fund public service broadcasting. Retrieved from www.thejournal.ie/poll-would-you-support-rte-device-charge-tv-licence-4882399-Nov2019/ (accessed October 2020).

O'Hagan, J. and Jennings, M. (2003). Public broadcasting in Europe: Rationale, licence fee and other issues. *Journal of Cultural Economics*, *27*, 31-56.

Picard, R. (2001). *Expansion and Limits in EU Television Markets: Audience Advertising and Competition Issues. Discussion Paper C2/2001*. Turku: Turku School of Economics.

Połońska, E. (2019). Watchdog, lapdog, or attach dog? Public service media and the Law and Justice government in Poland. In E. Połońska and C. Beckett (eds), *Public Service Broadcasting and Media Systems in Troubled European Democracies* (pp. 227-255). Basingstoke: Palgrave Macmillan.

Ramsey, P. (2018a). The BBC Ideas Service: The Corporation's Search for Universalism Online. Paper presented at the 2018 RIPE Conference 'Universalism and PSM', 18–20 October, Madrid.

Ramsey, P. (2018b). In search of reform for public service media funding. In C. Herzog, H. Hilker, L. Novy and O. Torun (eds), *Transparency and Funding of Public Service Media: Deutsche Debatte im internationalen Kontex* (pp. 77-90). Wiesbaden: Springer.

Renner, K.-H. (2007). Gebührensheriff unter Beschuss. *Die Zeit*, 1 February. Retrieved from www.ziet.de/2007/06/P-Buchholz (accessed October 2020) [*Licence fee sheriff under threat*].

Saurwein, F., Eberwein, T. and Karmasin, M. (2019). Public service media in Europe: Exploring the relationship between funding and audience performance. *Javnost – The Public, 26*(3), 291-308.

Schüller-Keber, V. (2009). Die Kommunikationsfreiheiten in der Verfassung. In D. Dörr, J. Kreile and M.D. Cole (eds), *Handbuch Medienrecht: Recht der elektronischen Massenmedien* (pp. 63-82). Frankfurt am Main: Verlag Recht und Wirtschaft. [*The freedoms of communication in the Constitution – Handbook media law: electronic mass media law*].

Stacey, P. (2019). RTÉ is a mess but public service broadcasting is still essential. Retrieved from www.independent.ie/entertainment/television/pat-stacey-rte-is-a-mess-but-public-service-broadcasting-is-still-essential-38382020.html (accessed October 2020).

Vlaamse Regering (2019). *Regeerakkoord 2019–2024*. Brussels: Vlaamse Regering. [*Government Agreement*].

Von Blazekovic, A. (2020). Mehrheit darf bei uns eben nicht alles. In *Süddeutsche Zeitung*, 17 June. Retrieved from www.sueddeutsche.de/medien/rundfunkbeitrag-2020-gez-1.4939087 (accessed October 2020) [*The majority is not allowed to do everything with us*].

VRT and Vlaamse Regering (2001). *Beheersovereenkomst 2002–2006*. [*Public service contract 2002*-2006].

Waterson, J. (2019, October 24). BBC at risk of losing young audiences, according to Ofcom. *The Guardian*. Retrieved from www.theguardian.com/media/2019/oct/24/bbc-at-risk-of-losing-young-audiences-according-to-ofcom (accessed October 2020).

Weeds, H. (2016). Is the television licence fee fit for purpose in the digital era? *Economic Affairs, 36*(1), 2-20.

11 Governance

Optimising for societal value or political control

Introduction

Manuel Puppis (2010: 137–138) makes a distinction between governance in the narrow or broad sense. Governance in the narrow sense 'refers to changing polities, politics, and policies'. It concerns regulation by government, but also more collaborative forms of regulation. Laws, governmental decisions, co-regulation, and so on, can be considered part of a narrow conceptualisation of governance. Puppis defines governance in the broad sense as all forms of collective coordination. This can involve various actors with different objectives. This broad form of governance also encompasses the narrow form: 'it is a mix of governing efforts by public and private actors occurring at different levels and in different modes'. Puppis opts for the broad definition of governance, which in his opinion does not imply a smaller role for governments but rather that their 'capacity for conventional "command and control" regulation is said to be complemented and gradually replaced by a capacity for influence'. Broad governance hence also concerns governance *from within*, that is the way in which public broadcasters regulate and steer themselves (Ingenhoff and Koelling, 2012). The broad definition of governance is somewhat similar to Dennis McQuail's conceptualisation, albeit that McQuail was rather pragmatic in his approach, considering media governance 'an umbrella term because it "covers all means by which the mass media are limited, directed, encouraged, managed or called into account, ranging from the most binding law to the most resistible of pressure and self-chosen disciplines"' (quoted in Lund, 2016: 104). Whereas the concept of media governance has been criticised for being a catch-all notion, it is commonly used within media policy research and the definition above – even with its shortcomings – is accepted by most scholars (Karppinen and Moe, 2013).

The key argument in this chapter will be that Public Service Media policies are still to a large extent determined by a narrow conception of governance and that attempts to broaden governance in most countries show a reinforcement of the traditional power structures (Donders, Van den Bulck and Raats, 2019). There are several reasons for that, not in the least the difficulty of moving beyond the birth of public broadcasters directly under the administration of the State in many European countries (Campos-Freire, Rodríguez-Castro and

Blasco-Blasco, 2020). My second argument is that there are different forces at play and varying directions within Public Service Media governance, which makes it difficult to tell what the ultimate goal of governance of public broadcasters is.

The aim of this chapter is not to provide a full overview of governance structures of public broadcasters across Europe. Rather, I want to discuss some trends, which point at the (re-)politicisation of public broadcasters in Europe. The first trend is the political capture of public broadcasters in Western Europe, not through straightforward censorship, but rather through a mix of a market-driven policy agenda, outside pressure from extreme right populism, budget cuts and a multitude of control mechanisms. The second trend is the strengthening of political capture in Central and Eastern Europe with the emergence of illiberal democracies or neo-authoritarian systems.

While the tone of voice as well as findings in this chapter might be somewhat pessimistic on Public Service Media governance, it is important to stress that some countries or regions such as Valencia (Cano Cejalvo, 2020) have shown the ability to progress not towards near-perfection, but at least to a situation whereby governance has become more professional, transparent and respectful of editorial independence.

Methodology

The chapter, similar to the previous chapters on online media regulation and funding, zooms in on several national cases, with a focus on governance in Flanders and Poland. The selection of cases we focus on has been inspired mainly by relevant scientific literature on the matter and actual changes in countries' public broadcasters' governance. Findings are based on a triangulation of data sources including scientific literature, policy documents, coverage of popular and more specialised press outlets, and a limited amount of complementary interviews with experts (notably for our discussion on Flanders and Poland). I talked with 11 experts on Polish Public Service Media, including (former) TVP or Polish Radio journalists, civil society and media activists, academics, and previous members of regulatory bodies. I talked with 17 experts on the Flemish case. Those are academics, consultants, former management staff or CEO's of public broadcaster VRT, politicians and policy-makers, management staff or CEO's of private media, and public broadcaster journalists. Quotes have been anonymised.

Where is the trust? Governance of Public Service Media in Flanders

The governance of Flemish public broadcaster VRT rests on four pillars. First, the media decree and management contract – the latter renewed every five years – are the legal basis for the public broadcaster to act upon. The management is autonomous regarding operational manners. The politically appointed

Board of Governors is competent for strategic issues. The composition of the Board changes after elections and reflects the political representation in Flemish Parliament. That system is the consequence of the so-called *Cultuurpact*. In 1972 Flemish political parties agreed that the governance of public institutions had to be pluralistic. Boards of governance would from that moment onwards consist of members that were appointed by political parties; each party being entitled to a certain number of Board Members depending on their electoral weight. The law from 1973 was adapted several times, most recently in 2009. Its contents have not changed fundamentally though.[1] There are 12 members in the Board of Governors of VRT. One of them serves as chairman. Who acts as chairman is a political decision as well. The Flemish Government decides on this. The chairman is always affiliated with one of the political parties in the Flemish Government. In meetings of the Board there is also a representative from the Flemish Government present. That person has no voting rights, but is entitled to access all internal information.

A second pillar of governance are the multiple bodies in charge of controlling VRT. Next to its Board of Governors and the representative from the Flemish Government, there are five more actors that have a say in the public broadcaster. The Flemish Parliament can ask questions to the minister of media and, upon invitation, directly to the management of VRT. Its most explicit task is the discussion of VRT's annual report. The Flemish Government itself also has a controlling function. It has extensive access to information from the public broadcaster. It also negotiates the management contract with VRT and determines its funding. Audit Flanders is a body that assists the Flemish Government in inspecting the financial operations of institutions such as VRT. The Court of Auditors checks compliance with principles of good governance. There is an internal audit as well, scrutinising financial performance, management and organisational efficiency. Members of the Board of Governance oversee the internal audit. Finally, the Flemish Regulator for the Media assesses whether VRT lives up to key performance indicators. It is also in charge of public value tests for new media services, even though the regulator does not take decisions. It can only provide advice to the Flemish Government (Donders and Raats, 2018).

There is a third, more flexible and also broader, governance pillar and that relates to the inclusion of stakeholders as well as the audience every time legislation related to the public broadcaster is changed. When the management contract is renewed or when VRT wants to launch a new service, respectively the Flemish Council for Media (an advisory body for the Flemish Government) and the Flemish Regulator for the Media organise stakeholder consultations and audience studies to evaluate whether the public broadcaster's plans are a good idea or not. Essentially, these tools – even if envisaging more inclusive methods of governance – have been shown to re-produce power inequalities in Flemish media policy-making and providing an additional playing ground for intense, often oppositional, lobbying from the public broadcaster and commercial adversaries direct at government (Donders, Van den Bulck and Raats,

2019). Commercial media by the way also question the efficacy of stakeholder consultations, which they find unfocused and unrelated to eventual outcomes of policy processes (Respondent Q, Flanders).

Fourth, there is also an internal governance structure within VRT. Management is planning activities both financially as well as operationally for several years in a row. There are diverse ethical codes, for journalistic content specifically and for the public broadcaster's media services at large. There is an ombudsman for news as well as a complaints office where the audience can approach the public broadcaster with both positive remarks or more critical statements.

What is noticeable when studying the governance of VRT is, first and foremost, the strong involvement of Flemish Government. That is something one would not so easily expect in a Western European country. It in practice does not result in a public broadcaster that is from an editorial point of view immensely under pressure from politics. That editorial independence is also protected by Article 7 of the media decree. Nonetheless, there is a constant scrutiny of what is happening. The relations between members of the Board of Governors and 'their' political parties are rather close even though the media decree specifies that some political functions (e.g., member of a cabinet of a minister) are incompatible with membership of the VRT's Board of Governors. It happens regularly that discussions within the Board of Governors are leaked to the press – a problem, definitely given the Board's access to all documents of VRT. There is no intent to de-politicise the Board of Governors, which could be done in compliance with Article 12 of the media decree as the latter provides that three more members of the Board of Governors can be appointed based on their knowledge of media policy or business economics. That has never been done though. Interestingly, the Board of Governors needs to approve dismissals of members of VRT's executive committee. In other words: in case the CEO wants to fire someone from this committee, the Board of Governors needs to agree. The Board of Governors cannot lay-off the CEO. That is a competence of the Flemish Government.

The composition as well as competencies of the Board of Governors was a topic frequently addressed by experts I interviewed on the Flemish case. Some people said that the Board of Governors' composition made sense in the 1990s, but that reform was needed to match contemporary society. A more independent Board of Governors with experts on media and business was advocated for by several interviewees (Respondent M, Flanders). Members should serve for a limited period of time as to avoid people being on the Board for 15 years or more. Such a Board of Governors should be qualified to select a CEO itself, taking that competence away from the Flemish Government. In case of a genuinely independent Board of Governors, acting in the interest of the company, discussions were said to become tougher, but ultimately VRT would be better off (Respondent F, Flanders). Others held the view that the CEO of the public broadcaster has to be firmer, and has to insist on the Board of Governors behaving independently, ethically and with an eye on the goals of the public broadcaster (Respondent E, Flanders). Some interviewees defended the current governance structure though, arguing the principle of ensuring pluralism within the Board of Governors through political appointees in combination with a clear division of competencies between Management and Board still makes sense (Respondents J, L, Flanders).

The multitude of controlling bodies and instruments is another element that is telling. It reflects a constant demand for more transparency from the public broadcaster on a variety of aspects of its functioning. That also shows in the 2019 Flemish Government agreement which asks for more concrete goals in the new management contract of VRT and a more scrupulous control of these objectives (Vlaamse Regering, 2019: 136). Of course, transparency, accountability and control are important, but the management contract 2016–2020 counts 63 pages of which 13 relate to transparency, reporting and evaluation. It moreover lists approximately 100 key performance indicators, ranging from required audience shares to the amount of meetings VRT has to have with representatives from the cultural, educational or even religious fields in society (Vlaamse Regering and VRT, 2015).

Experts were divided on the evaluation of the governance system in place. Former and current management of the public broadcaster in general argued that the governance structure is largely focused on control and measurement and this to disadvantage the public broadcaster. The objective is not to know more and to optimise VRT's functioning, but rather the contrary (Respondents D, G, Flanders). Private sector respondents were of the opinion that some elements require more control. VRT's activities in advertising were, for example, said to be highly untransparent. Also its behaviour in the market, choices to engage with certain practices and also decisions not to do things, were said to deserve more scrutiny. At the same time, government was considered two-faced in this regard: supporting private sector claims on the need to limit market distortion while at the same time allowing and even pushing VRT to get 40 per cent of its revenues out of the market (Respondent A, Flanders). Furthermore, policymakers are considered to have too limited knowledge of what is going on in the media market. A commission of experts to advise the Flemish Government and even the VRT's Board of Directors on media market developments and VRT's behaviour therein was advocated for (Respondent M, Flanders). In a way such an idea corresponds to broader conceptions of governance.

To sum up, the governance system is Flanders is flawed in two ways. It is, at its core, much too politicised. It is, moreover, too complicated and unfocused. This results in a lot of actors that have some competencies over VRT, a lot of reporting and a considerable amount of stakeholder consultations. However, at the end of day everyone is still unsatisfied with the result of the entire system. That consensus might wrongly be seen as evidence of the system being the best of poor systems. It is really necessary to rethink the governance of VRT with a focus on de-politicisation, a management that is accountable for strategic decisions, and expert opinion and evidence being used for optimising Public Service Media instead of cherry-picking from study reports when convenient. Most importantly, VRT and the Flemish Government should be able to trust each other more. That might sound a bit naïve, but ultimately the system as it stands today is built on the idea that the public broadcaster cannot be trusted with tax payers' money. At the same time, VRT has no trust that politicians are in fact in favour of a strong public broadcaster, which most Flemish politicians to date are.

Re-politicisation of public broadcasters towards national media: the Polish case

Until 1989, Poland's media were subject to communist rule. State broadcasting followed party ideology. A limited number of other media titles, also some with divergent views, were allowed though. Post-communism Poland has adopted characteristics of the liberal, democratic corporatist and polarised pluralist media systems (Hallin and Mancini, 2004). Private media, often from Germany, entered the market. These launched new television, radio as well as print services. Commercialisation and even tabloidisation entered the Polish media market. At the legal level, values such as media freedom and independence of Public Service Media became safeguarded. Practice showed rather high levels of political parallelism though with both right-wing and centrist parties trying to secure control over Public Service Media and, albeit less successfully so, over private initiatives as well (Dobek-Ostrowska, 2012). Sparks (1997) observes a high degree of political parallelism, low autonomy of journalists and high intervention from government. At the same time he also finds a free market in media, showing external pluralism. Klimkiwiecz (2017) is firm when saying the 'normative Western model as a point of departure was implemented only partially'. Definitely, some legal norms were in place. Nonetheless, political control remained present, showing among others through regular replacements of the National Broadcasting Council's members and subsequent changes in Public Service Media organisations' management – usually after elections (Respondents A, H, Poland).

Dobek-Ostrowska (2012: 33) thus concludes that politicisation was definitely visible from 1989 onwards, but intensified with the first victory of the Law and Justice Party (*Prawo i Sprawiedliwość*, 'PiS') in 2005 and its majority rule from 2015 onwards. Eva Połońska (2019: 227) agrees, marking 2015 and PiS's majority government as a turning point. PSM organisations became as an essential instrument for 'social engineering' from that moment onwards. PiS has pushed Polish Public Service Media back from a system that might have been flawed in many respects, but improving on essential Public Service Media values, nonetheless, to a State broadcaster (Klimkiwiecz, 2017). Content is made in line with 'the ideology of the governing party' (Respondent C, Poland).

In 2016 several legal changes were made that amended the Broadcasting Act of 1992. Laws, such as the 'Small Media Act', the 'Big Media Act' and the 'National Media Council Act', all which increased political power over Public Service Media organisations as well as over the Polish National Press Agency. The Polish Government created the National Media Council, a body that took over competencies from the National Broadcasting Council and of which the dedicated task is the oversight of the public broadcasting organisations, both the national and regional ones. The National Media Council's members are directly appointed by government and they in turn appoint members of the Board of Governors as well as the Executive Committee. The period of mandates was shortened and running mandates were ended. Polish Television and Polish Radio were renamed 'national media'. Also the Polish National Press Agency is categorised under that heading. A National Media Fund was, moreover, created, to oversee and organise funding of Polish Public Service Media organisations (Połońska, 2019). The mission of Public Service Media organisations was adapted. Objectives such as the 'cultivation of national tradition, patriotic values and human values, as well as contributing to the spiritual needs of listeners and viewers' and 'maintaining national community and strengthening responsibility for the common good' are included in the legal framework for Public Service Media in Poland. At the same time also editorial autonomy and independence of the 'national media' are recognised – seemingly the concept itself is in contradiction with that (Klimkiwiecz, 2017). Consequently, about 100 journalists were laid off to be partly replaced by younger journalists trained at ultra-conservative, Catholic universities.

Concurrent events indicate an eagerness to control commercial media also. Certain media outlets such as Radio Maryia and Gazeta Polska have expressed political support for PiS already since 2005 and have been awarded with financial support, directly through grants or indirectly via State advertising budgets (Glowacki and Kus, 2019: 8). The 'Re-Polenisation' of the media, high on the government's agenda since 2015, is definitely a course of policy to please those befriended media players, but also to limit the power of American groups such as Discovery Communications. The latter owns, among others, TVN, a commercial broadcaster that reaches more Polish people with its daily news bulletin than TVP1 (Glowacki and Kus, 2019). Surprisingly (or not so), the National Broadcasting Council fined TVN with a 350,000 euros fine in 2017 for contributing to threats to society. Because of international pressure, the Council came back on its earlier decision in 2018. This shows an increase of political interference with the National Broadcasting Council as in 2016 the Council, that has always been politicised yet critical at the same time, concluded that TVP1 had engaged in biased reporting. Glowacki and Kus (2019: 9) cite the Broadcasting Council's conclusion that TVP1:

> shows the monocentric world, narrowed down to the political sphere, with strong tensions between the power and the political opposition. ... There is a strong tendency to build a sense of threat from external forces (immigrants, Russia) as well as internal (opposition, previous government) which in total creates the image of the world as a double-besieged fortress.

The portrayal of a unified culture under threat from immigrants, the EU, LGBTQ+ communities, liberal media, and so on, by TVP and PR was often raised by interviewed experts as one of the most manifest consequences of the heightened government control over Public Service Media in Poland (Respondents A, D, I, Poland). Employees (former and current) from the Polish public broadcaster organisations said that they experienced much more pressure from politics and straightforward censorship since 2015. Politicians, according to one interviewee, 'wanted to have influence during all those years' (i.e. from 1989 onwards), but 'this desire is very strong now, more strong than it was ever before' (Respondent B, Poland).

The contemporary situation of Polish Public Service Media is attributed to 'low level of commitment to civic values in political culture, passivity of society and, in general, an unprofessional media' and, moreover, partisan journalists that strongly believe that their responsibility lies in promoting the best political course for Poland (Dobek-Ostrowaska, 2012: 48). In this, countries such as Poland differ from polarised pluralist systems in Southern Europe where politicisation of Public Service Media is less ideological and more inspired by pragmatism, clientelism and party-political benefits.

The criticism of the Polish Government seems to make Polish leaders even more determined to stick to their guns. While showing a huge divide between rural and urban Poland, the re-election of President Duda in the summer of 2020 reinforces this determination. It shows how illiberal trends are marking Polish politics.

Admittedly, the criticism from, among others, the European Commission, the Council of Europe, the European Federation of Journalists, the European Broadcasting Union and Reporters without Borders, while justified, is selective as the legal changes made to the governance structure of Polish Public Service Media can be found in other countries as well. Nowhere besides Hungary has criticism has been so fierce and unrelenting. Again well-deserved, but somewhat discriminatory in focus.

Having said that, the trends in Poland are worrisome, to say the least. They show how populist and illiberal, neo-authoritarian rule attacks the status of independent media, both public and private, for the purpose of creating an 'illiberal bubble'.

> We suggest that the changes to media policy in Poland can be extended to 'boundary-breaking' – dismantling of democratic rules governing public media. This logic of breaking and pushing the boundaries of the public media is linked to populist style through the creation of political demand to revisit media system in Poland, first public and later private media. This is a continuation of the ongoing trend, in which political actors do not inform the making of media policy on empirical evidence, but on the basis of political speculations, which, ex ante, assumes particular outcomes of the proposed public media policy without any explicit analysis of its design. This way, media policy in Poland is driven by the logic of conditioning of citizens to mechanisms for the creation of an institutional space designed on the principles of political monism.
>
> (Surowiec et al., 2008: 38–39)

Despite differences between Hungary and Poland, one cannot but see the similarities between the PiS and Fidesz regimes, both right-wing populist, rejecting liberal democracy and putting the rights of the nation above those of individuals. Both parties, albeit PiS is more committed to an ideology of populism than Fidesz which has been more instrumental in this regard, have had a history of conflict with both public and private media and use their power base to remedy that issue (Kerpel, 2017: 70). The PiS and Fidesz governments 'used the available maximum of its legislative power to restructure public media oversight system and to put its own people in key decision-making board positions' (2017: 74). An oversight of private media has to date been stricter in Hungary than in Poland, but largely public broadcasters MTV and TVP face similar forms of political interference at the level of laws, governance and day-to-day journalistic practices.

All of this might call to question the idea of 'ontogenesis', that is, 'the development of particular institutions of democracy, replicating (in whole or in part) the historical sequence of their earlier development in other societies'. Ontogenis, so Jakubowciz and Sükösd (2008: 12-13) continue, 'refers to a long societal learning process, with all the attendant crises and conflicts, in which democratic rules ultimately become accepted as the only game in town and respect for media independence finally wins the day'. Jakubowicz and Sükösd (2008: 10) hold that 'media system change is, of course, part and parcel of the general process of what may be called systemic social transformation'. Societal makeover might point in other directions than democracy though.

The drivers of governance

When studying governance of Public Service Media organisations in Flanders and Poland, a lot of similarities crystallise. Boards of Governors and the appointment of the CEO are in the hands of government. Public broadcasters VRT, TVP and PR face political pressure and budget cuts. All struggle with populist trends in society, the rejection of elites and how to align that with their mission in terms of political citizenship. Does that mean the situation of Public Service Media is equally precarious in Flanders and Poland? No. In Poland several policy decisions, not in the least the creation of the National Media Council and the adoption of public interest objectives related to patriotism, mark a very clear and explicit desire for media capture (Bajomi-Lazar, 2015: 62).

The evolution from a Public Service Media to a state or national broadcasting system, as will be elaborated upon further in Chapter 14, basically is a bit at odds with the very notion of media governance. The basic meaning of media governance as something that 'includes restrictions as well as prescriptions' to some extent clouds that the concept, as such, and definitely also in relation to Public Service Media, is 'fundamentally grounded, in the West at least, in the normative framework that prioritises freedom of speech traditions' (Lund, 2016: 104-105). Autonomy, media that act in the public interest and the legal

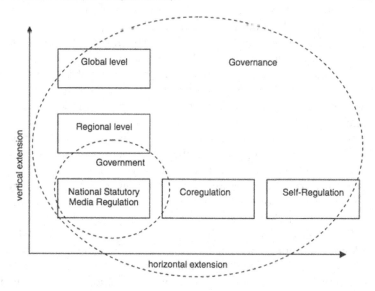

Figure 11.1 Analytical model of media governance
Source: Puppis (2010:140).

protection of press freedom are key in this respect. Trends in Western Europe, Central and Eastern Europe, but also in several Mediterranean countries, show that that dominant normative framework has been on shaky ground for decades and is in some cases being replaced by a free market place of an ideas paradigm that erodes the idea of public service, on the one hand, and a neo-authoritarian vision on media as part of the state, on the other.

The first push for a free market place of ideas paradigm has taken place at the national as well as regional, European Union, level (Michalis, 2010). It started with the upsurge of neoliberalism in the 1980s (Donders, 2012). Even organisations such as the WTO at the global governance level provide an impulse for the free market place of ideas paradigm through agreements such as GATS that consider audiovisual media as economic goods and services (Pauwels and Loisen, 2003; see Figure 11.1).

At the same time, the move towards a neo-authoritarian model is resisted by international institutions such as UNESCO and also by the European Commission through the use of Article 7 of the Treaty on the Functioning of the European Union and the Council of Europe which has adopted several resolutions that underpin the independence of public broadcasting organisations (see Chapter 7).

Governance thus seems to pull in different directions and with varying strength. The lack of self-regulation and thus internal governance within public broadcasters, beyond also the newsrooms, is not aiding in terms of balancing the forces at stake. Indeed, while there is a definite need for legal and institutional support for independence (Połońska and Beckett, 2019: 6), four other factors play a tremendous role in optimising governance.

First, there has to be a political willingness to allow public broadcasters to do their job, to fulfil Public Service Media as well as possible. Such an attitude requires political elites' conviction that an independent, public interest-driven media system is important. They should not see it as a mouthpiece of government, as a conveyor of 'the truth', nor should they pragmatically try to control the public broadcaster because 'it's their turn'. That change of mindset seems particularly difficult to achieve as Petros Iosofidis and Stylianos Papathanassopoulos (2019: 145-148) compellingly show in their study of Greek public broadcasters ERT and NERIT. When NERIT was founded after shutting down ERT against the background of austerity measures, the new government promised to do better. However, it soon became clear that there was no real commitment to install a genuine public broadcaster as had been promised to the electorate. Also the Tsipras government, which re-instated ERT in 2015, did not do much better. Political appointments remained the name of the game, inefficiency still rules and meddling with the editorial line of the newsroom is not uncommon. In a similar vein, legal changes in Poland as well as practices of censorship demonstrate political eagerness to control Public Service Media organisations. Sehl et al. (2020b: 9-10) illustrate how political control over Public Service Media institutions is typically, but not exclusively, the ambition of populist parties. They show tendencies of increased pressure from right-wing populists in Germany, Sweden and Austria. In the latter country, the government with right-wing populist party FPÖ augmented its say in *Rotfunk* ORF, among others, through cutting budgets.

Second, while multistakeholderism has not per se been a success story across Europe (Donders et al., 2019), the inclusion of citizens in Public Service Media governance is important to make sure public broadcasters behave in an accountable manner towards citizens instead of governments. That is not the job of government, although it should at least enable this. Public broadcasters 'should increase their efforts to include citizens in their governance structure and as part of a broader agenda to increase participation and legitimacy of public broadcasting' (Lowe, 2010; Donders and Raats, 2018). Michal Glowacki (2015: 26) argues for adopting 'user-centric approaches, which are based on openness, responsiveness and transparency'. Those, he says, 'are of critical importance for Public Service Media, which has been tasked to serve the societal and cultural needs of each member nation and to promote democracy and participation within the national geographical boundaries'. A first step in the right direction could be the inclusion of social groups in Boards of Governors, something that happens in Germany, but not in most other European countries – a fact criticised by Fernández Alonso and Fernández Viso (2012) in their study of national and regional Spanish public broadcasters' governance bodies.

Third, public broadcasters themselves have to become more resistant against negative evolution in their governance model. In their discussion of media governance, Ingenhoff and Koelling (2012: 156-157) focus on governance not as an outside force, but something from within a media organisation. They differentiate between the responsibility of media organisations regarding conduct and content. They relate this to employees, society and the work environment. While their work focuses on private media organisations, it is important to consider governance from within also when talking about public broadcasters. When researchers, for example, study the difficulty of integrating newsrooms because of staff resistance, a lack of digital profiles or a lack of vision with management (Larrando et al., 2016), all of these pertain to internal governance. Nonetheless, internal governance is crucial to face the challenges of the digital era as well as political threats.

> The current challenge for Public Service Media is to be able to adapt to the new ecosystem dominated by Internet networks and platforms without losing impact on the traditional means of distribution – digital terrestrial television, cable and satellite – which find themselves stagnated or in recession due to the changes in the access and consumption ways preferred by some types of audiences, like young people. This adaptation requires additional investments and strategies to reinforce the social legitimacy and reputation of Public Service Media through the reincarnation of its core, foundational principles – the Reithiantriad based on informing, educating and entertaining – as well as the application of other new, differentiating values linked to a quality service, such as the ones established by the European Broadcasting Union: universality, excellence, independence, diversity, innovation and accountability.
>
> (Campos-Freire, Rodríguez-Castro and Blasco-Blasco, 2020: 672)

Public broadcasters are, moreover, not per se separate entities from *the political* or from *society*. They can be, but are not necessarily victims of neo-authoritarian government regimes. They are often actively shaped by, as well as shaping, their environment. In other words, when Karol Jakubowicz (2011: 210) said that 'it would be hard to find another media segment that is as much a product of – and hostage to – public policy as Public Service Broadcasting', he is right 110 per cent when adding that public broadcasters are also a product of themselves and in some cases entangled with government to the extent that the two are not easily to be separated and soft institutions within the public broadcaster can, even when legal safeguards are in place, resist parting from dear State friends. Internal governance can strengthen public broadcasters or weaken them – an aspect insufficiently studied in the research field.

Finally, governance today is not always goal-oriented. Are control mechanisms, performance indicators, laws, regulatory oversight, and so on, always aiding the optimal performance of public broadcasters? Does governance increase the value that public broadcasters deliver to society? The analysis above, however partial it might be, as suggested in line with other research (see several contributions in Połońska and Beckett, 2019), shows otherwise.

Note

1　www.cultuurpact.be/nl/wetgeving/wet-van-12-mei-2009.

References

Bajomi-Lazar, P. (2015). Variations in media freedom: Why do some governments in Central and Eastern Europe respect media freedom more than others. *Central European Journal of Communication*, 8(1), 4–20.

Campos-Freire, F., Rodríguez-Castro, M. and Blasco-Blasco, O. (2020). Public service media's funding crisis in the face of the digital challenge. In: Á. Rocha, C. Ferrás, C. Montenegro Marin and V. Medina García (eds), *Information Technology and Systems. ICITS 2020. Advances in Intelligent Systems and Computing* (pp. 671–680). Cham: Springer.

Cano Cejalvo, H. (2020). *Has Political Intervention Eroded the Fourth Estate Role of the Valencian Public Broadcaster? The Valencians' Perspective*. Master thesis submitted in partial fulfilment of the requirements for the diploma Master of Science in Journalism and Media in Europe, Vrije Universiteit Brussel, Brussels.

Dobek-Ostrowaska, B. (2012). Italianization or Mediterraneanization of the Polish media system: Reality and perspective. In D. Hallin and P. Mancini (eds), *Comparing Media Systems Beyond the Western World* (pp. 26–50). Cambridge: Cambridge University Press.

Donders, K. (2012). *Public Service Media and Policy in Europe*. Basingstoke: Palgrave Macmillan.

Donders, K. and Raats, T. (2018). Flanders: Increasing transparency of public service media through stakeholder involvement in policy-making? In C. Herzog, H. Hilker, L. Novy and O. Torun (eds), *Transparency and Funding of Public Service Media – Die deutsche Debatte im internationalen Kontext* (pp. 41–53). Berlin: Springer.

Donders, K., Van den Bulck, H. and Raats, T. (2019). The politics of pleasing: A critical analysis of multistakeholderism in public service media policies in Flanders. *Media, Culture & Society*, 41(3), 347–366.

Fernández Alonso, I. and Fernández Viso, A. (2012). Internal pluralism in the governance of public service broadcasters in Spain and the role of social groups and professionals: The case of RTVE. *Communication & Society*, 25(2), 203–230.

Glowacki, M. (2015). Governance of public service media in Poland: The role of the public. *Media & Communication*, 3(4), 26–34.

Glowacki, M. and Kus, M. (2019). Media accountability meets media polarisation: A case study from Poland. In T. Eberwein, S. Fengler and M. Karmasin (eds), *Media Accountability in the Era of Post-truth Politics: European Challenges and Perspectives*. London: Routledge.

Hallin, D.C. and Mancini, P. (2004). *Comparing Media Systems: Three Models of Media and Politics*. Cambridge: Cambridge University Press.

Ingenhoff, D. and Koelling, A.M. (2012). Media governance and corporate social responsibility of media organizations: an international comparison. *Business Ethics: A European Review*, 21(2), 154–167.

Iosofidis, P. and Papathanassopoulos, S. (2019). Greek ERT: State of public service broadcaster?. In E. Połońska and C. Beckett (eds), *Public Service Broadcasting and Media Systems in Troubled European Democracies* (pp. 129-153). Basingstoke: Palgrave Macmillan.

Jakubowicz, K. (2011). Public service broadcasting: Product (and victim?) of public policy. In R. Mansell and M. Raboy (eds), *The Handbook of Global Media and Communication Policy* (pp. 210-229). Malden: Wiley-Blackwell.

Jakubowicz, K. and Sükösd, M. (2008). Twelve concepts regarding media system evolution and democratization in post-communist societies. In K. Jakubowicz and M. Sükösd (eds), *Finding the Right Place on the Map: Central and Eastern European Media Change in a Global Perspective* (pp. 9-40). Bristol: Intellect.

Karppinen, K. and Moe, H. (2013). Critique of "media governance". In M. Löblich and S. Pfaff-Rüdiger (eds), *Communication and Media Policy in the Era of the Internet* (pp. 69-80). Baden-Baden: Nomos.

Kerpel, A. (2017). Pole and Hungarian cousins be? A comparison of State media capture, ideological narratives and political truth monopolization in Hungary and Poland. *Slovo, 29*(1), 68-93.

Klimkiwiecz, B. (2017). State, media and pluralism: Tracing roots and consequences of media policy change in Poland. *Publizistik, 62*, 197-213.

Larrondo, A., Domingo, D., Erdal, I.J., Masip, P. and Van den Bulck, H. (2016). Opportunities and limitations of newsroom convergence. *Journalism Studies, 17*(3), 277-300.

Lowe, G.F. (ed.) (2010). *The Public in Public Service Media.* Göteborg: Nordicom.

Lund, A.B. (2016). A stakeholder approach to media governance. In G.F. Lowe and C. Brown (eds), *Managing Media Firms and Industries. Media Business and Innovation.* Cham: Springer.

Michalis, M. (2010). EU broadcasting governance and PSB: Between a rock and a hard place. In P. Iosifidis (ed.), *Reinventing Public Service Communication: European Broadcasters and Beyond* (pp. 36-48). New York: Palgrave Macmillan.

Pauwels, C. and Loisen, J. (2003). The WTO and the audiovisual sector: Economic free trade vs cultural horse trading? *European Journal of Communication, 18*(3), 291-313.

Połońska, E. (2019). Watchdog, lapdog, or attach dog? Public service media and the Law and Justice government in Poland. In E. Połońska and C. Beckett (eds), *Public Service Broadcasting and Media Systems in Troubled European Democracies* (pp. 227-255). Basingstoke: Palgrave Macmillan.

Połońska, E. and Beckett, C. (2019). Introduction. In E. Połońska and C. Beckett (eds), *Public Service Broadcasting and Media Systems in Troubled European Democracies* (pp. 1-20). Basingstoke: Palgrave Macmillan.

Puppis, M. (2010). Media governance: A new concept for the analysis of media policy and regulation. *Communication Culture & Critique, 3*(2), 134-149.

Sehl, A., Simon, F.M. and Schroeder, R. (2020b). The populist campaigns against European public service media: Hot air or existential threat. *International Communication Gazette.* Retrieved from https://doi.org/10.1177/1748048520939868 (accessed October 2020).

Sparks, C. (1997). Post-Communist media in transition. In J. Corner, P. Schlesinger and R. Silverstone (eds), *International Media Research: A Critical Survey* (pp. 96-122). London: Routledge.

Surowiec, P., Kania-Lundholm, M.K. and Winiarska-Brodowksa, M. (2008). Towards illiberal conditioning? New politics of media regulations in Poland (2015–2018). *East European Politics, 36*(1), 27–43.

Vlaamse Regering (2019). *Regeerakkoord 2019–2024.* Brussels: Vlaamse Regering. [*Government Agreement*].

VRT and Vlaamse Regering (2015). *Beheersovereenkomst 2016–2020.* [*Public service contract 2016–2020*].

Part III

Practice

12 Multi-platform strategies of public broadcasters in Ireland, the United Kingdom, Flanders and the Netherlands

From public broadcaster to public media organisation

Public Service Media, in most literature, refers to public broadcasters' provision of services that contribute to the democratic, cultural and social objectives of society and this on multiple devices and across varied technologies. Ample attention has been devoted to the evolution from Public Service Broadcasting to Public Service Media (see Lowe, Van den Bulck and Donders, 2018; Lowe and Martin, 2013). Scholarly work has zoomed in on the theoretical foundations of the Public Service Media concept, the ways in which public broadcasters have moved into the digital arena (or not) and the extent to which governments have enabled or inhibited them from doing so (Burri, 2015). Also public broadcasters' own multi-platform strategies have been researched, albeit mainly from a citizen- and services-oriented (Moe, 2013) perspective. Several scholars also researched the difficulty of integrating news rooms (Van den Bulck and Tambuyzer, 2013; Larrondo et al., 2016). Few research exists on the strategic positioning of public broadcasters in a rapidly evolving multi-platform market though. Besides assessments of national governments' or the European Union's (Ward, 2008) evaluation of public broadcasters' market-distortive behaviour, there is little attention for the way in which public broadcasters position themselves as Public Service Media strategically in internationalising media markets that are increasingly characterised by American-driven platformisation tendencies (Evens and Donders, 2018).

Main questions

Are public broadcasters making the transition from a radio and television to a media organisation, how are they doing this, and with what objectives in mind? Is there a clear strategy underlying what they are doing in the online realm or are actions directionless? These are the core questions I seek to answer in this chapter.[1]

Methodology

This chapter is based on desk research of public broadcasters' policies and strategies in Ireland, the United Kingdom, Flanders and the Netherlands and, complementary, expert interviews with one to two academics in each of the countries studied (carried out in the second half of 2018 and the beginning of 2019). I adopted a case study approach (Vennesson, 2008), focussing on broadcasters in the West of Europe. The Irish, Flemish and Dutch public broadcasters are funded on the basis of both public resources and commercial communication revenues whereas the BBC relies largely on public funds, complemented with revenues from exports. The selection of cases is to a large extent inspired by Hallin and Mancini's (2004) taxonomy. Ireland and the United Kingdom can be situated in the liberal model, at the crossroads with the democratic corporatist model. Both have a strong public broadcasting system, but are very open to market forces. Ireland is a small language neighbour of the United Kingdom, which comes with specific competitive issues such as high competition from UK broadcast channels. The United Kingdom is the biggest audiovisual market in Europe, exporting to other countries worldwide (Donders and Van den Bulck, 2016). Flanders and the Netherlands are part of the democratic corporatist group, showing strong levels of government intervention and a historical inclination to protect domestic content industries. They are open to market forces as a consequence of European liberalisation processes. Both the Flemish and Dutch public broadcasters are active in radio, television and online advertising. The BBC might, in comparison with RTE, VRT and NPO, be considered a bit of an outlier here because of its size, but can therefore also be expected to have more developed strategies for the digital platform era than other public broadcasters.

The case studies rely largely on qualitative content analysis, a method used to 'elicit meaning, gain understanding and develop empirical knowledge' (Bowen in Puppis, 2019). The qualitative content analysis, used frequently in media policy research (Puppis, 2019), first focuses on four key aspects of Public Service Media theory (as also elaborated in Chapter 3) when the transition to 'digital' is concerned:

- No exclusive focus on radio and television, but public service provision making use of all media. Other media are in fact considered of equal importance to radio and television and can, hence, not be considered accessory activities (Donders, 2012).
- More attention for audiences and audience engagement: public broadcasters should be more service-oriented, taking into account the needs and wants of their audiences. They should accept audiences are more so an integral part of Public Service Media than with Public Service Broadcasting. This means using the opportunities of the digital world to cater for minority interests better and adopting a more inclusive approach towards, for

example, urban and migrant audiences (Horsti and Hultén, 2011). It also means using these opportunities to allow for co-creation, participation and interaction (Bakker, 2011; Enli, 2008), albeit that these should not be ends in themselves (Vanhaeght, 2019).

- Internal reorganisation with an eye on embodying and dealing with convergence: public broadcasters should leave behind their silo-based organisations, certainly in their news departments (Larrondo et al., 2016). But also innovation departments should become more connected to the work floor. There seems to be a disconnect to the 'playground' of the tech people and those making television, radio and online services.
- A remaining and strengthened dedication to 'public service', providing services to the public regardless of their appeal to advertisers or their willingness-to-pay. Not just online service delivery for the sake of it and with an eye on competing with global giants, but services in the public interest, which are contributing to the realisation of socially beneficial goals such as the strengthening of cultural identity and diversity, social cohesion, media literacy, emancipation, informed citizenship, and so on. The main distinguishing feature of Public Service Media from Public Service Broadcasting might not be its multi-platform nature or the fact that it allows for interaction, participation or even co-creation of content. It might be its genuinely public service-driven agenda in a world of clickbait, non-transparent algorithm-driven personalisation, datafication, and so on. It ought to be the achievement of its democracy-centric ambitions in an international and converged media market.

These four aspects were operationalised further into a set of labels. Management contracts from 2013 until 2017 were analysed on this basis, as well as other relevant strategic documents like vision documents on innovation, digital strategies and new media services. In total, 32 documents were analysed.

On top of that I carried out theory testing expert interviews, which can be regarded as interviews that mainly look for tacit, explanatory knowledge from experts that have some distance from the policy process and/or corporate strategies and activities (Bogner, Littig and Menz, 2014). Academics and retired politicians are usually considered useful respondents for this type of interview. The six interviewees were academics, all of whom have a deep understanding of their national Public Service Media system. Some have a background in media policy studies; others are more knowledgeable about audience research or media management and economics. The experts interviewed were: Professor Dr Hilde Van den Bulck (Drexel University), who is an expert on Public Service Media in Belgium and Europe, media policy and celebrity culture; Professor Dr Tom Evens (Ghent University), who is an expert on Flemish media policy and economics and is a member of the sectoral body that advises the Flemish Government on legislative changes regarding public broadcaster VRT; Professor Dr Yaël de Haan (Utrecht University College), who specialises in Public Service

Media, journalism and multi-platform consumption in the Netherlands; Dr Phil Ramsey (Ulster University), who researches Public Service Media in the United Kingdom, with recent publications on the digital strategies of the BBC; Dr Sally Broughton-Micova (University of East Anglia and Media Policy Project, London School of Economics), who is an expert on Public Service Media in the United Kingdom and the Balkans; and Professor Dr Gavan Titley (Maynooth University), who studies the future of Public Service Media, digital media environments and the integration of social theory into media theory. Not in line with other chapters, I do relate experts' names with quotes and opinions they shared with me. I have their consent to this. Other chapters make use of stakeholders' opinions, many of which still occupy key positions in the media or policy field. That sensitivity does not play out here.

The main objective of the interviews was to cross-check the findings of the document analysis by using a more interpretative and evaluative approach, while at the same time attempting to identify the different stages of 'multi-platform development' of the four public broadcasters included in the analysis. Indeed, when reading scientific literature on this topic, scholars have identified different stages of 'multi-platform development'. First, there is the experimental stage in which public broadcasters realise the Internet and new possibilities in terms of interactivity, co-creation, app development, and so on, exist. They experiment, try to see what works, what does not work and what can be improved. Several pilots are created. Second, public broadcasters enter a panic stage, obsessed with the idea they need to be where their audiences are. Remarkable similarities can be drawn with this phase and public broadcasters' focus on market share post-liberalisation of the broadcasting sector (Nossiter, 1991). Subsequently and related, public broadcasters aim to maximise their presence online. Not per se the what, but the how much is an important motivator for developing online activities. Expansionist strategies value more online activities over the relation of these services with the public service mission (Donders, 2012). Fourth, and often while being confronted with budget cuts, public broadcasters need to critically evaluate what is a priority in terms of online service delivery and what is not. They are in a state of consolidation. Emphasis is put on the offer of video-on-demand as a basic service that consumers expect. Regulation is also limiting online expansion to some extent. Public broadcasters devote attention to integrating 'the digital' in their internal organisation, not only by integrated newsrooms, but also by shifting budget away from linear service provision to new services and by hiring staff with digital competencies (Raats, 2013: 128). Finally, there is the maturity phase in which public broadcasters have developed an online strategy that relates not to the idea of online service delivery as such but to the public service proposition of each of their brands. They have decided where they will distribute their content and under what conditions. They are more conscious of competitive trade-offs between them and, for example, Netflix. That does not mean strategies are completely coherent in all respects as the digital environment is very much a moving target (Ramsey, 2018b). While this presentation of phases might give the impression of a rather linear process, public broadcasters can in fact situate themselves in multiple of these phases, albeit that intensity will differ.

In the interviews, I used a semi-structured topic list, focussing on the distinctive features of each phase of Public Service Media development. I also confronted the experts with the preliminary findings from the document analysis (for expert interview techniques, see Herzog and Ali, 2015). In the past, media policy scholars have pointed out that issues such as 'cultural otherness' (Ganter, 2017) and a lack of familiarity with the complex interplay of historical, social, economic, political and cultural factors that determine national Public Service Media systems have had an impact on research (Raats and Pauwels, 2011). The complementary expert interviews were intended to mitigate any such possible impact.

I present the findings below, structuring insights from the data around the four main distinguishing features of Public Service Media compared to Public Service Broadcasting.

Radio and television as 'safe zones' of Public Service Media

Online distribution of radio and television content or full-fledged multi-media company

NPO, VRT, RTE and BBC all report on a multitude of online services. Whereas there was an explosion of websites in the early 21st century, there seems to be a consolidation now. The emphasis is on the news website, the offer of online children's services and the development of mature radio and video players. The latter are seen as a necessary step to provide audiences with the 2016 programmes they want, whenever they want it (e.g., VRT, 2015: 49; NPO, 2015b: 29; 2016; 2017: 12; BBC, 2017: 2;). The annual reports analysed all contain information on the aforementioned online services of public broadcasters. It can be noted that the state of play of these services is different from country to country. The BBC's news website, children's offerings and radio and video player are very advanced. They receive considerable budgets to work with, have a high reach and are an integral part of its service delivery (being mentioned in all annual reports studied). While RTE, NPO and VRT also have video and radio players, some of these are still fairly recent or require re-investments to ensure they are up to date with current audience expectations (Evens, 14 November 2018; Titley, 18 December 2018; see also NPO, 2018: 32). Whereas NPO, VRT and RTE are focused on online distribution of existing content and, complementarily, some new activities, the BBC has the ambition to become a genuine all-round media company. For smaller public broadcasters, services innovation and experiment (RTE, 2015: 37; VRT, 2017: 128), on the one hand, and doing something with principles such as curation, on the other hand (VRT, 2015: 5), are important also. However, there is a need to 'realign resources and refocus investment' (RTE, 2014a: 4) as resources are admittedly more limited. As Gavan Titley (18 December 2018) stated:

The axis of RTE's approach is on online distribution of programming. ...
Theoretically, they understand what a digital media environment is, but
they have difficulties translating this. There are a lot of aspirational ideas
... They talk about a new strategy and they do that very well. But little of
that can be seen.

Lack of coordination on online activities

When talking about bigger broadcasters such as the BBC, experts mainly
pointed at the relative maturity of BBC's online strategies (Broughton-Micova,
7 January 2019), but at the same time also at the remaining difficulties to align
media production, aggregation and distribution strategies between different
brands. In other words: what one of the BBC's generalist channels is doing
might be very different from what CBeebies is doing and could be very
different for legitimate reasons. The differences are not always due to thought
through considerations of, for example, audience needs though. They are very
often caused by a lack of coordination between divisions. Ramsey (18 October
2018) argues: 'the sheer scale of the corporation makes a centralised vision
impossible' and results in a competitive disadvantage when comparing the BBC
to more unified companies such as Netflix and Amazon.

The certainty of excelling in radio and television

While offering important online services such as news websites and video and
radio players, the main emphasis of public broadcasters – also in their reporting –
remains on radio and television. Annual reports, in so far they are transparent
regarding budgets, also show that the majority of public broadcasters' budget
is still invested in radio and television. Their evaluation is focused on performance in these areas as well. For example, RTE's performance commitments
deal mainly with radio and television. Weekly reach has to be maintained or
increased for each of their radio and television brands. Perceptions on quality
and/or trust are important evaluation criteria for television channels RTE One
and RTE2. Websites such as RTE.ie, RTE Player and RTE News Now are also
mentioned, but performance indicators are softer or focused on issues such as
audience perception or satisfaction, in the case of RTE.ie, and the offer of a
good range of content, for RTE Player (RTE, 2017a: 2ff). These are more service oriented and only implicitly relate to the core values of Public Service
Media. Of course, it can be argued that quality of programming is evaluated
when people's satisfaction with the quality of RTE One is measured. However,
younger audiences might access RTE content mainly via the RTE Player,
which makes it important to assess not only their satisfaction with the variety
of services offered via the video player, but also their opinion about the quality
of content offered. Similar observations can be made when analysing the BBC's
annual reports. While the BBC is admittedly the most digital-oriented public
broadcaster of the four analysed, it also puts most emphasis on its outstanding

news, documentary, drama … programmes and the prizes it wins with these (BBC, 2017: 2, 2018: 2-5). Several experts expressed related opinions. Hilde Van den Bulck (7 December 2018), for example, said (referring to te Walvaart et al.,) that 'even when management is ready to embrace digitisation, production is 2018 not always as ready to follow suit as television producers still primarily care about delivering a top television programme to the linear channels and see social media as something they have to do on the side'. Also Gavan Titley (18 December 2018) stated that RTE still sticks to broadcast programming, rarely going into genuinely innovative domains. Furthermore, Yaël de Haan (17 January 2019) stresses public broadcasting organisations as a whole have difficulties in transforming from radio and television broadcasters into something less broadcast focused. That would require a systemic change.

Of course, it is hard to make the transition from Public Service Broadcasting to Public Service Media. Financial and organisational reasons can be named. But, there is also an issue of risk-taking. Why put less emphasis on what you do very well? In 2013, RTE (2013: 3) reported that they broadcasted 19 out of the 20 most popular television programmes in Ireland. VRT (2017: 22, 25) held a market share of 63.7 per cent in radio and 37.1 per cent in television. NPO (2017: 15, 2018) attracts 29.2 per cent of listening time and 31.2 per cent of market share in television in 2018. BBC (2017: 24) states 32 per cent of television viewing in the UK is directed towards BBC television channels. The BBC and RTE are taking the lead in online also. The BBC's iPlayer was at the time of introduction highly innovative and set standards at the technical, but also at the use level (Broughton-Micova, 7 January 2019). Nowadays iPlayer faces a hard time dealing with Netflix and other US-led streaming services. RTE News Now is the top news app in Ireland (RTE, 2015: 2). For public broadcasters such as VRT the situation is different. They are not the market leader in online news, but see main newspaper publishers De Persgroep and Mediahuis taking the lead with hln.be and nieuwsblad.be respectively.

From experiments to consolidation and back again

At the same time, it was also argued that RTE, VRT, NPO and BBC have made significant progress in evolving to broadcasting companies that are active (and often successfully so) online. Hilde Van den Bulck (7 December 2018), Tom Evens (18 November 2018), Phil Ramsey (18 October 2018) and Sally Broughton-Micova (7 January 2019) considered VRT and BBC as situated in the phases of public service consolidation and, for some aspects, also in the maturity phase. Yaël de Haan (17 January 2019) was less optimistic about where NPO and its member organisations are to be situated. Public Service Media is still in an experimental and expansionist stage with sometimes signs of consolidation and, more often, intermediate moments of panic. According to Gavan Titley (18 December 2018) the situation in Ireland is complex as well with RTE being 'spread over' the different phases from experiment to maturity. He says that an online-first strategy is not per se reflecting an evolution to

Public Service Media, at least when taking into account the definition of the Public Service Media concept in scientific literature. The document analysis indeed shows that RTE, in terms of content distribution, has consolidated and focuses on optimising its offering of non-linear services through its player, on the one hand, and through commercial partnerships, bringing in revenues, on the other. At the level of both production and aggregation it is still very much in an experimental stage, seeing what digital-only services might work and what might not. The analysis of policy, strategy and annual report documents of VRT and NPO show similar results. For example, VRT only introduced a full-fledged on-demand audiovisual service (vrt.nu) two years ago. And both VRT and NPO have development labs in place that are still considering how to spread their news and current affairs offer more effectively to users, including youngsters. At the same time, both VRT and NPO have a rather developed, 360-degree content production, aggregation and distribution strategy for children. Besides, consolidation does not necessarily mean the mature embrace of the Public Service Media concept in practice. It might equal consolidating at something that is not the ideal, but from a practical and budgetary point achievable.

More consideration of audiences, but …

All documents analysed emphasise there is a different relation with the audience because of technological change. BBC, NPO, RTE and VRT stress that they still need to understand this changed relationship better (see, for example, RTE, 2014b: 10; BBC, 2014: 3; VRT, 2015: 4). Audience aspects that have changed concern the flexibility required when consuming content, the audience's capacity to interact with and even co-create content and the declining or not sufficiently increasing reach of some minorities in society.

Changed consumption behaviours as a given

First, the need for public broadcasters to deliver content anytime, anywhere and anyhow is more and more presented as a given. Whereas the management contracts from 2013, 2014 and 2015 still present this as something to be done (see NPO, 2015a: 14), management contracts from 2017 consider this a basic feature of Public Service Media and mention a radically different consumption behaviour of audiences. For example, in the 2014 NPO annual report, one can read there is a need 'to respond to changing audience needs' (NPO, 2015a: 16). In RTE's annual report of 2017 it is stated that 'While broad patterns of media consumption endure, with linear television and radio remaining very strong, major changes in the market are shifting audience behaviour and expectations (particularly among younger people) towards online and mobile services' (RTE, 2017b: 8).

Whereas personalisation was considered something that could happen in the future or was not even mentioned in earlier documents, it is now more or less a given, albeit that some public broadcasters problematise this more than others. They do not only consider personalisation an opportunity, but also relate it to issues such as fake news (NPO, 2018: 14) and filter bubbles (Van den Bulck, 7 December 2018; see also, Van den Bulck and Moe, 2018: 879). Tom Evens (14 November 2018) adds that most public broadcasters, including the Flemish one, are still struggling with taking a user-driven perspective on service delivery and meeting high consumer expectations.

Lip service to interaction, co-creation and participation

Second, audience interaction and co-creation are presented as parts of 'a more personalised, social and mobile BBC, offering individual recommendations, participation and a two-way relationship with our audiences' (BBC, 2014: 55). VRT (2015: 70, 75) aspires to strengthen participation in programmes as well as participation in, for example, culture and the arts through its programming. NPO mentions in its main strategic plan for 2016-2020 that it wants to strengthen audience interaction, offering 'numerous opportunities for the audience to interact and to participate ... through program sites and apps of broadcasters, through broadcast portals and through social media' (NPO, 2015b: 38). In its annual report of 2013 it also stated that participation and personalisation to meet audience needs is a necessity (NPO, 2014: 7). But a genuine view on what that could mean in terms of legitimacy for public broadcasters or for the empowerment of audiences is lacking still. The focus seems to be on pilot projects, often for a very limited part of the audience (e.g., VRT, 2014: 19).

A more audience-centred approach seems difficult to uphold for Public Service Media organisations' activities (de Haan, 17 January 2019). That, relating back to the elaboration of a citizenship-centric to Public Service Media in Chapter 4, has to do with a too limited understanding of what online, beyond connecting public broadcasters' services to users, can mean in terms of strengthening citizenship.

The difficulty of reaching youngsters

Third, all public broadcasters talk about the difficulty of reaching youngsters (NPO, 2015a: 27) and children. The focus on mobile is often argued for, pointing at the changing needs of the youngster audience (RTE, 2014b: 2-3). The use of social media such as Instagram is experimented with. For example, Dutch news broadcaster NOS has invested considerable resources in connecting to youngsters via Instagram news stories (de Haan, 17 January 2019). The BBC took one of the most drastic decisions of all four public broadcasters studied: it turned its BBC Three television channel into an online only service in a 'journey to ensure that the service meets the needs of young people today, and innovates with new ways to create and deliver content that keeps pace with young people's lives in the future' (BBC, 2016: 66). The decision has been criticised for being a cost-cutting measure mainly and not living up to expectations though (Ramsey, 18 October 2018). And indeed in May 2020 rumours surfaced on the BBC planning to bring BBC Three back on linear television (Waterson, 2020). Observing the reach of its CBBC channel dropped below 25 per cent in the age group 6 to 12 years old in 2017, the BBC also increased investments in its children's services (Ramsey, 18 October 2018; BBC, 2018: 24). Regardless, NPO, VRT, RTE and BBC have a 360-degree strategy in place for children that both in terms of reach and satisfaction (also of parents) performs well (VRT, 2016: 54; RTE, 2015: 61). When it concerns other minorities public broadcasters stress how good they are doing things. However, here it seems that the annual reports are largely used for PR purposes (e.g., VRT, 2013: 19ff, 2015: 17ff) and do not offer a genuine reflection on the rather low reach of some minority groups and a sense of lack of representation with these groups. That is, as I discussed in Chapters 4 and 5 of this book, problematic and largely goes against public broadcasters' role to strengthen political, social, cultural and civic citizenship with all groups in society.

What has stayed the same is audience trust in public broadcasters, at least according to themselves. Several annual reports stress that public broadcasters remain the most trusted, most watched, most listened to companies in media markets (NPO, 2015a: 13; VRT, 2016: 11). BBC, RTE, NPO and VRT also investigate this and point at high scores on traditional values such as trust, pluralism, quality, and so on (NPO, 2015a: 10; VRT, 2016: 14). This aspect will be further studied in the case study chapters.

An increased public service awareness, but commercialism is boosted too

More recent documents also show an increased public service awareness in terms of what public broadcasters should do in an international and converged media market. That comes with more commercialism at the same time as well. Public broadcasters indeed regard the online realm as a world of possibilities for new revenues that should complement public income.

Strengthening public broadcasters' legitimacy in an international and converged media market

In Ireland and the United Kingdom, there is an increased emphasis on public broadcasters' task in a commercialised, internationalised and platform-based digital environment. The offer of public broadcasters, particularly online, should add quality, creativity, value ... to what is done by others. Being online is not a goal in itself; there should be a reason for being there. As said by RTE: 'our digital approaches and tactics, all of what we do must be underpinned by a clear sense of purpose – a purpose that is rooted firmly within RTE's overall public service remit' (RTE, 2014b: 6). Whereas BBC seems to be more experimental, exploring the possibilities new kinds of services offer to achieve public service objectives (see also Ramsey, 2018a), RTE's focus is still on programming, on 'doing what it does best' (RTE, 2014b: 2): commissioning or making high-quality Irish programming and being a trusted source for news and current affairs programming.

On top of the attention for GAFA (Google, Apple, Facebook and Amazon) and the damages it can do to the local culture and domestic media markets, the Flemish public broadcaster defines its remit more and more against the background of societal trends such as polarisation, populism, an ageing population, urbanisation, the environmental issues at play, and so on (VRT, 2016: 11). The annual reports of VRT spend considerable attention to events where the public broadcasters bring together children, youngsters or elderly people; initiatives that bridge the gap between citizens and politicians; collaboration with the educational, cultural and social field. In short, they aim to show societal impact, emphasising also that international conglomerates are not interested in taking up that citizenship-centric role (VRT, 2014: 21; 2015: 5, 10; 2016: 28). In the case of the BBC, NPO and RTE lesser attention is devoted to these issues. According to Gavan Titley more attention for societal shifts and even fractures is necessary if Public Service Media wants to remain relevant. He called the Iris situation 'socially dislocating' and argues RTE appeals largely to urban elites. It fails to present a national narrative in which a majority of Irish people can recognise themselves. That fracture is aggravated by digitisation, but the latter is not the cause of it.

'Older' issues regarding public service remain. There is particularly with the Dutch a focus on distinctiveness from commercial offers at the level of genres. For example, the one NPO annual report states that 'the focus of programming is on journalism, music and the arts, education and information, series and film of Dutch origin, documentaries and children's programming' (NPO, 2015b: 5). This focus on distinctiveness has been omnipresent in Dutch debates since the 1980s when commercial broadcasting started. Also the BBC has emphasised the distinctiveness of its offers, including those services that are online only. With its BBC Ideas initiative, the BBC is commissioning for the creation of digitally native content for social media, competing thus with social media players, but driven by public interest objectives (Ramsey, 18 October 2018). Evens (14 November 2018) takes this a step further and claims that public broadcasters should think more about how technology as a tool can enhance its distinctiveness. How can public broadcasters use technology to further empowerment, participation in society … and not only reach as such.

Friction between public service awareness and commercial pragmatism

There is some friction between the abovementioned public service awareness, on the one hand, and public broadcasters' commercial strategies, on the other. While VRT and BBC remain silent on this, RTE (2017a: 1) says that

> as the organisation strives to fulfil its public service remit, it must content with the tensions of securing public service goals while remaining

dependent on a high level of commercial funding, and catering for popular interests, while serving minority cultures and interests'.

NPO mentions, even if briefly so, that its collaboration with third parties exploiting its content requires a 'balance between the increase of revenues on the one hand and the recognisability and attractiveness of its offers on the other hand' (NPO, 2015b: 57). While not stated as such in published documents, VRT and BBC also struggle with balancing public service goals and commercial objectives. They limit the universality of their offers (for example, by not streaming all of their offers or through boxing some of it in pay-services) because they do not want to jeopardise the generous income they receive from television distributors. The huge success of BBC content abroad has affected the British public broadcasters' commissioning strategies. Ramsey (18 October 2018) holds the opinion that the collaboration between the BBC and Netflix might erode the public broadcasters reason of existence. He says 'we are talking about two very different beasts: you cannot compare the BBC and Netflix ... the BBC could endanger itself by going too far down that road'.

The position of public broadcasters as economic entities is most explicitly addressed in the policy documents and annual reports concerning VRT and the BBC. The former's management contract for 2016-2020 (Vlaamse Regering and VRT, 2015: 31ff) contains a full chapter on the economic role VRT should play to strengthen domestic content production, start-ups, newspaper publishers, commercial broadcasters, and so on. The idea thereof is to instrumentalise the public broadcaster as a lever for growth in the whole media market (VRT, 2017: 131). The annual reports of VRT provide an increasing amount of information on partnerships with a diversity of companies, emphasising its increased investments in external production (over 70 per cent for prime time television programmes, see VRT, 2017: 7) and its role as facilitator for start-ups (VRT, 2018: 126). At the same time, in the annual reports from 2014 to 2016 little to no information is provided on how the public broadcaster positions itself in an increasingly commercialising, international media market. It's 2017 annual report marks a change as it refers explicitly to the difficulty of financing drama production in a market with powerful international competitors and raises the possibility to 'create together with other European public broadcasters a development platform for fiction' (VRT, 2017: 125). VRT might be positioned increasingly as a tool for market development, its own public service activities are increasingly curbed from a market distortion point of view (Van den Bulck, 7 December 2018; Evens, 14 November 2018).

The BBC operates as an economic entity on the basis of its charter agreement. Public purpose four (out of six main public purposes) explicitly states that the BBC's task is 'To reflect, represent and serve the diverse communities of all of the United Kingdom's nations and regions and, in doing so, support the creative economy across the United Kingdom.' As is the case with the VRT, the BBC invests significantly in external production and has even decided to turn its own production facilities into a fully commercial branch BBC Studios

(Ramsey, 18 October 2018). Moreover, its subsidiary, BBC Worldwide (which has now been combined with BBC Studios), sells BBC and non-BBC content to other public broadcasters and streaming platforms such as Netflix. It has also agreed to several co-production deals with the latter. Whereas VRT's task is also to strengthen direct, domestic competitors such as commercial broadcasters and newspapers – that is, those companies advocating for the limitation of its remit (Van den Bulck, 7 December 2018) – such a task cannot be found in the agreement, charter and annual reports of the BBC.

Interestingly, the Dutch and, albeit to a lesser extent, Irish policy and strategy documents do not elaborate on the international media environment and what that means in terms of content distribution until 2017. NPO's 2014 annual report mentions research carried out on the future of Public Service Media. While the need for a more distinctive offer, organisational changes, consumer behaviour, and so on, are all mentioned, no reference is made to issues such as internationalisation and platformisation. In the 2016 annual report, globalisation, consolidation of ownership structures and the powerful position of companies such as Apple, Netflix and Spotify are mentioned (NPO, 2016: 5). However, there is no elaboration on what this means for the public service remit, nor for the content production, aggregation and distribution strategies of NPO. Distinct public broadcasting organisations are looking for ways to valorise content. VPRO, for example, considers international co-productions and licensing of content to international platforms (de Haan, 17 January 2019).

There is an acknowledgement that the rules of the game have changed and this to the benefit of international, online-first companies. However, this trend is approached in different ways by the public broadcasters studied. First, it is seen as a trend and treated as a contextual factor. That was the approach apparent in the earlier annual reports (2013, 2014, 2015) and resulted in rather vague statements on the need to change strategies. RTE (2014a: 4) says it 'can't stand still' if you 'can see how challenging the competitive environment is becoming'. Second, the internationalising media environment is used in a rather instrumental manner to argue for preserving a strong public broadcaster. NPO says government should strengthen Public Service Media in response to 'the increasing role of wealthy international undertakings that control both the production and distribution of media services within the value chain' (NPO, 2015a: 42). More recently, in its 2017 annual report, Irish public broadcaster RTE says 'Public media has never been more necessary. In a media world dominated by the international, the commercially driven and the false, it is increasingly important to give authority and voice to the indigenous and to the creative' (RTE, 2018: 8). The public broadcaster emphasises the lack of accountability of the new players it is competing with and their lack of focus on or dedication to the production on distinctive, high-quality Irish content (RTE, 2018: 22). Third, public broadcasters are positioning ongoing economic changes more and more as a strategic issue. While doing their public service task and without having the adequate means to do so, they need to compete with international conglomerates (NPO, 2017: 31). How public broadcasters subsequently strategically position themselves is less clear. VRT, so Tom Evens (14 November 2018) argues, is thinking more carefully about where it puts what content and how to deal with new distributors. However, both the management contract and annual reports are silent on this matter. It is an issue the public broadcaster prefers to deal with behind the scenes. In contrast with that approach, the Irish public broadcaster communicates explicitly on partnerships with Sky, Netflix, Amazon, Acorn TV and Hulu, stressing mainly how important these are from a financial perspective (RTE, 2015: 36, 74, 2017b: 96). Of course, this business practice is related also to the Irish diaspora and the reach of audiences abroad (RTE, 2017b: 48). Overall, commercial strategies and distribution strategies specifically are not elaborated upon in important strategic documents, nor are there substantial explanations (in spite of some fair trading guidelines) to be found in the policy frameworks. The expert interviews revealed aspects of strategies though. While most public broadcasters embrace social media as an additional channel to reach citizens, they all realise that there are some ethical issues and competitive trade-offs to be dealt with. In competitive relationships with on-demand players, cable giants or Internet service providers relations are largely based on negotiation dynamics. However, in dealing with all these companies, public broadcasters do not have the upper hand. They have less power, less money and overall more to lose when not collaborating (Van den Bulck, 7 December 2018).

Internal reorganisation as the Achilles heel of Public Service Media strategies

In each management contract, strategy document and annual report the need for organisational reform is mentioned. A digital environment requires a flexible and efficient organisation. This line usually serves as a legitimation of budget cuts and staff reductions. Most documents refer to strengthening leadership within public broadcasters. Whereas budgetary issues are elaborated upon in a quite specific manner, that is less the case for everything that deals with leadership, stronger internal communication, stimulating collaboration across departments, and so on. For the latter type of issues, statements such as 'The HR department has focused on strengthening leadership and supporting collaborative dynamics' (VRT, 2017: 148) and 'The NPO finds education, training and coaching important. On the one hand to develop the knowledge, capacities, behaviour and attitude of employees in line with the goals of the organisation; on the other hand to enable them to tackle new challenges' (NPO, 2014: 125) are common place. The only area for which more specificities are provided is innovation and, in addition, newsroom integration. RTE is rather clear on the purpose of RTE Digital as a unit that structures all digital and innovation related activities, such as the radioplayer and the RTE Incubator (RTE, 2014b). It elaborates on reorganising its news and current affairs resources 'to deliver a digital-first news service alongside broadcast news and current affairs output' (RTE, 2017b: 28). Also VRT mentions the functions of its innovation department (R&D, external communication, collaboration with other public broadcasters), its Open Innovation initiative (inviting talent from outside the VRT to workshops, co-creation sessions) and VRT Sandbox, which is a test bed for new services from VRT and start-ups. Also the Dutch public broadcasting organisations have several innovation labs in place (de Haan, 17 January 2019). So, while there seems to be an awareness of the need to break up silos within public broadcasters, to work together and to nurture talent, it remains unclear whether that is really taking place and what the effect of reform is on digital content and distribution strategies.

The Netherlands are a bit peculiar when it comes to internal reorganisation as all documents analysed mainly refer to the changes made in the pluralistic structure of their Public Service Media system. In the Netherlands, several public broadcasters with different ideological or societal representations share a number of television channels and are to some extent coordinated by umbrella organisation NPO. It is thus a de-centralised public broadcasting system. The political consensus on this distribution of public service dissolved however. The opinion was that there were too many organisations (13) and that some merging activity was necessary, also because the membership-based existence of the different organisations was clearly under pressure in a society where more and more people disconnect from belonging to 'the' Christian public broadcaster or 'the' liberal public broadcasting organisation. Some of the biggest organisations merged and broadcasting organisations' existence does not depend on membership anymore. The process is still ongoing, very challenging and, while being necessary to streamline strategies in a digital age, it might also take away attention from the transition to Public Service Media (de Haan, 17 January 2019).

A focus on democracy, not on commercial revenues

There is more focus on digital content and distribution strategies. RTE, VRT and NPO seem to focus most on the online distribution of programmes. They invest also in some experimental, digital-only content. But these experiments are rather limited in scope and budget. The BBC takes a more ambitious approach, moving BBC Three online (thus not a success) and investing considerable resources in services such as BBC Ideas. The different focus is largely due to the difference in budget, on the one hand, and political limitations on the remit (formal or informal), on the other (Van den Bulck, 7 December 2018; de Haan, 17 January 2019; Gavan Titley, 18 November 2018). All in all, one could argue that our analysis shows that the digital strategy of the studied Public Service Media organisations shows the glass is half empty or half full. As Public Service Media is an ideal and its scientific definition also evolves along technological, economic and social developments, public broadcasters are pursuing a moving target. Others are more rapid in that pursuit, in some cases perhaps too fast. Others need more time and are faced with challenges (Evens,

14 November 2018). Taking a half-full perspective one could argue in line with Phil Ramsey (18 October 2018):

> If you would have said when the Internet was starting to get popular in the mid 1990s, in 20 years time the BBC will not have been undermined by the Internet, but will have thrived on it, many people would have said that that would not happen.

As producers, aggregators and distributors of content, public broadcasters have undeniably become more aware of the highly complex and competitive international media environment in which they operate. As said by Sally Broughton-Micova (7 January 2019) public broadcasters 'are quite aware of the platformisation and are working on adapting it; though they may be inhibited by resource constraints and legal barriers to cooperation, they do not seem to be held back by a lack of understanding'. They consider the surrounding environment to be a justification of their continued existence. Few of them are explicit about their competitive positioning in this environment though. Some would argue that makes sense from an economic point of view. Why share your strategic orientation with everyone? But, this secretiveness should be criticised. The way in which public broadcasters position themselves in a market has not only economic, but also public service implications. In case public broadcasters work together with Netflix and services are offered on a pay-per-view basis, this impacts the universality of public broadcasters' offers. If they decide with Netflix to modify editorial lines of drama series to make sure these appeal to international audiences, there is a possible impact on values such as quality, editorial independence, cultural diversity and identity, and so on. That is not to say that public broadcasters are mainly guided by economic motivations. On the contrary, both the analysed documents and experts interviewed indicate a strong public service awareness, but a friction between this and budgets that are across the four cases analysed under pressure. Admittedly, the competitive positioning of public broadcasters is a bit unclear at best and in most cases also a bit unfocused. There is not sufficient alignment of strategies between different brands and departments in public broadcasters. That is normal as all media companies need to adapt to the changing environment as well as competitors adapting to their changing strategies. One could thus argue that focus will never be observed given the moving target under investigation. What can be observed is NPO's, VRT's and RTE's bigger vulnerability given their lower budget and, perhaps even more so, their higher independence on commercial fundings, including advertising. All of this should not take away focus from a much-needed and long-term oriented reflection on what kind of organisation they want to be in an international and highly competitive media market. We should, however, be aware that the transition from Public Service Broadcasting to Public Service Media is quite difficult and taking place in a context that does not often facilitate that transition. De Haan (17 January 2019) explains, in line also with insights from Chapter 5:

A public broadcaster is such a robust entity. It is a big mammoth that needs to produce lots of content every single day. At the same time, it needs to stop and do things differently. That is terribly complicated, especially in a context where the political climate is not helping either.

Having said that, it is necessary that public broadcasters approach the digital environment less from a technological perspective and more from a societal perspective. How do they want to contribute to political, social, cultural and civic citizenship online? That reflection is not terribly present whereas it is exactly their public service role that will make the difference in struggling societies.

Of course, documents and interviews do not tell everything. More research, specifically through participatory observation, would be interesting to find out how exactly digital content production, aggregation and distribution strategies are being shaped at the level of management, but also through the day-to-day practices of producers, journalists, and so on. Because the focus of today's management contracts, annual reports and other strategy documents is largely on what public broadcasters have to do (in terms of output), there is too little focus on how they do this and with what impact. These two elements might actually become important in terms of distinguishing public broadcasters and their public service ethos from what commercial companies are doing in a datafied and further commodifying media environment. Some of this is addressed in the subsequent case study chapters on Flanders and Poland.

Note

1 Several key findings, albeit mainly focused on distribution, presented here, have also been published in *Media, Culture & Society* with the title 'Public Service Media beyond the digital hype: An analysis of digital content and distribution strategies in Europe', Donders, 2019.

References

Bakker, P. (2011). Expectations, experiences & exceptions: Promises and realities of participation on websites. In G.F. Lowe and J. Steemers (eds), *Regaining the Initiative for PSM* (pp. 237-251). Göteborg: Nordicom.
BBC (2014). *Annual Report*. London: BBC.
BBC (2016). *Annual Report*. London: BBC.
BBC (2017). *Annual Report*. London: BBC.
BBC (2018). *Annual Report*. London: BBC.
Burri, M. (2015). Contemplating a 'public service navigator': In search of new (and better) functioning public service media. *International Journal of Communication, 9*, 1341–1359.
Donders, K. (2012). *Public Service Media and Policy in Europe*. Basingstoke: Palgrave Macmillan.
Donders, K. (2019). Public service media beyond the digital hype: Distribution strategies in a platform era. *Media Culture & Society, 41*(7), 1011-1028.

Donders, K. and Van den Bulck, H. (2016). Decline and fall of public service media values in the international content acquisition market: An analysis of small public broadcasters acquiring BBC Worldwide content. *European Journal of Communication*, 31(3), 299–316.

Enli, G.S. (2008). Redefining public service broadcasting: Multi-platform participation. *Convergence: The International Journal of Research into New media Technologies*, 14(1), 105–120.

Evens, T. and Donders, K. (2018). *Platform Power and Policy in Transforming Television Markets*. New York and Basingstoke: Palgrave Macmillan.

Ganter, S.A. (2017). Perception and articulation of own cultural otherness in elite interview situations: Challenge or repertoire? *The Qualitative Report*, 22(4), 942–956.

Hallin, D.C. and Mancini, P. (2004). *Comparing Media Systems: Three Models of Media and Politics*. Cambridge: Cambridge University Press.

Herzog, C. and Ali, C. (2015). Elite interviewing in media and communications policy research. *International Journal of Media and Cultural Politics*, 11(1), 37–54.

Horsti, K. and Hultén, G. (2011). Directing diversity: Managing cultural diversity media policies in Finnish and Swedish public service broadcasting. *International Journal of Cultural Studies*, 14(2), 209–227.

Larrondo, A., Domingo, D., Erdal, I.J., Masip, P. and Van den Bulck, H. (2016). Opportunities and limitations of newsroom convergence. *Journalism Studies*, 17(3), 277–300.

Lowe, G.F. and Martin, F. (2013). *The Value of PSM*. Göteborg: Nordicom.

Lowe, G.F., Van den Bulck, H. and Donders, K. (eds) (2018). *Public Service Media in the Networked Society RIPE@2017*. Göteborg: Nordicom.

Moe, H. (2013). Public service broadcasting and social networking sites: The Norwegian broadcasting corporation on Facebook. *Media International Australia*, 146(1), 114–122.

Nossiter, T.J. (1991). British television: a mixed economy. In J.G. Blumler and T.J. Nossiter (eds), *Broadcasting Finance in Transition: A Comparative Handbook* (pp. 95–143). New York: Oxford University Press.

NPO (2014). *Jaarverslag 2013*. Hilversum, NPO. [*Annual report 2013*].

NPO (2015a). Jaarverslag 2014. Hilversum: NPO. [*Annual report 2014*].

NPO (2015b). *Het Publiek Voorop: Concessiebeleidsplan 2016–2020*. Hilversum: NPO. [*Audience first: Management contract 2016–2020*].

NPO (2016). *Jaarverslag 2015*. Hilversum, NPO. [*Annual report 2015*].

NPO (2017). *Jaarverslag 2016*. Hilversum, NPO. [*Annual report 2016*].

NPO (2018). *Jaarverslag 2017*. Hilversum, NPO. [*Annual report 2017*].

Puppis, M. (2019). Analyzing Talk and Text I: Qualitative content analysis. In H. Van den Bulck, M. Puppis, K. Donders and L. Van Audenhove (eds), *Handbook on Media Policy Research Methods* (pp. 367–384). Basingstoke: Palgrave Macmillan.

Raats, T. (2013). *And now for something completely different? De rol en positie van de publieke omroep in een genetwerkte samenleving: onderzoek naar de publieke omroepopdracht en – organisatie aan de hand van een comparatieve analyse van de culturele missie* (Unpublished Ph.D. thesis). Vrije Universiteit Brussel, Brussels. [*And now for something completely different? The role and position of the public broadcaster in a networked society: A comparative analysis of the public service remit and organisation in the cultural domain*].

Raats, T. and Pauwels, C. (2011). In search for the holy grail? Comparative analysis in public broadcasting studies. In K. Donders and H. Moe (eds), *Exporting the Public Value Test* (pp. 17–28). Göteborg: Nordicom.

Ramsey, P. (2018a). The BBC Ideas Service: The Corporation's Search for Universalism Online. Paper presented at the 2018 RIPE Conference 'Universalism and PSM', 18–20 October, Madrid.

Ramsey, P. (2018b) It could redefine public service broadcasting in the digital age: Assessing the rationale for moving BBC Three online. *Convergence, 24*(2), 152-167.

RTE (2013). *Annual report 2012 and group financial statements.* Dublin, RTE.

RTE (2014a). *Annual report 2013 and group financial statements.* Dublin, RTE.

RTE (2014b). *Extending public values in the digital age: Digital priorities 2015–2016.* Dublin, RTE.

RTE (2015). *Annual report 2014 and group financial statements.* Dublin, RTE.

RTE (2017a). *Extending public value in the digital age RTE.* Dublin, RTE.

RTE (2017b). *Annual Report 2016.* Dublin, RTE.

RTE (2018). *Annual Report 2019.* Dublin, RTE.

Van den Bulck, H. and Moe, H. (2018). Public service media, universality and personalisation through algorithms: Mapping strategies and exploring dilemmas. *Media, Culture & Society, 40*(6), 875-892.

Van den Bulck, H. and Tambuyzer, S. (2013). Collisions of convergence: Flemish news workers' and management's perceptions of the impact of PSB newsroom integration on journalistic practices and identities. *International Communication Gazette, 75*(1), 54-75.

Vanhaeght, A.-S. (2019). The need for not more, but more socially relevant audience participation in public service media. *Media, Culture & Society, 41*(1), 120–137.

Vennesson, P. (2008). Case studies and process tracing. In D. Della Porta and M. Keating (eds), *Approaches and methodologies in the social sciences* (pp. 223-239). Cambridge: Cambridge University Press.

VRT (2013). *Jaarverslag 2012.* Brussels: VRT. [*Annual report 2012*].

VRT (2014). *Jaarverslag 2013.* Brussels: VRT. [*Annual report 2013*].

VRT (2015). *Jaarverslag 2014.* Brussels: VRT. [*Annual report 2014*].

VRT (2016). *Jaarverslag 2015.* Brussels: VRT. [*Annual report 2015*].

VRT (2017). *Jaarverslag 2016.* Brussels: VRT. [*Annual report 2016*].

VRT (2018). *Jaarverslag 2017.* Brussels: VRT. [*Annual report 2017*].

VRT and Vlaamse Regering (2015). *Beheersovereenkomst 2016–2020.* [*Public service contract 2016–2020*].

Walvaart, M. (2019). Translating PSM policy into production practices. *View,* 8(16).

Ward, D. (2008). The European Commission's state aid regime and PSB. In D. Ward (ed.), *The European Union and the Culture Industries* (pp. 59-80). London: Ashgate.

Waterson, J. (2020). BBC Three could return to TV four years after online-only switch. *The Guardian,* 6 March. Retrieved from www.theguardian.com/media/2020/mar/06/bbc-three-could-return-tv-channel-broadcast (accessed October 2020).

13 A prominent market and cultural logic in Public Service Media policies in Flanders

Public broadcasting in Flanders

Public Service Broadcasting in a divided country

Public broadcaster VRT provides media services to the Dutch-speaking community in Belgium. It is regulated by the Flemish Government. Media policy is an autonomous competence of the language communities in Belgium. Besides VRT, there are two other public broadcasters in Belgium: RTBF that services the French-speaking community and BRF for the minor German-speaking population in the East of the country (see Donders, Van den Bulck and Raats, 2019b). The distinct public broadcasters have the objective to contribute to the cultural identity of their linguistic community, not to some sort of unified Belgian identity. That might seem odd to outsiders, but is a natural consequence of the governance structure of Public Service Media in Belgium and is in line with the social, economic and cultural reality of separate language communities. Brussels, the capital, is the exception as it hosts Dutch- and French-speaking citizens as well as a big group of people that do not fit either one of these two language communities.

Admittedly, public broadcaster VRT faces more external pressure from both politics and commercial competitors than is the case for RTBF in the French-speaking part of Belgium. Experts we talked to (cf. infra) noticed a different 'consensus' around Public Service Media in the French and Dutch-speaking communities in Belgium.

> Wallonia is a place where people find it normal that half of the economy is in the hands of government. You usually have a rather leftist government. It is a small area where besides RTBF there are no big media players. They are the only meaningful company. For politicians, it is the only platform they have. You thus do not go against RTBF. Even rightwing parties in Wallonia don't do that. Well, MR [liberal part in the French speaking community] is a rightwing party in Wallonia; in Flanders they would be at the center. The public broadcaster and the way it functions reflect the culture and society in which the public broadcaster is active. For Flanders, that means that VRT

should be good, but not too successful. That is typically Flemish. While we say we aim for excellency, we feel most comfortable with mediocracy. You cannot excel too much or they destroy you. That is *the* issue for VRT. It cannot have too much power.

(Respondent H, Flanders)

Nonetheless, the performance of VRT is – compared to other public broadcasters in Europe – very good. It reaches most people on a weekly basis, has the lead radio and television channel, is widely recognised for its local children's programming, spends nearly 20 per cent of its production budget to independent producers, and coordinates several European-level public broadcasting collaboration initiatives in the domains of innovation and drama production (Suarez-Candel, 2020; Raats, Van den Bulck and d'Haenens, 2015). Its budget is – compared to other public broadcasters in Europe – rather low at an annual cost of 42 euros per Flemish citizen per year. That figure will decrease further as the Flemish Government that was elected in 2019 immediately announced it would cut further in VRT's subsidies (Vlaamse Regering, 2019).

Critique on the public broadcaster is situated partly in academic corners as well. Some scholars criticise VRT for not being courageous enough in its transition from a Public Service Broadcasting to a Public Service Media organisation (Donders, 2019a), failing to reach out to citizens in a genuinely interactive manner (Vanhaeght, 2019) and representing minorities adequately (Panis, Paulussen and Dhoest, 2019). Most criticism can be detected with politicians and commercial competitors though. Several claim that VRT distorts the market, its offers are not sufficiently distinctive, does not spend enough money on culture and documentary, and fails to report neutrally on political matters (Donders, Raats and Tintel, 2020).

Having said that, there remains a political consensus on the need for a strong public broadcaster, albeit that there is serious disagreement on what 'strong' actually means, how much money that implies, and the width of the remit of a Public Service Media instead of a Public Service Broadcasting organisation. Discussions on this matter are vivid in Flanders and seem captured by two ideological fields of tension. First, a neoliberal, but at the same time also protectionist, market logic versus a more society and democracy-centric conceptualisation of Public Service Media (see also Donders, Van den Bulck and Raats, 2019b). Second, there is tension on the identity project Public Service Media should embody: unity versus diversity captures that tension the best. My analysis shows that public broadcasting policies in Flanders are constantly navigating between these logics. That has to do with politicians pleasing stakeholders, but also with a genuine dedication to safeguarding both public and commercial local media that can contribute to Flemish culture and economic growth. The growing importance of commercial funding of the public broadcaster compared to its declining subsidy basis makes that navigation exercise almost a mission impossible from the outset and might risk to take attention away (also with the public broadcaster itself) from the core of Public Service Media today: that is to contribute to political, cultural, social and civic citizenship in times when society risks to disintegrate. That does not necessarily mean that politicians or commercial media are opposed to Public Service Media as such, nor does it mean that the public broadcaster is flawless and cannot be blamed for imperfections. Rather, this chapter illustrates that a more consistent, value-based grounding of Public Service Media as a policy project is needed to sail straight ahead.

Main questions

The main aim of this chapter is to analyse what Public Service Media actually means in Flanders? Does it connect with the citizenship-centric conceptualisation I present in this book or is it defined in other manners? While I will provide some information on how VRT functions, the main focus of the analysis below is on the meaning of Public Service Media as a policy project in Flanders today and, specifically, tomorrow. Are the views of the public broadcaster, private media, politicians, civil society and scholars in this regard the same or do we see significant differences in terms of where VRT should stand in ten or even 20 years time? And if there are differences, what accounts for this? Are there diverging viewpoints on Public Service Media or on whether VRT should become a Public Service Media organisation at all?

Methodology

This chapter is based on a triangulation of data sources, including expert interviews, documents, participatory observation and complementary insights from coverage of popular press. First, I carried out 17 expert interviews with management and journalists of the public broadcaster, management of private media companies, policy-makers, former CEOs of the public broadcaster, academics, consultants, and so on. I asked them about the past, present and future of Public Service Media in Flanders, focussing on the public broadcaster's relationship with audiences, civil society, commercial media, politicians and its own organisation. I do not attribute specific opinions or quotes to these experts. Their names are mentioned in the introduction of this book though. I restate my appreciation for their contribution to this chapter and their willingness to talk to me in an open and constructive way. That was not evident, definitely since private media are aware that I have been assisting the public broadcaster with several policy-related dossiers.

The purpose of the expert interviews was to find out not so much what is going on factually as research on that exists, but why certain things are happening and how experts see VRT's future. The focus was thus on uncovering explanatory knowledge and to find out what experts thought was likely, but also desirable to happen. Typically, this knowledge resides with people involved in the decision-making process, but also with other stakeholders that hold some power over that process (e.g., media companies, public broadcaster's management).

Explanatory knowledge can be defined as the subjective opinions, points of views, interpretations, explanations, and so on, held by an expert on the basis of her expert knowledge (Bogner, Littig and Menz, 2014). When multiple experts adhere to similar interpretations, that does not mean that their beliefs are factual, but at least they offer value for the interpretation of highly contextual, often complex phenomena that are studied in case studies (Van Audenhove and Donders, 2019: 185).

I added documents to the set of rich data from the expert interviews. Documents included in the analysis are: all management contracts of VRT, the annual reports from 2013 until 2019, the 2019 Agreement of the Flemish Government, the 2019 Policy Note of the Minister of Media, reports from hearings in the Flemish Parliament (with a focus on the hearings concerning Public Service Media in 2015 and 2020), and the audience survey and stakeholder consultation reports of 2011, 2015 and 2019 that preceded new management contracts. I also engaged in participatory observation. Both in 2015 and Autumn 2019-Winter 2020, I acted as an adviser to the public broadcaster concerning the management contract negotiations with the Flemish Government. In that capacity I participated in over 50 meetings with government staff and public broadcaster management. In both periods, I had weekly meetings with the management committee and CEO of the public broadcaster, regular meetings with VRT staff dealing with children's television, diversity, production of Flemish content, journalism, innovation, and so on, and several get-togethers with members of parliament from all political factions, notably those members that were/are part of the Committee for Media. That role has the advantage of access to information researchers otherwise do not have access to. At the same time, it comes with a bias as well. That is why the method of data analysis has been crucially important to ensure an objective assessment of Public Service Media policies in Flanders.

All data derived from this intense role in the negotiation of the management contracts of VRT and the Flemish Government, expert interviews and documents were analysed on the basis of the method used for the case study on Poland as well: a combined qualitative content and thematic analysis. Qualitative content analysis allows for 'a systematic, step-by-step approach to interpreting interview transcripts, observation notes and documents' (Puppis, 2019: 367). Using the concept of (political, cultural, social and civic) citizenship (described in Chapter 4), all sentences in the fully transcribed interviews and relevant phrases in the documents were assigned to a category (for an illustration, see Table 13.1). After that, to structure the process of interpretation, I engaged in a thematic analysis, looking for themes and patterns of recurrence outside the citizenship-based framework of analysis. Themes can be defined as 'an abstract entity that brings meaning and identity to a recurrent experience and its variant manifestations' (DeSantis and Ugarr, 2000, in Herzog, Handke and Hitters, 2019: 394). Herzog, Handke and Hitters (2019: 385) say that the method is 'particularly suitable for analysing experiences, perceptions and understanding'. In combining a deductive analysis with a more inductive analysis, I ensured not

Table 13.1 Excerpt from the codebook

Main category	Subcategory	Definition	Sentence assigned to this code
Citizenship	Political citizenship	Political citizenship is about being informed and having access to different interpretative frameworks and deliberative fora. It requires a place for dialogue among citizens, internal and external pluralism.	"There is a danger that journalism becomes a bubble in its own right. We try to do it as well as possible, but some journalists are convinced they are right. We are the first to say we provide a forum to all opinions, but is that always true? There is room for improvement there" (Respondent G, Flanders).

to overlook relevant aspects of Public Service Media in Flanders. Insights from the participatory observation were added to the findings from the qualitative content and thematic analyses.

Citizenship as an implied goal of Public Service Media

Public Service Media is a recognised concept in Flanders. The management contract 2016-2020 sets out from the observation that media technology and use are changing dramatically and that in light of these changes a definition of VRT's role on the basis of radio, television and online does not make sense (Vlaamse Regering and VRT, 2015: 9). The management contract identifies strategic objectives and ambitions that VRT needs to achieve in domains such as information, culture, education, entertainment and sports. Essentially, those objectives and ambitions can be dealt with through any means necessary. Having said that, there is a chapter on new media services, requiring public value tests for entirely new channels or significantly new services (Vlaamse Regering and VRT, 2015: 50-51). Moreover, a lot of performance indicators are still tied to reach via radio and television, investments in television content, and the need for television or radio 'programmes' on history, religion, Flemish music, and so on (2015: 52ff). And also VRT itself is still organised along the silos of radio, television and digital media. So, while in principle the evolution from Public Service Broadcasting to Public Service Media is recognised as a fact and innovation on the side of the public broadcaster is encouraged, the management contract at the same time makes clear that online is a different animal when it comes to defining what VRT has to do or not. That approach can also be found in the Flemish Government Agreement of 2019. The document emphasises that VRT should refrain from competition in areas such as sports rights and celebrities, be more impartial and neutral in its political reporting, collaborate with a sector initiative to offer paid on-demand services, and stop offering text-based services (Vlaamse Regering, 2019). The policy note of the minister of media is admittedly more nuanced. It also emphasises the importance of neutrality, but subsequently defines this as 'impartiality, independence and editorial autonomy' (Dalle, 2019: 26). That is not the definition of neutrality, but seems to be a practical manner of dealing with what was written in the government agreement. The minister of media also mentions, in line with the government agreement, that there is need for internal and external quality control regarding neutrality (2019: 26). That is a sensitive matter for the public broadcaster as external control over (news) content is in general considered a breach of its editorial autonomy. Based on my involvement in the negotiation of VRT's new management contract, it seems that the Flemish Government is aware of this tension and therefore opts for independent scientific research on this matter, also in dialogue with the public broadcaster. Nonetheless, one should keep in mind that also the policy note on media from former Minister of Media Sven Gatz (2014: 28) mentioned pluralism *and* neutrality as important key features of Public Service Media. In other words: the issue is not new. There is rather an enduring emphasis on neutrality and an explicit desire against bias. While the policy note of Minister for Media Benjamin Dalle says that the focus of VRT's news site should be on audiovisual services and that longreads are prohibited, other parts are more progressive in their approach to Public Service Media. Dalle, for example, says that VRT should 'adapt its services to the changing media environment, with content on relevant own and external platforms' (2019: 27). I will develop these aspects further in the sections below.

Most of the interviews I conducted took place before the Flemish Government announced the changes to public broadcaster VRT. That was in hindsight a good thing as it de-politicised the interviews I did significantly. They were not yet captured fully by a 'lobby logic' on the side of the people I interviewed. The analysis of the interviews as well as documents shows that most emphasis is put on political and social citizenship. Politicians are admittedly more concerned with cultural citizenship as well, especially after the new Flemish Government pushed for a Flemish 'canon' in 2019 and also given the migration/integration issue that generates more discussion on what Flemish culture is and what is not. Civic citizenship was much less considered, unless in relation to media literacy. The latter is in line with our findings concerning Poland where strengthening civic citizenship is not a priority either. On the contrary, empowering citizens to employ their rights is in fact discouraged within the political setting in Poland (see Chapter 14). The latter is a finding that does, as might be expected, not correspond with the situation in Flanders.

Political citizenship

Information is one of the most important, if not the most important, task of VRT. All policy documents confirm the importance of the public broadcaster to inform citizens. The focus is on VRT being *the* source for impartial and trustworthy information being 'the only one in the Flemish media landscape that acts fully independent from commercial, political or ideological interests' (VRT, 2015: 8; see also VRT, 2014: 10, 24; VRT, 2017: 52; Vlaamse Regering and VRT, 2011: 25; 2006: 15).

The management contract 2012-2016 is more traditional. It defines news as the 'core task of the public broadcaster'. It mentions values such as quality, reliability, factual, correct, nuanced, trustworthy, impartial and credible. But no reference to the abovementioned trends can be found (see Vlaamse Regering and VRT, 2011: 25ff). That is also the case for the annual reports of the public broadcaster in 2014 and 2015. These have a rather neutral view on information. It is a task of all public broadcaster brands, of some more than others. Here and there annual reports mention spreading information via Facebook (e.g., VRT, 2014: 43) and websites (e.g., VRT, 2015: 10, 24). The online news offer is seen as something that supports the radio and television brands (VRT, 2015: 42). In general, the focus is on being *the* source for impartial and trustworthy information being 'the only one in the Flemish media landscape that acts fully independent from commercial, political or ideological interests' (VRT, 2015: 8).

While the information task is positioned largely in relation to the Flemish market until, more recent policy documents relate the obligation to inform people firmly to the 2015 internationalisation of the news media market, the rise of social media, polarisation and disinformation (e.g., Vlaamse Regering, 2019; Dalle, 2019; VRT, 2017: 52; VRT, 2018: 42). The management contract 2016-2020, for example, provides:

> In a rapidly internationalising media environment with an over-supply of information, the public broadcaster is the guarantee for impartial, independent and reliable information ... Trustworthiness is not acquired, but a permanent point of attention. VRT invests in independent and quality journalism. Core values are: trustworthiness, quality, accuracy, independence from political parties and interest groups, free from commercial interests, impartial and diepgaand [thorough].
>
> (Vlaamse Regering and VRT, 2015: 17)

That approach gradually changes as can be seen from the 2016 annual report (VRT, 2016: 61-62). Performance is still captured by the 2012-2016 management contract, but at the same time influenced by the negotiations on the new management contract. No reference to internationalisation or disinformation either, but more − although still limited − attention for the online offer of news, including podcasts, thematic websites, the use of platforms such as YouTube and Spotify, and so on.

While the prominence of the information task can be derived from all analysed documents, the goal of informed citizenship is often implicit and the strengthening of democracy is not mentioned at all. The only exception to this: the public broadcaster's own vision document on the management contract 2021-2025. Published at the end of 2019, the document portrays VRT as 'a necessary instrument for democracy' (VRT, 2019a) through impartial and trustworthy information, domestic programming, and educational and cultural programming (VRT, 2019b: 8).

Our interviewees also pointed at the important role of VRT in terms of information *as such* and, in line with many of the analysed documents, that VRT adds to the overall quality of the journalistic landscape. The public broadcaster, so it was said repeatedly, has to be impartial and show a strong dedication to its information task (e.g., Respondents G, J, N, Flanders). Commercial media, notably print media, have a slightly different function. While they inform about what has happened, they also at times take an ideological course and in so doing contribute to external pluralism in the news landscape (Respondents M, Q, Flanders). Internal pluralism, offering a forum to a variety of voices, was considered an important task for Public Service Media, but far from a given. One interviewee said that VRT often invites the same people. When there is a problem with the capital, Brussels, they have a name in mind. When there is an issue related to religion, they have another name in mind. But 'they do not adequately research who has something new to add, a fresh perspective'. VRT misses opportunities to 'get nuance back into a society that polarises increasingly' (Respondent F, Flanders).

Admittedly, some respondents also criticised VRT for not taking adequate action against journalists that jeopardise the impartiality or the perception of impartiality of the news room. Indeed, some journalists are rather active on social media and in so doing sometimes give the impression to be biased. There the opinion was that 'if you want to take individual standpoints, do not work with a public broadcaster because you undermine your own and the institution's credibility, even when exercising your right to freedom of expression'. These mistakes on social media 'give an easy weapon to opponents' (Respondent E, Flanders). They, at the core, also jeopardise the journalistic ethics (Respondent F, Flanders).

Another point of criticism from commercial media concerns the online news provision of the public broadcaster. While accepted, the reliance on text as a medium of communication was rejected as the core business of print media (Respondents A, G, M, Q, Flanders). Equally so, the free offer of news was considered market distortive, even though research shows that there is no correlation between willingness-to-pay and a free online news offer of public broadcasters (Fletcher and Kleis Nielsen, 2017; Sehl, Fletcher and Picard, 2020). Several interviewees said that the idea that more news online means a smaller need for Public Service Media news is false (Respondents B, P, O, Flanders). On the contrary, 'the more news there is online, the bigger the need for the public broadcaster as a beacon for objective, pluralistic and societally relevant information' (Respondent L, Flanders). The discussion is more complex and multi-layered though. There is no demand with politicians or commercial media (at least in Flanders) to eliminate online news from the public broadcaster's task. Interventions in Parliament, also by stakeholders, the interviews as well as several of the meetings between politicians and the VRT on its management contract show that the focus is largely on the amount of text on the news website of the public broadcaster, the presence of opinions and the fact that all public broadcaster news is offered for free. Text and opinions are considered the 'playground' of commercial media. Lack of payment is seen as a discouragement of users to pay for online news provided by newspapers (Respondents M, Q, Flanders). While all of these assumptions are debatable at a factual level, public broadcasters can actually, without much problem, focus their news provision on audio and audiovisual formats, making use of text as a supportive means to inform the audience. They can do so without any problem and without jeopardising losing their relevance. On the contrary, both audio and video are on the rise online. Public broadcasters such as VRT, one could also argue, have too easily used text to fill their news websites, they followed the trend instead of being distinctive (Respondent C, Flanders) and were largely concerned with attracting audiences instead of focusing attention on innovating and even reinventing their audio and audiovisual formats for the online age (Respondent M, Flanders). Having said that, offering – and one can discuss the format – a diversity of opinions on topics online is a task of public broadcasters and private media alike. Prohibiting public broadcasters to offer different viewpoints on issues would endanger pluralism of societal discussions and touch upon the core of public broadcasters' function to strengthen democracy. Even more problematic, taking a democracy-centric view on public broadcasting, is the assumption – albeit evident that private media take this position – that public broadcasters should not do text or opinions because others are doing it. The question should be whether they need it to perform their role in democracy and answering that question might in some cases come to answers that are mutually beneficial for public broadcasters as well as commercial media.

The continued need for VRT to perform well in times of disinformation, abundance and also polarisation was addressed by most (former) policy-makers and public broadcaster staff we talked to. VRT has to be trustworthy across platforms. Checking quotes, prioritising truth over speed and taking some distance from fast news facts were seen as necessary actions for the public broadcaster. The idea that that is needed to strengthen democracy was explicitly mentioned on several occasions (e.g., Respondents B, E, G, I, J, P, Flanders).

A shared concern among all respondents, no matter their background, was polarisation in society and the role some politicians play in this. Some politicians were said to 'manufacture' polarisation and to put VRT as well as other 'mainstream media' 'in the corner of fake, not to be trusted' (Respondent M, Flanders). Through social media, 'politicians have their own channels for communication'. That results increasingly in 'a discourse of polarisation', also against journalists 'that we have to deal with' (Respondent P, Flanders). The public broadcaster faces the challenge to be transparent about all the editorial choices it makes and to admit when mistakes have been made.

At the same time, public broadcaster respondents said they do not necessarily face more direct pressure from politicians. As long as we are 'critical for everyone and do our job', there is no issue (Respondent P, Flanders; also Respondent G, Flanders). Criticism is moreover not only limited to politicians, but extends to other actors in society whenever you touch upon a sensitive issue concerning climate, geopolitics, ethics, and so on. While most respondents indicated that these trends have little impact on editorial choices, some indicated that they 'fear this has an impact, unconsciously' and might thus result in phenomena such as self-censorship (Respondent O, Flanders). It might cause VRT to go along with polarisation or to refrain from taking a stance against it.

Another concern of various people I talked to was the societal divide on information that seems to grow. The public broadcaster itself, so several internal meetings I attended revealed, has a justified concern on a disconnect with lower educated citizens, people with a migration background and youngsters. While several initiatives try to tackle the challenge of connecting with these groups (e.g., through being more aware of language use, providing more context, using shorter formats of digital news on Instagram or YouTube), media industry representatives observe (in line with research of Hendrickx and Ranaivoson, 2019) that 'better informed citizens get more and better journalism today' while 'it is the big group of people, those that are not reading and will not read newspapers that are informed by social media and that are completely captured by fake news, also from politicians' (Respondent M, Flanders). While this might be too much of a vision of doom as research shows that digital news consumption in general is more diverse news consumption than could be observed 20 years ago (Newman et al., 2017; Dubois and Blank, 2018), there is evidence of certain groups in society consciously or not knowingly choosing to be part of filter bubbles, not buying newspapers, not visiting websites of print media or public broadcasters, and relying on biased and selective news blogs and/or social media for their information. Sinnott-Armstrong (2018: 41) says that 'few people want to get their news from sources that abuse and distort their political views'. He continues that a big part of the audience would 'reject such sources as subjective or even "fake news"'.

The concern on societal divides and polarisation to some extent also relates to populism. Several respondents argued that impartiality cannot justify a too-feeble stance against populism.

> Public broadcasters need to act against populism. If they do not do that, they are not necessary anymore.
>
> (Respondent L, Flanders)

> While public broadcasters need to be impartial, they do not have to provide a forum for lies, let alone provide equal speaking time to the liar and those that speak the truth. The public broadcaster should also act as a moral compass. I realise that is a dangerous discussion. But nevertheless, it is important that the public broadcast acts like this in a changing world.
>
> (Respondent E, Flanders)

Public broadcaster should thus not be the megaphone of populism. When it is news, they have to cover it. When it is not, they should refrain and not engage with sensationalism. The public broadcaster should, furthermore, while being critical of politics, refrain from feeding anti-political sentiments. That also is a risk for democracy, definitely in countries or regions where 'people do not realise anymore how it is to live in a society that is not free, where you have no say' (Respondent L, Flanders).

Social citizenship

Next to its contribution to political citizenship, VRT's role in terms of strengthening society is at centre stage of policy documents and the interviews as well. The qualitative content analysis and thematic analysis result in three main findings. First, VRT should reach everyone in Flemish society, with an emphasis on children, youngsters and the elderly, but also Flemish citizens with a migration background, refugees, the visually impaired, deaf people, and so on (VRT, 2014; 2015; 2016; 2017; 2018; Vlaamse Regering and VRT, 2011; 2015). The inclusive nature of the public broadcaster is a constant factor throughout the years. Second, 'society' as such is only implicitly referred to until 2018. Especially VRT annual reports refer to social cohesion, showing multiple examples of events that bring people together. Third, and related to the former, the societal role of the public broadcaster has become more of an explicit concern as of 2019. The public broadcaster has to be a unifying force in a disintegrating society. Also interviewees focused on the latter aspect considerably.

First, the inclusive nature of Public Service Media is emphasised in all documents whether authored by the public broadcaster (VRT, 2014: 14; 2016: 18) or policy-makers (Dalle, 2019; Vlaamse Regering and VRT, 2011; 2015).

> The VRT wants to reach everyone in Flanders. That is only possible when everyone feels represented in the offer of the public broadcaster. That is why VRT has more attention for certain groups in the population in its programs (people with a migration background, a mental of physical impairment, women). Besides it has a specific offer for certain groups (children, youngsters, foreigners in Flanders, Flemish people living abroad, deaf people, people with a disabling hearing loss, the visually impaired).
>
> (VRT, 2015: 21)

There is thus attention for reaching all, representing everyone and specific offers for some target groups. That is also a tricky thing as the ambition might be to reach everyone over being relevant to all.

> Of course, you want to be loved and attest that you are consumer-centric. It is easy to work with the dominant formats of the medium to get that done. You want to please the audience and hence adopt popular formats. It is a combination of consumer-centric and society-centric thinking though.

You have a certain responsibility. The public broadcaster must be creative, it must be able to transcend dominant formats and be creative in a value-driven manner. It should unite people.

(Respondent C, Flanders)

VRT has a diversity policy, which it discusses on a regular basis with researchers and groups representing minorities in society. While being a strategic objective, research has also shown that specifically ethnic minorities do not feel represented by the public broadcaster (Panis, Paulussen and Dhoest, 2019). Several interviewees also raised this. Some of VRT's brands such as children's channel Ketnet and youth radio brand MNM were said to be very diverse. Other brands such as generalist channels één and Canvas are not on top of the fact that society is more diverse.

We reach a turning point. Whether people like it or not, our society is getting more diverse. We cannot risk to loose that group [people with a migration background] because it is becoming bigger.

(Respondent O, Flanders)

Indeed, VRT faces difficulties to represent ethnic minorities along demographic trends. The Flemish Government insists on increasing the current quota of 7.5 per cent of ethnic minorities on screen to a number that reflects presence in society better. VRT seems committed to picking up on that challenge.

Second, society has been a relevant, yet fairly implicit element in Public Service Media policies. The public broadcaster has raised it though in several annual reports. Flemish content is 'important from a cultural, societal and economic point of view'. It 'brings media users together around a shared identity, supports Flanders as a cultural community and stimulates media production' (VRT, 2015: 16). VRT lists events and programmes that have created a sense of 'togetherness' (VRT, 2017: 14) among people or that have enabled coverage of difficult societal topics such as euthanasia, abortion, sexuality, and so on, in an accessible and approachable manner. Entertainment, soap, drama, sports and its generalist radio brands are considered the vehicles to get this done.

In 2016, VRT aired high-quality entertainment programs that have a unifying function, because they generate societal value for a large part of the audience and support our offer in domains such as information, culture and education.

(VRT, 2017: 14)

High-quality entertainment programs are important within VRT's portfolio because they contain informative, cultural and educational elements that allow to cover societal topics in an accessible manner and to enable discussion. Moreover, they have a unifying force.

(VRT, 2018: 15)

Policy documents are relatively silent on society, with three exceptions. First, the public broadcaster is important to trigger societal debate on several of the issues mentioned above. Second, its entertainment and sports programming are admissible in so far as programmes in these categories contribute to something more than mere entertainment. Indeed, the management contract 2016-2020 says that 'entertainment is a crucial means for social cohesion and bringing people together'. VRT can and should thus invest in entertainment provided 'informational, cultural and/or education elements are part of entertaining programmes'. Moreover, VRT should 'invest in entertainment that puts societal topics on the agenda and makes them negotiable' (Vlaamse Regering and VRT, 2015: 22). Third, collaboration with civil society is encouraged to ensure a societal layer in programmes. Several management contracts mention collaboration, with a clear emphasis on the need to work together from the management contract 2012-2016 onwards.

> VRT strengthens society and the media sector through collaboration. VRT develops a stakeholder management strategy and creates collaboration agreements.
>
> (Vlaamse Regering and VRT, 2011: 10)

The management contract 2016-2020 reinforces the focus on collaboration, stressing even more than was the case in 2011 the need for VRT to support the Flemish media ecosystem. VRT should be a lever to 'stimulate a qualitatively strong and economically viable media landscape with an eye on preserving a pluralistic and diverse offer' (Vlaamse Regering and VRT, 2015: 31). A little bit more than two full pages are spent on what that means, apparently with VRT in a juxtaposition with the media ecosystem while one can legitimately argue it is part of that landscape, not an outsider to it. The Flemish Government, as well as the Minister of Media Benjamin Dalle, have reaffirmed the importance of VRT aiding the media ecosystem, acknowledging though this is a shared responsibility among companies and not an exclusive task for the public broadcaster (see also Donders, Raats and Tintel, 2020).

VRT has always stressed the importance of collaboration. Nevertheless some public broadcasting staff are more sceptical and question whether the goal of collaboration is still in sight or whether collaboration itself has become an objective. There is a fear that collaboration does not leave adequate room for creativity and imagination (Respondent C, Flanders). This tension comes to the forefront in research of Tim Raats as well. He shows that while collaboration is in the DNA of VRT, there is indeed always the risk of it becoming a goal in itself. In case there is no clear societal objective and shared ambition underlying collaboration, his message is to refrain from it. Importantly, collaboration is usually a financial cost. That makes the need for a societal benefit even higher (Raats, 2020).

A third finding of our analysis is that society comes at the forefront of discussions on Public Service Media in a really explicit manner from 2019 onwards. The public broadcaster itself is the main trigger for that. Its vision document 'Co-creating Flanders' in preparation of its management contract for 2021-2025, identifies Flemish society as the basis for the public broadcaster's service delivery. Indeed, VRT has said for several years it is there to 'feel and feed' society. However, its vision paper is more explicit on this, saying:

> VRT should invest more strongly and structurally in its societal role, its role as public broadcaster. That remit is more topical, relevant and necessary than ever. VRT is dedicated to tackle the challenges of the Flemish society. She does that through informing, providing a for diverse opinions and inspiring people.
>
> (VRT, 2019a: 2)

VRT's approach is in alignment with the European Broadcasting Union's *Contribution to Society* vision whereby its member organisations are also actively encouraged to explain, measure and legitimise how and with what impact they play their role in strengthening societies (EBU, 2019).

The increased attention for the societal task of the public broadcaster was reflected in the interviews too. First and foremost, several interviewees (Respondents C, D, I, N, Flanders) pointed at the disintegration of society (not in the least because of disinformation). They mentioned the socio-economic inequality in society and the positioning of groups opposite to each other. In such a context it is not only important to contribute to social cohesion, but also to represent all of these groups without polarising. The challenge is to reach people not only mechanistically, but also mentally. That is an issue for public broadcasters today. People that think in a nuanced manner, might find discussions on the public broadcaster's channels too extreme; people with more extreme opinions will find coverage not extreme enough (Respondent O, Flanders). Related to this, experts pointed at a mental disconnect between the public broadcaster and several groups in society, including youngsters, minorities and extreme right voters (Respondent N, Flanders). The public broadcaster 'is not in the heart of everyone, it does not always connect with normal Flemish people' (Respondent D, Flanders). Some experts acknowledged that there is an issue in terms of connecting with society while at the same time stressing the valuable job VRT is doing still. Others were more critical, saying that VRT and in fact all public broadcasters struggle with societal changes. VRT is not everybody's public broadcaster. While it has the responsibility to understand changing demography and society, it fails to do that at the moment (Respondents B, Nn Flanders). It is a remark made by Irish, British, Dutch and Swiss experts we talked with for the purpose of this book as well. Nonetheless, fully understanding societal change is – next to innovating in the digital domain – a necessary condition though to bring about social cohesion. Indeed, several programmes such as *Taboe* (a humoristic television show that talks about sexuality, ethnicity, poverty, and so on) succeed in this. Nevertheless, not only programmes, but also the public broadcaster as an institution 'must work value driven with a focus on social cohesion, democracy and what makes society healthy, one expert said' (Respondent C, Flanders). Notably, several experts connected these observations to informed citizenship as well (e.g., Respondents B, D, Flanders). People that feel part of a society want to be informed. People that feel left behind and/or that cannot follow contents intellectually, disconnect from society and thus from information. While research (Picone and Donders, 2020) shows that the information offer of VRT still reaches a lot of citizens, there is a decline with youngsters and lower educated people. This confirms concerns expressed by experts. It also shows, as I said in Chapter 4, that the different types of citizenship are intimately linked to one another. High performance on political and cultural citizenship from an output-oriented perspective might thus be eroded through low performance in certain areas of social citizenship. There might also be a tension between different aspects of strengthening citizenship. A highly informative programme on politics and/or corruption might add to people's knowledge of politics. It might erode their sense of belonging to society or even their belief in democracy. Reflecting ethnic diversity might bring certain minorities closer to the public broadcaster and increase their contact with domestic culture or, even better, innovate cultural programming which should not reflect some sort of static canon. At the same time, it might alienate other groups that have difficulties identifying with a multicultural society. This shows that next to massive changes because of the transition to a digital media market, public broadcasters must also cope or at least be more sensitive to societal ruptures as well.

Cultural citizenship

Next to political and social citizenship, cultural citizenship is an important aspect of VRT's role as well. Historically, the small language community that Flanders is has paid considerable attention to the public broadcaster's task in strengthening Flemish identity, attention for language use and the local arts. Those aspects have been part of each and every management contract since 1996. They are also found in annual reports of VRT as well as policy documents from several ministers of media. From the outset the project of Flemish as a cultural community was also explicitly linked to the protection of local production and sustainability of the media ecosystem. It was even connected to innovation as also in the domain of new media services, VRT has been expected to safeguard Flemish identity.

> VRT must invest in new media products on the one hand and offer a technological media platform with quality content on the other hand to safeguard Flemish cultural identity in the domain of new media services.
>
> (Van Mechelen, 2002: 16)

> The offer of Flemish content is important from a cultural, social and economic perspective. It brings people together around a shared identity, it supports Flanders as a cultural community and stimulates media production.
>
> (VRT, 2015: 15)

It is noticeable that there are some tensions in defining and shaping the cultural task of VRT. That has to do with what culture is in the first instance and whether that is something unified or not.

Discussions on 'high culture' and 'popular culture' are not new and have been extensively addressed by Raymond Williams (among others in his work *The Sociology of Culture*, 1995) already decades ago. Whereas government usually focuses on the importance of Culture and the arts ('high culture') (e.g., Lieten, 2011: 17), the public broadcaster takes a view that corresponds more with the idea of 'popular culture', that is the habits, customs, ways of doing things … that have been developed by 'normal' people, usually to be situated within the dominant group in a certain region or country. Both high culture and popular culture are selective as well as dynamic. When looking at high culture, VRT usually emphasises the distinctive offer of its classical music radio channel *Klara* as well as its attempts to *universalise* high culture through popular programmes. *Klara* is even explicitly named *the cultural channel* of VRT (VRT, 2015: 10). Flemish culture is moreover also reflected through fictional series, soap and the diversity of music genres broadcast across its radio channels: from local Flemish music, over urban, to jazz and folk. Whereas aspects of informed citizenship and social citizenship take central stage in its vision document in the period 2021-2025, the same cannot be said for culture, which is mentioned largely sideways (VRT, 2019a). There has always been a push from successive Flemish governments to focus more on the arts, for example, through the creation of a dedicated Cultural channel, more digital offers in the Cultural domain (e.g., Bourgeois, 2006: 13). Some experts also emphasised that VRT is falling short in providing high-quality, distinctive content for arts lovers (Respondent B, Flanders). Actually, the task of VRT to strengthen aspects of cultural citizenship is also a subject of conflict within the public broadcaster. In preparation of the management contract 2021-2025, VRT employees in charge of the public broadcaster's strategy on Culture/culture repeatedly complained that top-level management of the public broadcaster had no vision for its task in this domain and focused too much on popular culture – the latter thus not per se a conscious decision. Obviously, those executives differed in opinion, emphasising the manifold initiatives VRT takes in the cultural domain. What I conclude from this is the rather static view also on both culture as well as Culture. Popular culture in itself also innovates, becomes more diverse, gets new forms of expression … and all but a few brands really pick up on that.

Another issue, besides the tension between high culture and popular culture, concerns the nature of culture whether with a capital C or not. Is it something unified, something that all inhabitants of Flanders share and that is based on a common set of values? Or is it something dynamic, highly unstable and possibly even divisive? Whereas most policy and strategy documents are in agreement on the importance of the *Flemishness* of VRT and its offers, usually defined in terms of the origin of production and operationalised through quotas for music as well as television programmes (e.g., Bourgeois, 2006: 12-13), there is different view among politicians and also within VRT on Flemish identity. Not surprisingly, the Flemish nationalist party as well as the extreme right party have a more unified view on Flemish identity, which is very unambiguously linked to citizenship: being part of a community (e.g., De Wever, 2019). That legitimate view is opposed by others for two reasons. First, some experts said that the public broadcaster indeed needs to reflect Flemish identity, but not necessarily Flemish identity as defined by nationalists.

> We need to have a public broadcaster for Flanders and it should reflect Flemish identity ... Nationalists want a public broadcaster that is favorable to them though and that reflects their nationalist ideology in day-to-day programming. That is something entirely different.
>
> (Respondent L, Flanders)

Second, some experts stressed that identity is not something unified – even if we want it to be cohesive. The public broadcaster was said to struggle with that itself and was incapable of walking an apparently thin line between polarising political sentiments on the issue on the one hand and reflecting identities and different opinions and forms of expression on the other. In other words: the tense nature of *the identity* question in Flanders makes the public broadcaster hesitant to deal with it while it should in fact provide a forum for a much-needed discussion on and reflection of identity/identities in society.

Having said that, and in spite of VRT being an important cultural vehicle for the Flemish Government – also abroad – cultural citizenship is not a huge priority for Flemish politicians as well as VRT. It is an assumed task, rather than an explicit priority of both government policies and the public broadcaster's strategies. Even the Flemish nationalist party, for whom the cultural task of VRT is admittedly most important and which adopts a rather static and unified view on Culture/culture, has a fairly brief and under-developed view of the public broadcaster's task in terms of cultural citizenship. In its 2019 political programme, the party says that 'VRT should have more attention for our identity, for a correct use of Dutch across programmes, for smaller sports, for new talent, for the collaboration with the Netherlands as well as a more intense and in-depth coverage and promotion of our common culture' (N-VA, 2019: 70). All in all, most experts I talked to also focused on elements of political and social citizenship. I do not want to downplay the importance of VRT as a cultural actor in Flanders, nor the fact that politicians talk a lot about the cultural role of VRT. However, that is not fully reflected in policy and public broadcaster strategy.

It is noticeable that civic citizenship receives considerably less attention in comparison with political, social as well as cultural citizenship. Strengthening the individual, emancipation, empowerment ... these are hardly mentioned in documents and also interviewees did not raise these issues frequently. While that conclusion was also reached in my case study on Poland, the situation in Flanders is of course different. While VRT should focus more on this aspect of citizenship, the absence of such focus is not due to an authoritarian view on citizens or rather the role of 'subjects' in society. So, while the Polish public broadcasters are in fact contributing to an erosion of civic citizenship, it can be said that VRT contributes to a strengthening of civic citizenship, but not per se on the basis of a certain vision, let alone a strategy, and that the contribution it makes might be suboptimal for that reason. It is something they do almost incidentally along the way.

Overall, Public Service Media is regarded as something that adds value to Flemish society. Most experts we talked to, also those working in the private sector, acknowledged this. Nonetheless, some experts indicated that there are more powerful voices these days that would, behind close doors, argue for a much smaller Public Service Media model or even the gradual abolition of the system (Respondent F, Flanders). Two ideological views underpin the more critical stances on Public Service Media as well as the way in which VRT transposes that idea into practice on a day-to-day basis. First, some defend a market failure perspective on Public Service Media: VRT should do less and refrain from actively pursuing activities that private media are engaged in. This view clashes with a democracy-centric view that sees Public Service Media as an essential pillar of a media market next to private initiative. There are of course different shades of grey between the black and white perspectives on the matter. Second, some would argue for less VRT because of its assumed left-wing bias. That criticism is fairly 'alive and kicking' with the extreme right party, but also with the Flemish nationalist party, which has positioned itself more to the right also on the political spectrum in relation to economic policies as well. That position is fuelled also by the difficult relationship that the public broadcaster has with the *identity issue*. While both the (neo)liberal and also populist view on Public Service Media are dreaded by the public broadcaster and those defending it, citizenship as a concept might in fact offer a conceptual tool to navigate the troubled waters between a market failure and democracy-centric perspective on Public Service Media, on the one hand, and the more progressive versus conservative and unification political agendas, on the other hand.

In the subsequent section, I want to spend a bit more time on other issues that interviewees devoted considerable attention to, outside of the conceptual framework of political, social, cultural and civic citizenship. I will consider documents as a complementary source here. The three main issues I want to address here are the difficult transitions to the digital era, the economic protectionism and influence of private media over Public Service Media policies in Flanders, and the deficient governance structure of VRT.

Difficult transition to the digital era

All of the experts I interviewed agreed that VRT is, in line with any other media company, facing difficulties to make the transition to the digital age. Largely this was perceived as a problem for the sustainability of the Public Service Media model in Flanders. Experts emphasised that some brands were doing 'better' in digital than others. Reference was often made to Ketnet, the children's brand that has rather successfully adopted a 360-degree strategy. While VRT regards radio brands such as StuBru (alternative music, younger audience) as successful in the digital domain, people I talked to were less enthusiastic. Several experts said that online services were too commercial, not public interest-driven and in general more focused on online expansion instead of meaningful service delivery (e.g., Respondents D, N, Flanders). Brands such as generalist television channels één and Canvas were applauded for their quality content, but at the same time criticised for being averse to risk-taking. The online player VRT NU was considered crucial, but under-used by several experts – an observation that the public broadcaster would agree with entirely, facing opposition from the private sector and Flemish Government to invest too heavily in the platform. One expert remarked that the brand strategy that has worked very well for VRT might not be suitable for the digital age: 'The philosophy of VRT is that through brands we reach the audience ... the question is whether that is still true today' (Respondent D, Flanders). Most brands are still very much focused on *the* linear. Some work with very big budgets; others have less means. That also creates imbalances in terms of money that can be spent on, for example, a documentary for the generalist channel or the more specialist channel. The latter takes a small portion of the budget for documentaries while serving documentary 'fans'. The former takes more budget for human interest-like documentaries because they reach a bigger audience. Brands have been important to build a reputation, to ensure connection with audiences. But the 1990s logic and needs have changed.

Somewhat related to these reflections on the hitherto successful brand strategy of VRT is the focus on reach through linear means. Of course, as discussed also in Chapter 12, one should also not demolish what still works well. But there is need for more risk-taking: 'We do not have to abandon the linear, but we have to make sure that there is sufficient direction to the online story' (Respondent P, Flanders). That also involves strategies that are more user-centric. The dominant line of thinking is still focused on making media for a mass audience though. On this issue there are two possibly conflicting, but potentially also complementary logics. After being involved in several strategic exercises within VRT over the last 10 years, you can see three perspectives on the move from an analogue to a digital media landscape. First, there is the very traditional way of thinking. Linear works well, there is decline, but let's not exaggerate things. That view is not really helpful when you want to transition from a Public Service Broadcasting to a Public Service Media organisation. The second view sets out still from homogeneous needs in the audience (for example, for high-quality drama shows), but you can no longer address the media user as part of a mass audience in a homogeneous manner. The real innovation lies in aggregation and distribution (e.g., Respondent C, Flanders). A third view is more radical and says that innovation is needed also at the level of content formats itself. Interactivity, user-generated content and the likes are coming to the forefront in such a view (e.g., Respondent P, Flanders). Actually, the second and third view can be combined but the weight of each view in implementation should gradually shift from innovation at the level of aggregation and distribution to content innovation.

Regardless of the diverging views on the digital transition that VRT stands for, several experts also emphasised the difficulty of the organisational change that is needed to make such a transition possible at all. Again, we elaborated on that already in Chapter 12, this is a challenge all public broadcasters are confronted with. And in fact, also private media companies struggle with this when looking at management, communication, work floor resistance, and so on (see, for example, Hendrickx and Picone, 2020). Some considered the glass half full: 'I think we already act quicker than 10 to 15 years ago…, the role of Bert De Graeve (former VRT CEO) is legendary in this regard' (Respondent C, Flanders). Others were more pessimistic or rather eager to reform more quickly and at the structural level (Respondent N, Flanders). Similarly, while some focused on the incredibly dedicated work force of VRT, on a 'stronger sense of contribution and belonging' (Respondent H, Flanders) and considered under-performing staff as an exception, rather than the rule, others took the view that a big part of VRT staff is rather complacent and not sufficiently aware of the comfortable circumstances in which it is working (Respondents A, G, M, Q, Flanders). While until a couple of years ago the discussion on VRT's organisation was largely focused on the size of its work force, that debate has – at least internally – re-focused more on whether the number of employees, their profile as well as the structural organisation of the public broadcaster is fit to make flexible adjustments within a media as well as societal context that has become more complex. The answer to that question is *uni sono*, no.

To sum up, when talking about the transition from a Public Service Broadcasting to a Public Service Media organisation, VRT is both at the content as well as organisation level, somewhere between a rock and a hard place. You cannot abandon linear television nor radio because a lot of people still use it intensely. At the same time, you need to innovate new distribution platforms as well as content formats. How do you do these things with employees that are good at making, aggregating and branding television programmes, a budget that is considerable but since 2007 continuously in decline, regulation that discourages the launch of new services (see also Donders and Van den Bulck, 2020) and within a setting that is – in contrast with the theory of Public Service Media – disinclined to risk-taking?

Protectionist logic on the rise (again)

While some might argue that there is a more hostile, even neoliberal political climate towards Public Service Media in Flanders, I do not entirely agree with that view. Experts had a lot to say about the relationship between VRT and the subsequent Flemish governments and from their opinions as well as my own experiences in government and VRT, I see three main issues when it comes to economics and VRT.

First, the Flemish Government has consistently raised the relative as well as absolute levels of commercial revenues of VRT. In 1996, television advertising was prohibited. When radio advertising and/or television sponsoring revenues fell below what was expected, the Flemish Government compensated for that loss (Vlaamse Regering and VRT, 1996). In subsequent management contracts the amount of television sponsoring that was allowed was increased, limited forms of online advertising became permissible, and the provisions for the compensation procedure were strengthened. At the same time, as from 2007 onwards, the subsidies from government were lowered (Vlaamse Regering and VRT, 2006; 2011; 2015). As a result thereof, the behaviour of the public broadcaster, perhaps not at the level of content, has become more assertive in commercial markets. The level of commercial revenues is now almost 40 per cent of VRT's budget, compared to not even 30 per cent 20 years ago. You reap what you sow. Few politicians will agree with that conclusion, but it is what several – not all – experts that have worked for VRT in the past acknowledged in my talks with them and it is definitely also the opinion of private media companies, some of which even support claims for higher public funding provided that there is a lower dependence on commercial money. To some extent, my argument is that the constant conflict between the public broadcaster and commercial media is organised by government. This confirms what one of the respondents said:

> Dual funding is not our choice. The current arrangement puts stress on the pax media. Government does not take its responsibility there. ... It is their choice, not ours.
>
> (Respondent C, Flanders)

Second, lobbying against VRT is quite intense. There are quite a lot of complaints about the activities of the public broadcaster online (notably for news, but also related to its video player) and its behaviour in advertising markets.

> There has never been so much free news as today. That news improves in terms of quality because fake news has become such a big problem on social media. You can notice that HLN, Het Nieuwsblad, De Standaard, De Morgen, ... offer a lot of news for free. ... I think it is a false argument to say that news should be free for the sake of democracy. Government has to monitor the behavior of the public broadcaster and they should make the assessment when they are de-stabilising a commercial market with subsidies. The end consumer is prepared to pay, also in mass markets.
>
> There is need for a checks and balances system with experts that inform the government. That has nothing to do about stopping public broadcasters' development online. The public broadcaster *has* to develop itself online, but setting out from its core: audio and audiovisual. Those are their growth poles, not news. Do that, but in a way that is not market distortive.
>
> (Respondent M, Flanders)

Private media have voiced these concerns, some of them relentlessly with government and politicians in general. That results among others in discussions in the Flemish Parliament that are mainly concerned with the position of VRT in *the* market and the harm that VRT could do to other players. While these concerns are definitely not illegitimate, they are most often not sustained by any empirical evidence. It is also apparent that some industry voices are more equal than others. Lobbying from companies such as DPG (biggest commercial newspaper publisher and commercial broadcaster) and independent television production companies has been quite impactful over the last decade.

The focus of government on commercial media's interests where Public Service Media is concerned was said to be 'outright ridiculous'. Politicians, according to the same expert, who is not employed by VRT, 'should be ashamed' for going along with purely commercial interests. The public broadcaster should do its job and, yes, that might annoy private media companies from time to time (Respondent E, Flanders). Others considered the idea of market strengthening as an empty promise, which 'has been instrumentalised to the benefit of VRT and how *they* think that the market has to be strengthened' (Respondent A, Flanders).

Third, and perhaps as a consequence of the former two elements, both the Flemish Government and VRT have since the management contract 2012-2016 increased emphasis on the public broadcaster's task to strengthen the Flemish media ecosystem (see Vlaamse Regering and VRT, 2011; 2015; Dalle, 2019). That might seem a bit odd as private media oppose an overly intrusive public broadcaster in the market. However, at the same time this idea of the public broadcaster being an essential 'partner' in the market could alleviate some of the concerns regarding its potentially market-distortive nature. I have analysed the discourse on VRT's market strengthening nature elsewhere and concluded that to date this rhetoric is a dangerous one. Indeed, the more public broadcasters take up their 'positive', economic role, the more they engage with a market-driven agenda that is somewhat inconsistent and also often hostile to the very existence of public broadcasters. Pleasing other media companies might also have the adverse effect of not putting the interests of users and society first. It should also be noted that while Flemish public broadcaster VRT has attempted to demonstrate a multiplier effect on the market as a whole (Ballon et al., 2018; Donders, Raats and Tintel, 2020), private news media as well as commercial broadcasters have considerable doubts about all of this. They will call for collaboration notably when it suits their agenda. But they do not necessarily see a bigger partnership agenda (see Enli et al., 2019). They also question whether VRT is interested in a *pax media*, some sort of *entente* with private media at all: 'You could say that we have lost our mental connection with VRT' (Respondent A, Flanders). Other respondents were admittedly less pessimistic, having reservations about the existence of a peaceful understanding with VRT, but dismissing the idea of a war between public and commercial media at the same time as well (Respondent Q, Flanders). One could argue that predictability helps in creating 'peace'; instruments to ensure this might come at the expense of flexibility that is much needed to make the transition from Public Service Broadcasting to Public Service Media – a transition so Chapter 12 shows does not exactly run smoothly for the Flemish public broadcaster. Public broadcaster experts seemed more divided on how they behave or ought to behave vis-à-vis their commercial colleagues. Some complained that too much emphasis was put on VRT's market distortive as well as strengthening role. Others, however, said that the public broadcaster should be more aware of its privileged position and show more generosity towards others (Respondent C, Flanders).

There is thus, so it seems, a paradox surrounding the role of VRT in the Flemish media market. On the one hand, government and commercial media want to see a less commercial VRT. On the other hand, its dependence on commercial revenues increases year after year. And against that background, there is a desire for more collaboration between the public broadcaster and commercial media, while the former – in spite of all the talk about the threat of international platforms – has in fact become a direct competitor of the latter not only on content, but also for revenues. That is not to say that a public broadcaster cannot earn commercial revenues, but the balance seems lost. Moreover, this strategy if continued further is problematic also because it commodifies Public Service Media in an international and digital media environment in which the project should stand for the opposite. While collaboration might seem fashionable and can solve conflicts and tensions for a short period of time, there is a progressiveness to this issue that will result in more conflicts.

An unfit governance environment

Another issue that was raised on multiple occasions during interviews was the governance of VRT. That was considered deficient by interviewees with various backgrounds. Whereas VRT respondents largely felt victims of an unfit governance environment, other experts related the governance structure to the inefficiency of VRT, organisational defects and a lack of trust between government and VRT. I will develop these points a bit further below.

Questioning the politicised Board of Governors

Admittedly, most interviewees pointed at VRT's Board of Governors. This Board is composed of 12 members, all of which are appointed by a political party in accordance with their relative weight in the Flemish Parliament. That approach is part of the so-called 'Cultural Pact' that determines the pluralistic composition of Boards of Governors of multiple organisations (Respondent L, Flanders). The Board is in charge over high-level strategic issues. It is an oversight body for management. Members of the Board cannot be ministers, members of parliament, management of private media companies, and so on. That is stipulated by Article 12 of the Flemish Media Decree. Nonetheless, members of the Board can be retired members of parliament, people occupying advisory or administrative functions in Flemish politics, collaborators of politicians, and so on. This also frequently happens. When multiple members have been appointed by a political party, they also informally form a 'faction' in the Board. This creates a particular, highly political dynamic in the Board that stands at odds with the entire idea of an independently functioning Board that acts in the best interest of the public broadcaster and the task it is assigned with (Respondent J, Flanders).

One private sector respondent said that VRT 'is not managed efficiently and government inhibits it from being managed efficiently'. The respondent continues to say that 'the majority of the board of governors is not competent to be there ... half of them are checking their e-mails when they should be listening to a management presentation' (Respondent M, Flanders). The subsequent Boards of Governors are said not to challenge the CEO and the management. It is often picky on symbolic issues and hardly contributing anything on strategic choices to be made.

> I think our Board of Governors is not composed well. I do not think that all members should represent government. A part, yes. I get that. But it would be much more useful to have some members that know something about media. I experience the Board as a body that controls us instead of steers us towards the future. The Board checks whether we stay within the 'lines'. It is a bureaucratic body. It does not add anything beyond that.
>
> (Respondent C, Flanders)

Other experts passionately argued for a de-politicisation of the Board of Governors. That should not be an arm of government. Members of the Board of Governors should believe in the institution. They should be critical of it at the same time, but they should not actively act against it. Such a construction will not work (Respondent B, Flanders). Moreover, the members of the Board should select a new CEO instead of the Flemish Government: 'that would automatically create more distance with the political level' and 'you will get more discussion in the board' (Respondent F, Flanders). A two-thirds majority of the Board could also terminate the CEO's position. That would create more responsibility on the side of the Board. It would also generate a more equitable relationship between the Board and the management. At the same time, it makes VRT more independent from government, but also more accountable. In any case, most interviewees stressed the importance of management autonomy. The 1990s were considered crucial because they already enhanced this (Respondents J, L, Flanders). But several experts stressed the need to move further (Respondents B, E, F, Flanders).

A lack of trust between government and VRT

Regardless of the Board of Governors, some experts also criticised VRT itself. The organisation was, in spite of a lot of highly motivated people and a strong dedication to the Public Service Media project (Respondent H, Flanders), said to be bureaucratic, rather hierarchical and lacking strong leadership. The public broadcaster was frequently said to be to complacent and insufficiently critical of own choices. One expert said that he was 'not always convinced that there is enough ethical self-consciousness with all programme makers when you look at the choice of guests and the use of social media' (Respondent F, Flanders).

Several others criticised VRT for its public broadcaster-centric thinking. Also private media struggle with digital challenges, with a changing demography and revenue loss (Respondents D, M, N, Q, Flanders). The continuous stress on the need for more public funding was considered arrogant by some.

Interference from politicians can and should never be accepted. At the same time, leadership needs to engage with other people. There should be an open dialogue with politicians on the project Public Service Media is, fails to be in practice and can be in the future. Someone said that 'you can be ideologically rigid in terms of the importance of Public Service Broadcasting or you can relate to other people' (Respondent E, Flanders).

All in all, VRT can be its own worst enemy, but 'it at the same time has the power to be its own biggest supporter' (Respondent H, Flanders).

A lot of the abovementioned statements reflect a lack of trust from commercial media as well as politicians in VRT. At the same time, there is considerable frustration from VRT employees and management in 'political elites'. The latter were said to have limited knowledge of media, to be interested in symbolic policy-making, and to react outrageously to a valid question for adequate funding (e.g., Respondents G, J, Flanders). The perception exists that the public broadcaster is expected to change, but at the same time is not allowed to make decisions. The management contract is more and more regarded as an armour, instead of a document that embodies a vision, rather than a list of brands and services, for a period of five years and beyond. In fact, discussions preceding the subsequent management contracts were considered increasingly 'marginal', touching upon the fundamental questions regarding media policy only sideways (e.g., Respondent E, Flanders).

To some extent, one can argue that this mutual lack of trust stands in the way of a basic, evidence-based debate on the role of Public Service Media in democratic societies as well as media markets. Reference to the *entente* between former Minister of Media Eric Van Rompuy and former VRT CEO Bert De Graeve (CEO between 1996 and 2002) was frequently made in talks. After the near-collapse of the Public Service Broadcasting system following the arrival of commercial television station VTM, their shared ambition was to maximise the potential of VRT and Bert De Graeve essentially got the freedom needed to achieve that objective. There is indeed a need to move beyond the oppositional talks on Public Service Media. Of course one can have a different opinion and be critical of Public Service Media as an idea as well as institution. But ultimately politicians need to decide whether they are still in favour of a relevant public broadcaster, dedicated to delivering the public interest in media (Respondent K, Flanders). And my involvement in Public Service Media policies in Flanders for over a decade tells me that most of them are. Similarly, the public broadcaster at some point needs to open up to policy-makers more, not to allow editorial interference, not for the sake of publishing yet another report on societal impact or economic multiplier effects, but with the genuine intent 'to listen to one another' (Respondent N, Flanders).

> As long as VRT does not threat the political level as an up to par partner that is legitimately in charge of defining the bigger mission of Public Service Media, the distrust in VRT will continue to persist.
>
> (Respondent L, Flanders)

The public broadcaster should not be naïve of course. Politics is what it is. Editorial interference should never be accepted, nor is there need for a cheer-leader squad when government is cutting the budget. A more mature relationship is nonetheless necessary, also taking into account that multiple former CEOs of VRT I talked to indicated that meddling with actual programmes is fairly limited and a line that most Flemish politicians do not so easily cross.

Glass half full or half empty

What is the view on Public Service Media in Flanders for 2030? Is there a consensus on the project or not? It is abundantly clear that Flanders has a strong public broadcaster in terms of reach and societal impact. VRT is far from perfect though. Diversity on the screen, dealing with polarisation in political debates, an organisation that cannot yet cope with the digital environment … These are all issues no adequate answer has been formulated to yet. Government clearly has a love-hate relationship with the public broadcaster, valuing its importance as a cultural, societal and economic agent in a small language community such as Flanders, but also struggling with its (too) big success and complaints from commercial media on the activities of VRT in advertising, online news, sports rights, and so on.

In spite of the consensus on the high-level idea of Public Service Media and the entrustment of that project to VRT, there are also issues that are quite fundamentally so dividing opinions. That is reflected in existing literature on Public Service Media in Flanders, the analysed documents as well as the transcripts from the expert interviews.

First, there is no clear view on the position and strength of VRT compared to private media. There is a clash between a democracy-centric and market failure perspective on Public Service Media. More accurately, there is a marked desire to protect domestic media companies not only against international platform companies, but also against the public broadcaster. That political aspiration is not so much inspired by an objective, scientifically grounded market failure paradigm. It is based on economic protectionism of a small selection of 'more worthy' media companies. One could argue that this is a clear example of the intertwinement of political and media elites. That holds only partially though. Several private media companies in Flanders perform well, not only economically, but also in terms of the production of domestic content and valuable journalism. And policy-makers feel a responsibility to protect (part of) the ecosystem as a whole. That is a legitimate desire but in practice results too often in the ad hoc pleasing of stakeholders (see Donders, Van den Bulck and Raats, 2019a) and the idea that the public broadcaster and the media ecosystem are two separate entities whereas the opposite is true. The public broadcaster is an integral and very important part of the ecosystem. Transposing that observation into the obligation for VRT to strengthen the market might in fact, when this means VRT servicing individual demands of competitors, undermine that strategic hub-position of VRT.

Second, the role of VRT in Flemish culture and society is giving rise to less prominent, but nonetheless important disputes. Outsiders as well as insiders criticise VRT for insufficiently focussing on Culture, including Flemish film, documentary and the arts. Again, a large set of policy documents assigns considerable importance to this task. And VRT annual reports are testimony to the tremendous job the public broadcaster does in this domain. However, repeatedly the impression exists that Culture is seen as something VRT *has* to do instead of wants to do. In all fairness, this relates to a bigger discussion on what is Culture and whether culture in the broadest sense is not more suitable to showcase via television and radio. Undoubtedly, digital distribution might overcome such issues and allow the public broadcaster to service niche audiences better. In a similar vein, some politicians are of the opinion that VRT has a tense relationship with 'Flemish identity'. The public broadcaster should contribute to strengthening Flemish, not Belgian identity. Whereas VRT programming is in terms of proximity very close to Flanders, Flemish society and culture, it is of course not inspired by a Flemish nationalist agenda, nor should it be. Of course, it should also not be biased against such a political belief but be impartial towards it. The growing diversity in Flemish society is adding to these matters. There are issues with adequately reflecting diversity, in spite of it being a priority in management contracts for over a decade. Some VRT collaborators as well as politicians and independent observers find this a big shortcoming of the public broadcaster to date. Others are, however, conflicted as more diversity on screen might also alienate a part of the audience that is moving to the right and opposing 'multiculturalism' in society. In reflecting diversity the public broadcaster might risk to add to polarisation. Not reflecting diversity is not an option either. Societal and cultural citizenship are thus on a tectonic field.

Another conclusion on Public Service Media in Flanders is the difficult transition to digital. The management contract 2007–2011 (Vlaamse Regering and VRT, 2006) is entitled 'The mission of the public broadcaster in a digital age'. Nonetheless, VRT is still a radio and television broadcaster. It is far from a Public Service Media organisation. That has to do with a lack of resources, but more so with a lack of vision and organisational changes contributing to the achievement of a coordinated vision on digital media making, also in interaction and co-creative efforts with the audience. Admittedly, government has been a slowing factor here. On the one hand there is a plea for progressing into the digital realm (e.g., Dalle, 2019). On the other hand, there is no clear view on what that means with policy-makers either and not such a progressive attitude when the public broadcaster's digital plans intervene with commercial media's interests.

Finally, the *apparatus* of the Public Service Media system in Flanders needs to be revisited. One should rationalise control systems, measure performance with the objective of knowing and evaluating, and de-politicise bodies such as the Board of Governors. The public broadcaster itself should push for such a change and argue vigorously for the inclusion of independent members as well as citizens in its governance. Especially the latter will not be welcomed by VRT, but is a crucial aspect of Public Service Media compared to Public Service Broadcasting.

Concluding, theory, the law and practice of Public Service Media do not match in Flanders. VRT is as any organisation imperfect. Government should accept this and VRT should work on that.

References

Ballon, P., Van Looy, B., Raats, T., Wauters, D. and Tintel, S. (2018). *De economische meerwaarde van de VRT: Een onderzoek in opdracht van de VRT.* Brussels: VUB & KU Leuven. [*The added economic value of the VRT: An analysis on behalf of the VRT*].

Bogner, A., Littig, B. and Menz, W. (2014). *Interviews mit Experten: eine praxisorientierte Einführung.* Wiesbaden: Springer-Verlag.

Bourgeois, G. (2006). *Beleidsnota Media.* Brussels: Vlaamse Regering. [*Policy brief: Media*].

Dalle, B. (2019). *Beleidsnota Media.* Brussels: Vlaamse Regering. [*Policy brief: Media*].

De Wever, B. (2019). *Over identiteit.* Antwerpen: Borgerhoff & Lamberigts. [*About identity*].

Donders, K. (2019). Public service media beyond the digital hype: Distribution strategies in a platform era. *Media Culture & Society, 41*(7), 1011-1028.

Donders, K. and Van den Bulck, H. (2020). Universality of public service media and pre-school audiences: The choice against a dedicated children's channel in Flanders. In P. Savage, M. Medina and G.F. Lowe (eds), *Universalism in Public Service Media* (pp. 49–68). Göteborg: Nordicom.

Donders, K., Van den Bulck, H. and Raats, T. (2019a). The politics of pleasing: A critical analysis of multistakeholderism in public service media policies in Flanders. *Media, Culture & Society, 41*(3), 347-366.

Donders, K., Van den Bulck, H. and Raats, T. (2019b). Public service media in a divided country: governance and functioning of public broadcasters in Belgium. In E. Połońska and C. Beckett (eds), *Public Service Broadcasting and Media Systems in Troubled European Democracies.* Basingstoke: Palgrave Macmillan.

Donders, K., Raats, T. and Tintel, S. (2020). (Re)defining public service media from an economic perspective: Damned if they do, damned if they don't. In B. Van Rimscha and S. Kienzler (eds), *Management and economics of Communication* (pp. 203-222). Berlin: Mouton De Gruyter.

Dubois, E. and Blank, G. (2018). The echo chamber is overstated: The moderating effect of political interest and diverse media. *Information, Communication & Society, 21*(5), 729–745.

EBU (2019). Investing in European Content and Culture. Retrieved from www.ebu. ch/news/2019/01/investing-in-european-content-and-culture (accessed October 2020).

Enli, G.S., Raats, T., Syvertsen, T. and Donders, K. (2019). Media policy for private media in the age of digital platforms. *European Journal of Communication, 34*(4), 395-409.

Fletcher, R. and Kleis Nielsen, R. (2017). Paying for Online News. *Digital Journalism, 5*(9), 1173-1191.

Gatz, S. (2014). *Beleidsnota Media*. Brussels: Vlaamse Regering. [*Policy brief: Media*].

Hendrickx, J. and Picone, I. (2020). Innovation beyond the buzzwords: The rocky road towards a digital first-based newsroom. *Journalism Studies, 21*(1), 1-17.

Hendrickx, J. and Ranaivoson, H. (2019). Why and how higher media concentration equals lower news diversity: The Mediahuis case. *Journalism*. Retrieved from https:// doi.org/10.1177/1464884919894138 (accessed October 2020).

Herzog, C., Handke, C. and Hitters, E. (2019). Analysing Talk and Text II: Thematic analysis. In H. Van den Bulck, M. Puppis, K. Donders and L. Van Audenhove (eds), *The Palgrave Handbook of Media Policy Research Methods* (pp. 385-401). Basingstoke: Palgrave Macmillan.

Lieten, I. (2011). *Beleidsbrief media*. Brussels: Vlaamse Regering. [*Policy brief: Media*].

N-VA (n.d.) *Verkiezingsprogramma*. Retrieved from www.n-va.be/sites/default/files/ verkiezingsprogramma.pdf (accessed October 2020) [*Program elections*].

Newman, N., Fletcher, R., Kalogeropoulos, A., Levy, D.A.L. and Kleis Nielsen, R. (2017). *Digital News Report*. Oxford: Reuters Institute for Journalism.

Panis, K., Paulussen, S. and Dhoest, A. (2019). Managing super-diversity on television: The Representation of ethnic minorities in Flemish non-fiction programmes. *Media and Communication, 7*(1), 13--21.

Picone, I. and Donders, K. (2020). Reach or trust optimisation? A citizen trust analysis in the Flemish public broadcaster VRT. *Media and Communication, 8*(3). Retrieved from https://doi.org/10.17645/mac.v8i3.3172 (accessed October 2020).

Puppis, M. (2019). Analyzing Talk and Text I: Qualitative content analysis. In H. Van den Bulck, M. Puppis, K. Donders and L. Van Audenhove (eds), *Handbook on Media Policy Research Methods* (pp. 367-384). Basingstoke: Palgrave Macmillan.

Raats, T. (2020). Sustaining small television ecosystems: Lessons from policy-driven research in Flanders. In U. Rohn and T. Evens (eds), *Media Management Matters: Challenges and Opportunities for Bridging Theory and Practice* (pp. 138-154). London: Routledge.

Raats, T., Van den Bulck, H. and d'Haenens, L. (2015). *Benchmark van de publieke omroep in Europa: een analyse van het aanbod, financiering en publieksbereik*. Brussels: VUB, UA, KUL [*Benchmark of public service media in Europe: An analysis of the offer, funding and audience reach*].

Sehl, A., Fletcher, R. and Picard, R. (2020). Crowding out: Is there evidence that public service media harm markets? A cross-national comparative analysis of commercial television and online news providers. *European Journal of Communication*. Retrieved from https://doi.org/10.1177/0267323120903688 (accessed October 2020).

Sinnott-Armstrong, W. (2018). *Think Again How to Reason and Argue*. London: Oxford University Press.

Suarez-Candel, R. (2020). Intervention in Flemish Parliament Committee for Culture, Media, Youth and Sports Hearing on VRT's management contract, 3 April. Brussels: Vlaams Parlement.

Van Audenhove, L. and Donders, K. (2019). Expert and elite interviews. In H. Van Den Bulck, M. Puppis, K. Donders and L. Van Audenhove (eds), *Handbook on Media Policy Research Methods* (pp. 179-197). Basingstoke: Palgrave Macmillan.

Van Mechelen, D. (2002). *Beleidsnota media*. Brussels: Vlaamse Regering. [*Policy brief: Media*].

Vanhaeght, A.-S. (2019). The need for not more, but more socially relevant audience participation in public service media. *Media, Culture & Society, 41*(1), 120–137.

Vlaamse Regering (2019). *Regeerakkoord 2019–2024*. Brussels: Vlaamse Regering. [*Government Agreement*].

VRT (2014). *Jaarverslag 2013*. Brussels: VRT. [*Annual report 2013*].

VRT (2015). *Jaarverslag 2014*. Brussels: VRT. [*Annual report 2014*].

VRT (2016). *Jaarverslag 2015*. Brussels: VRT. [*Annual report 2015*].

VRT (2017). *Jaarverslag 2016*. Brussels: VRT. [*Annual report 2016*].

VRT (2018). *Jaarverslag 2017*. Brussels: VRT. [*Annual report 2017*].

VRT (2019a). *Vlaanderen mee-maken: Visietekst ter voorbereiding van de beheersovereenkomst 2021–2025*. Brussels: VRT. [*Co-creating Flanders: Vision text in preparation of the management contract 2021–2025*].

VRT (2019b). *Jaarverslag 2018*. Brussels: VRT. [*Annual report 2018*].

VRT and Vlaamse Regering (1996). *Beheersovereenkomst 1997–2001*. [*Public service contract 1997–2001*].

VRT and Vlaamse Regering (2001). *Beheersovereenkomst 2002–2006*. [*Public service contract 2002–2006*].

VRT and Vlaamse Regering (2006). *Beheersovereenkomst 2007–2011*. [*Public service contract 2007–2011*].

VRT and Vlaamse Regering (2011). *Beheersovereenkomst 2012–2016*. [*Public service contract 2012–2016*].

VRT and Vlaamse Regering (2015). *Beheersovereenkomst 2016–2020*. [*Public service contract 2016–2020*].

Williams, R. (1995). *The Sociology of Culture*. Chicago: The University of Chicago Press.

14 State broadcasting in Poland

From a post-communist to a competitive authoritarian state

The Party of Law and Justice changed it all

The 1989 elections in Poland opened a window for democratic transformation. It ended communism. Poland entered a transition phase to democracy and became a member of the Council of Europe in 1991 and a Member State of the European Union in 2004. Massive reforms were undertaken to leave behind communist and authoritarian rule in general. Several of these reforms also impacted the media. Private initiative was allowed, the State broadcaster was turned into a public broadcaster, and press freedom became a part of the Polish Constitution in 1997. The Broadcasting Act that was approved in 1992 made several of these changes more explicit. It provided that the public broadcasting system should be independent from the government and ruling political parties, that it should inform Polish citizens in an independent and impartial manner, that it would invest in high-quality programming and, in so doing, add to an informed citizenry and social cohesion. The rules that were adopted are rather similar to what can be found in countries such as Belgium, Sweden and Germany.

The public broadcaster remained politicised though. Systems of political capture persisted, specifically for the TVP (*Telewizja Polska*), the public broadcasting organisation in charge of national television. This has been documented by scholars such as Karol Jakubowicz (2007), who fought for an independent public broadcaster throughout his entire academic career. Poland was not unique in this regard. It was seen as one of the post-communist countries that shared characteristics with polarised pluralist media systems such as Italy and Spain: a fairly low sales of newspapers, limited income from advertising, politicisation of public broadcasters and a lack of professionalisation in journalism (Terzis, 2007).

Nevertheless, there was a process of trial and error to come to more independence of public broadcasters and freedom of speech was ensured through commercial media in both print, radio and television. Government control was far from absolute, a lot of journalists were determined to achieve 'real'

Public Service Broadcasting and the inclusion of many academics in supervisory bodies such as the National Broadcasting Council ensured some level of non-alignment with government.

When the Party of Law and Justice (*Prawo and Sprawiedliwość* – 'PiS') gained majority after the 2015 elections, the trend towards more independence and less government intervention was reversed. The key question that will, exploratively, be answered in this chapter is how that trend was reversed and what explains this. I will thus not only describe what has happened, but, and more elaborately so, explain why Poland might be falling back into the abyss of State broadcasting. The next section of this chapter focuses on what has factually changed post-2015 to Polish Public Service Broadcasting. Subsequently, I study the impact this has had on Polish society. On the basis of expert interviews, I explain what the impact of several changes has been on political, social, cultural and civic citizenship. That is an interpretative endeavour, backed up with evidence from available studies on, for example, the propaganda in news programmes. After that, the structural barriers to Public Service Media in Poland are discussed, with the aim of explaining why the trend towards more independence could be so easily undone by PiS. That is a crucial section in this chapter as these structural barriers will lead me to the somewhat provocative conclusion that the achievement of the public interest in media in Poland cannot happen by relying on a centralised public broadcasting/state organisation.

Methodology

The case study on Poland is based on a triangulation of methods: relevant secondary data, *in casu* scientific literature, on the state of play of Public Service Media in Poland, documents such as the media law, and expert interviews. I interviewed ten people on the basis of semi-structured interview protocols. Those were not focused on the political situation in Poland, but rather on the present and future of Public Service Media in relation to audiences, other public institutions, private competitors, government and the own organisation. That way, I avoided steering experts in a certain way. The expert interviews were carried out between April and November 2019. I talked to a variety of experts with a civil society, Public Service Media or academic background. Several interviewees were actively involved in the practice or regulation/oversight of Public Service Media. Nobody representing the government was willing to talk to me. While I had scheduled an interview with the managers of *TVP National* and *TVP Kultura* on 12 April, these were cancelled the evening before by the head of international affairs of TVP, Mr Clayton Reklewski. He explained to us that they had no interest in talking to researchers. Those were, in their opinion, only out to show there was no press freedom in Poland and not interested in studying the real truth (paraphrasing personal communication on 11 April 2019).

The composition of the group of experts is thus markedly different than, for example, the group interviewed for the case study on Flanders. That has various reasons. First, the existence of a bigger personal network in Flanders. Second, the focus of the research on explanatory factors for the situation *as is* in Poland. That type of expert interview relies more on experts that can distance themselves mentally from the research subject, more so than stakeholders. Third, the unwillingness of Public Service Media management as well as government officials to talk with me. I anonymised the experts as requested by several.

The purpose of the expert interviews was to find out not so much what is going on, but why certain things are happening and whether experts see a way out of the precarious situation that Polish Public Service Media organisations are in today. The focus was thus on uncovering context knowledge and explanatory knowledge. The former, according to Kaiser (2014), is knowledge about the context, power and interest structure interfering in solving societal conflicts. Typically, this knowledge resides with people involved in the decision-making process such as members of broadcasting councils and other types of regulatory bodies, but also government. Explanatory knowledge can be defined as the subjective opinions, points of views, interpretations, explanations, and so on, held by an expert on the basis of her expert knowledge (Bogner, Littig and Menz, 2014). When multiple experts adhere to similar interpretations, that does not mean their beliefs are factual, but at least they offer value for the interpretation of highly contextual, often complex phenomena that are studied in case studies (Van Audenhove and Donders, 2019: 185).

The data was analysed on the basis of a combined qualitative content and thematic analysis. Qualitative content analysis allows for 'a systematic, step-by-step approach to interpreting interview transcripts, observation notes and documents' (Puppis, 2019: 367). Using the concept of (political, cultural, social and civic) citizenship (described in Chapter 4) and the barriers to Public Service Media in competitive authoritarian countries (described in Chapter 6), all sentences in the fully transcribed interviews were assigned to a category (for an illustration, see Table 14.1). After that, to structure the process of interpretation, I engaged in thematic analysis, looking for themes and patterns of

Table 14.1 Excerpt from the codebook

Main category	Subcategory	Definition	Sentence assigned to this code
Citizenship	Political citizenship	Political citizenship is about being informed and having access to different interpretative frameworks and deliberative fora. It requires a place for dialogue among citizens, internal and external pluralism.	'Right wing media, that is okay, but not in public media, not in public broadcasting. Public broadcasting is not the place where you can do that. The public media, it should be something in between' (Respondent G, Poland).

recurrence. Themes can be defined as 'an abstract entity that brings meaning and identity to a recurrent experience and its variant manifestations' (DeSantis and Ugarr, 2000, in Herzog, Handke and Hitters, 2019: 394). Herzog, Handke and Hitters (2019: 385) say that the method is 'particularly suitable for analysing experiences, perceptions and understanding'. In combining a deductive analysis with a more inductive analysis, I ensured not to overlooked relevant aspects of Public Service Media in Poland.

I am greatly indebted to Michal Glowacki, Professor at the University of Warsaw, for hosting me multiple times at the University of Warsaw (in Spring and Autumn 2019) and collaborating with me on the research that is the basis of this chapter. I want to stress that this chapter presents explorative findings. I do not want to pretend that my knowledge on Polish Public Service Media is bigger than scientists that have studied Polish media policy for decades from within. Nonetheless, the research presented below has been executed meticulously and set out from the idea that there is an added value of researchers going outside of their comfort zone of studying Public Service Media within the Western-centric paradigm.

Changes to Polish public broadcasting post-2015

Poland's Public Service Media system is largely based on two pillars: TVP (*Telewizja Polska*) and PR (*Polskie Radio*). TVP coordinates the two main television channels *TVP1* and *TVP2*, 16 regional television channels, a 24 hour news channel *TVP Info*, a satellite channel for Polish citizens living abroad (*TVP Polonia*) and several specialised channels such as *TVP Kultura, TVP Historia, TVP Sport* and *TVP Seriale*. Polish Radio has four radio channels and one channel dedicated to Polish people living abroad. Both TVP and Polish radio have their own Internet portals. Next to these organisations, there is also the Polish press association that is owned by the State and distributes news directly to the audience online. Poland was one of the EU Member States that necessitated quite some time to make the switch to digital terrestrial television. That has not per se fastened the uptake of cable or satellite television viewing as the commercial channels Polsat and TVN (Discovery Communications) are not available throughout the country, whereas the coverage of TVP is excellent.

The market share of radio is rather low. The market leader is the German company, Bauer Media Group. Its lead radio channels have a market share of over 25 per cent, sometimes even going up to 30 per cent. TVP's main generalist channel *Radio Jedynka* has less than 6 per cent. The public television channels had a market share of about 29 per cent in 2017, compared to 24 per cent for Polsat and 21 per cent for TVN (Połońska, 2019: 235) – even though these aggregated figures hide the popularity of the separate channels of the broadcasting groups (with Polsat and TVN channels being equally popular as TVP's channels), and moreover the geographical and socio-economic stratification of Polish Public Service Media audiences. People in rural areas of Poland watch TVP much more; often they do not have access to competitors such as Polsat and TVN. It is noticeable that the audience shares of TVP have dropped quite considerably after the changes introduced by the Party of Law and Justice. The main channels TVP1 and TVP lost about 10 per cent market share; in the age group 16-49 years that figure is climbing towards 20 per cent (Piechota, 2017).

Until 2015 Polish media law was clear on the task of Public Service Media and in accordance with theory. Public broadcasters should inform the audience, independently from government. The Broadcasting Act of 1992 was modelled after Western European countries such as the UK and France. Its main aim was to safeguard freedom of expression, a liberalised media market and a public broadcaster contributing to the wellbeing society (Dzięciołowski, 2017: 26ff). The theory did not crystallise in full in reality as shown by several scholars (e.g., Połońska, 2019; Dobek-Ostrowska, 2015), but at least there was an aspiration both in the law and in practice to aim for a Public Service Broadcasting project that contributed to the strengthening of citizenship. In fact, after communism, Poland even used TVP and specifically Polish Radio to advocate for the values of liberal democracy abroad, among others in Belarus (see Ociepka, 2016).

Changes to the Polish Public Service Media system post-2015

However, in 2015 after the election of the Party of Law and Justice, several changes to the Public Service Media system were made. These exemplified a manifest desire to abandon also at the legal and governance level core principles of liberal democracy. The so-called 'Small Media Act', 'Big Media Act' and the National Council Act' introduced considerable alterations, most – if not all – negatively impacting the independence, but also the operational flexibility of the public broadcasters. Several of these have been discussed more in detail in Chapter 11:

- The public broadcasters became 'national broadcasters', a far from innocent name change. Also the Polish Press Agency is covered under that heading.
- Government can directly appoint managers in TVP and Polish radio. The same goes for members of the Management Boards. In 2016, this changed and this competence was transferred to the National Media Council (which basically is the same in practice).
- Abolishment of open competition for public service jobs, criticised by Połońska (2019: 231) as it gives 'government the right to appoint public servants without reference to any other authority or external criteria'.
- Creation of the National Media Council that took over competencies from the National Broadcasting Council, which was admittedly more independent. Oversight by the National Media Council is in the hands of members that have been appointed by the Parliament, proportionate to the representation of political parties therein (hence PiS takes three out of five members of the National Media Council). The Council in turn appoints

members of the Board of Governors as well as executive committee. Running mandates of the National Broadcasting Council were ended.

- Creation of a National Media Fund to oversee and organise funding of Polish Public Service Media, which is an important and powerful thing to do given the permanent financial problems of the Polish public broadcasters and the fairly generous ad hoc compensations from government.
- The adaptation of the mission of the public broadcasters with more attention to patriotism, national community building and vague notions such as 'the common good'.
- Lay-off of approximately 100 journalists and hiring of less experienced staff trained at conservative, Catholic universities. Overall, 230 journalists left, some because they were fired, others out of protest.

Additional State funding

The main source of revenue for Polish Public Service Media organisations ought to be the license fee. Complementarily, all organisations also rely on state funding and advertising. The license fee system operates on the basis of registering the ownership of a television or radio set with a postal office. After registration, households receive a bill to pay the license fee. In practice, few people register a device. Even fewer pay the license fee. There is no enforcement of registration nor of payment. Poland is Europe's champion in terms of license fee avoidance with only about 15 per cent of Polish households paying, compared to 32 per cent in 2010 and 43 per cent in 2006 (Krajewski and Diakite, 2012). That also results in a situation whereby slightly more than 20 per cent of TVP's revenues come from the license fee. The remainder consists of direct, often ad hoc, government grants and advertising income.

The Polish Government has provided additional subsidies amounting to over 220 million euros since 2017. Some have argued that these subsidies amount to illegal State aid. However, it is unclear whether that is indeed the case. Is it the lack of independence of a public broadcaster that can qualify a subsidy as illegal? State aid law does not consider that question, albeit it could argue that State aid to public broadcasters should contribute in line with the wording of the Amsterdam Protocol to the democratic, cultural and social goals of democracy (see Chapter 7). In 2020, complaints about the Hungarian public broadcasting system were effectively issued with the European Commission. Complainants (apparently a Hungarian member of Parliament, an NGO and commercial radio) have argued that illegal state aid in the form of state advertising has been granted to the Hungarian public broadcaster since 2016. The process of deciding on the expenditure of State advertising budgets is highly untransparent and in full ignorance of 'regular' market processes (Personal communication with journalist on EU affairs, 29 July 2020). However, no further news is publicly available on this.

Not so shocking is that 'politicians, journalists and the experts have a negative view of TVP' which is 'heavily criticised for its lack of political independence in providing content, not living up to its public service mission and its lack of financial sustainability, which results in commercialisation' (Krajewski and Diakite, 2012).

The use of government funding to impact media output is not isolated to public broadcasters only. Tadeusz Kowalski has shown that newspapers such as *Gazeta Polska*, *Sieci* and *Do Rzeczy* receive considerable revenues from State advertising, amounting to 45 per cent, 40 per cent and 23 per cent of commercial revenues of the named titles (Makarenko, 2019). This increased power of government over media has also been reinforced by limiting foreign ownership through the so-called 'Re-Polinisation' of the media sector. Essentially, the argument is that concentration and consolidation have resulted in media being in the hands of foreign owners, alien to Polish identity and its way of life. TVP has accused foreign media of being biased against PiS.

Changes to Public Service Media at the level of the law, governance and funding has contributed to the erosion of the system and the emergence of a state, government-led broadcasting system. There is no longer politicisation because of pragmatic reasons: 'it is our turn to control TVP'. Rather, an ideological, competitive authoritarianist logic has surfaced that impacts Public Service Media in Poland in all domains of citizenship. The section below will illustrate this further.

Erosion of citizenship

Political citizenship

Political citizenship was most intensely referred to during my interviews. While most experts mentioned that Polish Public Service Media were never fully independent from government, there was consensus on the increased professionalisation, the emergence of editorial policies and pluralism in news and current affairs programming after the collapse of communism. Indeed, political capture continued to exist after post-Solidarity parties came into power in the early 1990s. And elections were always followed by smaller or bigger 'earthquakes' in the various public broadcasting organisations. Nevertheless, all interviewees emphasised that this system of political parallelism did not prevent TVP and other public radio reporting factually on issues and facilitating discussion on different opinions in society. A journalist we interviewed (Respondent J, Poland) indeed stressed that the different public broadcasters strived after independent reporting post-communism. He said the institutions 'were not free from political influence, but at least they tried to be independent', whereas TVP no longer pretends and in practice admits to being a propaganda channel of the government. Some also pointed at civil society-driven changes in Polish media law between 2008 and 2010 and the involvement of university professors in the different media regulatory bodies. All of this ensured a 'system of checks and balances', a public broadcaster that not only enjoyed absolute levels of independence, but was 'independent enough to criticise government, not to be a servant of government' (Respondents D, E, Poland). That has shifted. Public Service Media no longer exists in Poland. The PiS government 'destroyed it' (Respondents F, D, G, Poland). TVP has become a full-blown state broadcaster (Respondent C, Poland) or national broadcaster (Respondent H, Poland). The former deputy minister of culture is now the head of TVP. One also refers to TVP and Polish radio as national broadcasters, admittedly with radio still being in a slightly more advantageous position (Respondent J, Poland). After this legal change, the PiS government became explicit in requiring the public broadcasting organisations to report in the national interest, which was subsequently defined as the interest of PiS and not the public interest (Respondent B, Poland). The word propaganda was frequently mentioned by respondents: they talked about visible manipulation of the news, and parallels with communist rule (e.g., Respondents E, H, Poland). The PiS government, on the other hand, claims that this is the first real public broadcaster Poland has ever had, restoring the progressive and liberal bias in commercial media and, in so doing, ensuring genuine pluralism in the whole Polish media sector. For obvious reasons, experts disagreed with that view, saying government 'does not understand that Public Service Media should be plural inside' (Respondent H, Poland).

Importantly, several respondents said that the idea of government is by no means to strengthen political citizenship, but to address PiS voters and make sure that they remain in favour of the ruling government. Reference was frequently made to lower educated people and the rural population (Respondent C, Poland). More complex issues such as the historical development of Poland and, relatedly, different ideological orientations in various parts of the country were said to play a role besides education and professional occupation (Respondent A, Poland). In any case, PiS was said to consider media as a part of government and uses TVP in particular as a means to address subjects, not citizens. That implicitly relates to civic citizenship, which was hardly mentioned at all and was, when asked, not considered an aspect of past and present Public Service Media in Poland. Empowering citizens, giving them a voice, allowing for contributions, and so on, were considered relevant though, but expert opinion was that it has never been key to Polish media policy and not of the public broadcasting strategy either.

Social citizenship

The critical evaluation of how Public Service Media in Poland is not adding to political citizenship was pronounced in relation to cultural and social citizenship too. While literature largely defines these aspects of citizenship as a means to hold society together, all experts observed TVP 'adding to a divided society' (e.g., Respondent C, Poland) with 'audiences being very strongly polarised' (Respondent H, Poland). While the agenda of TVP, Polsat and TVN news used to be rather similar, that was said to have changed, resulting in viewers of TVP, Polsat and TVN living in 'different news bubbles' (Respondent H, Poland). These companies and their audiences have become "media tribes" (Respondent

A, Poland). They are selling their truth as the only truth. Polarisation on topics such as migration and environmental issues was mentioned, not only in news and current affairs programming. Experts mentioned soaps and telenovelas with anti-immigration and anti-LGBTQ+ community story lines (Respondent I, Poland). Largely, the idea thereof is to protect Polish identity against outside enemies, which can be different at different times (Respondent C, Poland).

Cultural citizenship

Culture was seen to be instrumentalised with the purpose of creating an adjusted, exclusively positive view of Polish history (Respondents G, J, Poland). Some mentioned culture became a 'propaganda of patriotism' (Respondent F, Poland), even though some respondents acknowledged that thematic channels such as TVP Kultura still made valuable content, perhaps also because they could operate under less government scrutiny than the journalistic programme teams. In any case, culture has become a site of contestation, whereby the exclusion of some groups, whether migrants, LGBTQ+ communities, progressives, and so on, from Polish society is a guiding principle. Those groups do not correspond with some sort of unified, homogeneous Polish culture that relies on rather conservative ideas on family life and set out from the idea that 'everyone who is an outsider, is the enemy' (Respondent A, Poland).

Civic citizenship

Empowerment of citizens or civic rights in general were rarely addressed by the people I interviewed. It was very clear for them that the Polish Public Service Media system was never really about that and certainly not under the rule of the Party of Law and Justice. One of the experts said the party programme is 'quite explicitly authoritarian in nature'. He said the party does not make a secret out of the fact they are not incredibly pro-democracy. So, 'in their ideology, it might seem very well legitimate to use the public broadcaster as a mouthpiece' (Respondent A, Poland). In other words, the PiS party, and to a lesser extent previous Polish governments, sees the inhabitants of Poland as subjects, not so much as citizens. They do not want to strengthen citizenship in the sociological sense, but want to increase barriers for citizenship in the legal way – all of this under the pretence of representing 'the voice of the people' (Respondent A, Poland).

All of this progressively gives the idea of Polish Public Service Media becoming more similar to the Hungarian state of play, even if private media are still more independent with American company Discovery Communications owning the biggest commercial television channel TVN. The latter is more critical of government, with some experts arguing that criticism was at times also somewhat biased against the PiS government. Besides TVN, commercial television company Polsat was considered considerably more neutral than TVP, but devotes less time to news and current affairs because of government pressure to take away licenses in other sectors where the company is active such as telecommunications and energy (Respondent G, Poland).

Structural barriers to Public Service Media in Poland

While PiS completely eroded the idea and practice of Public Service Media in Poland, one should not overlook the structural factors that inhibit the successful transposition of a citizenship-centric Public Service Media project into practice. Those factors existed long before PiS came to power and will most likely persist for some time. The problematic state of play of Public Service Media in Poland was attributed to four main issues.

Lack of political willingness to make Public Service Media work

First and foremost, experts said that there is no political willingness to make Public Service Media happen. While opposition parties protest against the PiS changes of the Public Service Media system, most experts we interviewed all said those parties kept in place far-going levels of politicisation themselves (Respondent I, Poland). There is a common conviction that it is your turn when you are in power to control the public broadcaster. The public broadcasting organisations have always been 'a kind of political battle ground' with politicians that find it 'natural' that when 'they win the elections, they will get ownership over the Public Service Media system' (Respondent A, Poland).

The repeated replacements of management and journalistic staff would in that sense most likely continue also in a post-PiS era (Respondents B, E, Poland). Some respondents were rather pessimistic in their evaluation, stressing that politicians 'never had the idea to cut the strings between public broadcasting organisations and government' (Respondent C, Poland), not even right after the collapse of communism, though the extent to which one party controls TVP can differ. Having said that, most, if not all, experts agreed that PiS took matters very far. Because of their majority in Parliament, they managed to undermine the progress in the Public Service Media system in a matter of weeks (Respondent D, Poland). Their involvement goes further than was the case before. That shows, first, in the replacement of staff from very high to lower ranks among the different public broadcasters. Second, they give explicit instructions on what language to use when talking about issues such as, for example, migration (Respondent J, Poland).

Lack of legal safeguards

Secondly, legal reforms have undermined some of the progress made in the 1990s and after the millennium change regarding independence. The creation of the National Council for the Media, which oversees changes of media laws and appointments in the public broadcasting organisations, was seen as a means to concentrate power over media and add Public Service Media as a department within government. At the same time, several experts raised a point that the law is on several levels very good and explicit about the task of Public Service Media to reach the whole of society, to be impartial, to be objective and to build social cohesion. That formulation of Article 21 of the broadcasting law is not adhered to in practice, referring back to the lack of political will to translate law into practice when it does not fit the political agenda (Respondent G, Poland). We observed some disagreement between experts on the positivity of evolutions in Public Service Media after communism and before the PiS majority rule. Some (e.g., Respondent C, Poland) insist that in spite of legal reforms the system has always been corrupt, even if the situation might be worse these days. Others, however, pointed at coalitions of politicians, academics, artists, unions and journalists from left to right, from liberal to conservative, from urban to rural … coalitions with a genuine dream and intention to modernise Public Service Media as a means to contribute to liberal democracy (e.g., Respondent F, Poland). Overall, the legislative changes under PiS rule were evaluated negatively. Pleas for strengthening the independence of the regulatory bodies and a more contractual relationship between the Polish state and the public broadcaster were made (Respondent E, Poland). Related to this, a journalist with the Polish public broadcaster also insisted that a legal strengthening of journalists' and newsroom independence from government was necessary to allow journalists to be more courageous and say 'no' (Respondent B, Poland). That is far from evident these days as the journalist experienced herself, refusing to report on the murder of an Italian priest in the prescribed manner and subsequently facing a decision to be moved to the archival services of Polish Radio as a consequence.

Lack of a sustainable financing system

Third, the financial system is said to enable political influence over Public Service Media. Polish public broadcasting organisations are paid on the basis of a license fee, commercial revenues and ad hoc government subsidies. Very few people actually pay the license fee. People need to register a television or radio set at the post office, after which they will receive an invitation to pay. In the absence of such a registration, no payment will be asked and nobody will check whether you have a television set or not. There is no enforcement of payment after you are registered either (Respondent, D, Poland). That obviously increases dependence on advertising revenues, often also coming from government, and ad hoc subsidies of government.

> Unfortunately, the license fee system is a completely destroyed component, which means that in practice, the public gives money directly from the government through law, so simply donations.
>
> (Respondent G, Poland)

The direct donations of government have increased dramatically during the PiS government with sums amounting to approximately add amount Polish zloties (Respondent G, Poland). It is 'the salary for propaganda' (Respondent F, Poland) While several political and civil society actors have brought this issue to the attention of the European Commission, asking for an assessment on the basis of the Communication on the application of the State aid rules to Public Service Broadcasting (European Commission, 2009; Donders, 2015), no in-depth investigation has followed. The European Commission seems to agree the ad hoc subsidies for TVP are part of the existing State aid regime and hence compatible with the internal market provisions. Having said that, the increasing dependency on direct government grants aggravates the situation described above. It plays into the hands of those that consider TVP their own political party playground and this within a context that has for decades been very susceptible to political influence.

Lack of citizen identification with Public Service Media

Finally, experts said that citizens do not identify with Public Service Media. They and average Polish citizens find it normal that Public Service Media is in fact State media, and those that cannot accept that situation do not watch TVP. There is a continuously declining trust in Public Service Media (Makarenko, 2019), and, more importantly so, no belief that such a system can actually exist in Poland. One respondent firmly stated that 'Younger audiences do not iden-tify with the theoretical idea of Public Service Media' and consider it normal that public broadcasters are in fact state broadcasters. A new approach, a renewal of the conceptualisation is much needed (Respondent E, Poland). Even journalists, with some exceptions, were said to go with the flow of the parties in government.

> And what's dramatic, what's tragic for me, when I see those people [journalists], they have no problem with that. They come and they do their job, what the chiefs say. And they also think it is okay, there is nothing wrong with that. They think: we have this government now, so we will follow the rhetoric of this government.
>
> (Respondent B, Poland)

The younger generation, especially the higher educated urban group, were said not to watch TVP a lot. People do not see where Public Service Media stands out, what added value it offers to society. Also experts themselves find it 'evident' that politicisation of Public Service Media is happening: 'when you win the elections, the media are yours, and that is a kind of natural right' (Respondent C, Poland). While not agreeing with it, the existence of political capture, regular politically driven management swaps, lay-off of journalists, and so on, were considered common practice that would continue for many decades to come.

The 'of course-ness' of this was expressed on many occasions by interviewees (e.g., Respondent B, Poland). Regardless of that defeatism, the sharp decline in market share of TVP since the PiS election victory in 2015 shows the audience is not completely indifferent. One-third of viewership was lost between 2015 and 2019. TVP has lost its credibility to some of the people (Respondent B, Poland, 9 April 2019). They 'generally do not trust Public Service Media right now, after four years of such actions' (Respondent I, Poland). This to some extent implies that not all audiences find the government intervention self-evident. That, one can argue, goes against the idea that audiences do not identify with Public Service Media as a theoretical construct or, alternatively and less optimistically, that a part of the population seeks television programmes that contain the opinions they adhere to.

Aggravating factors

There were also some issues that emerged during interviews. These issues fall outside the scope of our citizenship-centric and barriers framework, but surfaced through the thematic analysis nonetheless. They add to the analysis above and can be seen to aggravate some of the structural barriers to Public Service Media.

Catholic Church – PiS alliance

First, the close ties between government and the Catholic Church were mentioned in each of the interviews. Experts pointed to the education of journalists at Catholic, highly conservative private universities and their employment after the PiS government came into power. They also said that the PiS government and notably TVP united around a discourse of exclusion against LGBTQ+ communities and the alleged pornification of society. Scandals related to sexual abuse within the Catholic Church receive hardly any attention from TVP on top of that.

The limited reach of non-public service offers in rural areas

Second, while consumption of Public Service Media offers is relatively low, some experts also worried about the fact that in some areas of Poland most people can only receive information from TVP as Polsat and TVN channels are not available free-to-air (Respondent F, Poland). That, moreover, contributes to a very fragmented media consumption behaviour in the population and further erodes social cohesion. While some experts said that the commercial TVN channel was in fact more 'public service' than TVP and that freedom speech and the press existed not because of Public Service Media but because of private media (e.g., Respondent D, Poland), others thus partly dismissed that idea because of the limited availability of the channel in rural areas (Respondent B, Poland) and, moreover, counterargued that a 'good' Public Service Media system is still to be preferred over a system that relies on commercial imperatives only (Respondent J, Poland).

Interestingly, the issue of reach was also related to a kind of mental, normative division – more difficult to measure – in Polish society with people from Warsaw and also the part of Poland that was closer to German influences being more progressive, while the East of Poland that has been much more impacted by Russian Soviet ideology is, in general, also more Catholic, and more reliant on agriculture. The surroundings of Krakow and the city itself are considered more mixed (Respondent A, Poland). The nationalist agenda of the Party of Law and Justice is mainly targeting the people that have been used to Soviet rule, are anti-Russian, more nationalist and thus more open to their agenda. This shows how complex and multi-layered the issues surrounding Public Service Media in Poland are and how the manifestation or practice of Public Service Media can be intertwined with political, economic, but also socio-cultural features of a society. This also makes it so difficult to explain the differences among Central and Eastern European countries in terms of Public Service Media development post-communism (Respondent K, Poland).

Experts' orientation to the West

Third, when discussing Polish Public Service Media, experts repeatedly mentioned Western systems such as the United Kingdom, Germany or Sweden as examples. For example, one of the people I talked to said that the National Broadcasting Council worked very hard around 2010 to 'build Polish media as parallel to Western media systems'. The Council has the legally entrusted role to act as the guardian of a pluralistic media system, to protect the public interest in media. The same respondent said he could no longer tell 'what that means, public interest in media' in Poland (Respondent F, Poland). Also other interviewees pointed at foreign public broadcasters such as the BBC as inspirational examples for Poland, not only in terms of independence, but also when looking at digital innovation (Respondent E, J, Poland). Some experts questioned the relevance of Public Service Media in a Western context for Poland, saying that such a system 'is not born yet in Poland' and that, while laws were developed in line with models such as British public broadcaster BBC or Swedish Sveriges Television in the 1990s, the distance between law and practice is enormous (Respondent B, Poland).

The mission impossible of achieving Public Service Media in Poland

My research to a large extent confirms what others have researched before me: Polish Public Service Media is dead (e.g., Połońska, 2019; Glowacki and Kus, 2019; Jaskiernia and Pokorna-Ignatowicz, 2017). It in fact never existed, even though some evolution away from the state broadcasting model could be observed after the collapse of communism in 1989. There are structural barriers that inhibit the emergence of a Public Service Media model. Several experts pointed at the role of Jarosław Kaczyński in all of this. One respondent said that laws, independent regulators, professional journalism, and so on, cannot protect a Public Service Media system from 'these kind of people' (Respondent D, Poland). The leader of the biggest political party in Poland was said to pull all the strings. He enforced a party logic, which is largely determined by him (Respondents H, I, Poland).

But, regardless of the importance of figures such as Kaczyński, the structural barriers to Public Service Media are not caused by PiS, but in fact instrumentalised to a very grave extent. As already contended by Karol Jakubowicz (2007) the lack of independence and professionalism in Polish Public Service Media is intertwined with a lack of dedication to democracy. With the weak legal safeguard in place, the lack of political willingness to make Public Service Media work and also the erosion of the normative belief in such a system with not only politicians, but also experts and parts of the audience all explain why 'it' is not working in Poland. Indeed, audience research on Public Service Media in South East Europe (thus not including Poland, but focussing on Albania, Bosnia-Herzegovina, Bulgaria, Croatia, Kosovo, Moldova, Montenegro, Macedonia, Romania and Serbia), shows that many citizens still believe in a Public Service Media system (over 60 per cent) but a similar percentage does not think that their public broadcaster is delivering Public Service Media and is independent (over 60 per cent also)(Car et al., 2019: 18ff). That could mean that Public Service Media as an idea and project might be achievable, but not per se with a centralised public broadcaster.

Several experts indeed suggested getting rid of the current public broadcaster altogether (Respondent C, Poland) or to downsize it significantly (Respondent D, Poland). There is no public service DNA that can serve as the basis for improvement. One of the interviewed experts said: 'if you want public interest media, the public broadcaster is not the place to start: bomb it and start from scratch' (Respondent C, Poland). Another one added: 'if you would want some sort of public broadcaster, leave it [TVP] there and start something else' (Respondent B, Poland). There was little hope that change would come from the inside (Respondent E, Poland), not because most journalists or employees support what is going on, but because they are not inclined to actively protest against the situation and basically want to survive or tolerate the situation until a new government is elected and things improve (Respondent J, Poland).

I agree to a large extent with this, even though arguing for the abolishment of TVP and Polish radio can be considered somewhat provocative. I agree with Eva Połońska (2019: 231) that TVP is 'both the victim and an instrument of the new government's political engineering', but at the same time it is also an active agent within a system that is, at its very base, hostile towards Public Service Media as a theoretical concept. Thus, why not invest time and resources of organisations such as UNESCO and the European Broadcasting Union in grassroots initiatives, professionalising these, while at the same time preparing EU legislation that safeguards the independence of such initiatives at the European level, including also monitoring and enforcement instruments?

References

Bogner, A., Littig, B. and Menz, W. (2014). *Interviews mit Experten: eine praxisorientierte Einführung.* Wiesbaden: Springer-Verlag.

Car, V., Gogu, N., Ionescu, L., Londo, I., Qeriqi, D., Radojkovic, M., Ruzic, N., Sekuloviski, D., Spassov, O., Surugiu, R., Turcilo, L. and Wolter, D. (2019). *A Pillar of Democracy on Shaky Ground: Public Service Media in South East Europe.* Berlin: Konrad-Adenauer-Stiftung.

Donders, K. (2015). State aid to public service media: European Commission decisional practice before and after the 2009 Broadcasting Communication. *European State aid Law Quarterly, 1*(15), 68-87.

Dzięciołowski, K. (2017). Is there a chance for a non-partisan media in Poland? Retrieved from https://reutersinstitute.politics.ox.ac.uk/sites/default/files/2017–12/Is%20 there%20a%20chance%20for%20non-partisan%20media%20in%20Poland%20- %20Krzysztof%20Dzieciolowsk%20Paper.pdf (accessed October 2020).

European Commission (2009). Communication of 2 July 2009 on the *Application of the State Aid Rules to Public Service Broadcasting.*

Glowacki, M. and Kus, M. (2019). Media accountability meets media polarisation: A case study from Poland. In T. Eberwein, S. Fengler and M. Karmasin (eds), *Media Accountability in the Era of Post-truth Politics: European Challenges and Perspectives.* London: Routledge.

Herzog, C., Handke, C. and Hitters, E. (2019). Analysing Talk and Text II: Thematic analysis. In H. Van den Bulck, M. Puppis, K. Donders and L. Van Audenhove (eds), *The Palgrave Handbook of Media Policy Research Methods* (pp. 385-401). Basingstoke: Palgrave Macmillan.

Jakubowicz, K. (2007). Public service broadcasting: A new beginning, or the beginning of the end. Retrieved from www.knowledgepolitics.org.uk (accessed October 2020).

Jaskiernia, A. and Pokorna-Ignatowicz, K. (2017). Public Service Media vs. Sovereign National Media. In M. Głowacki and A. Jaskiernia (eds), *Public Service Media Renewal: Adaptation to Digital Network Challenges* (pp. 171-192). Frankfurt am Main: Peter Lang.

Kaiser, R. (2014). *Qualitative Experteninterviews: Konzeptionelle Grundlagen und praktische Durchführung.* Wiesbaden: Springer. [*Qualitative expert interviews: Conceptual basis and practical implementation*].

Krajewski, A. and Diakite, K. (2012). Mapping digital media: Poland. Retrieved from www.opensocietyfoundations.org/uploads/17183ef3–3aba–486f–a168–4877e021317d/ mapping-digital-media-poland-20130722.pdf (accessed October 2020).

Makarenko, V. (2019). *Poland. Reuters Institute Digital News Report 2019.* Retrieved from www.digitalnewsreport.org/survey/2019/poland-2019/ (accessed October 2020).

Ociepka, B. (2016). International broadcasting by a middle-size country: The case of Belsat TV from Poland to Belarus. *Global Media and Communication, 12*(2), 111-126.

Piechota, G., 2017 [online]. *Digital Media Report. Poland.* Retrieved from www. digitalnewsreport.org/survey/2017/poland-2017/ (accessed October 2020).

Połońska, E. (2019). Watchdog, lapdog, or attach dog? Public service media and the Law and Justice government in Poland. In E. Połońska and C. Beckett (eds), *Public*

Service Broadcasting and Media Systems in Troubled European Democracies (pp. 227-255). Basingstoke: Palgrave Macmillan.

Puppis, M. (2019). Analyzing Talk and Text I: Qualitative content analysis. In H. Van den Bulck, M. Puppis, K. Donders and L. Van Audenhove (eds), *Handbook on Media Policy Research Methods* (pp. 367-384). Basingstoke: Palgrave Macmillan.

Terzis, G. (ed.)(2007). *European Media Governance: National and Regional Dimensions.* Bristol: Intellect.

Van Audenhove, L. and Donders, K. (2019). Expert and elite interviews. In H. Van Den Bulck, M. Puppis, K. Donders and L. Van Audenhove (eds), *Handbook on Media Policy Research Methods* (pp. 179-197). Basingstoke: Palgrave Macmillan.

15 Conclusions

Explaining the (mis)match between theory, the law and practice

The purpose of this book is to contribute to the lively scholarship on Public Service Media, confronting theoretical perspectives with insights on rules, policies and practice. My main aim is to contribute to the conceptual thinking on Public Service Media in a bottom-up manner. In this conclusion, I will provide the reader with a brief synthesis of what I consider the main findings of this book. I will subsequently make a modest and explorative attempt in adding to the reconceptualisation of Public Service Media at the level of values, rules and practice.

Synthesis of findings

The first question I tried to answer is whether a shared set of theoretical values is still necessary and feasible for Public Service Media. My answer was twofold. First, the international media landscape confronts us with far-going forms of commodification (including datafication of the user) that necessitate a form of intervention for the public interest. Whereas that intervention can at the conceptual level take the form of public service algorithms or public service platforms, public broadcasters are institutions that could embody these newer manifestations of the public interest in media. Simultaneously, I already argued that in some countries the crystallisation of Public Service Media, public service algorithms and/or public service platforms in the established organisational form might not be a solution to a pertinent problem, but an aggravation of a precarious situation. In any case, I think that few scholars would dispute that some level of intervention (government or not government-led) in favour of delivering the public interest in media is much needed. Second, I put forward a set of values and goals that can be a re-boot of the conceptual discussions on Public Service Media. The sociological, not legal notion of citizenship is key to the model I elaborated. Admittedly there are shortcomings to this model. Some might consider it too old-fashioned, that I set out too much from democracy theory, and also from a Western-centric liberal democracy model. I have to say I did the latter intentionally because my investigation of a lot of Public Service Broadcasting and Public Service Media literature reveals that we assign the denominator Public Service Media to institutions that are, at their very

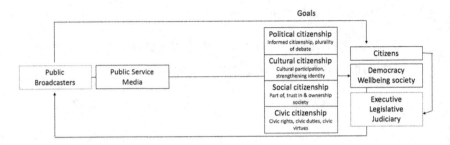

Figure 15.1 Public Service Media as a democracy- and citizenship-centric project

core, not occupied with that idea at all. That might be a provocative statement and dismissive of nuance, but I think it is a necessary addition to the debate on Public Service Media.

The model I put forward rests on four notions of citizenship: political, cultural, social and civic citizenship. Some of these notions are focused on the individual (e.g., civic citizenship), others on the collective (e.g., social citizenship) and in fact most, if not all, of these types of citizenship embody elements at the individual, family, community and larger societal level. Some aspects of citizenship might, moreover, be related to knowledge transfer, others to attitude and still others to behaviour. What they all have in common or should have in common is that they are citizen- and democracy-centric instead of media maker-centric. They definitely do not set out from a market failure perspective. Nonetheless, contributing to these forms of citizenship can also be an effect of commercial media delivery, but not the principal objective (see Figure 15.1).

The second main question was whether the law as well as Public Service Media practice corresponds with those values. To analyse and evaluate that in a more purposeful manner, I added elements to Public Service Media's overall ambition of strengthening citizenship and democratic societies, being the means and necessary conditions to make the ideal or something close to it happen (see Figure 15.2).

As hypothesised, and unsurprisingly, both the law and practice clash with the model above and this at the level of goals, means and necessary conditions. Not only are EU legal frameworks and their implementation biased towards objectives of market integration at the expense of aspirations that relate to democracy, social cohesion, cultural identity, and so on. They are also, at least when public broadcasters' funding is involved, indifferent to the massive changes in the international media landscape. There is inadequate enforcement of principles such as independence of public broadcasters. National legislative frameworks, too, are deficient. They are first and foremost patchworks; the result of a path-dependent and historical process of policy-making regarding Public Service Media, subject

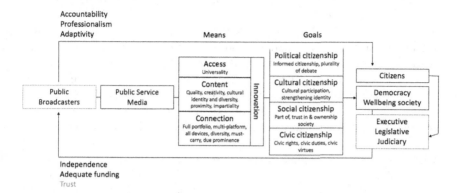

Figure 15.2 Public Service Media as a citizenship- and democracy-centric project: goals, means, and necessary conditions

to lobbying from all sorts of interest groups, and at least in the cases investigated often incoherent and overly focused on details, rather than the fundamentals of Public Service Media. In spite of positive evolutions such as the transition from a license to a household fee in countries such as Finland and Germany, other countries struggle to engage in balanced discussions on the future of Public Service Media and public broadcaster and to disconnect the former from the latter. I have to admit that I have also struggled to do that throughout the book as the institution is so much intertwined with the idea, at least in Western and Northern Europe.

At the level of practice, and based on a smaller set of cases, I have concluded first that the transition from Public Service Broadcasting to Public Service Media when looking at the offer of online content, digital distribution, organisational change and commercial strategies is not in an advanced stage at all. Findings from Ireland, the Netherlands, the UK and Flanders demonstrate that the ideals from mainstream Public Service Media theories are not achieved. And also when relating the findings to a citizenship-centric conceptualisation of Public Service Media, serious issues can be observed. For example, distribution strategies seem oriented more at the attraction of additional revenues than on the achievement of the public service remit. My case studies on Poland and Flanders, which had a gaze wider than 'the digital' only, moreover showed that the view on Public Service Media in these parts of Europe is highly conflicted. In Poland, the majority PiS government has effectively turned TVP and Polish radio into state broadcasters. At the level of funding, independence, accountability, and other means, there are tremendous deficiencies that result in a system that contributes to polarisation, division in society and an erosion of political, social, cultural and civic citizenship. At the same time, that is not a linear process. Equally so, the current manifestation of Public Service Media in Poland is caused by an ideological view on the State that sets aside the basic ideas of liberal democracy. The public broadcasting organisations in Poland are not per se passive victims of that highly complex process, but also in part participants in it. That left me with doubts on whether a centralised Public Service Media system in Poland is a good idea at all. The Flemish case showed a system with more affinity to the model I and other authors in the field have elaborated. Nonetheless, this model is also conflicted. VRT reaches many citizens, but does not have an inclusive view on citizens as part of Public Service Media (making or governance). It collaborates with other public institutions, but often from a moral high ground. Furthermore, in spite of the longstanding focus of policy-makers and VRT on collaboration to strengthen the market, relations are tense, to say the least. That can be attributed to commercial media, to the public broadcaster itself, but – so I argue – mostly to the subsequent Flemish governments that have organised a deep-rooted conflict between the public and commercial media scene by making VRT increasingly dependent on commercial revenues. Related, there is a lack of open dialogue between the Flemish government and VRT. Something I experienced in the period I have been involved with Public Service Media policy-making in Flanders is that a basic level of trust in Public Service Media as a project, the institution that takes care of it and the government that should enable, safeguard and control it, has to some extent dissolved. To me that is one of two main issues VRT needs to resolve to ensure a sustainable future. The other issue is a more clear view on its mission in society, looking at the digital (r)evolution as well as, too often neglected, societal ruptures.

Conceptual (re)thinking of Public Service Media

How do these findings feed into our thinking on Public Service Media? First, at the level of values, it is striking how little attention is going to civic citizenship and also how much conflation there is between means such as quality and diversity on the one hand and goals such as social cohesion, informed citizenship and user empowerment on the other hand. Regarding civic citizenship, work on communication rights, alternative and community media, and emerging media organisations can be highly insightful. Also the citizen itself at the individual as well as collective level needs to find a place in my framework. It is one of the topics discussed often with Polish experts: what do the Polish expect from their public broadcaster in terms of these democracy-centric values? Do they have any expectations there? Perhaps PiS voters do not align with the model I elaborate; most likely other Polish citizens will find the Polish public broadcasters a poor starting place for the achievement of that model. When introducing citizens into the equation it is important to find a balance between a political sciences, sociological and even consumerist perspective on where citizens 'belong' in Public Service Media. The first perspective focuses on meaningful participation, often with an axis on political citizenship. It corresponds with a media-centric, top-down perspective. The second perspective values interaction in itself. It can have value, even when there are no grand ambitions concerning political, social and cultural citizenship involved (Vanhaeght, 2019; Picone et al., 2019). The consumerist perspective, often alien to Public Service Media literature, is nonetheless needed because a continuation of consumption is necessary for public broadcasters or any other organisation form in charge of delivering the public interest in media to remain relevant. While some might argue for a stronger presence of digital technology, algorithms, data, and so on, in my view on Public Service Media, I would resist that argument. The design and use of algorithms to enhance the serendipity and diversity of content consumption corresponds with notions of quality and diversity as well as with the ambition of strengthening cultural citizenship. In other words, the model I propose might need further updates at the level of means, but not necessarily at the level of goals, albeit that these goals might be operationalised in more detail.

The rules on Public Service Media are in need of an update too, not per se only in the legal frameworks of public broadcasters, but also in the way we as scholars think about them in our work. Rules can have three impacts on how public broadcasters deliver the public interest in media. First, they can enable this, ensuring editorial independence, elaborating on a key mission for public broadcasters and foreseeing adequate oversight and evaluation, which feeds into continuous reflection and adaptation of what public broadcasters do to achieve political, social, cultural and civic citizenship. Second, rules can do the opposite. They can be an effective means of inhibiting anything close to the ideal of Public Service Media from emerging. They facilitate and even legitimise government intervention with content; they make it impossible for public broadcasters to innovate and adjust quickly to the digital media environment; they stifle the renewal of funding arrangements and keep in place outdated models, and so on. Third, they can be a bit of both. While policy is always a messy process and also organisations will be imperfect, the idea should be to strive after rules that enable Public Service Media. That is not necessarily to the detriment of commercial media as some of the things public broadcasters do are not per se necessary to achieve the public interest in media. Because of the focus of scholars on the rules that exist, rather than on the legal frameworks that are absent and also the underlying and overall conceptualisation of those legal frameworks, we have also added to deficient legislative frameworks or at least insufficiently contributed to more optimal conditions under which Public Service Media could be achieved. Important therein is to strengthen legal scholars on the interdependent relationship between independence from economic and political forces, on the one hand, and accountability to elected members of parliament, government and above all citizens, on the other. I already referred to Des Freedman's work on policy silences that explain my point very well. In his work Freedman (2010: 347) says:

> There is, however, an entirely different approach, rooted in debates in social and political science that emerged in the 1960s (e.g., Bachrach and Baratz, 1962; Crenson, 1971; Lukes, 2005) that seeks to locate power in less visible arenas of decision making and indeed to focus instead on examples of

non–decision making and policy neglect. Instead of dwelling on the evidence provided by key participants, the content of white papers and regulatory orders, the detail of draft bills and congressional acts, and the flavor of parliamentary debates, this approach examines the means by which alternative options are marginalized, conflicting values delegitimized, and rival interests derecognized. This flows from an understanding of decision making as an ideological process structured by unequal access to power and where power itself 'is at its most effective when least observable' (Lukes, 1974/2005: 1).

So, whereas Public Service Media scholarship is concerned most with what has been and is happening with public broadcasting organisations, there is much less consideration of what is not happening or what cannot easily be studied on the basis of content analysis, document analysis or expert interviews.

The practice of Public Service Media needs continuous improvement. This book might seem critical of Public Service Media and the institutions that have been entrusted with it. That was also my purpose. A lot of public broadcasters perform well; a lot of them are under-achievers or complete failures when it comes to achieving the public interest in media. The first group can become better provided they focus on a genuine transformation from Public Service Broadcasting to Public Service Media, not only from a technological point of view, distributing traditional radio and television shows via other platforms, but also through the development of new services, a firm dedication to their public service assignment and an acknowledgement of and working with the social ruptures of society. There is a reported move away from the values of liberal democracy in Europe. That trend is most outspoken in several Central and Eastern European countries, but there is a marked surge of populist and anti-democratic parties in other parts of Europe as well. Public broadcasters struggle with this trend for obvious reasons. More research is needed in this domain. What is important to me is not only a changing mindset with politicians on Public Service Media and public broadcasters, but also a mentality shift with public broadcasters. They are not the centre of the universe and while there is a definite commercialisation of the private media scene, they are not the only ones pursuing objectives that go beyond sales and profit. In that regard, bottom-up, less large-scale initiatives to inform people, to bring citizens together or to educate children through games should be embraced by public broadcasters as elements that add to some sort of 'digital commons' (Murdock, 2004) instead of seeing these initiatives as a possible threat to the apparent monopoly public broadcasters have over public service. In this regard, Vilde Schanke Sundet and Trine Syvertsen's (2020: nn) highly interesting study on public broadcasters' strategies in management contract re-negotiations shows a talent to resist change, 'to inhibit change, and find ways to un-couple or at least redefine the problem and policy streams'. While that might be a successful approach in the short run, that strategy will not be beneficial for the survival of a genuine Public Service Media project.

While I am rather pessimistic about the desirability of keeping state broadcasters with the legal obligation to serve the audience and the public interest in place, I do think that the means, values and objectives of Public Service Media need government or, alternatively, civil society intervention to crystallise in practice. In case public broadcasters perform rather well, one should strive for continuous improvement. In case they under-perform, there is the need for other scenarios – to be developed more in collaboration and even co-creation with citizens.

To me, the big absentees in this discussion on Public Service Media practice are the European Broadcasting Union and even more so the European Commission. While I know that the European Broadcasting Union tries to professionalise its members and also raises issues of (in)dependence with the European institutions, it has so far refrained from terminating the membership of some organisations. At some point, also to maintain your credibility as an organisation and the integrity of your members, such an action is indispensable though even if it comes at the cost of losing a membership fee. More importantly and structurally, the European Union has so far failed to uphold basic values of democracy in its own household. From Spain, over Greece to Poland and Hungary: there are Member States that have eccentric views on what liberal democracy stands for. While an Article 7 procedure provides a starting point for acting against transgressions, it is noteworthy that this procedure is used only selectively, that some countries with more 'conventional' political parties in charge are usually left off the hook, and that things move incredibly slowly. The European Union should strengthen the legal basis to act against violations of liberal democracy, including in the area of media. That legal basis should be on a par with the legal safeguards that protect the internal market (see Figure 15.3).

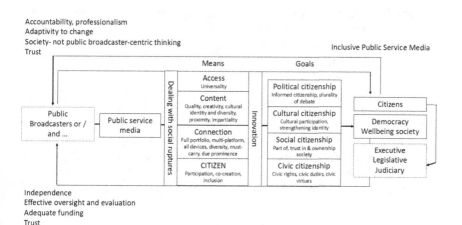

Figure 15.3 Public Service Media as a citizen(ship)- and democracy-centric project

Reflection on this book

This book sets out from very high ambitions and admittedly those have not been achieved. A lot of research went into all of the chapters. Most of the research in this book has not been published elsewhere. My aim was not only to answer the research questions, which I have done only partially. A bigger aim was to contribute to Public Service Media scholarship in novel ways and to provide a basis, next to a lot of other valuable scholarship in the field, for new and more out-of-the-box research on Public Service Media. My hope is that my work will be criticised. I see many possible elements of criticism myself. First, the volume of Public Service Media systems included is limited. Second, while I study multiple cases, this is not a comparative research as such. There is thus no basis for developing an explanatory theory on Public Service Media, which I intended to do, but which will require more research on more Public Service Media systems and this in relation to the conceptual model I developed. Third, the blind spot in the theoretical parts of this book relate to the vast amount of literature on alternative media, emerging media organisations, community media, journalism outside mainstream media, and so on. The more I read work in these fields of scientific enquiry, the more I was convinced that there is a need to relate it more to research on Public Service Media. Fourth, my involvement in Flemish Public Service Media policies can be seen as a strength as well as a weakness. It provided me with rich insights into Public Service Media strategies and policies. It at times made me a bit (too) cynical about policy-making, which by its very nature is imperfect, messy and subject to *real politik* movements. It might also have resulted in a pro-public broadcaster bias or, also and alternatively, in a tendency to be overly critical of public broadcasters. Let me be clear: I am still a firm believer in Public Service Media and in a lot of the organisations working on its achievement on a day-to-day basis. Public broadcasters' output of high-quality output, domestic drama, local children's programming, investigative journalism, and so on, does not mean that several aspects of its organisation, processes, output as well as relations with others, be it public institutions, politicians or private media, do not need fundamental revision. Nor can we defend, setting out from a misplaced superiority on Western and Northern public broadcasters, the public broadcasters from these more wealthy parts of Europe simply because they accomplish more than public broadcasters in previously fascist or communist countries. If public broadcasters want to continue their central role in delivering the public interest in media, they need to be open to change, be more self-critical and prepared to open up Public Service Media to others. Not only the digital, but also the societal changes we witness should be key to that entire process.

References

Freedman, D. (2010). Media policy silences: The hidden face of communications decision making. *The International Journal of Press/Politics, 15*(3), 344–361.

Murdock, G. (2004). Building the Digital Commons: Public Broadcasting in the Age of the Internet. Paper presented at the 2004 Spry Memorial Lecture, 22 November, Montreal.

Picone, I., Kleut, J., Pavlíčková, T., Romic, B., Møller Hartley, J. and De Ridder, S (2019). Small acts of engagement: Reconnecting productive audience practices with everyday agency. *New Media & Society*, *21*(9), 2010-2028.

Schanke Sundet, V. and Syvertsen, T. (2020). From problem to solution? Why it is difficult to restrict the remit of public broadcasters. *International Journal of Cultural Policy*. Retrieved from https://doi.org/10.1080/10286632.2020.1807522 (accessed October 2020).

Vanhaeght, A.-S. (2019). The need for not more, but more socially relevant audience participation in public service media. *Media, Culture & Society*, *41*(1), 120–137.

Index

subscription 27, 196
subsidies 7, 13, 47, 50, 90; cultural and
    economic policies 130; funding laws
    and policy instruments 90, 189–192,
    197–202; ideological divisions in policy
    109, 111, 121; online services regulation
    167, 177; polarised pluralist countries
    111; State aid rules, internationalisation
    and convergence 144; TVP (Poland)
    277, 282–283; VRT (Flanders, Belgium)
    243, 262
Sweden: governance 216; ideological
    divisions 110, 120–121; Sveriges
    Television 285
Switzerland 6, 8, 255; democracy- and
    citizenship-centric project 72; ideological
    divisions 109, 110, 120, 121; *No Bilag*
    referendum 2; online services regulation
    168, 180, 182; SRG 73
Syr 112

technology neutrality 157
Telecinco 130
Telefonica 27, 28
Telemedia (Germany) 178
Television without Frontiers directive and
    successors 127–129
TF1 (France) 121, 126
thematic analysis 148–149, 245–246, 252,
    274, 284
'think global, act local' strategies 21–22
top-slicing 49, 92
transparency: accountability and
    professionalism 93–94; achieving
    public service media 96; Broadcasting
    Communication (2001 and 2009) 133;
    culture and freedom of speech 138;
    funding laws and policy instruments
    194–195; gaps in public service
    media theory 41; governance 207,
    216; independence and professional
    governance 89; market integration 134;
    multi-platform strategies 228; platforms
    and algorithms 52; State aid rules 149,
    153–154, 161; VRT (Flanders, Belgium)
    210, 250
Treaty on European Union 134
Treaty on the Functioning of the European
    Union (TFEU) 115, 129–131, 133;
    culture and freedom of speech 136,
    139; democracy-centric policies 140;
    governance 215; market integration
    134–135

trust 14, 292; accountability and
    professionalism 94; alternative media
    120; democracy- and citizenship-centric
    project 67; funding 91; legitimacy 116,
    117; multi-platform strategies 228,
    232; social capital 66; VRT (Flanders,
    Belgium) 248–250
Tsipras, A. 112, 216
Tudou 128
TV Lab (France) 32
TV2 (Denmark) *146*, 150
TVN (Poland) 275, 279, 280, 284
TVP Historia (Poland) 275
TVP Info (Poland) 275
TVP Kultura (Poland) 275, 280
TVP (Poland) 9–10, 32, 68, 201–202,
    214, 272–287, 291; aggravating factors
    284–285; authoritarian state 272–275;
    Catholic Church-Party of Law and
    Justice (Pis) alliance 284; changes post-
    2015 275–278; citizenship, erosion of
    278–284; civic citizenship 273–274,
    279–281; cultural citizenship 273–274,
    280–281; experts' orientation to the
    West 285; governance 207, 214; legal
    safeguards, lack of 281–282; methodology
    273–275; non-public service offers in
    rural areas 284–285; political apathy 281;
    political citizenship 273–274, 278–279;
    social citizenship 273–274, 279–280; state
    funding, additional 277–278; structural
    barriers 281; sustainable financing system,
    lack of 282–283
TVP Polonia (Poland) 275
TVP Seriale (Poland) 275
TVP Sport (Poland) 275
TVP1 (Poland) 212, 275–276
TVP2 (Poland) 275
Twitter 33, 119

undercompensation 153
UNESCO 215, 286
unethical treatment of data
    24
United Kingdom 6, 7, 8, 14, 26, 255, 291;
    BritBox 179; Discovery Communications
    28; funding laws and policy instruments
    90, 190, 192, 195; ideological divisions
    107, 108, 110, 120, 121; ITV 179; market
    integration 126, 129, 130; online services
    regulation 168, 171, 172; State aid rules
    145; *see also* BBC; on-demand offer of
    audiovisual content in United Kingdom;

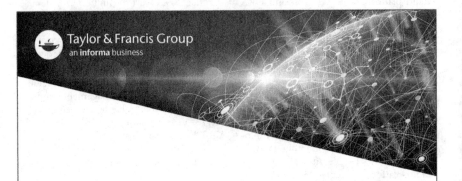

Printed in the United States
by Baker & Taylor Publisher Services